THEY WORE RED SOCKS
AND PINSTRIPES

THEY WORE RED SOCKS AND PINSTRIPES

Players Who Went to the Enemy

Todd Stanley

McFarland & Company, Inc., Publishers
Jefferson, North Carolina

All photographs are from the Library of Congress unless otherwise noted.

Library of Congress Cataloguing-in-Publication Data

Names: Stanley, Todd, 1972– author.
Title: They wore red socks and pinstripes : players who went to the enemy / Todd Stanley.
Description: Jefferson, North Carolina : McFarland & Company, Inc., Publishers, 2017. | Includes bibliographical references and index.
Identifiers: LCCN 2017008113 | ISBN 9780786497515 (softcover : acid free paper) ∞
Subjects: LCSH: Boston Red Sox (Baseball team)—History. | New York Yankees (Baseball team)—History. | Sports rivalries—United States—History.
Classification: LCC GV875.B62 S73 2017 | DDC 796.357/640974461—dc23
LC record available at https://lccn.loc.gov/2017008113

British Library cataloguing data are available

**ISBN (print) 978-0-7864-9751-5
ISBN (ebook) 978-1-4766-2125-8**

© 2017 Todd Stanley. All rights reserved

No part of this book may be reproduced or transmitted in any form or by any means, electronic or mechanical, including photocopying or recording, or by any information storage and retrieval system, without permission in writing from the publisher.

Front cover: Babe Ruth as a Red Sox (left) and a Yankees (right) player (Library of Congress)

Printed in the United States of America

*McFarland & Company, Inc., Publishers
Box 611, Jefferson, North Carolina 28640
www.mcfarlandpub.com*

To W.P. Kinsella, the author of *Shoeless Joe*, *The Iowa Baseball Confederacy*, and *Box Socials*. These books instilled in me a love for baseball that I have carried for a lifetime.

I would also like to thank my wife, Nicki, who once spring comes around knows what it means to be a baseball widow.

Table of Contents

Preface	1
Introduction	11
1. A Friendly Relationship: The Deadball Era (1907–1919)	15
2. The Curse Was About More Than the Bambino: The Live Ball Era (1920–1941)	44
3. The Trade That Almost Happened: The Integration Era (1942–1960)	91
4. Managing for the Enemy: The Expansion Era (1961–1973)	111
5. The Shot Heard Round the Nation: The Free Agency Era (1974–1993)	129
6. The Lightning (A-)Rod: The Steroid Era (1994–2005)	147
7. The Evil Empires: The Present and Future (2006–present)	172
Appendix: Which Team Fared Better?	191
Bibliography	197
Index	199

Preface

The Greatest Rivalry in Sports

The Celtics and Lakers, Michigan and Ohio State, Real Madrid and Barcelona, Toronto and Montreal—all leap to mind when one thinks of the greatest rivalries in sports. Baseball has more than its share of rivalries, of course, from the traditional—the Giants and Dodgers, the Cubs and Cardinals—to the more recent—the Mets and Braves, the Angels and A's. But the national pastime's most intense rivalry is the long-running one between the Boston Red Sox and the New York Yankees. It may in fact be the most storied rivalry in all of sports.

It would seem like a natural fit, this rivalry. It involves two major East Coast cities, separated by a four-hour drive—a fact that makes it easy for fans to travel into enemy territory. (The front line appears to run across Connecticut, from the northwest to the southeast, with towns north of the line tending to favor the Sox.) They have also been in the same league for more than a hundred years, finishing first and second 19 times. Here is a statistical look at the rivalry as it has played out over that time, through the 2016 season:

Meetings: 2,121

Yankee victories: 1,145

Red Sox victories: 960

Ties: 14

Longest New York winning streak: 12 in a row in both 1936 and 1953

Longest Red Sox winning streak: 17 in a row in 1912

Yankees playoff berths: 51

Red Sox playoff berths: 22

Yankees World Series titles (27): 1923, 1927, 1928, 1932, 1936, 1937, 1938, 1939, 1941, 1943, 1947, 1949, 1950, 1951, 1952, 1953, 1956, 1958, 1961, 1962, 1977, 1978, 1996, 1998, 1999, 2000, 2009

Red Sox World Series titles (8): 1903, 1912, 1915, 1916, 1918, 2004, 2007, 2013

Red Sox and Yankees placed 1st and 2nd in the division (19): 1904, 1938, 1939, 1941, 1942, 1949, 1978, 1986, 1995, 1998, 1999, 2000, 2001, 2002, 2003, 2004, 2005, 2007, 2009

Yankees finished in first and the Red Sox in second (15): 1938, 1939, 1941, 1942, 1949, 1978, 1998, 1999, 2000, 2001, 2002, 2003, 2004, 2005, 2009

Red Sox finished in first and the Yankees in second (4): 1904, 1986, 1995, 2007

Looking at these numbers, one could easily argue that the Yankees have the upper hand in this rivalry. After all, it is difficult to argue with 27 World Series championships. Others may give the edge to the Yankees in the 20th century but quickly point out that Boston has won three World Series in the 21st century while the Yankees have one. One thing that no one would argue is the dislike these two teams harbor for each other. Many times this dislike has led to violence on the field. Here are some notable skirmishes.

- On May 30, 1938, Joe Cronin (Boston) and Jake Powell (New York) got into a fight that began on the field and continued underneath the stands. At this time Cronin was the player-manager of the Sox. Imagine a manager in current day baseball challenging an opposing player to a fist fight. While no clear winner was declared in this particular fight, the Yankees won the war as they finished first in the league with the Red Sox right behind.
- On May 24, 1952, rookie infielder-outfielder Jimmy Piersall, whose emotional and behavioral issues would later come to light, went toe to toe with Yankees second baseman Billy Martin, who was likewise quick to anger, in the clubhouse tunnel at Fenway. Piersall then carried his anger into the clubhouse and began a fight with one of his own teammates, Mickey McDermott.
- During the first game of a 1967 doubleheader, Red Sox third baseman Joe Foy hit a home run; in the second game, Yankees pitcher Thad Tillotson beaned him. In retaliation, Tillotson was beaned by Sox pitcher Jim Lonborg the very next inning, instigating a brawl in which Boston outfielder Reggie Smith body-slammed Tillotson.
- A battle of the catchers took place in 1973 when Carlton Fisk and Thurman Munson went at it after Munson barreled into Fisk on a failed squeeze play. After the two were separated, shortstop Gene Michael, who had missed on the bunt attempt, attacked Fisk, who eventually had to be pulled from the smaller Michael. The skirmish lasted roughly 10 minutes.
- Fisk's dislike for the Yankees carried over to 1976 when he got into a fight with third baseman Lou Piniella, who slid into the catcher. No sooner had that fight been quelled than Red Sox pitcher Bill Lee and Yankees third baseman Graig Nettles got into a fight in which Lee suffered a separated shoulder.
- In one of the ugliest scenes in their bitter rivalry, during the third game of the 2003 League Championship Series, three different fights broke out. Perhaps the most shocking moment came when 72-year-old Yankees bench coach (and former Boston manager) Don Zimmer charged Red Sox pitcher Pedro Martinez, who grabbed Zimmer by the head and used the coach's momentum to toss him to the ground.
- July 24, 2004, stands as the day many believe was the beginning of the end for the Curse of the Bambino. Sox catcher Jason Varitek and Yankee Alex Rodriguez went at it after Rodriguez took umbrage at being hit by a curveball. It was a turning point in the season, and the rivalry, as the Sox finally won their first World Series in 86 years.

To say that the Yankees and BoSox do not get along is quite an understatement. They hate each other. And so do their fans. One of the popular sayings in Red Sox Nation is "My two favorite teams are the Red Sox and whoever is playing the Yankees." Vendors outside of Fenway sell t-shirts emblazoned with the slogan "Yankees Suck," which is also a cheer that frequently issues from the stands at Fenway. For their part, Yankees fans used to wear shirts that read simply "1918"—the last year, until 2004, that the Sox had won a Series. As in Boston, this popular taunt was also shouted from the stands. While New York fans can no longer tease the Sox about a decades-long championship dry spell, they can and do point to their dominance of both the Sox and all of baseball since 1923 ("Twenty-Seven Rings, Bro!").

Can you imagine being a player in this rivalry? So ingrained is the us-vs.-them outlook that hands are wrung, teeth are gnashed, and editorials are written anytime the rivalry appears to have lost heat. The other team has always been the enemy—and, if the world is to make sense, must always be the enemy.

But what happens when you find yourself playing for the other side, whether because you were traded or signed as a free agent. What then? It would be like fighting in battles for the Confederacy and having them transfer you to the Union Army. How do you put all that anger, that hatred, that animosity you feel for the other team aside and now trying to help them win ballgames? And not only to win ballgames, but to win them against the side you once played for.

Some would argue that in the age of free agency, it is no longer a big deal to switch teams. With relatively few exceptions, after all, players move around, starting out in one city, moving on during their prime contract years, and maybe making brief stops elsewhere as their careers wind down. And yet the rivalry between the Yankees and Red Sox has perhaps become more intense over the past decade as both franchises have fielded top-flight clubs. Consider this fact: In the decade beginning with 2000, the Yankees and Red Sox finished first and second eight times. When both teams are in contention, it makes sense that the games between them take on added significance.

So how could someone play for both of these teams? As of the end of the 2014 season, more than 200 players have taken the field for both the Yankees and the Red Sox. Some stayed a single season, or less, on the enemy's roster, others—Wade Boggs, Roger Clemens, anyone?—for meaningful chunks of their careers. Such a player brings up several questions. What was it like to see both sides of this intense rivalry? Did the players enjoy or value their time with one team more than the other? Did the different parks, teammates, and managers materially affect their careers? And then there's what might be the most important question for fans: Which of the two teams got the better of the player? This is the debate we will seek to settle.

Understanding the Numbers

Statistics are an undeniable part of baseball. A player's entire career can be boiled down to a cold, hard number, which does not take into account the effort the player put in, the times he played hurt, the sacrifices he and his family made. Numbers may not tell the entire story, but they never lie. (That's not the same as saying they cannot, if misread, mislead.) If a player at an offensive position—say, third base or right field—struggles at the plate over a meaningful number of at-bats or seasons, no intangibles can make up for it. For management (and for baseball researchers), numbers are the basis for evaluation, used to size up a player relative to his peers. Who hit a similar number of home runs, got on base at roughly the same clip, or hit into as many double plays? Because understanding these numbers gives one a better awareness of the context of a player's career, it is necessary to understand what all the numbers mean. Throughout this book we will be looking at the statistics of pitchers and hitters.

Although these days there seems to be an endless number of statistics compiled for players, this book will consider a mix of standard or old-school measures and the more broadly recognized among sabermetric stats. The intention is to establish, in a way readily understood by both casual and serious fans, the approximate worth of a player, and in particular his worth during stints with the Red Sox and Yankees.

Here are the biographical details and statistics used for hitters, each accompanied by a brief discussion of its relevance:

Year The year or years that the player spent with a particular team. These years are known as seasons and a player has to have at least ten seasons in the major leagues to be considered for the Hall of Fame.

Age The age of the player at the time the statistic was recorded. Age is relative in baseball. A player usually hits his prime at around age 27 and shows signs of decline by age 35. There are exceptions to this rule, but there are very few players whose careers last into their 40s or start before their 20s.

G—Games The number of games a player appeared in over the course of the year. This does not mean the player played the entire game. He might have been brought in to pinch-hit or pinch-run, as a defensive replacement, as an injury replacement, or in a myriad of other scenarios in which a coach makes a switch. There are now 162 games a year in baseball; before 1962 there were only 154 games. Postseason games, which can number as many as 20 in a year, are not included. Players rarely appears in all 162 games in a season, let alone play every inning of every game.

AB—At Bats The number of plate appearances a player makes minus walks, hit-by-pitches, sacrifice hits or bunts, catcher's interferences, or instances in which he is replaced by another batter mid–plate appearance because of an injury. Each of these outcomes excluded for at-bats does count toward plate appearances. Five hundred at-bats is a very rough average for starting players.

R—Runs A player is credited with a run scored every time he crosses home plate and it is counted as a run for his team. The single-season all-time leader in runs scored is Babe Ruth at 177, and the career leader is Rickey Henderson at 2.295. Only seven players in the history of the game have scored 2,000 runs in their career.

H—Hits A hit is credited when the player puts the ball into play in fair territory and is able to reach at least first base without benefit of an error or fielder's choice. The all-time single-season record for hits is 262, established in 2004 by Ichiro Suzuki; the all-time hits leader is of course Pete Rose, who had 4,256. In a 500-at-bat season, starting players often have 125 or more hits.

2B—double Credited when a player hits the ball and is able to reach second base safely without the benefit of an error. Forty or more doubles will generally land a player among the MLB top 10 in a given season. Earl Webb in 1931 set the single-season record with 67 doubles. Tris Speaker is the career leader in doubles with 792.

3B—triple Credited when a player hits the ball and is able to reach third base safely without the benefit of an error. The rarest of all the hits. The most anyone has ever hit in a season is 36, by Chief Wilson. In order to hit a triple a player will generally need to shoot the ball into a gap and be quick enough to make it three-quarters of the way around the bases. Only three active players (Carl Crawford, Jose Reyes, and Jimmy Rollins) have more than 100 triples in their careers.

HR—Home Run Credited when a player is able to make it all the way around the bases in a single play without the benefit of an error. The most common way to hit a home run is to knock the ball over the outfield fences in fair play. The single-season home run record is held by Barry Bonds, who hit 73 during the 2001 season. He is also the career leader with 762 home runs. The career leader in inside-the-park home runs is Sam Crawford, whose record of 51 is unlikely ever to be broken. The most in a single season is Sam Crawford with 12. Power hitters frequently top 20 home runs in a season, league leaders 35 home runs in a season.

RBI—Run Batted In Credited when a hitter, as an outcome of his plate appearance, allows a teammate or himself to cross home plate in a single play. A player can achieve an RBI by a hit; being hit by a pitch with bases loaded; walking with the bases loaded; hitting a sacrifice fly, groundout, or bunt; or hitting into a fielder's choice. No RBI is credited when a run scores because of an error, wild pitch, passed ball, balk, or steal of home. A player can achieve multiple RBIs if more than one person crosses home plate on a play. The most RBIs a player can achieve in a single plate appearance is four, as the result of a grand slam home run. The career leader in RBIs is Hank Aaron with 2,297, and the single season leader is Hack Wilson, who knocked in 191 in 1930. League leaders generally top 100 RBI in a season.

SB—Stolen Base A stolen base is credited when a player advances to a base he is not entitled to, arriving without being tagged with the ball. Players can steal first to second, second to third, and, very rarely, third to home. A player cannot steal to first. The career stolen base leader is Rickey Henderson with 1,406 stolen bases, nearly 500 more than the second-place finisher (Lou Brock). Steals are down in the present era, in part because of the prevailing philosophy that stolen-base attempts lead to too many outs. League leaders will often swipe 50–70 bases in a season.

CS—Caught Stealing A steal attempt that ends in the runner's having been put out before safely reaching the attempted base. The lower the number of times caught stealing, the higher a runner's success rate or stolen-base percentage. (A success rate of roughly 70 percent or more is needed to outweigh the risk of an out.) Ironically, the very same man who has the career stolen bases record is also the leader in caught stealing, as Rickey Henderson was thrown out 335 times.

BB—Base on Balls (Walk) A base on balls, or walk, occurs when a pitcher throws four balls to a batter, allowing the batter to advance to first base. A walk can be as valuable as a hit, in the sense that both result in the offense's landing a man on base (and, sometimes, in advancing baserunners). A walk does not count as an at-bat but does count as a plate appearance. League leaders often top 100 walks in a season. The all-time walks leader is Barry Bonds with 2,558 walks. He is also the single-season record holder at 232 walks in 2004.

SO—Strikeout A strikeout is recorded after a batter accumulates three strikes. A player can strikeout looking at a called third strike, swinging and missing, or attempting to bunt when there are two strikes and the ball goes foul. Reggie Jackson has the most career strikeouts at 2,597. Until 2008 a player had never struck out more than 200 times in a season; since then it has been done six times, three times by Mark Reynolds.

BA Batting Average: This is the number of hits a player has divided by the number of at-bats, reported to three decimal places. A .300 average, whether over a season or a career, has long been a benchmark for success. The last time a player finished a season with a .400 average or better was 1941 when Ted Williams did it. If a player is under .200 they are said to be below the Mendoza Line, named after shortstop Mario Mendoza, who hit .198 or lower multiple times in his career. The implication is that anyone hitting below the Mendoza Line is a weak hitter.

OBP—On-Base Percentage This is similar to batting average but takes into account walks and hit-by-pitches. A player's OBP is almost always higher than his average. On-base percentage is calculated by adding hits, walks, and hit-by-pitches and dividing the total by the number of at-bats, walks, hit-by-pitches, and sacrifice flies. The all-time leader in career OBP is Ted Williams at .482; in other words, he reached base nearly half of the time (48.2 percent) that he stepped to the plate. Barry Bonds in 2004 had a season OBP of .609. On-base percentage is now generally considered a better indicator of a batter's worth than batting average.

SLG—Slugging Percentage This measure is similar to batting average but incorporates total bases and thereby provides an indication of power. It is arrived at by dividing total bases by the number of at-bats. A slugging percentage of .400 is fairly common, while elite power hitters will generally top .500. Babe Ruth has the highest career slugging percentage at .689. Barry Bonds finished the 2001 seasons with an .863 slugging, racking up 411 total bases out of 476 at-bats.

OPS—On-base Plus Slugging The sum of a player's on-base and slugging percentages, OPS measures both a player's ability to get on base and his power. An average OPS according to sabermetric guru Bill James is .700 to .766. League leaders are frequently at or above .900. The top career OPS is Babe Ruth's 1.163. The top four career OPS scores are all by left-handed hitters, as are the top 10 single-season OPS scores.

OPS+—Adjusted On-Base Plus Slugging A similar statistic to OPS, but OPS+ also takes into account the parks a player hits in and the league in which he played. A 100 OPS+ is considered average, a 125 very good, and a 150 elite. The career leader in OPS+ is Babe Ruth, who finished with a mind-boggling career score of 206.

TB—Total Bases Total bases is, as the name implies, the total number of bases a player accumulates in a season. A single counts for one, a double for two, a triple for three, and a home run for four. Total bases does not take into account any further advancement on the basepaths, such as a steal, passed ball, or another batter moving the player up a base. So a player that hits a single, double, and a home run in a game has accumulated seven total bases. The single-season leader in total bases is Babe Ruth, who racked up 457 in 1921. But the career leader is Hank Aaron with 6,856 total bases.

SH—Sacrifice Hits Better known as sacrifice bunts, these plays involve a player who lays down a bunt with the intention of advancing a runner already on base. Typically this results in an out but puts the runner in scoring position. A sacrifice bunt does not count as an at-bat and thus cannot negatively impact a player's batting average. If the official scorer of the game determines the player was bunting to try and get on base rather than sacrificing himself to advance the runner, the player will be charged with an at-bat. Pitchers or weaker hitters are frequently called upon to perform a sacrifice bunt. Bill James and, later, the influential book *Moneyball* discount the value of a sacrifice bunt, arguing that it gives away the offense's most valuable possession, its outs. Eddie Collins leads in career sacrifice bunts with 512.

For pitchers, this book considers the following pieces of information:

Year As with batters, year here refers simply to the year that the player played for a particular team. These years are known as seasons and a player has to have at least ten seasons in the major leagues to be considered for the Hall of Fame.

Age This is the age of the pitcher at the time the statistic was recorded. Age is relative in baseball. A pitcher generally hits his prime at around age 26, a year or so earlier than a position player, and has become a shadow of himself by age 35. There are exceptions to this rule but there are very few pitchers who remain active into their 40s and only a handful who were promoted to the majors before they were in their 20s.

W—Wins Wins is self-explanatory; it is simply the number of wins a pitcher accumulates over the course of a season or over his career. A win is awarded to a starter only if that pitcher pitches five complete innings or more. A win can be awarded to a reliever if that pitcher was in the game when his team took the lead. A winning pitcher is defined as the pitcher who last pitched prior to the half-inning when the winning team took the lead for the last time. Through the decades, a pitchers who win 300 games have been considered a lock for the Hall of Fame; in the age of four- and five-man rotations, pitch counts, and specialization, that benchmark appears to be all but out of reach. Twenty-win seasons are less and less common. Modern-day statisticians now downplay the importance of wins for a pitcher, since he has no control over how many runs his team scores, only how many runs the other team scores. The career wins leader is Cy Young, who won 511 games in a long career that spanned the late-nineteenth and early twentieth centuries. Old Hoss Radbourn notched 59 wins in 1884 to set the single-season record.

L—Losses A loss is assigned to the pitcher who allows the run that gives the opponent a lead that is never relinquished. A pitcher can be awarded a loss even though another pitcher gives up the go-ahead hit if the runner on base who scores was put there by the original pitcher. There is no minimum number of innings a pitcher must pitch to receive a loss and a reliever can be awarded the loss without ever retiring a single batter. The career leader in losses is Cy Young with 316, but he had 511 wins for a .618 winning percentage. John Coleman in 1883 had 48 losses, which established the single-season record.

Pct.—Winning Percentage The percentage of a pitcher's career decisions represented by wins is his winning percentage. If a pitcher wins more than he loses, his winning percentage will be over .500 (that is, over 50 percent). If he has more loses than wins it will be below. He had only 152 decisions, but Spud Chandler career .717 winning percentage is nevertheless recognized as the best in baseball history.

ERA—Earned Run Average Earned run average, as most fans know, is the number of earned runs a pitcher would be projected to give up per nine innings pitched. (Especially in recent decades, few pitchers routinely go nine innings in a start.) It is calculated by multiplying earned runs by nine and then dividing by innings pitched. A good ERA is determined by the era in which the pitcher played. In the Deadball Era (1900–1919), an ERA below 2.00 was good; in the Live Ball Era that followed, it was a sub-4.00 ERA. In the 1960s it went back to below 2.00 until the mound was lowered in 1969. In recent decades, an ERA between 3.00 and 4.00 ERA has generally been regarded as respectable. Ed Walsh has the best career ERA with a 1.82 from 1904 to 1917. The best modern-day ERA belongs to closer Mariano Rivera, who posted a 2.21 ERA from 1995 to 2013. Many would argue ERA is a more useful gauge of pitcher performance than wins and losses since a pitcher has complete control over the number of earned runs he gives up. (It's not quite as simple as that, of course; league, ballpark, and era can influence ERA.) Note that earned runs are not the same as runs; when a fielder makes an error that results in a run scored, that run is considered "unearned," and the pitcher is not penalized.

G—Games The number of games a pitcher appears in. Whereas a batter can appear in all 162 games in a season, a starting pitcher takes the mound only every four or five days and will generally appear in two or at most three dozen games a season. A reliever might appear in more games, but he will accumulate fewer innings than a regular starter. The single-season record for most appearances for a pitcher is reliever Mike Marshall who had 106.

GS—Games Started The number of starts a pitcher starts a pitcher makes. This is a statistic designed to determine whether the pitcher was used as a starter or a reliever in the game. The leader for most career starts is Cy Young with 815, which he accumulated over a 22-year span. In 1883, Pud Galvin started an amazing 75 games.

CG—Complete Games When a starting pitcher goes the entire game, he is credited with a complete game. This statistic has evolved over the years; it used to be that a starting pitcher was expected to throw the entire game. With the advent of specialization among pitchers, it has become increasingly uncommon for a starter to last nine innings. In 1904, pitchers completed 87 percent of the games they started; by 1954, it was 34 percent; and by 2004, it was a mere 3 percent. Cy Young is the career leader in complete games with 749. The top active complete games leader is C.C. Sabathia with 38 complete games in 15 seasons (as of the end of the 2015 season).

SV—Saves The save came about in 1969. A save is credited to the pitcher who finishes a game in which his team wins. There are, however, other requirements: The pitcher must be someone other than the winning pitcher, must work at least one third of an inning (represented in pitching lines as .1, as in 7.1 innings), and must either enter the game with no more than a three-run lead; with the potential tying run on base, at bat, or on deck; or pitch for at least three innings. Typically it is the designated closer that a team will turn to for saves, and he will enter the game in either the eighth or, more often these days, the 9th inning. A save can be earned by other pitchers, though. Mariano Rivera is the career saves leader with 652. The record for most saves in a single season is held by Francisco Rodriguez of the Anaheim

Angels, who saved 62 in 2008. Note that saves credited, ex-post facto, for seasons before 1969 might not meet today's requirements for the stat; they are often awarded to the non-starter who entered the game with a lead and, in most instances, pitched the last out of a game.

IP—Innings Pitched This is simply the number of innings pitched in a game, broken down by thirds. So if a pitcher faces one batter and gets him out, he has pitched a third—often expressed, oddly enough, as .1—of an inning. (Likewise, two-thirds of an inning can be expressed as .2.) A pitcher can come in and get no one out, resulting in an appearance but no credit for innings pitched. A starting pitcher averages around 200 innings pitched a season, a reliever around 80 innings. Mike Marshall set the all-time record for relievers in 1974 when he threw 208.1 innings. Cy Young pitched 7,356 innings in his career as a starter.

H—Hits Batters want this statistic to be high, but pitchers want it to be low. For a pitcher, this is the number of hits he allows. The average pitcher gives up roughly one hit for every inning he pitches. If a pitcher allows fewer hits than innings pitched, that is usually a good indicator that he has enjoyed a solid season. John Coleman in 1883 allowed 772 hits in a single season, the most ever.

R—Runs When a batter crosses home plate safely, a run is charged to the opposing pitcher responsible for him. This statistic can include both earned and unearned runs. Pitchers are judged on the number of runs they allow, as runs are what win and lose games. Cy Young, who leads many pitching categories such as innings pitched, wins, and losses, also leads this one, having given up 2,994 runs in his career.

HR—Home Runs This is another of those categories that is a plus for a batter, minus for a pitcher. Jamie Moyer, a soft-throwing but crafty pitcher, gave up 522 home runs in his 25-year career, the most ever. The most home runs given up by a pitcher in a single season is Bert Blyleven, who surrendered 50 in 1986. The league leaders tend to be in the 30–40 range.

BB—Base on Balls (Walk) After four pitches in one at-pat are declared balls, the pitcher is charged with a walk, or a base on balls. This results in a batter being given first base and, potentially, other runners advancing (if the batter-runner's arrival at first forces them along). The sturdy Nolan Ryan, who pitched for 27 seasons, set the record not only for strikeouts but for walks, amassing 2,795, nearly a thousand more than the pitcher occupying second place (Steve Carlton, who pitched for 24 seasons).

SO—Strikeouts A strikeout is credited to the pitcher when he records three strikes in one at-bat. Although strikeouts are a coveted statistic, they are not the only way—or even the most desirable way—to get an out. Pitchers who specialize in groundball outs or fly ball outs can be as effective as someone who relies on strikeouts. (Consider that the leader in career strikeouts, Nolan Ryan, had a winning percentage of .526, which ranks 544th in major league history.) The benefit of strikeouts is that they allow a pitcher to record outs independent of the defense behind him. League leaders in the present era frequently compile 200 or more strikeouts in a season.

ERA+—Adjusted ERA This statistic adjusts the pitcher's ERA to account for the ballpark and the league ERA. A league-average ERA+ is 100; the higher the number above that, the better the performance. Pedro Martinez holds the modern single-season record for ERA+ with a 291, a mark set when he finished with a 1.74 ERA while the league average was 4.92. The highest career ERA+ belongs to Mariano Rivera, who finished at 205. In second place is Pedro Martinez at 154.

WHIP—Walks plus Hits per Innings Pitched This statistic, which is expressed as an average, combines the number of walks and hits and divides by the number of innings pitched. What this leaves is the number of times a pitcher allows batters to reach base. Mariano Rivera's 1.00 is the lowest career WHIP since the Deadball Era ended. (Deadballer Addie Joss held batters to a 0.96 WHIP over the course of his nine-year career at the turn of the 20th century.) Pedro Martinez holds the single-season record with a WHIP 0.73 during the 2000 season with the Red Sox.

H/9—Hits per 9 innings This statistic functions similarly to ERA but counts hits rather than runs. There's an important difference, however: Not all hits lead to runs, and a pitcher can space out a higher-than-average number of hits in a game and still emerge with both a win and a sparkling ERA. (There have been 12 instances in that last 50 years in which a team has had 13 hits but failed to score a single run.) Nolan Ryan, the strikeout king who threw seven no-hitters, has the lowest career average at 6.55. He also holds the best single-season mark at 5.26 in 1972.

BB/9—Walks per 9 innings This is the number of walks a pitcher gives up for every nine innings that he pitches. Again, this statistic is dominated by pitchers from earlier eras, the leader being Candy Cummings, who pitched in the 1870s and had a .473 BB/9. In other words, Cummings gave up less than half a walk per game—albeit it a time when it took up to nine balls to constitute a walk. To find BB/9, the number of walks a pitcher gives up is multiplied by nine and then divided by the total number of innings pitched. Through the end of the 2015 season, the active leader among pitchers with at least 1,000 innings pitched is Doug Fister, who walks 1.76 batters every nine innings. The highest single-season mark since 1900 belongs to Carlos Silva, who finished the 2005 season at .430.

SO/9—Strikeouts per 9 innings This is the average number of strikeouts a pitcher has over the course of a nine-inning game. To find a pitcher's SO/9, multiply his home runs given up by nine before dividing by the total number of innings pitched. Unlike the BB/9 and HR/9, this statistic is not dominated by pitchers from long ago. In fact, there are only three starters who have averaged more than 10.0 for strikeouts per nine—Randy Johnson, Kerry Wood, and Pedro Martinez—and all retired after the year 2000. Of the top ten single-season SO/9 records, Randy Johnson holds seven of the spots, including the top one at 13.4 in 2001.

SO/BB—Strikeout to Walks Ratio This is the number of strikeouts a pitcher has for every walk issued. Tommy Bond from the late 1800s is the career leader with a 5.03. (Bond, like Cummings above, pitched at a time when it took more than four balls to constitute a walk.) That means for every walk he gave up, he struck out five batters. Curt Shilling, the modern-day leader, sits at second with a 4.38 SO/BB ratio.

These statistics are, for better or for worse, the common measures of a player's performance and worth. This is why several of them appear on the backs of baseball cards. Many of these numbers will be considered when determining which team, the Yankees or Red Sox, enjoyed the better performance from players the two teams shared.

Introduction

A Brief History of the Red Sox–Yankees Rivalry

The Yankees and Red Sox played their first game against one another on May 7, 1903. Sure, some might argue that the two teams had met before, when the Yankees were located in Baltimore, Maryland, but this 1903 meeting was the first that pitted the two franchises against each other while each was located in the city with which we now associate it. It should be noted, though, that they were not called the Yankees and Red Sox. Boston at this time was best known simply as the Bostons or Americans, and the New York team was called the Highlanders. This first series provided a good indicator of what was to come between these two franchises. In the second game, played on May 8, a fight broke out when Boston pitcher George Winter was knocked down by a pitch. The Yankees would win the game, but Boston went on to take the pennant and the very first World Series, as they triumphed over the Pittsburgh Pirates that October.

The 1904 season heated things up in the rivalry as the two teams faced off in both of their home openers. It came full circle as the two went up against one another on the final day of the regular season. The winner of the game would clinch the American League Pennant. The loser was simply going home (there not being any such thing as a wild card back then or even different divisions for that matter). The New York starting pitcher was Jack Chesbro, who won 41 games during the season. However, number 42 was to elude him when he threw a wild pitch, allowing Boston to score and win the game.

Boston kept the upper hand between the two teams as they dominated the decade of the 1910s, winning the championships in 1912, 1915, 1916, and 1918. It seemed the Red Sox would dominate the twentieth century. Who knew that after that 1918 win, it would take them nearly a century to taste World Series victory again?

The Yankees, on the other hand, got a taste of it for the first time in 1923—and, boy, did they like it. They liked it so much they went on to win another 25 world championships before Boston won their next Series, ending their 86-year drought with a sweep of the St. Louis Cardinals. Some say that what changed the fate of these two clubs was the trading of Babe Ruth, who had been one of Boston's best pitchers and had recently established himself as a dominant hitter, to New York. The Yankees would go on to dominate baseball while Boston endured a long dry spell, winning the pennant again only twice (in 1946 and 1967) in the next four decades.

From 1919 to 1945, the Yankees finished ahead of the Red Sox every year. In fact, other than one aberration in 1925, in which the Yankees finished seventh to Boston's eighth place, the Yankees finished in the first division every year. With equal (but unenviable) consistency the Red Sox finished fifth or lower every season during that same period. They were dead last eight of those seasons. Needless to say, it wasn't much of a rivalry during this time. Some indication of why comes in a comparison of the lineups.

The 1927 Yankees, which boasted the famous Murderers' Row lineup, tore through the league, winning a record-setting 110 games. The second-place team finished 19 games back of these Bronx Bombers. Here is what the lineup did that year:

Player	Pos.	Hits	Bat. Avg.	On-Base	Home runs	RBIs
Earle Combs	CF	231	.356	.414	6	64
Mark Koenig	SS	150	.285	.320	3	62
Babe Ruth	RF	192	.356	.486	60	164
Lou Gehrig	1B	218	.373	.474	47	175
Bob Meusel	LF	174	.337	.393	8	103
Tony Lazzeri	2B	176	.309	.383	18	102
Joe Dugan	3B	104	.264	.321	2	43
Pat Collins	C	69	.275	.407	7	36
Totals		1,314	.319	.400	151	749

Here, for the sake of comparison, is what the lineup for the 1927 Red Sox did on its way to last place and 103 losses:

Player	Pos.	Hits	Bat. Avg.	On-Base	Home runs	RBIs
Jack Rothrock	SS	111	.259	.302	1	30
Buddy Myer	3B	135	.288	.359	2	47
Jack Tobin	RF	116	.310	.371	2	40
Ira Flagstead	CF	133	.285	.374	4	69
Phil Todt	1B	122	.236	.280	6	52
Wally Shaner	LF	111	.273	.311	3	49
Bill Regan	2B	128	.274.	.315	2	66
Grover Hartley	C	67	.275	.337	1	31
Totals		923	.275	.331	21	384

The most obvious disparity in statistics is home runs: The Yankees, at 151, had more than seven times as many. The most a Red Sox player hit was Phil Todt's six—or as many as the Yankees' leadoff hitter, Earle Combs. Ruth hit 60. New York's batting average was nearly as high as the Boston's on-base percentage. The Yankees also had nearly 400 more hits and nearly twice as many RBIs. Six of the Yankees—Combs, Ruth, Gehrig, Lazerri, and pitchers Herb Pennock and Waite Hoyt—are in the Baseball Hall of Fame, as is manager Miller Huggins. Among the Red Sox, none of the position players made it to Cooperstown, and only Red Ruffing, at the time a young, below-league-average pitcher, eventually earned enshrinement. (And which American League team enjoyed his peak seasons? The Yankees, of course.) Although an extreme case, this snapshot of the teams demonstrates the stark difference between the two franchises during this time period.

The fires in the rivalry, however, were stoked after the arrival of Red Sox outfielder Ted Williams. This was evident in 1941 when Williams batted .406, becoming the last man in baseball to accomplish that feat, and was still runner-up to Yankees center fielder Joe DiMaggio in the Most Valuable Player voting. He may not have batted .400, but DiMaggio did amass a 56-game hitting streak, another feat yet to be repeated. Boston finished second that year to the Yankees, and did so again the following season. In 1946 Boston not only caught up to the Yankees but finished 17 games ahead of them, leaving New York and the rest of the league well behind on their way to the pennant. They would lose the Series to the Cardinals, but it was a banner year for Beantown, as the team spent all but two days of the regular season in first place. The Sox struck again in 1948 when they eliminated the Yankees from the pennant chase on the penultimate day of the season. The next day, the Sox won again and, with first-place Cleveland's loss, forced a one-game playoff, the first ever, to decide whether the Red

Sox or Cleveland would go on to the World Series. Cleveland won, going on to defeat the Boston Braves in the World Series, the last time they captured the championship.

The rivalry came to a head during the 1949 pennant race when the teams again met for a two-game series to finish the year. Boston, which had a one-game lead on the Yankees, needed to win only one of the two games. The Yankees had other ideas, however, narrowly taking both games, toppling the Red Sox, and going on to win the World Series. It would be the first of five consecutive Series titles and part of 16-year stretch that saw New York win the pennant 14 times. The Red Sox, on the other hand, were going the other way, enduring eight losing seasons in a row from 1959 to 1966. An aging Williams was around for only the first two of those seasons, and a young Carl Yastrzemski had little help (until the emergence of Tony Conigliaro in 1964) in the effort to keep up with the Yankees.

That all changed in 1967. Not only did Yastrzemski win the Triple Crown and league MVP Award, he led the Boston team back to the World Series. And the Yankees put up little fight, finishing ninth out of ten teams. Boston nevertheless barely won the pennant, edging out the Minnesota Twins and Detroit Tigers by a single game, before losing again to the St. Louis Cardinals in the Fall Classic.

Neither Boston nor the Yankees managed to take the pennant again until in back-to-back years Cincinnati beat each of them in the World Series, Boston in the historic seven-game 1975 matchup and the Yankees in a sweep a year later. More painful for fans than the loss to the Big Red Machine in '75 was Boston's implosion in 1978. As of July 19, the Red Sox had a comfortable 14-game lead over the Yankees, who were then in fourth place behind Milwaukee and Baltimore, who were likewise well behind Boston. By the time New York and Boston met for a four-game series at Fenway starting September 7, the Yankees had climbed to second place and was only four games out. This series became known as the Boston Massacre because the Yankees swept Boston, moving into a tie with them atop the standings. The Yankees surged ahead as the month went on but the Red Sox then went on a tear and managed to win their final eight games of the regular season, giving the Yankees and Boston identical records. A one-game playoff would decide the division. The Sox held a 2–0 lead into the seventh inning when up strode light-hitting shortstop Bucky Dent. Despite hitting only four home runs on the year, he managed to loft a three-run homer over the Green Monster to put the Yankees ahead. From that moment on he became known to Beantowners as Bucky "Fucking" Dent. The Yankees would go on to win the World Series that year and the year following.

The 1980s and early 1990s were a dry spell for both teams. Neither one won a World Series although both teams played in one. The Yankees lost to the Los Angeles Dodgers in 1981 and Boston was beaten by the New York Mets in 1986. The latter was the Series of the infamous Bill Buckner play, in which a ball rolled between the hobbled first baseman's legs, allowing the Mets to score and eventually win the game. For the Yankees this period became known as the Curse of Don Mattingly, for the first baseman who played 13 seasons in pinstripes. During his tenure, and despite his sustained run of excellence at the plate and in the field, the Yankees won the division only once, in 1994, when the players' strike shortened the season and there was no playoffs or World Series. During this time Boston finished in first place four times.

Mattingly retired at the end of the 1995 season, when the Yankees machine began to heat up again. They won the World Series in 1996 and then again in 1998, 1999, and 2000. They were also World Series runners-up in 2001 and 2003. In 2003, Boston and New York fought it out for the American League championship. The battle went back and forth, Boston winning the first game, the Yankees the next two, Boston tying it up, and the teams splitting the next pair to set up a game seven. Things did not look good for the Yankees as Boston took a 5–2 lead into the eighth inning. But Pedro Martinez, the Boston ace, had thrown well over 100 pitches, and after retiring the first batter of the inning, he gave up a run on back-to-back hits. Boston manager Grady Little walked to the mound, and many expected him to take the ball from Martinez. But then, in what must later have seemed inevitable to Sox fans, he decided against removing his starter. The Yankees promptly scored two more runs, knotting the game, which would go to extra innings. Knuckleballer Tim Wakefield came in to pitch a scoreless tenth and then returned to the mound for the start of the eleventh. Midseason acquisition Aaron Boone strode to the plate for the Yankees. Wakefield threw one pitch and it was all Boone needed. He sent a laser beam into the left-field stands, giving the Yankees the victory. With the blast, the Yankees third baseman joined Bucky Dent as an agent of heartbreak for Red Sox Nation, and fans soon took to calling him Aaron "Fucking" Boone. It truly seemed as if the Boston team was cursed never to win the World Series again.

That all changed the very next year in the ALCS, which again pitted the Bombers and Beaners against each other. This time the series did not see-saw back and forth; in fact, the Yankees jumped out to a three-games-to-none lead, leaving them in need of only a single victory to move on to the World Series. Never in the history of baseball had a team overcome such a deficit in a seven-game playoff. It seemed just a matter of time before the Yankees ended Boston's season in frustration once again. And, sure enough, New York went into the ninth inning of game four carrying a one-run lead. All that closer Mariano Rivera had to do was what he did best—throw his cutter and get the save. Somehow, though, Boston managed to scratch out a run after Dave Roberts stole second and put himself in scoring position. The game went to extra innings. In the twelfth, David Ortiz, the Red Sox slugger who will go down in history as its greatest playoff player, hit a walk-off two-run home run to win it for Boston. But it just seemed to be delaying the inevitable. Game five saw the Yankees leading, 4–2, into the eighth. Boston again managed to tie it up, and as they had the night before, the teams played into extra innings. Five hours and forty-nine minutes into the game, David Ortiz did it again, knocking in the winning run with a single. Boston would live to fight another day. Only two teams before in playoff history had been down 0–3 and forced a game six. Both of them had lost that game. The Red Sox tapped Curt Schilling, the ace they acquired in the offseason, to start the game. Schilling had a torn tendon in his ankle, but the team doctor managed to stitch it into place before the game. The blood-stained sock Schilling wore would go down in baseball lore as he pitched Boston to a 4–2 victory, forcing a game seven. And this time, there was little suspense after the early innings, as Boston scored four runs in the second to go up 6–0 and added four more by game's end to rout the Yankees, 10–3, punching their ticket for the World Series. There they rode the momentum and swept the St. Louis Cardinals for their first World Series championship in almost a century.

With Boston at last ascendant, the rivalry now began to set itself on a level playing field. After the American League went to the three divisions in 1995, placing both Boston and New York in the Eastern Division, every postseason until 2014 featured at least one of the two teams. And since this same period saw the advent of the wild card, which made it possible for a strong second-place team to extend its season, the playoffs frequently included both teams. (Eight times, in fact.) It now seems odd when at season's end one team isn't in position to thwart the other's playoff hopes or to give itself the late edge heading into a potential postseason matchup. It is the greatest rivalry in sports.

1. A Friendly Relationship
The Deadball Era (1901–1919)

Even though the first-ever series between the Yankees and Red Sox almost erupted in violence, the relationship between the two teams in the early years was fairly cordial. In fact, the two teams did not officially become the Red Sox and Yankees until 1914. The Yankees had begun as the Baltimore Orioles, reviving the name of the National League team that had dominated the mid–1890s. But they were not long for the Maryland city, as the intention all along had been to locate an American League franchise in New York, something that the National League opposed at first. By 1903, the path to the Big Apple had opened, the Baltimore franchise was transferred, and the nickname Orioles gave way to Highlanders (a reference to their ballpark location at one of the highest points in Manhattan and, perhaps, a play on the name of their owner, Joseph Gordon, which recalled the famed Scottish military unit the Gordon Highlanders). Boston was known primarily as the Americans, a nickname that pointed to league affiliation and differentiated the franchise from the Boston Braves. The intense rivalry had not developed quite yet, and in the 11-year period between 1907 and 1919, the two franchises exchanged 27 players in 11 sales and five trades.

Year	Players	From	To
June 1902	George Prentiss	Americans	Orioles
July 1902	Tom Hughes	Orioles	Americans
December 20, 1903	Jesse Tannehill	Highlanders	Americans
	Tom Hughes	Americans	Highlanders
June 17, 1904	Bob Unglaub	Highlanders	Americans
	Pasty Dougherty	Americans	Highlanders
October 13, 1907	Frank LaPorte	Highlanders	Americans
November 5, 1907	Hobe Ferris	Americans	Highlanders
July 10, 1908	Jake Stahl	Highlanders	Red Sox
August 17, 1908	Harry Niles	Highlanders	Red Sox
	Frank LaPorte	Red Sox	Highlanders
May 10, 1910	Clyde Engle	Highlanders	Red Sox
May 26, 1910	Red Kleinow	Highlanders	Red Sox
February 1912	Rip Williams	Red Sox	Highlanders
May 13, 1914	Les Nunamaker	Red Sox	Yankees
May 27, 1914	Guy Cooper	Yankees	Red Sox
December 18, 1918	Ray Caldwell	Yankees	Red Sox
	Frank Gilhooney	Yankees	Red Sox
	Slim Love	Yankees	Red Sox
	Roxy Walters	Yankees	Red Sox
	Dutch Leonard	Red Sox	Yankees
	Duffy Lewis	Red Sox	Yankees
	Ernie Shore	Red Sox	Yankees
June 13, 1919	Bill Lamar	Yankees	Red Sox
July 29, 1919	Bob McGraw	Yankees	Red Sox
	Allen Russell	Yankees	Red Sox
	Carl Mays	Red Sox	Yankees

During the Live Ball Era (1920–1941) there were just as many transactions, but most of them came about because Boston sought to jettison payroll. New York was only too happy to help. After the Red Sox had improved their financial situation and improved their play, the trades began to dry up. From 1942 to the present, there have been only 15 trades. Nine of those trades were complete by 1972, with only six trades, involving 13 players, coming in the years since then. When the two teams swapped middle infielders (the Yankees received Stephen Drew, the Red Sox Kelly Johnson) on July 31, 2014, in fact, it was the first trade between the two teams since 1997. To put their relationship in perspective, here are the trades they made with their other division foes in the last forty years:

Boston	Toronto	6 trades, 11 players
Boston	Tampa Bay	1 trade, 2 players
Boston	Baltimore	10 trades, 17 players
New York	Toronto	15 trades, 39 players
New York	Tampa Bay	1 trade, 1 player
New York	Baltimore	12 trades, 32 players

The only opponent either has dealt with less often is the Tampa Bay Rays, who have been around for only the past 18 seasons.

Of course during the Deadball Era there was no free agency, and ballplayers were basically slaves to the club that controlled them. That often meant the only way a player switched teams was via trade or sale. And since the rivalry between the two had not yet risen to the level it is at currently, neither team thought too long or hard about sending a good player to another team. Until, that is, the Red Sox traded away Babe Ruth.

Players Who Spent Time with Both Teams, 1901–1920

Doc Adkins

Doc Adkins played for New York and Boston before they were the Yankees and Red Sox. The year he pitched for the Boston team, they were known as the Americans, and the very next year he pitched for the Highlanders. Most of his time in baseball was spent playing for the minor league Baltimore Orioles. (After Baltimore was jilted for New York, the city promptly established a franchise in the Eastern League.) He won 132 games over an eight-year span with the Orioles.

American Season

Year	Age	W	L	%	ERA	G	GS	CG	SV	IP	H	R	HR	BB	SO	ERA+	WHIP	H/9	BB/9	SO/9	SO/BB
1902	29	1	1	.500	4.05	4	2	1	0	20.0	30	20	2	7	3	89	1.850	13.5	3.2	1.4	0.43

Highlanders Season

Year	Age	W	L	%	ERA	G	GS	CG	SV	IP	H	R	HR	BB	SO	ERA+	WHIP	H/9	BB/9	SO/9	SO/BB
1903	30	0	0		7.71	2	1	0	1	7.0	10	8	0	5	0	43	2.143	12.9	6.4	0.0	0.00

Which Team Fared Better?

Neither team got a whole lot out of Adkins. He pitched only 20 innings with Boston, starting twice and making two appearances out of the bullpen, at a time in which most pitchers finished their games. He pitched even less with the New York squad, starting one game and coming in relief in another, for a total of 7 innings. Considering that he threw five walks in only seven innings, and had an ERA of 7.71, it isn't a matter of the Boston team getting the better of him but rather the New York team getting the worst of him.

Neal Ball

In a seven-year major league career, Ball played for New York, Boston, and the Cleveland Naps. He was primarily a shortstop but could also fill in at second and third. As a member of the Cleveland team, Ball turned baseball's first unassisted triple play, and against Boston. He was playing shortstop and caught a line drive from Boston hitter Amby McConnell, stepped on second base to double up Heinie Warner, and tagged Jake Stahl, who had been trying to advance on the play. The glove he used is now on display at the Baseball Hall of Fame in Cooperstown.

Highlander Years

Year	Age	G	AB	R	H	2B	3B	HR	RBI	SB	CS	BB	SO	BA	OBP	SLG	OPS	OPS+	TB	SH
1907	26	15	44	5	9	1	1	0	4	1		1	11	.205	.222	.273	.45	53	12	2
1908	27	132	446	35	110	16	2	0	38	32		21	91	.247	.284	.291	.575	87	130	15
1909	28	8	29	5	6	1	1	0	3	2		3	10	.207	.281	.310	.592	86	9	2
Totals		155	519	45	125	18	4	0	45	35		25	112	.241	.278	.291	.569	84	150	19

Red Sox Years

Year	Age	G	AB	R	H	2B	3B	HR	RBI	SB	CS	BB	SO	BA	OBP	SLG	OPS	OPS+	TB	SH
1912	31	18	45	10	9	2	0	0	6	5	1	3	4	.200	.250	.244	.494	39	11	1
1913	32	23	58	9	10	2	0	0	4	3		9	13	.172	.294	.207	.501	45	12	2
Totals		41	103	19	19	4	0	0	10	8	1	12	17	.184	.276	.223	.499	43	23	3

Which Team Fared Better?

Ball set two Yankees records that have yet to be broken, and both of them were the sort that no one hopes to break. In 1908, he led the major leagues with 81 errors, 80 of them as a shortstop. That same year he also led the majors with 91 strikeouts, which would have been an alarming number in the Deadball Era. He did set a good record for the Yankees: His 438 assists as a rookie was not eclipsed until Derek Jeter had 444 in 1996. After a few years in Cleveland he was purchased for $2,500 by Boston in 1912. He would win a World Series with the Red Sox that year, but as a utility man, not a starter. He had only one at-bat in the Series. The nod, then, goes to New York, for whom he played in three times as many games and contributed 125 hits, as opposed to the 19 he had over two years with Boston.

Ray Caldwell

A pitcher who spent 12 years in major league baseball, Caldwell logged time with Cleveland in addition to Boston and New York. His best pitch was his spitball, and he became one of the 17 pitchers who were allowed to continue to throw the spitter after it was made illegal in 1920. Starting pitchers back then were known for being tough, but Caldwell was a cut above the rest. He was struck by lightning while pitching for Cleveland, and despite being knocked unconscious, he refused to exit, finishing out the complete game and getting the win. He was also an alcoholic. In 1916 his drinking problem was so bad that the Yankees suspended him halfway through the season. When they had had all of his off-field behavior that they could tolerate, the team traded him to Boston along with three other players. In 1924, Miller Huggins said, "Caldwell was one of the best pitchers that ever lived, but he was one of those characters that keep a manager in a constant worry. If he had possessed a sense of responsibility and balance, Ray Caldwell would have gone down in history as one of the greatest of all pitchers."

Highlanders/Yankees Years

Year	Age	W	L	%	ERA	G	GS	CG	SV	IP	H	R	HR	BB	SO	ERA+	WHIP	H/9	BB/9	SO/9	SO/BB
1910	22	1	0	1.000	3.72	6	2	1	1	19.1	19	8	1	9	17	73	1.448	8.8	4.2	7.9	1.89
1911	23	14	14	.500	3.35	41	26	19	1	255.0	240	115	7	79	145	107	1.251	8.5	2.8	5.1	1.84
1912	24	8	16	.333	4.47	30	26	13	0	183.1	196	111	1	67	95	81	1.435	9.6	3.3	4.7	1.42
1913	25	9	8	.529	2.41	27	16	15	1	164.1	131	59	5	60	87	124	1.162	7.2	3.3	4.8	1.45
1914	26	18	9	.667	1.94	31	23	22	0	213.0	153	53	5	51	92	142	0.958	6.5	2.2	3.9	1.80
1915	27	19	16	.543	2.89	36	35	31	0	305.0	266	115	6	107	130	102	1.223	7.8	3.2	3.8	1.22
1916	28	5	12	.294	2.99	21	18	14	0	165.2	142	62	6	65	76	98	1.249	7.7	3.5	4.1	1.17
1917	29	13	16	.448	2.86	32	29	21	0	236.0	199	92	8	76	102	94	1.165	7.6	2.9	3.9	1.34
1918	30	9	8	.529	3.06	24	21	14	1	176.2	173	69	2	62	59	92	1.330	8.8	3.2	3.0	0.95
Totals		96	99	.492	3.00	248	196	150	4	1,718.1	1519	684	41	576	803	101	1.219	8.0	3.0	4.2	1.39

Red Sox Year

Year	Age	W	L	%	ERA	G	GS	CG	SV	IP	H	R	HR	BB	SO	ERA+	WHIP	H/9	BB/9	SO/9	SO/BB
1919	31	7	4	.636	3.96	18	12	6	0	86.1	92	49	1	31	23	77	1.425	9.6	3.2	2.4	0.74

Which Team Fared Better?

Caldwell played nine years with the Yankees and a single season for Boston. Even though he accumulated a losing record with New York, he won 96 games there. Five of the years he played for the Yankees he had a winning record, his best being 1914 when he went 18–9. He had respectable numbers for Boston but they released him after only half a season. After catching on with Cleveland, he would throw a no-hitter against the Yankees. Nevertheless, New York fared better with the pitcher than Boston did.

JACK CHESBRO

Nicknamed Happy Jack, Chesbro pitched 11 years in the majors, starting his career with the Pittsburgh Pirates before going to the Yankees for seven seasons and finishing with Boston. He was elected to the Hall of Fame by the Veterans Committee in 1946, and his induction has a bit of controversy attached to it. Many claim he got in because of one season, 1904, in which he won 41 games in 51 starts. In the years he was eligible for election to the Hall of Fame by the sportswriters, he received a total of nine votes, many of those years receiving not a single vote.

Highlanders Years

Year	Age	W	L	%	ERA	G	GS	CG	SHO	SV	IP	HR	BB	SO	ERA+	WHIP	H/9	HR/9	BB/9	SO/9	SO/BB
1903	29	21	15	.583	2.77	40	36	33	1	0	324.2	7	74	147	112	1.152	8.3	0.2	2.1	4.1	1.99
1904	30	41	12	.774	1.82	55	51	48	6	0	454.2	4	88	239	150	0.937	6.7	0.1	1.7	4.7	2.72
1905	31	19	15	.559	2.20	41	38	24	3	0	303.1	5	71	156	133	1.098	7.8	0.1	2.1	4.6	2.20
1906	32	23	17	.575	2.96	49	42	24	4	1	325.0	2	75	152	100	1.197	8.7	0.1	2.1	4.2	2.03
1907	33	10	10	.500	2.53	30	25	17	1	0	206.0	0	46	78	111	1.155	8.4	0.0	2.0	3.4	1.70
1908	34	14	20	.412	2.93	45	31	20	3	1	288.2	6	67	124	84	1.188	8.6	0.2	2.1	3.9	1.85
1909	35	0	4	.000	6.34	9	4	2	0	0	49.2	2	13	17	41	1.671	12.7	0.4	2.4	3.1	1.31
Totals		128	93	.579	2.58	269	227	168	18	2	1,952.0	26	434	913	109	1.120	8.1	0.1	2.0	4.2	2.10

Red Sox Year

Year	Age	W	L	%	ERA	G	GS	CG	SHO	SV	IP	HR	BB	SO	ERA+	WHIP	H/9	HR/9	BB/9	SO/9	SO/BB
1909	35	0	1	.000	4.50	1	1	0	0	0	6.0	1	4	3	62	1.833	10.5	1.5	6.0	4.5	0.75

Which Team Fared Better?

Chesbro did a lot of amazing things, most of them while playing for the Yankees. He pitched their first game in New York as the Highlanders. A year later, Chesbro won 41 games, a number no one has equaled since, and threw 48 complete games. He amassed 269 games pitched and 200 victories for the Yankees in the seven years he played for them, twice leading the league in wins. By contrast, he pitched only one game for the Red Sox, the final game of the 1909 season, which he lost. The Yankees definitely got more out of this Hall of Famer.

Right: Jack Chesbro pitched from 1899 to 1909, amassing nearly 200 wins in that time. He was a Hall of Famer who spent a good majority of his career with New York. When he played for them they were still known as the Highlanders and had yet to take on the moniker of the Yankees. For the Red Sox, he pitched precisely one game, going six innings and giving up three earned runs in a no-decision.

Guy Cooper

Though he spent 12 seasons in the minors, Cooper pitched for only two—or, rather, parts of two—in the major leagues. He garnered a total of one win in that time, spent with the Yankees and Red Sox. His nickname was the Rebel, most likely because he was from Georgia and spent time in the military. He joined the Navy at age 18 and rejoined to fight in World War I.

Yankees Year

Year	Age	W	L	%	ERA	G	GS	CG	SHO	SV	IP	HR	BB	SO	ERA+	WHIP	H/9	HR/9	BB/9	SO/9	SO/BB
1914	21	0	0		9.00	1	0	0	0	0	3.0	0	2	3	36	1.667	9.0	0.0	6.0	9.0	1.50

Red Sox Years

Year	Age	W	L	%	ERA	G	GS	CG	SHO	SV	IP	HR	BB	SO	ERA+	WHIP	H/9	HR/9	BB/9	SO/9	SO/BB
1914	21	1	0	1.000	5.32	9	1	0	0	0	22.0	1	9	5	52	1.455	9.4	0.4	3.7	2.0	0.56
1915	22	0	0		0.00	1	0	0	0	0	2.0	0	2	0		1.000	0.0	0.0	9.0	0.0	0.00
Totals		1	0	1.000	4.88	10	1	0	0	0	24.0	1	11	5	58	1.417	8.6	0.4	4.1	1.9	0.45

Which Team Fared Better?

Cooper's lone win came while playing with the Red Sox. He pitched a single game for the Yankees, giving up three runs in three innings. He cost New York $1,500 when they purchased him in January 1914 from the Petersburg Goobers of the Virginia League, for whom Cooper had gone 16–5 while also batting .360 in 37 games. By May, however, Cooper no longer figured in New York's plans, and he was sold to Boston, who the *New York Times* reported had "refused to let the Yankees have any of their players by trade." New York surely got less for their money.

Lou Criger

Criger spent 16 years in major league baseball, and a majority of that time with Boston. He also played for the Cleveland Spiders, the St. Louis Cardinals and the crosstown Browns, and the New York Highlanders. With the World Series–winning Boston Americans in 1903, Criger caught every inning of the eight-game showdown with the National League's Pirates.

Americans/Red Sox Years

Year	Age	G	AB	R	H	2B	3B	HR	RBI	SB	CS	BB	SO	BA	OBP	SLG	OPS	OPS+	TB	SH
1901	29	76	268	26	62	6	3	0	24	7		11	9	.231	.270	.276	.546	52	74	6
1902	30	83	266	32	68	16	6	0	28	7		27	18	.256	.324	.361	.685	88	96	5
1903	31	96	317	41	61	7	10	3	31	5		26	31	.192	.256	.306	.562	64	97	14
1904	32	98	299	34	63	10	5	2	34	1		27	27	.211	.283	.298	.580	79	89	8
1905	33	109	313	33	62	6	7	1	36	5		54	20	.198	.322	.272	.593	88	85	7
1906	34	7	17	0	3	1	0	0	1	1		1	4	.176	.222	.235	.458	44	4	1
1907	35	75	226	12	41	4	0	0	14	2		19	17	.181	.251	.199	.450	44	2	10
1908	36	84	237	12	45	4	2	0	25	1		13	14	.190	.232	.224	.456	47	0	7
Totals		628	1,943	190	405	54	33	6	193	29		178	140	.208	.279	.279	.558	68	12	58

Highlanders Year

Year	Age	G	AB	R	H	2B	3B	HR	RBI	SB	CS	BB	SO	BA	OBP	SLG	OPS	OPS+	TB	SH
1910	38	27	69	3	13	2	0	0	4	0	-	10	15	.188	.291	.217	.509	56	15	0

Which Team Fared Better?

Boston had Criger for a longer time, and earlier in his career. He played eight seasons for the Red Sox, averaging 79 games a season for a grand total of 628 games. He was also Boston's first Opening Day catcher and was behind the plate for most of Cy Young's 511 victories. He caught only 27 games for the Highlanders in his lone year with them. Although he never even sniffed the doors of the Hall of Fame, he did receive 8 percent of the writers' vote in 1937.

Patsy Dougherty

An outfielder, Dougherty has the distinction of being the first player in baseball history to hit two home runs in a single World Series game, doing so for Boston in 1903, during the first modern World Series. During the regular season, he had led the majors in hits (195) and runs (107), and led the Americans in batting average for the second straight year. Boston nevertheless shipped Daugherty off to New York in 1904 after 49 games for Bob Unglaub, whose career fit his name. At the time of the trade Unglaub was in the hospital for alcohol poisoning while Dougherty was leading Boston in hits. Americans fans were in an uproar at the trade, seeing the lopsidedness of it. He spent three years with New York before going to the Chicago White Sox where he finished out his career playing six years for the pale hose.

Americans Years

Year	Age	G	AB	R	H	2B	3B	HR	RBI	SB	CS	BB	SO	BA	OBP	SLG	OPS	OPS+	TB	SH
1902	25	108	438	77	150	12	6	0	34	20		42	41	.342	.407	.397	.805	121	174	3
1903	26	139	590	107	195	19	12	4	59	35		33	62	.331	.372	.424	.796	133	250	18
1904	27	49	195	33	53	5	4	0	4	10		25	20	.272	.355	.338	.693	114	66	3
Totals		296	1,223	217	398	36	22	4	97	65		100	123	.325	.382	.401	.783	126	490	24

Highlanders Years

Year	Age	G	AB	R	H	2B	3B	HR	RBI	SB	CS	BB	SO	BA	OBP	SLG	OPS	OPS+	TB	SH
1904	27	106	452	80	128	13	10	6	22	11		19	44	.283	.316	.396	.712	120	179	4
1905	28	116	418	56	110	9	6	3	29	17		28	40	.263	.319	.335	.654	98	140	7

Year	Age	G	AB	R	H	2B	3B	HR	RBI	SB	CS	BB	SO	BA	OBP	SLG	OPS	OPS+	TB	SH
1906	29	12	52	3	10	2	0	0	4	0		0	4	.192	.192	.231	.423	27	12	0
Totals		234	922	139	248	24	16	9	55	28		47	88	.269	.311	.359	.670	105	331	11

Which Team Fared Better

The Yankees thought they were getting an All-Star when they traded for Daugherty, and he played well enough his first two seasons for them. But he wasn't the offensive player he had been for the Americans, despite swatting nine home runs for the Highlanders, twice as many as he had in Boston. But if his time on the field was of more value to the Americans, his trade to the Highlanders greased the skids for other trades to come. Daugherty was merely the first of the peak-level players Boston would deal to New York over the next couple of decades.

CLYDE ENGLE

A utility player, Engle was in major league baseball for eight seasons, playing for the Cleveland Indians and Buffalo's Federal League team as well as the Red Sox and Highlanders. He played just about anywhere but pitcher and catcher, spending most of his time at first or third base. He entered the league with the Highlanders before being purchased by Boston during the 1910 season.

Highlanders Years

Year	Age	G	AB	R	H	2B	3B	HR	RBI	SB	CS	BB	SO	BA	OBP	SLG	OPS	OPS+	TB	SH
1909	25	135	492	66	137	20	5	3	71	18		47	55	.278	.347	.358	.705	122	176	19
1910	26	5	13	0	3	0	0	0	0	1		2	0	.231	.333	.231	.564	73	3	0
Totals		140	505	66	140	20	5	3	71	19		49	55	.277	.347	.354	.702	120	179	19

Red Sox Years

Year	Age	G	AB	R	H	2B	3B	HR	RBI	SB	CS	BB	SO	BA	OBP	SLG	OPS	OPS+	TB	SH
1910	26	106	363	59	96	18	7	2	38	12		31	47	.264	.326	.369	.695	115	134	12
1911	27	146	514	58	139	13	3	2	48	24		51	54	.270	.343	.319	.662	86	164	16
1912	28	58	171	32	40	5	3	0	18	12	7	28	19	.234	.348	.298	.647	82	51	6
1913	29	143	498	75	144	17	12	2	50	28		53	41	.289	.363	.384	.747	116	191	13
1914	30	59	134	14	26	2	0	0	9	4	9	14	11	.194	.275	.209	.484	45	28	2
Totals		512	1,680	238	445	55	25	6	163	80	16	177	172	.265	.341	.338	.679	97	568	49

Which Team Fared Better?

His offensive production might have been better for New York, but Engle was a valuable member of a World Series winner with Boston in 1912, playing three infield positions and contributing on offense to the tune of a 116 OPS+. He will forever be known in Red Sox lore as the man whose fly ball the Giants' Fred Snodgrass muffed, allowing the Sox to tie the score in the 10th inning of the Series' final game. His overall contribution to the Red Sox was greater.

FRANK GILHOOLEY

In nine seasons, Gilhooley played for three teams. He spent six years with the Yankees, one with the Red Sox, and two with the St. Louis Cardinals. He was primarily a right fielder but could play center and left as well.

Yankees Years

Year	Age	G	AB	R	H	2B	3B	HR	RBI	SB	CS	BB	SO	BA	OBP	SLG	OPS	OPS+	TB	SH
1913	21	24	85	10	29	2	1	0	14	6		4	9	.341	.378	.388	.766	124	33	3
1914	22	1	3	0	2	0	0	0	0	0	0	1	0	.667	.750	.667	1.417	326	2	0
1915	23	1	4	0	0	0	0	0	0	0	0	0	1	.000	.000	.000	.000	100	0	0
1916	24	58	223	40	62	5	3	1	10	16		37	17	.278	.383	.341	.724	116	76	2
1917	25	54	165	14	40	6	1	0	8	6		30	13	.242	.362	.291	.653	99	48	5
1918	26	112	427	59	118	13	5	1	23	7		53	24	.276	.358	.337	.695	108	144	12
Totals		250	907	123	251	26	10	2	55	35	0	125	64	.277	.367	.334	.701	110	303	22

Red Sox Year

Year	Age	G	AB	R	H	2B	3B	HR	RBI	SB	CS	BB	SO	BA	OBP	SLG	OPS	OPS+	TB	SH
1919	27	48	112	14	27	4	0	0	1	2		12	8	.241	.315	.277	.591	70	31	3

Which Team Fared Better?

Of his six years with the pinstripers, his best was 1918, when he set career highs for at-bats, RBIs, doubles, and runs. His value to the Yankees jumps further when one discovers he was traded to Boston for Duffy Lewis, who gave the Yankees some good seasons while Gilhooley spent only one with the Red Sox, batting .241, knocking in a single run in 127 plate appearances, and playing backup for Babe Ruth.

CHARLIE HEMPHILL

Eagle Eye, as he was known, spent 11 years in the majors, playing for six teams, including the St. Louis Perfectos, St. Louis Browns, Cleveland Spiders, and Cleveland Broncos. He has the distinction of playing for Cleveland in 1899, when the Spiders recorded the worst record in major league history, winning just 20 games while losing 134. In 1901 he became the first Opening Day right fielder in Red Sox history. Hemphill then spent 1902 in Cleveland and St. Louis where he had his most productive year at the plate, batting .308 with six home runs and 69 RBIs. He spent the majority of his career with the St. Louis Browns, playing five years for them.

Americans Year

Year	Age	G	AB	R	H	2B	3B	HR	RBI	SB	CS	BB	SO	BA	OBP	SLG	OPS	OPS+	TB	SH
1901	25	136	545	71	142	10	10	3	62	11		39	26	.261	.312	.332	.644	79	181	9

Highlanders Years

Year	Age	G	AB	R	H	2B	3B	HR	RBI	SB	CS	BB	SO	BA	OBP	SLG	OPS	OPS+	TB	SH
1908	32	142	505	62	150	12	9	0	44	42		59	43	.297	.374	.356	.730	137	180	14
1909	33	73	181	23	44	5	1	0	10	10		32	23	.243	.357	.282	.639	101	51	3
1910	34	102	351	45	84	9	4	0	21	19		55	27	.239	.350	.288	.638	95	101	8
1911	35	69	201	32	57	4	2	1	15	9		37	18	.284	.397	.338	.736	101	68	5
Totals		386	1,238	162	335	30	16	1	90	80		183	111	.271	.369	.323	.692	113	400	30

Which Team Fared Better?

While Boston got 62 RBIs, 142 hits, and 71 runs from him in 1901, Hemphill contributed considerably more to the Highlanders in his four seasons with that team, or in any one of them, for that matter: His adjusted OPS was higher every year from 1908 to 1911 than it was in 1901. New York gets the nod.

Tim Hendryx

In an eight-season career, Hendryx played for four teams, the additional two being the Cleveland Naps and the St. Louis Browns. An outfielder, Hendryx had 215 putouts and 17 assists with the Yankees in a career-high 125 games in 1917 before being traded to the St. Louis Browns. After being released by the Browns in 1919, he spent some time playing for Louisville of the American Association before being traded to the Red Sox.

Yankees Years

Year	Age	G	AB	R	H	2B	3B	HR	RBI	SB	CS	BB	SO	BA	OBP	SLG	OPS	OPS+	TB	SH
1915	24	13	40	4	8	2	0	0	1	0	3	4	2	.200	.289	.250	.539	61	10	1
1916	25	15	62	10	18	7	1	0	5	4		8	6	.290	.380	.435	.816	143	27	1
1917	26	125	393	43	98	14	7	5	44	6		62	45	.249	.359	.359	.717	118	141	16
Totals		153	495	57	124	23	8	5	50	10	3	74	53	.251	.356	.360	.715	117	178	18

Red Sox Years

Year	Age	G	AB	R	H	2B	3B	HR	RBI	SB	CS	BB	SO	BA	OBP	SLG	OPS	OPS+	TB	SH
1920	29	99	363	54	119	21	5	0	73	7	9	42	27	.328	.400	.413	.814	119	150	13
1921	30	49	137	10	33	8	2	0	22	1	1	24	13	.241	.362	.328	.690	79	45	6
Totals		148	500	64	152	29	7	0	95	8	10	66	40	.304	.389	.390	.779	108	195	19

Which Team Fared Better?

Although he played one more year for the Yankees, appeared in only five more games for New York. He had similar numbers in at-bats (+5 for New York), stolen bases (+2 for New York), and runs (+7 for Boston). But Hendryx was more efficient with Boston, amassing 28 more hits and knocking in 45 more runs, and he posted better on-base and slugging percentages. His best full season in the majors took place in Boston in 1920, when he batted .328 with 54 runs and 73 RBIs. Boston fared a little better.

Tom Hughes

Not to be confused with Tom Hughes the outfielder who played for the 1930 Tigers, this Hughes was a pitcher for 13 years, plying his trade for the Chicago Orphans, Baltimore Orioles, and the Washington Senators in addition to the Highlanders and Americans. In his rookie season with Chicago he struck out 225 batters, the third best ever for a National League rookie. He pitched in the 1903 World Series for the Americans, winning a ring with them. While playing for the Senators in 1906, he became the first pitcher ever to throw a shutout and hit a home run, which produced the only run in the game. It has only been done six times since, the last time in 1983. After going to the American Association and winning 31 games for the Minneapolis Millers, he eventually returned to the majors with the Senators. He finished his career with a 131–175 record.

Americans Years

Year	Age	W	L	%	ERA	G	GS	CG	SV	IP	H	R	HR	BB	SO	ERA+	WHIP	H/9	BB/9	SO/9	SO/BB
1902	23	3	3	.500	3.28	9	8	4	0	49.1	51	31	0	24	15	109	1.520	9.3	4.4	2.7	0.63
1903	24	20	7	.741	2.57	33	31	25	0	244.2	232	95	5	60	112	118	1.193	8.5	2.2	4.1	1.87
Totals		23	10	.697	2.69	42	39	29	0	294.0	283	126	5	84	127	116	1.248	8.7	2.6	3.9	1.51

Highlanders Year

Year	Age	W	L	%	ERA	G	GS	CG	SV	IP	H	R	HR	BB	SO	ERA+	WHIP	H/9	BB/9	SO/9	SO/BB
1904	25	7	11	.389	3.70	19	18	12	0	136.1	141	72	3	48	75	74	1.386	9.3	3.2	5.0	1.56

Which Team Fared Better?

Just glancing at the numbers it seems obvious Boston made out much better. The Red Sox got a 20-game winner for the 1903 season, while he was 7–11 for the 1904 Highlanders. His ERA while with Boston was 2.69; it was a full run higher with New York. His adjusted ERA (ERA+) was 42 points better in Beantown, too. Boston even made out fairly well when they traded Hughes to the Highlanders for Jesse Tannehill. Although the trade was initially unpopular in Boston, Tannehill accumulated a 62–38 record for Boston, while Hughes pitched so poorly for New York that they traded him halfway through the season, sending him and fellow right-hander to the Senators for Al Orth.

RED KLEINOW

Mostly used as a reserve catcher during his eight-year career, he played six and a half seasons for the Yankees, one and a half for Boston, and half a season for the Philadelphia Phillies. Although Kleinow was a solid defensive catcher, the highest his batting average ever climbed was .264, a peak he achieved in 1907. His career batting average was a backup-catcher-like .213, but he was of more value behind the plate than standing next to it.

Highlanders Years

Year	Age	G	AB	R	H	2B	3B	HR	RBI	SB	CS	BB	SO	BA	OBP	SLG	OPS	OPS+	TB	SH
1904	26	68	209	12	43	8	4	0	16	4		15	37	.206	.259	.282	.541	67	59	6
1905	27	88	253	23	56	6	3	1	24	7		20	34	.221	.284	.281	.564	71	71	3
1906	28	96	268	30	59	9	3	0	31	8		24	28	.220	.287	.276	.563	69	74	13
1907	29	90	269	30	71	6	4	0	26	5		24	25	.264	.327	.316	.643	98	85	7
1908	30	96	279	16	47	3	2	1	13	5		22	31	.168	.237	.204	.441	44	57	8
1909	31	78	206	24	47	11	4	0	15	7		25	31	.228	.315	.320	.635	100	66	9
1910	32	6	12	2	5	0	0	0	2	2		1	0	.417	.462	.417	.878	168	5	0
Totals		522	1,496	137	328	43	20	2	127	38		131	186	.219	.286	.279	.564	75	417	46

Red Sox Years

Year	Age	G	AB	R	H	2B	3B	HR	RBI	SB	CS	BB	SO	BA	OBP	SLG	OPS	OPS+	TB	SH
1910	32	50	147	9	22	1	0	1	8	3		20	26	.150	.251	.177	.428	33	26	2
1911	33	8	14	0	3	0	0	0	0	1		2	0	.214	.313	.214	.527	49	3	1
Totals		58	161	9	25	1	0	1	8	4		22	26	.155	.257	.180	.437	34	29	3

Which Team Fared Better?

His best year was spent with the Highlanders in 1907, for whom he set career highs in batting average (.264), on-base percentage (.327), slugging (.316), hits (71) hits, runs scored (30), and wins above replacement (1.6). Although he batted only .150 for Boston the year they traded for him, he did what he was acquired to do, which was to act as a serviceable backup catcher for the oft-injured Bill Carrigan. Overall New York got the better of him as he contributed a total of 328 hits, 127 RBIs, and 137 runs over the course of his seven seasons. Even if you average those numbers out he would be at 47 hits, 18 RBIs, and 20 runs; his best season for Boston saw those numbers at 25, 8, and 9, respectively.

John Knight

A shortstop for five teams across his eight-year major league career, Knight played for New York in two stints, once when they were the Highlanders and then when they had become the Yankees. He also spent some time in Philadelphia with the Athletics as well as with the Washington Senators.

Americans Year

Year	Age	G	AB	R	H	2B	3B	HR	RBI	SB	CS	BB	SO	BA	OBP	SLG	OPS	OPS+	TB	SH
1907	21	98	360	31	78	9	3	2	29	8		19	53	.217	.256	.275	.531	70	99	3

Highlanders/Yankees Years

Year	Age	G	AB	R	H	2B	3B	HR	RBI	SB	CS	BB	SO	BA	OBP	SLG	OPS	OPS+	TB	SH
1909	23	116	360	46	85	8	5	0	40	15		37	68	.236	.311	.286	.597	88	103	17
1910	24	117	414	58	129	25	4	3	45	23		34	55	.312	.372	.413	.785	140	171	19
1911	25	132	470	69	126	16	7	3	62	18		42	63	.268	.342	.351	.693	89	165	99
1913	27	70	250	24	59	10	0	0	24	7		25	27	.236	.310	.276	.586	72	69	6
Totals		435	1,494	197	399	59	16	6	171	63		138	213	.267	.338	.340	.678	99	508	61

Which Team Fared Better?

He played a single season for Boston, hitting only .217 and getting on base at a mere .256 clip. His two best seasons came while with the Highlanders, in 1910 and 1911. In those years he led the team in several offensive categories and even received four votes in the MVP balloting in 1911. In 1910 he batted .312 with a slugging percentage of .413, and a year later he knocked in 62 runs while scoring 69. Either of those two seasons alone would be worth more than his time with the Americans. When you factor in the fact he went back to New York in 1913 and contributed 24 RBIs, 59 hits, and 24 runs to his career totals with them, there is no doubt about which of the franchises got more out of Knight.

Bill Lamar

In the nine years he played major league baseball, Lamar played left field for four teams, the most time spent with the Philadelphia Athletics at four years. He was with the Yankees for three seasons as well as the Brooklyn Robins for two. He got to play for a World Series in 1920 as a member of the Robins but lost to the Cleveland Indians.

Yankees Years

Year	Age	G	AB	R	H	2B	3B	HR	RBI	SB	CS	BB	SO	BA	OBP	SLG	OPS	OPS+	TB	SH
1917	20	11	41	2	10	0	0	0	3	1		0	2	.244	.244	.244	.488	48	10	1
1918	21	28	110	12	25	3	0	0	2	2		6	2	.227	.267	.255	.522	56	28	3
1919	22	11	16	1	3	1	0	0	0	1		2	1	.188	.278	.250	.528	48	4	0
Totals		50	167	15	38	4	0	0	5	4		8	5	.228	.263	.251	.514	53	42	4

Red Sox Year

Year	Age	G	AB	R	H	2B	3B	HR	RBI	SB	CS	BB	SO	BA	OBP	SLG	OPS	OPS+	TB	SH
1919	22	48	148	18	43	5	1	0	14	3		5	9	.291	.314	.338	.652	87	50	6

Which Team Fared Better?

Lamar gave his best years to the Athletics, having a career year in 1925 when he hit for a .356 average, knocked in 77 runs, had 202 hits, and scored 85 runs. Even though he played for the Yankees for three years, they used him sparingly. He accrued only 38 hits, 15 runs, and 5 RBIs during that time. He was purchased by Boston in June of 1919, and in the half-season he played for them, he put up better numbers—43 hits, 18 runs, and 14 RBIs—in fewer at-bats. Because Boston used him as an everyday player, they were able to get more production out of him than the Yankees, who used him intermittently. While the Yankees placed him on waivers and essentially got the purchase price for him in return, the Red Sox flipped Lamar for Tim Hendryx, who for two seasons put up pretty decent numbers for Boston. This one belongs to the Red Sox.

Frank LaPorte

In his 11-year major league career, Frank LaPorte played a little second base, third base, and outfield. He started out with the Highlanders, who traded him that offseason to Boston, who traded him back to New York the following August. He stayed with the Highlanders through 1910, then spent his final seasons with the St. Louis Browns (1911–1912), Washington Senators (1912–1913), Indianapolis Hoosiers (Federal League, 1914), and Newark Peppers (Federal League, 1915).

Yankees Years

Year	Age	G	AB	R	H	2B	3B	HR	RBI	SB	CS	BB	SO	BA	OBP	SLG	OPS	OPS+	TB	SH
1905	25	11	40	4	16	1	0	1	12	1		1	4	.400	.415	.500	.915	177	20	0
1906	26	123	454	60	120	23	9	2	54	10		22	57	.264	.300	.368	.668	100	167	6
1907	27	130	470	56	127	20	11	0	48	10		27	35	.270	.317	.360	.676	109	169	9
1908	28	39	145	7	38	3	4	1	15	3		8	12	.262	.301	.359	.659	114	52	5
1909	29	89	309	35	92	19	3	0	31	5		18	36	.298	.340	.379	.719	126	117	8
1910	30	124	432	43	114	14	6	2	67	16		33	34	.264	.321	.338	.658	101	146	19
Totals		516	1,850	205	507	80	33	6	227	45		109	178	.274	.318	.363	.681	109	671	47

Red Sox Year

Year	Age	G	AB	R	H	2B	3B	HR	RBI	SB	CS	BB	SO	BA	OBP	SLG	OPS	OPS+	TB	SH
1908	28	62	156	14	37	1	3	0	15	3		12	8	.237	.296	.282	.578	86	44	3

Which Team Fared Better?

The Yankees must have thought he was valuable to their organization because less than a year after trading him to Boston, they traded to bring him back. It was the first time a player ever went from New York to Boston back to New York again. If the Yankees had been hoping for the production (15 RBIs and 37 hits in 62 games) he provided while with Boston, they weren't disappointed; he put up nearly the same numbers after returning to New York, but in only 39 games. Over the length of his Yankees career, LaPorte would contribute 507 hits and 227 RBIs. But then he was traded again, this time to the St. Louis Browns, who in 1920 had a career year from him. New York got the better overall numbers from LaPorte but twice traded him away when they could have gotten production from him.

Louis LeRoy

A pitcher from Wisconsin, LeRoy played for only the Highlanders and Red Sox in his big league career. Known as "Chief" because he was Native American (on his mother's side; his father was French-Canadian, according to SABR's Bill Nowlin), he spent two seasons with the Yankees before jumping ship to the minor league American Association. He did come back to the majors for one game with the Red Sox before eventually finishing out his career in the American Association, Pacific Coast League, and a few lower-level minor leagues.

Highlanders Years

Year	Age	W	L	%	ERA	G	GS	CG	SV	IP	H	R	HR	BB	SO	ERA+	WHIP	H/9	BB/9	SO/9	SO/BB
1905	26	1	1	.500	3.75	3	3	2	0	24.0	26	14	2	1	8	79	1.125	9.8	0.4	3.0	8.00
1906	27	2	0	1.000	2.22	11	2	1	1	44.2	33	19	0	12	28	135	1.007	6.6	2.4	5.6	2.33
Totals		3	1	.750	2.75	14	5	3	1	68.2	59	33	2	13	36	109	1.049	7.7	1.7	4.7	2.77

Red Sox Year

Year	Age	W	L	%	ERA	G	GS	CG	SV	IP	H	R	HR	BB	SO	ERA+	WHIP	H/9	BB/9	SO/9	SO/BB
1910	31	0	0		11.25	1	0	0	0	4.0	7	9	1	2	3	26	2.250	15.8	4.5	6.8	1.50

Which Team Fared Better?

Neither team got much out of LeRoy in his limited time. He pitched only 14 games with the Highlanders and a lone game with Boston. He went 3–1 with New York, pitching 68 innings and striking out 36. Because his ERA was inflated after he gave up seven hits and nine runs, five of them earned, in the four innings he pitched for Boston, the edge would have to go to the Highlanders.

Duffy Lewis

A left fielder who spent most of his career with Boston, Lewis was a solid all-around player who contributed heavily to some of the great early Red Sox teams. In eight seasons with Boston he put together several solid years, winning three world championships with the team in 1912, 1915, and 1916. He missed out winning the World Series with Boston in 1918 because he had joined the U.S. Navy for World War I.

Red Sox Years

Year	Age	G	AB	R	H	2B	3B	HR	RBI	SB	CS	BB	SO	BA	OBP	SLG	OPS	OPS+	TB	SH
1910	22	151	541	64	153	29	7	8	68	10		32	71	.283	.328	.407	.734	127	220	27
1911	23	130	469	64	144	32	4	7	86	11		25	49	.307	.355	.437	.792	121	205	23
1912	24	154	581	85	165	36	9	6	109	9	19	52	76	.284	.346	.408	.754	111	237	31
1913	25	149	551	54	164	31	12	0	90	12		30	55	.298	.336	.397	.734	112	219	29
1914	26	146	510	53	142	37	9	2	79	22	31	57	41	.278	.357	.398	.755	126	203	24
1915	27	152	557	69	162	31	7	2	76	14	7	45	63	.291	.348	.382	.731	121	213	28
1916	28	152	563	56	151	29	5	1	56	16		33	56	.268	.313	.343	.656	96	193	24
1917	29	150	553	55	167	29	9	1	65	8		29	54	.302	.342	.392	.735	125	217	33
Totals		1,184	4,325	500	1,248	254	62	27	629	102	57	303	465	.289	.340	.395	.735	117	1,707	219

Yankees Years

Year	Age	G	AB	R	H	2B	3B	HR	RBI	SB	CS	BB	SO	BA	OBP	SLG	OPS	OPS+	TB	SH
1919	31	141	559	67	152	23	4	7	89	9		17	42	.272	.293	.365	.658	84	204	26
1920	32	107	365	34	99	8	1	4	61	2	8	24	32	.271	.320	.332	.651	70	121	16
Totals		248	924	101	251	31	5	11	150	10	8	41	74	.272	.304	.352	.656	78	325	42

Which Team Fared Better?

His legacy is tied pretty firmly to the Red Sox. Along with Tris Speaker and Harry Hooper, he was a member of what some still argue was one of the best outfields in baseball history. In 1913 the three combined for a whopping 84 assists, 29 of them from Lewis. His defensive prowess

was such that the incline that used to exist in front of the Green Monster was known as "Duffy's Cliff," an unexpected hazard that could embarrass lesser defenders. He received some MVP votes for his 1914 season, but he put up similar numbers in all but one (1916) of his seasons in Boston. He did play well for the Yankees in the two years he was with them, with 150 RBIs, 251 hits, 11 home runs, and 101 runs combined, but he will forever be known as a Boston Red Sox due to his three rings with them.

Duffy Lewis had 793 RBIs and 1,518 hits during his eleven year career. The best of these years he gave to Boston, with whom he won three championships back when the Red Sox dominated the early twentieth century. He was inducted into the Boston Red Sox Hall of Fame in 2002.

Carl Mays

Mays will forever be known as the answer to the trivia question Who was the only pitcher to have killed a major leaguer with a beanball? The victim was Ray Chapman, whom Mays plunked on August 16, 1920. Chapman died 12 hours later. That tragic event notwithstanding, Mays enjoyed a fairly good career, winning 207 games and finishing with an adjusted ERA of 119 (which means he was 19 percent better than a league-average pitcher from his day). He played five years each for the Red Sox, the Yankees, and the Cincinnati Reds, finishing his 15-year career with the New York Giants.

Red Sox Years

Year	Age	W	L	%	ERA	G	GS	CG	SV	IP	H	R	HR	BB	SO	ERA+	WHIP	H/9	BB/9	SO/9	SO/BB
1915	23	6	5	.545	2.60	38	6	2	7	131.2	119	54	0	21	65	108	1.063	8.1	1.4	4.4	3.10
1916	24	18	13	.581	2.39	44	24	14	3	245.0	208	79	3	74	76	116	1.151	7.6	2.7	2.8	1.03
1917	25	22	9	.710	1.74	35	33	27	0	289.0	230	81	1	74	91	148	1.052	7.2	2.3	2.8	1.23
1918	26	21	13	.618	2.21	35	33	30	0	293.1	230	94	2	81	114	122	1.060	7.1	2.5	3.5	1.41
1919	27	5	11	.313	2.47	21	16	14	2	146.0	131	57	2	40	53	123	1.171	8.1	2.5	3.3	1.33
Totals		72	51	.585	2.21	173	112	87	12	1,105.0	918	365	8	290	399	124	1.093	7.5	2.4	3.2	1.38

Yankees Years

Year	Age	W	L	%	ERA	G	GS	CG	SV	IP	H	R	HR	BB	SO	ERA+	WHIP	H/9	BB/9	SO/9	SO/BB
1919	27	9	3	.750	1.65	13	13	12	0	120.0	96	34	3	37	54	194	1.108	7.2	2.8	4.1	1.46
1920	28	26	11	.703	3.06	45	47	26	3	312.0	310	127	13	84	92	125	1.263	8.9	2.4	2.7	1.10
1921	29	27	9	.750	3.05	49	38	30	7	336.2	332	145	11	76	70	138	1.212	8.9	2.0	1.9	0.92
1922	30	13	14	.481	3.60	34	29	21	1	240.0	257	111	12	50	41	111	1.279	9.6	1.9	1.5	0.82
1923	31	5	2	.714	6.20	23	7	2	0	81.1	119	59	8	32	16	64	1.857	13.2	3.5	1.8	0.50
Totals		80	39	.672	3.25	164	124	91	11	1,090.0	1,114	476	47	279	273	121	1.278	9.2	2.3	2.3	0.98

Which Team Fared Better?

He played an equal number of years with each team, compiling very similar statistics. He had 72 wins for Boston and 80 for New York, and he was a 20-game winner twice for each club. He pitched 1,105 innings for the Red Sox, 1,090 for the Yankees. When it comes to strikeouts and runs allowed, Boston gets the edge. His ERA, at 2.59, was a full run lower with Boston— it was 3.82 for New York—and that at first would seem significant; but then a look at the years he spent with each team puts those numbers in perspective. His time with the Sox was during the Deadball Era; four of his five Yankees seasons came after 1919, at a time when league offense was rebounding. The statistic that puts the Red Sox ahead is instead the number of World Series Championships. He won three with Boston: 1915, 1916, and 1918. He had a single championship with the Yankees in 1923—and was accused of helping to throw the 1921 World Series, which the Yankees lost to the Giants. The Red Sox got Mays for a relatively cheap minor league contract, while the Yankees paid $40,000 for his services. Not that all was perfect when Mays was with Boston.

Carl Mays had a reputation as a headhunter that, after a fateful game in 1920, he would never shake. Mays had a wicked spitball, and one of them hit Ray Chapman in August of that season, fracturing the shortstop's skull and leading to his death. (The fatal beaning was the most compelling reason for banning the spitball, which Major League Baseball had taken its first steps toward doing the season before.) Mays had a lot of success with both the Yankees and the Red Sox, however, winning three World Series with Boston and one with the Yankees.

Bob McGraw

McGraw played for nine seasons, taking a break from the majors when he left to play with the American Association from 1921 to 1924. After coming back to the majors he played for the Brooklyn Robins, the St. Louis Cardinals, and the Philadelphia Phillies. He served mostly as a relief pitcher early in his career, becoming a regular starter only once he had returned from his time in the American Association.

Yankees Years

Year	Age	W	L	%	ERA	G	GS	CG	SV	IP	H	R	HR	BB	SO	ERA+	WHIP	H/9	BB/9	SO/9	SO/BB
1917	22	0	1	.000	0.82	2	2	1	0	11.0	9	5	0	3	3	346	1.091	7.4	2.5	2.5	1.00
1918	23	0	1	.000		1	1	0	0	0.0	0	4	0	4	0	4					0.00
1919	24	1	0	1.000	3.31	6	0	0	0	16.1	11	6	1	10	3	99	1.286	6.1	5.5	1.7	0.30
1920	25	0	0		4.67	15	0	0	0	27.0	24	18	1	20	11	83	1.630	8.0	6.7	3.7	0.55
Totals		**1**	**2**	**.333**	**4.14**	**24**	**3**	**1**	**0**	**54.1**	**44**	**33**	**2**	**37**	**17**	**85**	**1.491**	**7.3**	**6.1**	**2.8**	**0.46**

Red Sox Year

Year	Age	W	L	%	ERA	G	GS	CG	SV	IP	H	R	HR	BB	SO	ERA+	WHIP	H/9	BB/9	SO/9	SO/BB
1919	24	0	2	.000	6.75	10	1	0	0	26.2	33	23	0	17	6	46	1.875	11.1	5.7	2.0	0.35

Which Team Fared Better?

He didn't log a lot of playing time with either team. In four years with the Yankees, he pitched in only 24 games. In the half-season he played for Boston, he appeared in 10 games. His ERA was pretty high for both teams, but his 4.14 (85 ERA+) for the Yankees was considerably better than the 6.75 (46 ERA+) for Boston. And the Yankees must have seen something in him: They kept bringing him back.

DEACON McGUIRE

McGuire was a career baseball man, spending 26 years in the majors and playing until he was 48. As a catcher, no less. He was a player-manager for parts of four seasons (including two in which his clubs won pennants) and non-playing manager for two others. He was also later a coach for the Detroit Tigers for six years. McGuire played for eleven different teams, a record that was only recently broken, in 2010, by Matt Stairs. These teams included the Toledo Blue Stockings, Detroit Wolverines, Philadelphia Quakers, Cleveland Blues, Rochester Broncos, Washington Senators, Brooklyn Superbas, Detroit Tigers, and Cleveland Naps in addition to the Highlanders and Americans/Red Sox. His career spanned four decades, and he holds the major league record for most assists by a catcher at 1859.

Highlanders Years

Year	Age	G	AB	R	H	2B	3B	HR	RBI	SB	CS	BB	SO	BA	OBP	SLG	OPS	OPS+	TB	SH
1904	40	101	322	17	67	12	2	0	20	2		27	45	.208	.276	.258	.533	66	83	5
1905	41	72	228	9	50	7	2	0	33	3		18	21	.219	.291	.268	.558	70	61	3
1906	42	51	144	11	43	5	0	0	14	3		12	17	.299	.365	.333	.698	110	48	0
1907	43	1	1	0	0	0	0	0	0	0		0	1	.000	.000	.000	.000	-100	0	0
Totals		225	695	37	160	24	4	0	67	8		57	84	.230	.299	.276	.575	76	192	8

Americans/Red Sox Years

Year	Age	G	AB	R	H	2B	3B	HR	RBI	SB	CS	BB	SO	BA	OBP	SLG	OPS	OPS+	TB	SH
1907	43	6	4	1	3	0	0	1	1	0		0	0	.750	.750	1.500	2.250	618	6	0
1908	44	1	1	0	0	0	0	0	0	0		0	0	.000	.000	.000	.000	-100	0	0
Totals		7	5	1	3	0	0	1	1	0		0	0	.600	.600	1.200	1.800	475	6	0

Which Team Fared Better?

He played the most for the Washington Senators, spending nine years with them. By the time he came to the Highlanders he was 40 years old—yet still caught 97 games. His number of games played decreased every year after that, however, and in his final season with the team, he played in a single game before he was placed on waivers. When the Red Sox claimed him, they did so with the idea of using him more as manager than as catcher, which accounts for his appearing in only six games for the that year and only one the year after. After going 53–62 as manager during the 1908 season, he was replaced. The edge goes to New York.

Marty McHale

In his six seasons in major league baseball, McHale played for three teams, the additional one being the Cleveland Indians. He pitched 358 innings in his career, most of them with the Yankees. While still a ballplayer he performed in Vaudeville, earning him the moniker "the Caruso of Baseball."

Red Sox Years

Year	Age	W	L	%	ERA	G	GS	CG	SV	IP	H	R	HR	BB	SO	ERA+	WHIP	H/9	BB/9	SO/9	SO/BB
1910	23	0	2	.000	4.61	2	2	1	0	13.2	15	8	0	6	14	58	1.537	9.9	4.0	9.2	2.33
1911	24	0	0		9.64	4	1	0	0	9.1	19	12	1	3	3	36	2.357	18.3	2.9	2.9	1.00
1916	29	0	1	.000	3.00	2	1	0	0	6.0	7	7	0	4	1	101	1.833	10.5	6.0	1.5	0.25
Totals		0	3	.000	5.90	8	4	1	0	29.0	41	27	1	13	18	51	1.862	12.7	4.0	5.6	1.38

Yankees Years

Year	Age	W	L	%	ERA	G	GS	CG	SV	IP	H	R	HR	BB	SO	ERA+	WHIP	H/9	BB/9	SO/9	SO/BB
1913	26	2	4	.333	2.96	7	6	4	0	48.2	49	21	1	10	11	102	1.212	9.1	1.8	2.0	1.10
1914	27	6	16	.273	2.97	31	23	12	1	191.0	195	82	3	33	75	93	1.194	9.2	1.6	3.5	2.27
1915	28	3	7	.300	4.25	13	11	6	0	78.1	86	45	1	19	25	69	1.340	9.9	2.2	2.9	1.32
Totals		11	27	.289	3.28	51	40	22	1	318.0	330	148	5	62	111	87	1.233	9.3	1.8	3.1	1.79

Which Team Fared Better?

McHale spent three seasons with each team, playing for Boston on two separate occasions, although in his second stint he was sent packing to Cleveland before the end of the season. In his time spent with the Red Sox he bounced back and forth between the majors and minors, accounting for the fact that he pitched only 29 innings in those three seasons. He logged much more time with the Yankees, pitching 318 innings in the three years there and winning 11 games. To determine which team got the most from McHale, one has to compare which is better: losing 27 games for the Yankees or winning no games for the Red Sox. The name of the game in baseball is winning, and McHale didn't do that very much for either team. In the end, the Yankees probably got more out of him, as evidenced by his 1.233 WHIP (1.862 with Boston). Even though his baseball career did not amount to much, he eventually became a stockbroker, opening his own firm and enjoying a 52-year career. In the end the real winner was McHale, who made a success of himself off the field.

Mike McNally

A utility infielder who played at second, third, and shortstop, McNally spent ten years in the majors, five with the Red Sox and another four with the Yankees before riding out his career with the Washington Senators. Interestingly enough, the Yankees had traded McNally back to Boston in December 1924, but a day later the Red Sox traded him to the Senators. He was never a starter, and the most games he ever appeared in over the course of a season was 93 for the 1920 Red Sox. He appeared in 492 games in his career, meaning he averaged about 50 games a season.

Red Sox Years

Year	Age	G	AB	R	H	2B	3B	HR	RBI	SB	CS	BB	SO	BA	OBP	SLG	OPS	OPS+	TB	SH
1915	21	23	53	7	8	0	1	0	0	0	2	3	7	.151	.196	.189	.385	17	10	0
1916	22	87	135	28	23	0	0	0	9	9		10	19	.170	.228	.170	.398	19	23	6
1917	23	42	50	9	15	1	0	0	2	3		6	3	.300	.375	.320	.695	113	16	7

Year	Age	G	AB	R	H	2B	3B	HR	RBI	SB	CS	BB	SO	BA	OBP	SLG	OPS	OPS+	TB	SH
1919	25	33	42	10	11	4	0	0	6	4		1	2	.262	.279	.357	.636	82	15	4
1920	26	93	312	42	80	5	1	0	23	13	10	31	2	.256	.326	.279	.604	64	87	20
Totals		278	592	96	137	10	2	0	40	29	12	51	55	.231	.293	.255	.549	56	151	37

Yankees Years

Year	Age	G	AB	R	H	2B	3B	HR	RBI	SB	CS	BB	SO	BA	OBP	SLG	OPS	OPS+	TB	SH
1921	27	71	215	36	56	4	2	1	24	5	6	14	15	.260	.306	.312	.617	56	67	11
1922	28	52	143	20	36	2	2	0	18	3	0	16	14	.252	.331	.294	.625	63	42	17
1923	29	30	38	5	8	0	0	0	1	2	0	3	4	.211	.268	.211	.479	26	8	3
1924	30	49	69	11	17	0	0	0	2	1	1	7	5	.246	.316	.246	.562	46	17	3
Totals		202	465	72	117	6	4	1	45	11	7	40	38	.252	.312	.288	.600	54	134	34

Which Team Fared Better?

He was on several pennant winning teams for both Boston and New York, appearing in the 1916 World Series with the Red Sox and the 1921 and 1922 fall classics for the Yankees. He had been with Boston for part of the 1915 championship campaign, too, but was sent down to the minors well before the post-season was under way. He missed out on another Series with the Yankees in 1923, the year of their first championship, when he was sidelined by an injury to his ankle. His most productive year was in 1920, when with Boston he had career highs in games played (93), runs scored (42), hits (80), stolen bases (13), and on-base percentage (.326). So who benefitted more by his play? He had more hits and runs with the Red Sox, along with a very slightly higher OPS+. With the Yankees he posted a better batting average and had more RBIs. It would seem this one is more or less a statistical tie, but his relationship with Babe Ruth might be the tiebreaker. The two became friends while playing for Boston, and when they both ended up on the Yankees together, McNally served as his roommate and essentially his babysitter. For that reason, the Yankees made out better.

Although he spent his entire career as a utility infielder, amassing only 85 RBIs over 10 big league seasons, McNally was a versatile infielder who provided defensive value at second base, third base, and shortstop, and that versatility accounts for the fact that he played on five pennant-winning teams and appeared in three World Series.

Fred Mitchell

In the seven years this right-handed pitcher-catcher played baseball, he bounced around to six teams. He spent the first five years as a pitcher, playing for the Boston Americans, Philadelphia Athletics and Phillies, and Brooklyn Superbas. He left baseball in 1905 only to return in 1910 as a catcher for New York. After finishing his playing career with the 1913

Boston Braves, he went on to become a manager for that team and the Chicago Cubs, with whom he won the 1918 pennant.

Red Sox Years

Year	Age	W	L	%	ERA	G	GS	CG	SV	IP	H	R	HR	BB	SO	ERA+	WHIP	H/9	BB/9	SO/9	SO/BB
1901	23	6	6	.500	3.81	17	13	10	0	108.2	115	67	2	51	34	94	1.528	9.5	4.2	2.8	0.67
1902	24	0	1	.000	11.25	1	0	0	0	4.0	8	5	1	5	2	35	3.250	18.0	11.3	4.5	0.40
Totals		6	7	.462	4.07	18	13	10	0	112.2	123	72	3	56	36	88	1.589	9.8	4.5	2.9	0.64

Yankees Year

Year	Age	G	AB	R	H	2B	3B	HR	RBI	SB	CS	BB	SO	BA	OBP	SLG	OPS	OPS+	TB	SH
1910	32	68	196	16	45	7	2	0	18	6		9	19	.230	.274	.286	.560	71	56	0

Which Team Fared Better?

This is an interesting debate because Mitchell played a different role for the two teams. It is like comparing apples to oranges. As a pitcher with Boston, his 6–7 record is less than impressive, but the same can be said of his time as a catcher with New York, for whom he had 18 RBIs, 45 hits, and a .230 batting average. But if he was a below-average player with both clubs, he might have been more nearly average with the Red Sox, as reflected by his 88 ERA+ in 1901. With the Yankees, he managed only a 71 OPS+, and none of the available stats (including wins above replacement, range factor, and fielding percentage) indicate that he contributed much behind the plate. (The one standout stat? He finished fourth in the league in passed balls.)

HARRY NILES

An outfielder-infielder whose career spanned five years and four teams, Niles first played for the St. Louis Browns, staying with them two years before being traded to New York ahead of the 1908 season. He spent a few months with the Highlanders, then in August moved on to Boston where he stayed for another two seasons. He ended his career with Cleveland Indians. A utility man who played nearly twenty games at six different positions, his greatest asset was his speed. He swiped 30 bases in his rookie year, and another 77 in the four years that followed.

Yankees Year

Year	Age	G	AB	R	H	2B	3B	HR	RBI	SB	CS	BB	SO	BA	OBP	SLG	OPS	OPS+	TB	SH
1908	27	95	361	43	90	14	6	4	24	18		25	29	.249	.305	.355	.660	114	128	10

Red Sox Years

Year	Age	G	AB	R	H	2B	3B	HR	RBI	SB	CS	BB	SO	BA	OBP	SLG	OPS	OPS+	TB	SH
1908	27	18	33	4	8	0	0	1	3	3		6	2	.242	.375	.333	.708	128	11	4
1909	28	145	546	65	134	12	5	1	38	27		39	48	.245	.311	.291	.602	88	159	18
1910	29	18	57	6	12	3	0	1	3	1		4	3	.211	.262	.316	.578	79	18	2
Totals		181	636	75	154	15	5	3	44	31		49	53	.242	.310	.296	.606	89	188	24

Which Team Fared Better?

The Red Sox had him for much longer, which accounts for the discrepancy in the number of plate appearances. That being said, he made better use of his time, at least offensively, with New York, hitting more home runs (four compared with three), nearly as many doubles (14 compared with 15), and one more triple (six to five). He became a fifth wheel in the Boston outfield, which had Harry Hooper, Tris Speaker, and Duffy Lewis, considered by some to be the best-fielding outfield ever. The final nail in the coffin for the Red Sox is the fact that in 1908 Niles was responsible for breaking up Boston pitcher Cy Young's perfect game, drawing a walk in the lead-off spot. Niles was thrown out trying to steal and Young retired the next 26 batters in order, having to settle for a no-hitter.

LES NUNAMAKER

A catcher who played for 12 years in the major leagues, Nunamaker split his time nearly equally between the Boston, New York, and Cleveland, while also making a single-season stop in St. Louis to play for the Browns. He was part of two world championship teams, the 1912 Boston and the 1920 Indians.

Red Sox Years

Year	Age	G	AB	R	H	2B	3B	HR	RBI	SB	CS	BB	SO	BA	OBP	SLG	OPS	OPS+	TB	SH
1911	22	62	183	18	47	4	3	0	19	1		12	34	.257	.303	.311	.614	72	57	12
1912	23	35	103	15	26	5	2	0	6	2	2	6	17	.252	.313	.340	.652	83	35	3
1913	24	29	65	9	14	5	2	0	9	2		8	8	.215	.311	.354	.665	92	23	2
1914	25	5	5	0	1	0	0	0	0	0	0	1	0	.200	.333	.200	.533	60	1	0
Totals		131	356	42	88	14	7	0	34	5	2	27	59	.247	.307	.326	.633	79	116	17

Yankees Years

Year	Age	G	AB	R	H	2B	3B	HR	RBI	SB	CS	BB	SO	BA	OBP	SLG	OPS	OPS+	TB	SH
1914	25	87	257	19	68	10	3	2	29	11	9	22	34	.265	.327	.350	.678	104	90	3
1915	26	87	249	24	56	6	3	0	17	3	2	23	24	.225	.293	.273	.566	69	68	4
1916	27	91	260	25	77	14	7	0	28	4		34	21	.296	.380	.404	.784	133	105	1
1917	28	104	310	22	81	9	2	0	33	5		21	25	.261	.310	.303	.613	86	94	6
Totals		369	1,076	90	282	39	15	2	107	23	11	100	104	.262	.328	.332	.659	98	357	14

Which Team Fared Better?

Although Nunamaker won a championship with Boston, his role in the Series was minimal; an injured finger relegated him to third-string status behind the plate, and he failed even to record an at-bat. He enjoyed his best season as a hitter with the 1916 Yankees, posting a .296 batting average, 77 hits, and 28 RBIs. His high in RBIs with the Red Sox was 19, which he bested nearly all four seasons spent with the Yankees, falling two short in 1915. He gave his best to New York.

ALLEN RUSSELL

An 11-year pitcher in the major leagues, Russell played five seasons for New York, four for Boston, and three for the Washington Senators. He won a World Series with the Senators in 1924 and followed that up by helping them to win the American League pennant in 1925. He was one of the 17 spitballers who were allowed to continue throwing the pitch after it was deemed illegal.

Yankees Years

Year	Age	W	L	%	ERA	G	GS	CG	SV	IP	H	R	HR	BB	SO	ERA+	WHIP	H/9	BB/9	SO/9	SO/BB
1915	21	1	2	.333	2.67	5	3	1	0	27.0	21	10	1	21	21	112	1.556	7.0	7.0	7.0	1.00
1916	22	6	10	.375	3.20	34	19	8	6	171.1	138	83	8	75	104	91	1.243	7.0	3.9	5.5	1.39
1917	23	7	8	.467	2.24	25	10	6	2	104.1	89	42	2	39	55	121	1.227	7.7	3.4	4.7	1.41

Year	Age	W	L	%	ERA	G	GS	CG	SV	IP	H	R	HR	BB	SO	ERA+	WHIP	H/9	BB/9	SO/9	SO/BB
1918	24	7	11	.389	3.26	27	18	7	4	141.0	139	68	6	73	54	86	1.504	8.9	4.7	3.4	0.74
1919	25	5	5	.500	3.47	23	9	4	1	90.2	89	48	5	32	50	92	1.335	8.8	3.2	5.0	1.56
Totals		26	36	.419	3.05	114	59	26	13	534.1	476	251	22	240	284	95	1.340	8.0	4.0	4.8	1.18

Red Sox Years

Year	Age	W	L	%	ERA	G	GS	CG	SV	IP	H	R	HR	BB	SO	ERA+	WHIP	H/9	BB/9	SO/9	SO/BB
1919	25	10	4	.714	2.52	21	11	9	4	121.1	105	38	1	39	63	121	1.187	7.8	2.9	4.7	1.62
1920	26	5	6	.455	3.01	16	10	7	1	107.2	100	44	3	38	53	121	1.282	8.4	3.2	4.4	1.39
1921	27	6	11	.353	4.11	39	14	7	4	173.0	204	92	10	77	60	103	1.624	10.6	4.0	3.1	0.78
1922	28	6	7	.462	5.01	34	11	1	1	125.2	152	81	6	57	34	81	1.663	10.9	4.1	2.4	0.60
Totals		27	28	.491	3.74	110	46	24	10	527.2	561	255	20	211	210	102	1.463	9.6	3.6	3.6	1.00

Which Team Fared Better?

He pitched his way to a 17–12 record in his time with the Senators, his only winning record with a team. You might think that would mean his ERA was lowest with them, but it was actually his highest, at 3.93. (To be fair, the run-scoring environment in the early twenties was not what it had been early in his career, and Russell's performance for the Senators was slightly better than average relative to the league.) In fact, it seemed the worse the record, the lower the ERA. He went 26 –36 for the Yankees for a .419 winning percentage, yet had his lowest (non-normalized) ERA at 3.05. He was almost .500 with Boston, winning 27 and losing 28, but his ERA was (again, before being normalized) 3.74. So what happens when ERA+ is considered? Russell's 95 for the Yankees is his worst mark, with Washington next at 101, and the Red Sox faring best at 102. Add in his winning percentage with the Sox, and it looks as if they might have had more to show for their time with the pitcher.

WALLY SCHANG

One of the better offensive catchers of the Deadball Era, Schang played 19 seasons for five different teams. His longest stop was with the Philadelphia Athletics, for whom he played six seasons. The Yankees had him for five years, the St. Louis Browns four, the Red Sox three, and the Detroit Tigers one. He had 1,506 hits in his career, with 710 RBIs and a .284 average. He played in a remarkable six World Series, on the winning side three times—once apiece with the A's, Yankees, and Red Sox. He is the only major leaguer to have won championships with three different teams.

Red Sox Years

Year	Age	G	AB	R	H	2B	3B	HR	RBI	SB	CS	BB	SO	BA	OBP	SLG	OPS	OPS+	TB	SH
1918	28	88	225	36	55	7	1	0	20	4		46	35	.244	.377	.284	.662	100	64	9
1919	29	113	330	43	101	16	3	0	55	15		71	42	.306	.436	.373	.809	133	123	7
1920	30	122	387	58	118	30	7	4	51	7	7	64	37	.305	.413	.450	.862	132	174	8
Totals		323	942	137	274	53	11	4	126	26	7	181	114	.291	.412	.383	.796	125	361	24

Yankees Years

Year	Age	G	AB	R	H	2B	3B	HR	RBI	SB	CS	BB	SO	BA	OBP	SLG	OPS	OPS+	TB	SH
1921	31	134	424	77	134	30	5	6	55	7	4	78	35	.316	.428	.453	.881	123	192	6
1922	32	124	408	46	130	21	7	1	53	12	6	53	36	.319	.405	.412	.816	111	168	23
1923	33	84	272	39	75	8	2	2	29	5	2	27	17	.276	.360	.342	.702	84	93	7
1924	34	114	356	46	104	19	7	5	52	2	6	48	43	.292	.382	.427	.809	108	152	13
1925	35	73	167	17	40	8	1	2	24	2	1	17	9	.240	.310	.335	.645	65	56	7
Totals		529	1,627	225	483	86	22	16	213	28	19	223	140	.297	.390	.406	.796	105	661	56

Which Team Fared Better?

Schang's timing was right when he jumped from the cellar-dwelling A's to the Red Sox, who won their last championship for 86 years in 1918. For Boston he had 274 hits, drove in 126 RBIs, and scored 137 runs over three seasons. When the Sox started giving all of its good players away to the Yankees, Schang was one of them, and in his five seasons with the Yankees he had 483 hits, 213 RBIs, and 225 runs. If you average out his time with each team, he had 91 hits, 42 RBIs, and 46 runs for Boston per year, and 97 hits, 43 RBIs, 45 runs for the Yankees, showing that he was the model of consistency—but perhaps ever so slightly better, at least offensively, for New York.

A stellar offensive catcher, Wally Schang was also an effective deterrent to basestealing, throwing out 46 percent of the runners who tried in his 19 years behind the plate. He played in 32 World Series games, batting .287, and in his time with the Red Sox (three years) and New York (four), proved as steady with the bat in his hands as either could have expected.

EVERETT SCOTT

A shortstop by trade, Scott played for 13 seasons and five different teams. He spent the bulk of his playing career (eight seasons) with Boston, although he spent significant time (four seasons) with the Yankees, too, before splitting his final two years with Washington, Cincinnati, and the White Sox. Like most shortstops of that time his primary value was in his defense and consistency, as Scott led the league in fielding percentage seven straight years. Reliability, in fact, could have been his middle name: He still ranks third all time for consecutive games played, his 1,307 games trailing only Ripken and Gehrig. Scott was a .249 career hitter who scored 552 runs and knocked in 551.

Red Sox Years

Year	Age	G	AB	R	H	2B	3B	HR	RBI	SB	CS	BB	SO	BA	OBP	SLG	OPS	OPS+	TB	SH
1914	21	144	539	66	129	15	6	2	37	9	14	32	43	.239	.286	.301	.586	75	162	26
1915	22	100	359	25	72	11	0	0	28	4	7	17	21	.201	.237	.231	.468	42	83	23
1916	23	123	366	37	85	19	2	0	27	8		23	24	.232	.283	.295	.578	73	108	30
1917	24	157	528	40	127	24	7	0	50	12		20	46	.241	.268	.313	.581	78	165	41
1918	25	126	443	40	98	11	5	0	43	11		12	16	.221	.242	.269	.510	54	119	26
1919	26	138	507	41	141	19	0	0	38	8		19	26	.278	.306	.316	.621	78	160	13
1920	27	154	569	41	153	21	12	4	61	4	11	21	15	.269	.300	.369	.669	79	210	21
1921	28	154	576	65	151	21	9	1	62	5	9	27	21	.262	.295	.335	.630	62	193	17
Totals		1,096	3,887	355	956	141	41	7	346	61	41	171	212	.246	.280	.309	.588	69	1,200	197

Yankees Years

Year	Age	G	AB	R	H	2B	3B	HR	RBI	SB	CS	BB	SO	BA	OBP	SLG	OPS	OPS+	TB	SH
1922	29	154	557	64	150	23	5	3	45	2	3	23	22	.269	.304	.345	.649	67	192	28
1923	30	152	533	48	131	16	4	6	60	1	3	13	19	.246	.266	.325	.591	54	173	20

Year	Age	G	AB	R	H	2B	3B	HR	RBI	SB	CS	BB	SO	BA	OBP	SLG	OPS	OPS+	TB	SH
1924	31	153	548	56	137	12	6	4	64	3	7	21	15	.250	.278	.316	.593	53	173	18
1925	32	22	60	3	13	0	0	0	4	0	1	2	2	.217	.242	.217	.459	18	13	3
Totals		481	1,698	171	431	51	15	13	173	6	14	59	58	.254	.282	.324	.606	57	551	69

Which Team Fared Better?

Everett Scott was a strong-fielding shortstop who proved to be valuable for the Red Sox and Yankees, serving as captain for both squads. His impressive resume includes four World Series championships and seven straight years of leading the league in fielding percentage, and stands behind only Cal Ripken, Jr., and Lou Gehrig for most consecutive games played.

Scott was a captain for both the Red Sox and the Yankees. His numbers between the two teams are fairly similar. What this comes down to is the sort of argument made by Jason Segel in the film *Bad Teacher*. When Segel and a student argue over who is a better basketball player, Michael Jordan or LeBron James, Segel places his central argument on Jordan's six championships, claiming it is the only argument he needs. By that line of reasoning, the Red Sox fared better with Scott, who won three championships with Boston (1915, 1916, and 1918) and one with the Yankees (1923). He is also in the Red Sox Hall of Fame.

ERNIE SHORE

A pitcher for seven years, Shore spent a majority of his career with the Red Sox, averaging 15 wins a season during his four seasons with them. He came up with the Giants in 1912, throwing a single, disastrous inning for them. (Shore faced 13 batters, gave up eight hits, and was tagged for 10 runs, though only three were earned.) After playing 1913 in the minors, he came up with another promising young Boston pitcher, Babe Ruth. His final two years were spent with the Yankees, pitching poorly enough to be sent down to the minors before retiring. Babe Ruth at one time said Shore was going to be the best pitcher in baseball, but he was never the same after returning, in 1919, from a year in the military.

Red Sox Years

Year	Age	W	L	%	ERA	G	GS	CG	SV	IP	H	R	HR	BB	SO	ERA+	WHIP	H/9	BB/9	SO/9	SO/BB
1914	23	10	5	.667	2.00	20	16	10	1	139.2	103	45	1	34	51	136	0.981	6.6	2.2	3.3	1.50
1915	24	19	8	.704	1.64	38	32	17	0	247.0	207	75	3	66	102	170	1.105	7.5	2.4	3.7	1.55
1916	25	16	10	.615	2.63	38	28	10	1	225.2	221	93	1	49	62	105	1.196	8.8	2.0	2.5	1.27
1917	26	13	10	.565	2.22	29	27	14	1	226.2	201	76	1	55	57	116	1.129	8.0	2.2	2.3	1.04
Totals		58	33	.637	2.12	125	103	51	3	839.0	732	279	6	204	272	128	1.116	10.7	4.2	2.3	0.55

Yankees Years

Year	Age	W	L	%	ERA	G	GS	CG	SV	IP	H	R	HR	BB	SO	ERA+	WHIP	H/9	BB/9	SO/9	SO/BB
1919	28	5	8	.385	4.17	20	13	3	0	95.0	105	50	4	44	24	77	1.568	9.9	4.2	2.3	0.55
1920	29	2	2	.500	4.87	14	5	2	1	44.1	61	31	1	21	12	79	1.850	12.4	4.3	2.4	0.57
Totals		7	10	.412	4.39	34	18	5	1	139.1	166	81	5	65	36	78	1.658	10.7	4.2	2.3	0.55

Which Team Fared Better?

Shore was with the Red Sox during their heyday, securing a World Series with them in 1915 and 1916, and winning three Series games along the way. He missed winning a third championship with them in 1918, having joined the military along with a few of his teammates (including Duffy Lewis) the previous fall. Before leaving, however, he pitched a no-hitter for Boston under odd circumstances. Babe Ruth had started the game, walking the first batter he faced. Then he proceeded to get into an argument with the umpire and got tossed from the game. Shore was brought in and after the leadoff hitter was thrown out trying to steal, Shore retired the next 26 batters. His time with the Yankees was not as memorable. He won seven and lost ten for a .412 winning percentage, results that pale alongside his 58–33 record with the Red Sox. The only significant mark he made with the Yankees was as part of the blockbuster, six-player trade between Boston and New York, the first of many moves that would declaw the Red Sox for decades.

Jake Stahl

A first baseman by trade, Stahl played for nine years, mostly with Boston. He had three stints with the club, one for only a season (1903), another for parts of three (1908–1910), and a final one for two (1912–1913). After his first stop with Boston, he spent three years with Washington, two of them as player-manager, before giving roughly half a season in 1908 to the Highlanders in advance of his re-signing with Boston. He retired after the 1910 season but was talked into coming back as a player-manager for the Red Sox in 1912. As a manager he accumulated a 263–270 record.

Americans/Red Sox Years

Year	Age	G	AB	R	H	2B	3B	HR	RBI	SB	CS	BB	SO	BA	OBP	SLG	OPS	OPS+	TB	SH
1903	24	40	92	14	22	3	5	2	8	1		4	24	.239	.286	.446	.731	112	41	0
1908	29	78	262	29	64	9	11	0	23	13		20	37	.244	.333	.363	.696	124	95	10
1909	30	127	435	62	128	19	12	6	60	16		43	94	.294	.377	.434	.812	153	189	12
1910	31	144	531	68	144	19	16	10	77	22		42	128	.271	.334	.424	.758	134	225	17
1912	33	95	326	40	98	21	6	3	60	13	22	31	51	.301	.372	.429	.801	124	140	17
1913	34	2	2	0	0	0	0	0	0	0		0	1	.000	.000	.000	.000	-100	0	0
Totals		486	1,648	213	456	71	50	21	228	65	22	140	335	.277	.350	.419	.769	134	690	56

Highlanders Year

Year	Age	G	AB	R	H	2B	3B	HR	RBI	SB	CS	BB	SO	BA	OBP	SLG	OPS	OPS+	TB	SH
1908	29	75	274	34	70	18	5	2	42	17		11	43	.255	.304	.380	.683	122	104	9

Which Team Fared Better?

With Boston, Stahl led the American League in home runs in 1910, socking 10. He is the only Red Sox player to be on World Series–winning teams in two different decades. He won with the Boston Americans in 1903 and then when they had become the Red Sox in 1912. He was also the manager for Boston during that 1912 campaign, before having issues with teammates and resigning halfway through the 1913 season. He played only half a season for the Yankees before the Red Sox bought him away from them. Boston definitely fared better with him.

Jesse Tannehill

During his 15 seasons, spent with five teams, Tannehill earned a reputation as one of the better hitting pitchers in the league. He was so good that over the course of his career he was used 87 times in the outfield, just to get his bat into the lineup. He pitched for two seasons with the Cincinnati Reds, his first and then his last; six for the Pittsburgh Pirates; five for the Red Sox; two for Washington Senators; and one for the Yankees. He had six seasons with 20 or more wins, on his way to 197 victories in his career. He won pennants in both leagues and was the ERA champ in 1901 with the Pirates. To this day he has the best winning percentage in Pirates history at .667

Yankees Year

Year	Age	W	L	%	ERA	G	GS	CG	SV	IP	H	R	HR	BB	SO	ERA+	WHIP	H/9	BB/9	SO/9	SO/BB
1903	28	15	15	.500	3.27	32	31	22	0	239.2	258	123	3	34	106	95	1.218	9.7	1.3	4.0	3.12

Red Sox Years

Year	Age	W	L	%	ERA	G	GS	CG	SV	IP	H	R	HR	BB	SO	ERA+	WHIP	H/9	BB/9	SO/9	SO/BB
1904	29	21	11	.656	2.04	33	31	30	0	281.2	256	89	5	33	116	131	1.026	8.2	1.1	3.7	3.52
1905	30	22	9	.710	2.48	37	32	27	0	271.2	238	91	7	59	113	108	1.093	7.9	2.0	3.7	1.92
1906	31	13	11	.542	3.16	27	26	18	0	196.1	207	91	9	39	82	87	1.253	9.5	1.8	3.8	2.10
1907	32	6	7	.462	2.47	18	16	10	1	131.0	131	59	3	20	29	104	1.153	9.0	1.4	2.0	1.45
1908	33	0	0		3.60	1	1	0	0	5.0	4	2	0	3	2	76	1.400	7.2	5.4	3.6	0.67
Totals		62	38	.620	2.50	116	106	85	1	885.2	836	332	24	154	342	107	1.118	8.5	1.6	3.5	2.22

Which Team Fared Better?

A .500 pitcher in his lone season with the Yankees, he fared much better with Boston. All but one (1906) of his four full seasons with the Red Sox was better, in fact. Even with a losing record in his fourth season with Boston, in 1907, his ERA was still a better-than-league-average 2.47, and easily better than his year with the Yankees. Boston got nearly four times as much from him as the Yankees did.

Jack Thoney

In his first three years as a player, Thoney played for five different teams. He started in 1902 with the Cleveland Broncos, playing in 28 games before being sold in September to the Baltimore Orioles, for whom he got into three games. In 1903 he went back to Cleveland for 32 games, then split time between the New York team and the Washington Senators in 1904. From 1905 to 1907, he toiled in the minors. But then Boston came calling, and he played his final three seasons (1908–1909, 1911) with the Red Sox. It might have been a four-year stop in Boston, but in 1910 he slipped on a banana peel and dislocated his shoulder, missing the season. As a reserve he played six different positions 10 times or more, spending the most time in the outfield.

Highlanders Year

Year	Age	G	AB	R	H	2B	3B	HR	RBI	SB	CS	BB	SO	BA	OBP	SLG	OPS	OPS+	TB	SH
1904	24	36	128	17	24	4	2	0	12	9		8	20	.188	.241	.250	.491	52	32	3

Red Sox Years

Year	Age	G	AB	R	H	2B	3B	HR	RBI	SB	CS	BB	SO	BA	OBP	SLG	OPS	OPS+	TB	SH
1908	28	109	416	58	106	5	9	2	30	16		13	62	.255	.282	.325	.607	95	135	9
1909	29	13	40	1	5	1	0	0	3	2		2	3	.125	.167	.150	.317	-1	6	1
1911	31	26	20	5	5	0	0	0	2	1		0	1	.250	.250	.250	.500	40	5	0
Totals		148	476	64	116	6	9	2	35	19		15	66	.244	.271	.307	.578	84	146	10

Which Team Fared Better?

Because he was with New York for only half the season, he saw only 128 at-bats. In his first year with Boston, he had 416 at-bats. In New York he managed only 24 hits for a .188 average; in that first year for Boston, he had 106 hits and a .255 average. Although his skills and numbers began to wane in the following two seasons with Boston, his one respectable season in 1908 is enough to put the Red Sox ahead.

FRANK TRUESDALE

A second baseman by trade, this switch-hitting sparkplug spent four years in the majors, with several stints in the minors breaking up those years. His first two seasons were spent with the St. Louis Browns, and in one of them Truesdale made 56 errors, a total that led the league and resulted in his .914 fielding percentage, the lowest ever compiled by a second baseman who appeared in over 100 games. It took him three years to make it back to the majors with the Yankees. He left professional baseball altogether for another three years before the Red Sox came calling for his services in 1918.

Yankees Year

Year	Age	G	AB	R	H	2B	3B	HR	RBI	SB	CS	BB	SO	BA	OBP	SLG	OPS	OPS+	TB	SH
1914	30	77	217	22	46	4	0	0	13	11	11	39	35	.212	.340	.230	.570	72	50	4

Red Sox Year

Year	Age	G	AB	R	H	2B	3B	HR	RBI	SB	CS	BB	SO	BA	OBP	SLG	OPS	OPS+	TB	SH
1918	34	15	36	6	10	1	0	0	2	1		4	5	.278	.350	.306	.656	98	11	2

Which Team Fared Better?

Although he was officially a member of the 1918 world champion Red Sox, he was released in July of that year and did not play in the postseason. He had only 36 at-bats with Boston, getting 10 hits for a .278 average. His batting average with New York was lower, at .212, but he had 217 at-bats and 46 hits. What decides this debate, however, is Truesdale's fielding. He committed 17 errors for the Yankees in 323 chances for a .947 fielding percentage. He continued his iron-mitt ways with the Red Sox, making four errors in only 46 chances, which dropped his fielding percentage still lower, to .913. Given those numbers the Yankees got the better part of him, if only because the Red Sox got the worst.

BOB UNGLAUB

Unglaub was a first baseman for six seasons. After getting into six games in the first three months of the 1914 season, he was traded by the Highlanders to the Americans in exchange for Patsy Dougherty. Unglaub spent parts of four years there in Boston, taking a year off to play in the Tri-State League in 1906. He finished his time in baseball with three years for the Washington Senators.

Highlanders Year

Year	Age	G	AB	R	H	2B	3B	HR	RBI	SB	CS	BB	SO	BA	OBP	SLG	OPS	OPS+	TB	SH
1904	22	6	19	2	4	0	0	0	2	0		0	0	.211	.211	.211	.421	30	4	0

Americans/Red Sox Years

Year	Age	G	AB	R	H	2B	3B	HR	RBI	SB	CS	BB	SO	BA	OBP	SLG	OPS	OPS+	TB	SH
1904	22	9	13	1	2	1	0	0	2	0		1	4	.154	.214	.231	.445	37	3	0
1905	23	43	121	18	27	5	1	0	11	2		6	15	.223	.269	.281	.541	71	34	7
1907	25	139	544	49	138	17	13	1	62	14		23	59	.254	.284	.338	.622	99	184	17
1908	26	72	266	23	70	11	3	1	25	6		7	28	.263	.287	.338	.626	101	90	9
Totals		263	944	91	237	34	17	2	100	22		37	106	.251	.281	.329	.610	95	311	33

Which Team Fared Better?

In his time with the Yankees, Unglaub is said to have suffered from blood poisoning, which perhaps accounts for his having made only 19 plate appearances. He would not only become a regular in 1907, enjoying one of his better seasons, but serve for a time in the unlikely role of Red Sox manager. Boston went through five skippers that season after Chick Stahl, hired in the offseason, committed suicide in spring training. Cy Young began the regular season as manager but stepped down after only six games. He was replaced with George Huff, who lasted longer, a whole eight days, before resigning as well. Their choices dwindling, the Red Sox tapped Unglaub. Although he won four of the first five games he managed, after 29 games he was 9–20. This prompted the Red Sox to replace him with Deacon McGuire, who finished out the season, and ship Unglaub off to the Senators in July. Because the Red Sox got his best season, they get the nod.

JIMMY WALSH

There were two Jimmy Walshes playing in the decade of the 1910s. One was an outfielder, the other an infielder. The one who played for both the Red Sox and Yankees was the outfielder. He was also one of the last native-born Irishmen to play in the major leagues. Walsh started with the Philadelphia A's, whom he helped win the pennant twice (1913 and 1914) and the Series once (1913). After the 1913 season, he became the player to be named later for a deal with the Yankees from earlier that summer. In July 1914, after half a season of little production, he was traded back to the A's in exchange for Tom Daley. A little more than two years later, he was shipped to Boston, where he played his final two seasons.

Yankees Year

Year	Age	G	AB	R	H	2B	3B	HR	RBI	SB	CS	BB	SO	BA	OBP	SLG	OPS	OPS+	TB	SH
1914	26	43	136	13	26	1	3	1	11	6	9	29	21	.191	.333	.265	.598	80	36	1

Red Sox Years

Year	Age	G	AB	R	H	2B	3B	HR	RBI	SB	CS	BB	SO	BA	OBP	SLG	OPS	OPS+	TB	SH
1916	28	14	17	5	3	1	0	0	2	3	2	4	2	.176	.333	.235	.569	70	4	2
1917	29	57	185	25	49	6	3	0	12	6		25	14	.265	.352	.330	.682	109	61	2
Totals		71	202	30	52	7	3	0	14	9	2	29	16	.257	.351	.322	.672	106	65	4

Which Team Fared Better?

Walsh played partial seasons with New York (1914) and Boston (1916) in which he failed to break the .200 mark in batting. He did, however, take part in the World Series Boston won in 1916, going 0 for 3 but recording a putout in center field during Game Two. A year later, still with the Red Sox, he batted .265, got on base at a .352 clip, had 49 hits, stole six bases, and knocked in 12 runs. This was his best season between the two teams, giving Boston the edge.

George Whiteman

Whiteman's big league career was a bit spotty. He played for the Boston Americans in 1907, the New York Yankees in 1913, and Boston again in 1918. In between he was in the minors, where he had a remarkable career, setting the record for most hits and games played.

Americans/Red Sox Years

Year	Age	G	AB	R	H	2B	3B	HR	RBI	SB	CS	BB	SO	BA	OBP	SLG	OPS	OPS+	TB	SH
1907	24	4	12	0	2	0	0	0	1	0		0	4	.167	.167	.167	.333	7	2	0
1918	35	71	214	24	57	14	0	1	28	9		20	9	.266	.335	.346	.681	106	74	12
Totals		75	226	24	59	14	0	1	29	9		20	13	.261	.327	.336	.663	101	76	12

Yankees Year

Year	Age	G	AB	R	H	2B	3B	HR	RBI	SB	CS	BB	SO	BA	OBP	SLG	OPS	OPS+	TB	SH
1913	30	11	32	8	11	3	1	0	2	2		7	2	.344	.462	.500	.962	181	16	2

Which Team Fared Better?

Although he had only one home run and 31 RBIs in his three-year career, he was a World Series hero in the 1918 Fall Classic with Boston. He batted only .250 during the Series but had crucial at-bats, driving in a run, scoring two others, and figuring into eight other runs as well. He also made game-saving catches, none bigger than in the final game, which the Red Sox won, 2–1, against the Cubs. Although there was no such thing as a World Series MVP at that time, he was clearly the hero. It is Whiteman's moment in the limelight that tells the tale. The nod goes to the Red Sox.

Harry Wolter

Wolter played seven years in the majors, four of them with the Yankees. He also spent time in Boston, Cincinnati, Pittsburgh, St. Louis, and Chicago, with the Cubs. Primarily used as an outfielder, he did pitch in 15 games, going 4–6. But his contributions came from his bat rather than his arm. He had 514 hits in his career, scoring 286 runs.

Red Sox Year

Year	Age	G	AB	R	H	2B	3B	HR	RBI	SB	CS	BB	SO	BA	OBP	SLG	OPS	OPS+	TB	SH
1909	24	54	121	14	29	2	4	2	10	2		9	24	.240	.292	.372	.664	107	45	5

Yankees/Highlander Years

Year	Age	G	AB	R	H	2B	3B	HR	RBI	SB	CS	BB	SO	BA	OBP	SLG	OPS	OPS+	TB	SH
1910	25	135	479	84	128	15	9	4	42	39		66	61	.267	.364	.361	.725	122	173	20

Year	Age	G	AB	R	H	2B	3B	HR	RBI	SB	CS	BB	SO	BA	OBP	SLG	OPS	OPS+	TB	SH
1911	26	122	434	78	132	17	15	4	36	28		62	37	.304	.396	.440	.836	127	191	10
1912	27	12	32	8	11	2	1	0	1	5	3	10	4	.344	.512	.469	.980	174	15	0
1913	28	127	425	53	108	18	6	2	43	13		80	50	.254	.377	.339	.716	110	144	12
Totals		396	1,370	223	379	52	31	10	122	85	3	218	152	.277	.382	.382	.764	121	523	42

Which Team Fared Better?

Wolter had the first hit in Fenway Park, and that's something; but the Yankees enjoyed a stronger performance from him. He had 379 hits for them, compared with the 29 he managed with Boston; scored 223 runs, compared with 14; and racked up 122 RBIs, compared with 10. When Boston bought his contract it was supposedly for a big price. New York got him from Boston for a reasonable $1,500—and got the most out of their money.

2. The Curse Was About More Than the Bambino
The Live Ball Era (1920–1941)

We often attribute the downfall of the early twentieth century's hot team, the Boston Red Sox, to the sale of George Herman "Babe" Ruth to the New York Yankees in 1919. At the time, Harry Frazee, the owner of the Sox, faced money problems. In his other line of work, he was a producer (as well as a theater owner and a director), and the recent profits from his plays left him struggling to meet financial obligations. He looked to Ruth, his star, who was said to be a large child, demanding higher pay, drinking uncontrollably, and acting as if he thought himself the best player in the world, which he was. Frazee sold him to the Yankees for $125,000, plus a loan for another $300,000.

The Ruth sale, however, was simply one sign of a team whose chances were quickly circling the drain. Between the years of 1918 to 1925, the Yankees and Red Sox made several transactions together. Here are the players the Red Sox sent to the Yankees:

Babe Ruth	Mike McNally	Elmer Smith
Duffy Lewis	Wally Schang	Harvey Hendrick
Ernie Shore	Bullet Joe Bush	George Pipgras
Carl Mays	Sad Sam Jones	Herb Pennock
Harry Harper	Everett Scott	Howie Shanks
Waite Hoyt	Joe Dugan	Alex Ferguson
		Bobby Veach

The Yankees paid out $349,000. In today's game that barely buys a passable middle reliever, but back then the highest paid player, Ruth, made only $7,000 a year. The Red Sox did more than sell, however. They traded, receiving the following players in return:

Ray Caldwell	Hank Thormahlen	Johnny Mitchell
Frank Gilhooley	Sammy Vick	Lefty O'Doul
Slim Love	Rip Collins	Al DeVormer
Roxy Walters	Roger Peckinpaugh	Norm McMillan
Bob McGraw	Bill Piercy	George Murray
Allen Russell	Jack Quinn	Camp Skinner
Del Pratt	Chick Fewster	Ray Francis
Muddy Ruel	Elmer Miller	

When you compare the production that these sets of players provided each team, it seems painfully obvious the Yankees made out on these deals and the Red Sox were simply saving money. Now consider the combined contributions for all of the players the Yankees and Red Sox swapped.

Hitters, New York

	Seasons	Games	AB	Hits	HR	RBIs	Runs	BA	OBP
Babe Ruth	15	2,084	7,217	2,518	659	1,978	1,959	.349	.484
Duffy Lewis	2	248	924	251	11	150	101	.272	.304
Mike McNally	4	202	465	117	1	45	72	.252	.312
Wally Schang	5	529	1,627	483	16	213	225	.297	.390
Everett Scott	4	481	1,698	431	13	173	171	.254	.282
Joe Dugan	7	785	3,043	871	22	317	426	.286	.326
Elmer Smith	2	91	210	61	8	40	31	.290	.363
Harvey Hendrick	2	77	142	38	4	23	16	.268	.293
Howie Shanks	1	66	155	40	1	18	15	.258	.343
Bobby Veach	1	56	116	41	0	15	13	.353	.400
Totals	43	4,583	15,597	4,851	735	2,972	3,029	.311	

Pitchers, New York

	Seasons	Games	Wins	Losses	IP	H	ERA	WHIP	Ks	BBs
Ernie Shore	2	34	7	10	139.1	166	4.39	1.658	36	65
Carl Mays	5	164	80	39	1,090.0	1,114	3.25	1.278	273	279
Harry Harper	1	8	4	3	52.2	52	3.76	1.462	22	25
Waite Hoyt	10	365	157	98	2,272.1	2,405	3.48	1.336	713	631
Bullet Joe Bush	3	115	62	38	783.0	765	3.44	1.374	297	311
Sad Sam Jones	5	202	67	56	1,089.1	1,149	4.06	1.427	363	405
George Pipgras	9	247	93	64	1,351.2	1,376	4.04	1.421	656	545
Herb Pennock	11	346	162	90	2,203.1	2,471	3.54	1.335	700	471
Alex Ferguson	3	39	7	3	112.1	149	6.73	1.958	30	71
Totals	49	1,520	639	401	9,094.0	9,647			3,090	2,803

Hitters, Boston

	Seasons	Games	AB	Hits	HR	RBIs	Runs	BA	OBP
Frank Gilhooley	1	48	112	27	0	1	14	.241	.315
Roxy Walters	5	268	764	156	0	62	62	.204	.272
Del Pratt	2	289	1,128	352	11	188	153	.312	.369
Muddy Ruel	3	262	802	216	1	79	81	.269	.345
Sammy Vick	1	44	77	20	0	9	5	.260	.269
Chick Fewster	2	113	367	91	0	24	40	.248	.337
Elmer Miller	1	44	147	28	4	16	16	.190	.222
Johnny Mitchell	2	151	550	129	1	27	60	.235	.304
Lefty O'Doul	1	36	35	5	0	4	2	.143	.189
Al DeVormer	1	74	209	54	0	18	20	.259	.282
Norm McMillan	1	131	459	116	0	42	37	.253	.299
Camp Skinner	1	7	13	3	0	1	1	.231	.231
	21	1,467	4,663	1,197	17	471	491	.257	

Pitchers, Boston

	Seasons	Games	Wins	Losses	IP	H	ERA	WHIP	Ks	BBs
Ray Caldwell	1	18	7	4	86.1	92	3.96	1.425	23	31
Bob McGraw	1	10	0	2	26.2	33	6.75	1.875	6	17
Allen Russell	5	110	27	28	527.2	561	3.74	1.463	109	159
Hank Thormahlen	1	23	1	7	96.1	101	4.48	1.401	17	34
Rip Collins	1	32	14	11	210.2	219	3.76	1.528	69	103
Bill Piercy	3	82	16	33	429.2	489	4.48	1.606	95	201
Jack Quinn	4	145	45	54	832.2	946	3.65	1.364	226	190
George Murray	2	67	9	20	258.0	287	5.48	1.574	67	119
Ray Francis	1	6	0	2	28.0	44	7.71	1.471	4	13
Totals	19	493	119	161	2,493.2	2,772			616	867

Note: Shortstop Roger Peckinpaugh and pitcher Slim Love were traded to Boston from New York but never played for them as Boston then traded them to another team.

Let us handicap the situation and take Babe Ruth out of the equation. His numbers for the time stack up well against whole teams, so evaluating the Yankees and Red Sox is unbalanced when considering him puts things squarely in favor of New York. Even with Ruth taken out, though, the trades seem lopsided. For instance, the average number of years the players were with their new team is nearly five for New York but only two for Boston. That means that, on average, for every player traded, the Yankees kept their new player for twice as long as the Red Sox did. They got 4,019 games out of the hitters and pitchers while the Red Sox got 1,960.

And then there is the production of the hitters. The combined total of home runs from players the Red Sox received in trade with New York was 17, and a single player, Del Pratt, accounted for 11 of those. Taking out the 659 home runs Ruth hit for the pinstripers, the players the Yankees received from the Red Sox put up a total of 76. Joe Dugan alone hit 22, five more than the total for the players Boston received. Of the twelve players Boston received, eight of them never hit a home run. Out of the ten players the Yankees received, only a single one failed to hit a home run. When it comes to RBIs, the Yankee players (again, minus Ruth) knocked in 994, compared with 471 driven in by the Boston players. The Yankees also double up on hits, having 2,333 of them (Ruth added 2,518 more) compared with the 1,197 that Boston players had. Finally, there is a vast difference in the batting averages of the players each team received. The Boston players hit for an average of .257, the numbers of a light-hitting shortstop basically. The Yankees hit to the tune of .278, and if we were to include Ruth's statistics, that figure would jump to .311.

Then there is the pitching. Pitchers that came from New York to Boston posted a losing record of 119–161. New York pitchers that came from Boston, on the other hand, went 639–401. New York received triple the number of games pitched (1,520 vs. 493), nearly four times the number of innings (9,094 vs. 2,493.2), and nearly five times the number of strikeouts (3,090 vs. 616). Another disturbing statistic from the Boston pitchers is that they walked more hitters (867) than they struck out (616). Out of the nine pitchers Boston received, in fact, only one had more strikeouts than walks. New York's pitchers punched out 3,091 batters and walked 2,803. When it comes to ERA, Boston pitchers averaged 4.89, New York pitchers 4.07.

Even though we left Ruth out of the above analysis, what cannot be discounted is what Boston lost when they traded him. Boston used the Sultan of Swat mostly as a pitcher. He had 89 regular-season wins for Boston in the six years he played for them, adding another three in the World Series. That is nearly the number of wins the nine pitchers Boston received from New York provided. Even if Ruth had stayed with the Red Sox, however, his value from this point in his career forward would have come mostly from offense. His number of innings pitched had already been sharply reduced in 1918 and 1919, and he was on his way to being a full-time position player.

Placing the blame for Boston's sliding fortunes on the Ruth sale is easy to do when he put up numbers like this in the Bronx:

	Seasons	Games	AB	Hits	HR	RBIs	Runs	BA	OBP
Babe Ruth	15	2,084	7,217	2,518	659	1,978	1,959	.349	.484

But the darkening clouds over Fenway were about more than Ruth. The 19 players New York received from Boston far outperformed the 23 they sent the other way. Harry Frazee made a number of bad moves, and in the time he was the majority owner and president, he hurt Boston so badly it would take them decades to recover. To put it in perspective, when the

Yankees won their first World Series in 1923, 11 of the 24 New York players had previously played for the Red Sox.

Players Who Spent Time with Both Teams, 1920–1941

IVY ANDREWS

A pitcher in major league baseball from 1931 to 1938, Andrews played for four teams. He was twice a Yankee, at the beginning and end of his career. In between he played two seasons with Boston, three with the St. Louis Browns, and one with the Cleveland Indians. His most productive year was 1935, with the Browns, with whom he compiled a 13–7 record and a 3.54 ERA (135 ERA+), eighth best in the league. His career record, established over 1,041 innings, was 50–59.

Yankees Years

Year	Age	W	L	%	ERA	G	GS	CG	SV	IP	H	R	HR	BB	SO	ERA+	WHIP	H/9	BB/9	SO/9	SO/BB
1931	24	2	0	1.000	4.19	7	3	1	0	34.1	36	17	2	5	10	95	1.282	9.4	2.1	2.6	1.25
1932	25	2	1	.667	1.82	4	1	1	0	24.2	20	8	0	9	7	227	1.176	7.3	3.3	2.6	0.78
1937	30	3	2	.600	3.12	11	5	3	1	49.0	49	19	2	17	17	145	1.347	9.0	3.1	3.1	1.00
1938	31	1	3	.250	3.00	19	1	1	1	48.0	51	25	3	17	13	153	1.417	9.6	3.2	2.4	0.76
Totals		8	6	.571	3.12	41	10	6	2	156.0	156	69	8	51	47	140	1.327	9.0	2.9	2.7	0.92

Red Sox Years

Year	Age	W	L	%	ERA	G	GS	CG	SV	IP	H	R	HR	BB	SO	ERA+	WHIP	H/9	BB/9	SO/9	SO/BB
1932	25	8	6	.571	3.81	25	19	8	0	141.2	144	76	4	53	30	117	1.391	9.1	3.4	1.9	0.57
1933	26	7	13	.350	4.95	34	17	5	1	140.0	157	96	8	61	37	89	1.557	10.1	3.9	2.4	0.61
Totals		15	19	.441	4.38	59	36	13	1	281.2	301	172	12	114	67	101	1.473	9.6	3.6	2.1	0.59

Which Team Fared Better?

Although he finished with a losing record in the two seasons he was with Boston, that fact is best considered in context. The 1932 Red Sox were considered by some to be the worst team in club history. They won only 43 games, losing 111, and finished 64 games out of first place. (Adding insult to injury, they watched the Yankees take the pennant with 107 wins.) In that season, Andrews won two games for the Yankees before being traded in June to the Red Sox, with whom he won another eight. That means he won nearly 20 percent of their games. He was the only Boston pitcher to have a winning record that year on the entire roster, starters and relievers. The Yankees on the other hand did not find his 2-1 record and 1.82 ERA to be good enough to keep him around, trading him for a 1 and 10 pitcher, Danny Mac-Fayden. Although Andrews went 7–13 for Boston the next year, his value in the 1932 season was greater than it was for his entire stint with the Yankees, which was spent mostly in relief in the last couple of years.

PETE APPLETON

Born Peter Jablonowski, Appleton's big league career spanned 14 seasons, lasting from 1927 to 1945, with time out for World War II. He played for seven teams, his longest tenure being five years with the Washington Senators. He also spent years with the Cincinnati Reds, Cleveland Indians, Chicago White Sox, and the St. Louis Browns. After playing for the Yankees and Red Sox as Jablonowski, he returned to the majors in 1936 as Appleton. So why the name change? Historian Bill James, in *The New Bill James Historical Baseball Abstract*, cites sportscaster Bill Stern as saying that the player did it to change his luck.

Red Sox Year

Year	Age	W	L	%	ERA	G	GS	CG	SV	IP	H	R	HR	BB	SO	ERA+	WHIP	H/9	BB/9	SO/9	SO/BB
1932	28	0	3	0.00	4.11	11	3	0	0	46.0	49	35	2	26	15	109	1.630	9.6	5.1	2.9	0.58

Yankees Year

Year	Age	W	L	%	ERA	G	GS	CG	SV	IP	H	R	HR	BB	SO	ERA+	WHIP	H/9	BB/9	SO/9	SO/BB
1933	29	0	0		0.00	1	0	0	0	2.0	3	0	0	1	0		2.000	13.5	4.5	0.0	0.00

Which Team Fared Better?

It is difficult to determine which team fared better in the limited time Appleton spent with both teams. He went 0–3 with a 4.11 ERA for Boston in 46 innings pitched, and he pitched in a single, meaningless game for the Yankees in 1933. True, he did not give up any runs as a Yankees pitcher, but over two innings he did allow three hits and issue a walk. The Red Sox win this one, if only because they were able to trot out a roughly league-average pitcher for 10 more games than the Yankees did.

George Burns

Not to be confused with the actor or the outfielder who played around the same time for the Giants, Reds, and Phillies. This George Burns was a first baseman who played for 16 seasons. He was awarded the MVP in 1926 while posting a .358 average and setting a major league record for doubles with 64. He also won World Series rings with the 1920 Cleveland Indians and 1929 Philadelphia Athletics. Other teams he played for were the Detroit Tigers, Yankees, and Red Sox. His longest stint was with Cleveland, where he played for a total of seven seasons. He was a .307 lifetime hitter with 2,018 hits and 1,641 games played at first base.

Red Sox Years

Year	Age	G	AB	R	H	2B	3B	HR	RBI	SB	CS	BB	SO	BA	OBP	SLG	OPS	OPS+	TB	SH
1922	29	147	556	71	171	32	5	12	73	8	2	20	28	.306	.341	.446	.767	104	249	15
1923	30	146	551	91	181	47	5	7	82	9	7	45	33	.326	.386	.470	.856	125	259	12
Totals		293	1,109	162	352	79	10	19	155	17	9	65	61	.317	.364	.458	.822	115	508	27

Yankees Years

Year	Age	G	AB	R	H	2B	3B	HR	RBI	SB	CS	BB	SO	BA	OBP	SLG	OPS	OPS+	TB	SH
1928	35	4	4	1	2	0	0	0	0	0	0	0	1	.500	.500	.500	1.000	165	2	0
1929	36	9	9	0	0	0	0	0	0	0	0	0	4	.000	.000	.000	.000	-100	0	0
Totals		13	13	1	2	0	0	0	0	0	0	0	5	.154	.154	.154	.308	-18	2	0

Which Team Fared Better?

Burns played very little for the Yankees, accumulating 13 at-bats in two seasons, compared with 1,109 with Boston, also over two seasons. In each of his two years with the Red Sox, the team managed only 61 wins, losing more than 90. Burns cannot be blamed for their woes, however; he batted .317 during that time with 155 RBIs, 19 home runs, and 352 hits, second only to outfielder Joe Harris on the team. He was a major contributor to the wins they did get.

BULLET JOE BUSH

A 17-year major leaguer, Bush is the pitcher often credited with creating the fork ball. He played for seven teams in his time, bookending his career with the Philadelphia Athletics and spending time with the St. Louis Browns, Washington Senators, Pittsburgh Pirates, and New York Giants. He finished with 195 wins and 183 losses, and he was a member of three world championship teams: the 1913 Athletics, 1918 Red Sox, and 1923 Yankees. In 1916, as a member of the A's, he threw a no-hitter against the Cleveland Indians.

Red Sox Years

Year	Age	W	L	%	ERA	G	GS	CG	SV	IP	H	R	HR	BB	SO	ERA+	WHIP	H/9	BB/9	SO/9	SO/BB
1918	25	15	15	.500	2.11	36	31	26	2	272.2	241	88	3	91	125	126	1.216	8.0	3.0	4.1	1.37
1919	26	0	0		3.56	2	2	0	0	7.0	9	3	0	4	2	84	1.657	11.6	5.1	2.6	0.50
1920	27	15	15	.500	4.25	35	22	16	1	243.2	287	136	3	94	88	86	1.657	10.6	3.5	3.3	0.94
1921	28	16	9	.640	3.50	37	32	21	2	254.1	244	111	10	93	96	121	1.325	8.6	3.3	3.4	1.03
Totals		46	39	.541	3.25	110	97	65	5	777.2	781	340	16	282	311	108	1.367	9.0	3.3	3.6	1.10

Yankees Years

Year	Age	W	L	%	ERA	G	GS	CG	SV	IP	H	R	HR	BB	SO	ERA+	WHIP	H/9	BB/9	SO/9	SO/BB
1922	29	26	7	.788	3.31	39	30	20	3	255.1	240	109	16	85	92	121	1.273	8.5	3.0	3.2	1.08
1923	30	19	15	.559	3.43	37	30	22	0	275.2	263	115	7	117	125	115	1.378	8.6	3.6	4.1	1.07
1924	31	17	16	.515	3.57	39	31	19	1	252.2	262	117	9	109	80	117	1.472	9.4	3.9	2.9	0.73
Totals		62	38	.620	3.44	115	91	61	4	783.0	765	341	32	311	297	118	1.374	8.8	3.6	3.4	0.96

Which Team Fared Better?

Even though he was only a .500 pitcher (15–15) in his first year with Boston, he had a career-best as well as a team-best ERA of 2.11. He would continue to pitch fairly well over his four years with the Red Sox, going 46–39 with a better-than-league-average ERA of 3.25 (108 ERA+). He was a little sharper still for the Yankees, compiling a 62–38 record to go along with his 3.44 ERA (118 ERA+). His best year as a pitcher was probably with New York in 1922, when he went 26–7 for a league leading .788 winning percentage.

Bush nearly won 200 games in his career, using the forkball that he made famous—there is some argument about whether he invented the pitch—much to his advantage. He pitched on six pennant winners, and helped three of them to World Series victories. His career spanned from 1912 to 1928; the Red Sox (1918–1921) and Yankees (1922–1924) were but two of his seven clubs.

He finished fourth in the MVP voting that year. Bush went to the World Series for both teams. In the 1918 World Series, he pitched one game for the Red Sox, which he lost despite not pitching poorly. For the 1922 New York Yankees, he pitched in two World Series games against the Giants, losing both and giving up 21 hits and 8 runs in them. The Yanks went on to lose the Series. The next year, in a rematch with the Giants, he fared much better, going 1–1 with a 1.08 ERA and the Yankees won the championship. Given that outcome, the favor falls on the side of the Yankees.

Roy Carlyle

A left-handed batting outfielder, Carlyle had only two years in the majors, playing for three different teams. He started the 1925 season with the Washington Senators but was traded to Boston at the end of April after only a single at-bat. The next season, the Red Sox released him and the Yankees picked him up off of waivers. In the 174 games he played in his career, he had a .312 batting average and drove in 76 runs. You would think these numbers would be good enough to keep him around, but he was apparently slow in the field and committed a lot of errors. He had 13 miscues with the Red Sox in 1925 and a .910 fielding percentage for his career, meaning he misplayed one out of every ten balls hit to him.

Red Sox Years

Year	Age	G	AB	R	H	2B	3B	HR	RBI	SB	CS	BB	SO	BA	OBP	SLG	OPS	OPS+	TB	SH
1925	24	93	276	36	90	20	3	7	49	1	1	16	28	.326	.365	.496	.862	118	137	7
1926	25	45	165	22	47	6	2	2	16	0	0	4	18	.265	.310	.382	.692	83	63	0
Totals		138	441	58	137	26	5	9	65	1	1	20	46	.311	.345	.454	.798	105	200	7

Yankees Year

Year	Age	G	AB	R	H	2B	3B	HR	RBI	SB	CS	BB	SO	BA	OBP	SLG	OPS	OPS+	TB	SH
1926	25	35	62	3	20	5	1	0	11	0	0	4	9	.323	.373	.435	.809	111	27	0

Which Team Fared Better?

The Red Sox benefited from 441 at-bats from Carlyle while the Yanks had only 62. His batting average for both teams was pretty good, .311 for the Sox and .323 for New York. Although Carlyle's rate stats were slightly better for New York, his counting stats for the Red Sox carry the day. He went to the plate far more often, hit nine home runs (as opposed to none for the Yankees), and drove in 65 runs (only 11 for New York), giving the Red Sox the advantage.

Ben Chapman

Chapman had an interesting fifteen years in major league baseball. He began as an outfielder, playing seven solid years for the Yankees. He then bounced around from the Senators to the Red Sox, on to the Indians, and finally to the White Sox. He then spent two years in the minors, returning as a pitcher to the majors. He became the manager for the Philadelphia Phillies in 1945 and was in that same position in 1947 when Jackie Robinson broke the color barrier with the Brooklyn Dodgers. Remembered today primarily as a bigot, Chapman informed his pitchers to bean Robinson whenever they got to a 3–0 count. He was so abusive to Robinson that it made headlines in the newspapers, and there was a lot of backlash toward Chapman.

Yankees Years

Year	Age	G	AB	R	H	2B	3B	HR	RBI	SB	CS	BB	SO	BA	OBP	SLG	OPS	OPS+	TB	SH
1930	21	138	513	74	162	31	10	10	61	14	6	43	56	.316	.371	.474	.645	116	243	6
1931	22	149	600	120	189	28	11	17	122	61	23	75	77	.315	.396	.483	.879	135	290	6
1932	23	151	581	101	174	41	15	10	107	38	18	71	55	.299	.381	.473	.854	125	275	5
1933	24	147	565	112	176	36	4	9	98	27	18	72	45	.312	.393	.437	.830	125	247	10
1934	25	149	588	82	181	21	13	5	86	26	16	67	68	.308	.381	.413	.795	110	243	8
1935	26	140	553	118	160	38	8	8	74	17	10	61	39	.289	.361	.430	.791	108	238	14
1936	27	36	139	19	37	14	3	1	21	1	2	15	20	.266	.338	.432	.769	91	60	2
Totals		910	3,539	626	1,079	209	64	60	589	184	93	404	362	.305	.379	.451	.830	119	1,596	51

Red Sox Years

Year	Age	G	AB	R	H	2B	3B	HR	RBI	SB	CS	BB	SO	BA	OBP	SLG	OPS	OPS+	TB	SH
1937	28	113	423	76	130	23	11	7	57	27	12	57	35	.307	.391	.463	.854	110	196	6
1938	29	127	480	92	163	40	8	6	80	13	6	65	33	.340	.418	.494	.912	123	237	8
Totals		240	903	168	293	63	19	13	137	40	18	122	68	.324	.405	.480	.885	117	433	14

Which Team Fared Better?

The Yankees got the first seven years of his career. During this time Chapman had a .305 batting average, more than 1,000 hits, and 60 home runs. He also led the league in stolen bases for three years, his best season being 1931 when he stole 61. Of course, he led the league in times caught stealing during those years as well. He was an All-Star four times for the Yankees, receiving some MVP consideration for his 1931 and 1933 seasons. He played well for the Red Sox, finishing his two years with them with a .324 average, including a career best .340 and 137 RBIs, but did not spend enough time with them to make the impact he did with New York. Sealing the deal for the Yankees was the fact that he won a World Series with them in 1932, batting .294 in the postseason.

RIP COLLINS

Surprisingly there were two players known as Rip Collins during this time. This one was a pitcher; the other was a backup catcher. This Rip Collins played two years with the Yankees, followed by a season with the Red Sox. Five of his 11 years were spent pitching for Detroit, and he finished up with the St. Louis Browns.

Yankees Years

Year	Age	W	L	%	ERA	G	GS	CG	SV	IP	H	R	HR	BB	SO	ERA+	WHIP	H/9	BB/9	SO/9	SO/BB
1920	24	14	8	.636	3.22	35	18	10	1	187.1	171	53	6	79	66	119	1.335	8.2	3.8	3.2	0.84
1921	25	11	5	.688	5.44	28	16	7	0	137.1	158	103	6	78	64	77	1.718	10.4	5.1	4.2	0.82
Totals		25	13	.658	4.16	64	34	17	1	324.2	329	186	12	157	130	96	1.497	9.1	4.4	3.6	0.83

Red Sox Year

Year	Age	W	L	%	ERA	G	GS	CG	SV	IP	H	R	HR	BB	SO	ERA+	WHIP	H/9	BB/9	SO/9	SO/BB
1922	26	14	11	.560	3.76	32	29	15	0	210.0	219	101	4	103	69	108	1.528	9.4	4.4	2.9	0.67

Which Team Fared Better?

He won 25 games for the Yankees over the course of two seasons, losing only 13 for a .658 winning percentage. He also went to the World Series with them in 1921. (They lost to the New York Giants.) He pitched only 2/3 of an inning and gave up four earned runs, giving him an inflated 54.00 ERA in the postseason. In his time in Boston he logged more innings than he did in either of his seasons with the Yankees. He had a 14–11 record for a 1922 Red Sox team that won only 61 games. Determining the value of his contributions to either team is basically a coin toss. The deciding factor, though, is the men each team got for him in their trade. He was part of a seven-player trade between Boston and New York, the Yankees getting Bullet Joe Bush, Sad Sam Jones, and Everett Scott, all of whom contributed solidly to New York. Bush piled up 62 wins, Jones 67, and Scott was a respectable hitter. When Boston traded Collins along with Del Pratt, they got Danny Clark, Howard Ehmke, Babe Herman, and Carl Holling. Clark and Ehmke had losing records in their time with Boston, and Herman and Holling never cracked the major league lineup with the Red Sox. The Yankees certainly got more for their trade of Collins.

Dusty Cooke

A good defensive player who made a career out of being the fourth outfielder, Cooke played for eight years. He spent the first three with the New York Yankees before going to the Red Sox for four seasons. He finished with the Cincinnati Reds. His career numbers include 229 RBIs, 324 runs, and a .384 on-base percentage. Perhaps his most impressive stat was his career 1.06 walk-to-strikeout ratio.

Yankees Years

Year	Age	G	AB	R	H	2B	3B	HR	RBI	SB	CS	BB	SO	BA	OBP	SLG	OPS	OPS+	TB	SH
1930	23	92	216	43	55	12	3	6	29	4	6	32	61	.255	.353	.421	.775	99	91	2
1931	24	27	39	10	13	1	0	1	6	4	1	8	11	.333	.447	.436	.563	138	17	0
1932	25	3	0	1	0	0	0	0	0	0	0	1	0		1.000				0	0
Totals		122	255	54	68	13	3	7	35	8	7	41	72	.267	.370	.424	.794	105	108	2

Red Sox Years

Year	Age	G	AB	R	H	2B	3B	HR	RBI	SB	CS	BB	SO	BA	OBP	SLG	OPS	OPS+	TB	SH
1933	26	119	454	86	133	35	10	5	54	7	5	67	71	.293	.386	.447	.833	118	203	8
1934	27	74	168	34	41	8	5	1	26	7	2	36	25	.244	.377	.369	.746	90	62	0
1935	28	100	294	51	90	18	6	3	34	6	8	46	24	.306	.400	.439	.839	112	129	6
1936	29	111	341	58	93	20	3	6	47	4	3	72	48	.273	.401	.402	.803	94	137	0
Totals		404	1,257	229	357	81	24	15	161	24	18	221	168	.284	.392	.422	.815	106	531	14

Which Team Fared Better?

After using him fairly regularly in 1930, the Yankees used him only intermittently the following two years, giving him a single plate appearance in the 1932 season. (He walked.) The Red Sox found more playing time for him, having 454 at-bats in his first season alone, more than his combined three years with New York. Appearing in nearly three hundred more games for Boston, he knocked in 161 RBIs (35 for NY), swatted 15 home runs (7 for NY), and scored 229 runs (54 for NY). It doesn't take a math genius to see Boston got more out of him.

Babe Dahlgren

In addition to Babe Ruth, there were 23 other Babes that played in the major leagues. Babe Dahlgren was an infielder who played for 12 years. He was a member of eight teams, spending the longest time, four years, with the Yankees. For each of the other teams—the

Boston Braves, Chicago Cubs, St. Louis Browns, Brooklyn Dodgers, Philadelphia Phillies, and Pittsburgh Pirates—he played for two or fewer seasons. Dahlgren's main claim to fame is that he is the answer to the trivia question Who replaced Lou Gehrig at first base to end the streak of 2,130 straight games played? He was named to the 1943 All-Star team as a member of the Phillies, and he won a World Series with the 1939 New York Yankees. Another claim to fame for Dahlgren? He became the first player to take a drug test when rumors about him pot smoking began to circulate. He tested negative.

Red Sox Years

Year	Age	G	AB	R	H	2B	3B	HR	RBI	SB	CS	BB	SO	BA	OBP	SLG	OPS	OPS+	TB	SH
1935	23	149	525	77	138	27	7	9	63	6	5	56	67	.263	.337	.392	.730	84	206	12
1936	24	16	57	6	16	3	1	1	7	2	1	7	1	.281	.359	.421	.780	88	24	1
Totals		165	582	83	154	30	8	10	70	8	6	63	68	.265	.340	.395	.735	84	230	13

Yankees Years

Year	Age	G	AB	R	H	2B	3B	HR	RBI	SB	CS	BB	SO	BA	OBP	SLG	OPS	OPS+	TB	SH
1937	25	1	1	0	0	0	0	0	0	0	0	0	0	.000	.000	.000	.000	-100	0	0
1938	26	27	43	8	8	1	0	0	1	0	0	1	7	.186	.205	.209	.414	4	9	0
1939	27	144	531	71	125	18	6	15	89	2	3	57	54	.235	.312	.377	.689	76	200	13
1940	28	155	568	51	150	24	4	12	73	1	1	46	54	.264	.325	.384	.709	86	218	3
Totals		327	1,143	130	283	43	10	27	163	3	4	104	115	.248	.314	.374	.688	78	427	16

Which Team Fared Better?

Even though he only had a single at-bat in the 1937 season for New York, he was a regular in 1939 and 1940, accumulating over 600 plate appearances both seasons. That is twice the number he had for the Red Sox. He also had nearly twice as many hits, almost three times as many home runs, and twice the number of RBIs. This ultimately makes him twice as valuable to the Yankees as Red Sox.

AL DEVORMER

DeVormer began his professional career in 1914 and played until 1932. During that time he spent five years in the major leagues as a backup catcher, beginning with a cup of coffee with the Chicago White Sox in 1918. After spending two seasons with the Yankees, he was traded in January 1923 to Boston. After another three years in the minors, he returned to the show with the New York Giants where he finished up in 1927. He spent five more years playing minor league baseball before hanging up his spikes.

Yankees Years

Year	Age	G	AB	R	H	2B	3B	HR	RBI	SB	CS	BB	SO	BA	OBP	SLG	OPS	OPS+	TB	SH
1921	29	22	49	6	17	4	0	0	7	2	0	2	4	.347	.373	.429	.801	102	21	2
1922	30	24	59	8	12	4	1	0	11	0	0	1	6	.203	.217	.305	.522	34	18	4
Totals		46	108	14	29	8	1	0	18	2	0	3	10	.269	.288	.361	.649	65	39	6

Red Sox Year

Year	Age	G	AB	R	H	2B	3B	HR	RBI	SB	CS	BB	SO	BA	OBP	SLG	OPS	OPS+	TB	SH
1923	31	74	209	20	54	7	3	0	18	3	0	6	21	.258	.282	.321	.603	58	67	6

Which Team Fared Better?

He was a third-string catcher for the Yankees, getting only 108 at-bats in two seasons. He was traded, the story goes, after jumping into Lake Michigan with an entire suit of clothes on to win a $10 bet. Miller Huggins, the Yankees boss, was not impressed and shipped DeVormer to the Red Sox for two minor leaguers. But one of those minor leaguers, right-hander George Pipgras, would win 93 games for the Yankees over parts of nine seasons, finishing nearly 30 games over .500. The other acquisition, first baseman and outfielder Harvey Hendrick, played two years for New York, contributing modestly, but went on to enjoy a solid 11-year career in the majors.

Joe Dugan

Considered one of the best third basemen in baseball during his time (1917–1931), Dugan played 14 seasons for five teams, spending parts of seven of them with the New York Yankees. He also played five years with the Philadelphia Athletics and one apiece with the Red Sox, Boston Braves, and Detroit Tigers.

Red Sox Year

Year	Age	G	AB	R	H	2B	3B	HR	RBI	SB	CS	BB	SO	BA	OBP	SLG	OPS	OPS+	TB	SH
1922	25	84	341	45	98	22	3	3	38	2	3	9	28	.287	.308	.396	.704	83	135	10

Yankees Years

Year	Age	G	AB	R	H	2B	3B	HR	RBI	SB	CS	BB	SO	BA	OBP	SLG	OPS	OPS+	TB	SH
1922	25	60	252	44	72	9	1	3	25	1	0	13	21	.286	.331	.365	.696	80	92	12
1923	26	146	644	111	182	30	7	7	67	4	2	25	41	.283	.311	.384	.695	81	247	13
1924	27	148	610	105	184	31	7	3	56	1	2	31	33	.302	.341	.390	.731	88	238	25
1925	28	102	404	50	118	19	4	0	31	2	4	19	20	.292	.330	.359	.689	76	145	14
1926	29	123	434	39	125	19	5	1	61	2	4	25	16	.288	.328	.362	.690	81	157	23
1927	30	112	387	44	104	24	3	2	43	1	4	27	37	.269	.321	.362	.683	78	140	12
1928	31	94	312	33	86	15	0	6	34	1	0	16	15	.276	.317	.381	.699	84	119	8
Totals		785	3,043	426	871	147	27	22	317	12	16	156	183	.286	.326	.374	.700	82	1,138	107

Which Team Fared Better?

It takes a mere glance to see that New York got many more productive years out of Dugan. Dugan was just another example of Harry Frazee dumping talented players into the laps of the Yankees without much in return. Even if you take all of his regular seasons with the Yankees away and look only at his postseason accomplishments, New York fares much better. He won the World Series with the Yankees in 1923, 1927, and 1928, and played for them in two more (1922 and 1926). In these games he batted .267 with 24 hits, 13 runs, and 8 RBIs—not much less than he provided in his one full season with the Red Sox. He was considered by some to be the hero of the 1923 World Series, the first one the Yankees won, playing great defense and knocking in five runs.

Cedric Durst

Known more as a defensive outfielder than a good hitter, Durst played seven seasons in the majors, four of them with the Yankees. He began his career with the St. Louis Browns before being traded to New York to act as the fourth outfielder to the Murderers' Row of Babe

Ruth, Bob Meusel, and Earle Combs. In May of 1930 the Yankees traded him to the Red Sox where he finished out the season and his career.

Yankees Years

Year	Age	G	AB	R	H	2B	3B	HR	RBI	SB	CS	BB	SO	BA	OBP	SLG	OPS	OPS+	TB	SH
1927	30	65	129	18	32	4	3	0	25	0	3	6	7	.248	.281	.326	.607	58	42	7
1928	31	74	135	18	34	2	1	2	10	1	0	7	9	.252	.289	.326	.615	62	44	4
1929	32	92	202	32	52	3	3	4	31	3	2	15	25	.257	.309	.361	.670	76	73	5
1930	33	8	19	0	3	1	0	0	5	0	0	0	1	.158	.158	.211	.368	-6	4	0
Totals		239	485	68	121	10	7	6	71	4	5	28	42	.249	.290	.336	.627	64	163	16

Red Sox Year

Year	Age	G	AB	R	H	2B	3B	HR	RBI	SB	CS	BB	SO	BA	OBP	SLG	OPS	OPS+	TB	SH
1930	33	102	302	29	74	19	5	1	24	3	1	17	24	.245	.290	.351	.641	65	106	9

Which Team Fared Better?

Although he did not see much playing time in his four years with the Yankees, having only 485 at-bats during that span, he filled his role nicely of spelling the big three outfielders for the Yankees. Durst was a member of the 1927 and 1928 world championship teams for New York. In addition to his contributions, he gave the Yankees Red Ruffing, who came over to the pinstripers in the trade. Ruffing would provide the Yankees with 231 wins in his 14 career with them, making Durst's unintentional contribution even greater.

Doc Farrell

A nine season major leaguer, Farrell was a utility infielder, mostly at shortstop. He played for six teams, having two tours with the New York Giants, three seasons with the Boston Braves, and a split season between the St. Louis Cardinals and the Chicago Cubs. He played for the Yankees for two seasons and the Red Sox for one. His career numbers are a .260 batting average, 467 hits, 10 home runs, and 213 RBIs. He did receive some MVP votes for his work with the Giants in the 1927 season.

Yankees Years

Year	Age	G	AB	R	H	2B	3B	HR	RBI	SB	CS	BB	SO	BA	OBP	SLG	OPS	OPS+	TB	SH
1932	30	26	63	4	11	1	1	0	4	0	0	2	8	.175	.212	.222	.434	15	14	1
1933	31	44	93	16	25	0	0	0	6	0	0	16	6	.269	.376	.269	.645	78	25	3
Totals		70	156	20	36	1	1	0	10	0	0	18	14	.231	.314	.250	.564	53	39	4

Red Sox Year

Year	Age	G	AB	R	H	2B	3B	HR	RBI	SB	CS	BB	SO	BA	OBP	SLG	OPS	OPS+	TB	SH
1935	33	4	7	1	2	1	0	0	1	0	0	1	0	.286	.375	.429	.804	102	3	0

Which Team Fared Better?

He received a World Series ring with the 1932 Yankees despite the fact he did not play in the postseason for them. He had only 36 hits with the Yankees, but they were 34 more than he had with the Red Sox. Perhaps his largest contribution came in the form of trade; he was one of the four players traded to the San Francisco Seals, of the PCL, to net the Yankees Joe DiMaggio. This is more significant than any numbers he could have put up himself.

ALEX FERGUSON

A pitcher known for having a nasty forkball, he had ten years in the major leagues with five different teams. He broke into the majors with the Yankees, before going to the Red Sox for four seasons. In 1925 he started with the Red Sox, was traded to the Yankees again, and then purchased by the Washington Senators, whom he helped win a pennant. He set a record for having the highest ERA, a 6.18, for a pitcher who started a postseason game. This was not broken until Oliver Perez started a playoff game for the 2006 Mets with a higher ERA. He finished his last few years with the Philadelphia Phillies and Brooklyn Robins.

Yankees Years

Year	Age	W	L	%	ERA	G	GS	CG	SV	IP	H	R	HR	BB	SO	ERA+	WHIP	H/9	BB/9	SO/9	SO/BB
1918	21	0	0		0.00	1	0	0	0	1.2	2	0	0	2	1		2.400	10.8	10.8	5.4	0.50
1921	24	3	1	.750	5.91	17	4	1	1	56.1	64	40	4	27	9	71	1.615	10.2	4.3	1.4	0.33
1925	28	4	2	.667	7.79	21	6	0	1	54.1	83	57	3	42	20	55	2.301	13.7	7.0	3.3	0.48
Totals		7	3	.700	6.73	39	10	1	2	112.1	149	97	7	71	30	63	1.958	11.9	5.7	2.4	0.42

Red Sox Years

Year	Age	W	L	%	ERA	G	GS	CG	SV	IP	H	R	HR	BB	SO	ERA+	WHIP	H/9	BB/9	SO/9	SO/BB
1922	25	9	16	.360	4.31	39	27	10	2	198.1	201	108	5	62	44	95	1.326	9.1	2.8	2.0	0.71
1923	26	9	13	.409	4.04	34	27	11	0	198.1	229	115	5	67	72	101	1.492	10.4	3.3	3.3	1.07
1924	27	14	17	.452	3.79	41	32	15	2	237.2	259	115	6	108	78	115	1.544	9.8	4.1	3.0	0.72
1925	28	0	2	.000	10.91	5	4	0	1	15.2	22	22	6	5	5	42	1.723	12.6	2.9	2.9	1.00
Totals		32	48	.400	4.20	119	90	36	5	650.0	711	360	22	242	199	100	1.466	9.8	3.4	2.8	0.82

Which Team Fared Better?

When you glance at the numbers it appears the Yankees got the better of him. He had a winning record with them, going 7–3. While with the Red Sox, on the other hand, he went 32–48 for a .400 winning percentage. But when you look at the numbers a little more closely, you find his record is not a good indicator of his pitching performance. For instance, he had a 4.20 ERA for Boston. Nothing spectacular, but certainly better than the 6.73 for New York. His WHIP for Boston was a 1.466 and was nearly a 2.000 for the Yankees, a 1.958. His strikeout-to-walk ratio was 0.82 for the Red Sox and only half of that, 0.42, for New York. Those numbers indicate that it was actually the Red Sox who got the better pitcher.

WES FERRELL

A 15-year major leaguer, Ferrell won 193 games in his career. He began with the Cleveland Indians, playing for seven seasons with the franchise before going on to the Red Sox for four. He rode out his career pitching for the Washington Senators, New York Yankees, Brooklyn Dodgers, and Boston Braves. He was a twenty-game winner six times, four times for the Indians and twice for the Red Sox. He was an All-Star in 1933 with the Indians and in 1937 with the Red Sox.

Red Sox Years

Year	Age	W	L	%	ERA	G	GS	CG	SV	IP	H	R	HR	BB	SO	ERA+	WHIP	H/9	BB/9	SO/9	SO/BB
1934	26	14	5	.737	3.63	26	23	17	1	181.0	205	87	4	49	67	130	1.403	10.2	2.4	3.3	1.37
1935	27	25	14	.641	3.52	41	38	31	0	322.1	336	149	16	108	110	134	1.377	9.4	3.0	3.1	1.02

Year	Age	W	L	%	ERA	G	GS	CG	SV	IP	H	R	HR	BB	SO	ERA+	WHIP	H/9	BB/9	SO/9	SO/BB
1936	28	20	15	.571	4.19	39	38	28	0	301.0	330	160	11	119	106	126	1.492	9.9	3.6	3.2	0.89
1937	29	3	6	.333	7.61	12	11	5	0	73.1	111	66	14	34	31	63	1.977	13.6	4.2	3.8	0.91
Totals		62	40	.608	4.11	118	110	81	1	877.2	982	462	45	310	314	120	1.472	10.1	3.2	3.2	1.01

Yankees Years

Year	Age	W	L	%	ERA	G	GS	CG	SV	IP	H	R	HR	BB	SO	ERA+	WHIP	H/9	BB/9	SO/9	SO/BB
1938	30	2	2	.500	8.10	5	4	1	0	30.0	52	33	6	18	7	57	2.333	15.6	5.4	2.1	0.39
1939	31	1	2	.333	4.66	3	3	1	0	19.1	14	10	2	17	6	95	1.603	6.5	7.9	2.8	0.35
Totals		3	4	.429	6.75	8	7	2	0	49.1	66	43	8	35	13	67	2.047	12.0	6.4	2.4	0.37

Which Team Fared Better?

The fact that Ferrell is in the Red Sox Hall of Fame speaks to his contributions to that team. When he went over to Boston, the catcher for the Red Sox was his brother Rick. The best season Wes had was 1935, when he went 25–14 with Boston, leading the league in wins, complete games (31), innings pitched (322.1), and batters faced (1,391), coming in second in the MVP voting behind Hank Greenberg. He followed that up with another twenty-win season for Boston, going 20–15 and again leading the league in complete games (28), innings pitched (301.0), and batters faced (1,341). After he arrived in New York in August of 1938, he pitched only five games. He was released by them the following year after throwing in only three games.

CHICK FEWSTER

A second baseman who spend 11 years in the major leagues, Fewster played his first six years with the Yankees. This was followed by two years in Boston, two in Cleveland, and two in Brooklyn. A widely touted prospect when first breaking into the bigs, Fewster impressed his Yankees manager, Miller Huggins, who claimed never to have seen a greater prospect. But a beaning by Jeff Pfeffer, who hit Fewster in the temple during a 1920 spring training game, had him at death's door. He eventually came back but was never the same player.

Yankees Years

Year	Age	G	AB	R	H	2B	3B	HR	RBI	SB	CS	BB	SO	BA	OBP	SLG	OPS	OPS+	TB	SH
1917	21	11	36	2	8	0	0	0	1	1		5	5	.222	.317	.222	.539	64	8	0
1918	22	5	2	1	1	0	0	0	0	0		0	0	.500	.500	.500	1.000	199	1	0
1919	23	81	244	38	69	9	3	1	15	8		34	36	.283	.386	.357	.743	109	87	8
1920	24	21	21	8	6	1	0	0	1	0	1	7	2	.286	.464	.333	.798	110	7	1
1921	25	66	207	44	58	19	0	1	19	4	4	28	43	.280	.382	.386	.768	95	80	7
1922	26	44	132	20	32	4	1	1	9	2	4	16	23	.242	.324	.311	.635	65	41	11
Totals		228	642	113	174	33	4	3	45	15	9	90	109	.271	.372	.349	.721	93	224	27

Red Sox Years

Year	Age	G	AB	R	H	2B	3B	HR	RBI	SB	CS	BB	SO	BA	OBP	SLG	OPS	OPS+	TB	SH
1922	26	23	83	8	24	4	1	0	9	8	3	6	10	.289	.344	.361	.706	85	30	3
1923	27	90	284	32	67	10	1	0	15	7	14	39	35	.236	.334	.278	.613	62	79	5
Totals		113	367	40	91	14	2	0	24	15	17	45	45	.248	.337	.297	.634	67	109	8

Which Team Fared Better?

Fewster was the first batter ever to step into the box at Yankee Stadium. He also was a part of a trade between the Yankees and Red Sox that sent Joe Dugan and Elmer Smith to New York, the 11th and 12th players to be moved to the Bronx in the infamously lopsided trades of the time that strengthened the Yankees and weakened the BoSox. In the six years that he did play for the Yankees, he topped triple digits in at-bats only three seasons. He did contribute to the Yankees 1921 World Series efforts, hitting a two-run homer in Game Six, but it was not enough to beat the Giants that year. Although he saw more at-bats after moving to Boston, his contributions were not impressive, and he even got into a fight with his own teammate on the bench. The Yankees get the advantage here, but only because of what they added in subtracting him.

Eddie Foster

Foster was a third baseman who also played some second in his 13 seasons in the majors. After breaking in with the Yankees, he spent the next eight seasons with Washington, with whom he became a regular. He led the league in at-bats four seasons with the Senators, putting up his career-best numbers, including a .266 average, 1,177 hits, 355 RBIs, and 166 stolen bases. Three of his last five years in baseball were spent with the Red Sox, and the final two were with the St. Louis Browns.

Yankees Year

Year	Age	G	AB	R	H	2B	3B	HR	RBI	SB	CS	BB	SO	BA	OBP	SLG	OPS	OPS+	TB	SH
1910	23	30	83	5	11	2	0	0	1	2		8	13	.133	.217	.157	.374	14	13	0

Red Sox Years

Year	Age	G	AB	R	H	2B	3B	HR	RBI	SB	CS	BB	SO	BA	OBP	SLG	OPS	OPS+	TB	SH
1920	33	117	386	48	100	17	6	0	41	10	4	42	17	.259	.336	.334	.671	81	129	11
1921	34	120	412	51	117	18	6	0	35	13	7	57	15	.284	.371	.357	.728	89	147	16
1922	35	48	109	11	23	3	0	0	3	1	1	9	10	.211	.277	.239	.516	36	26	3
Totals		285	907	110	240	38	12	0	79	24	12	108	42	.265	.345	.333	.678	79	302	30

Which Team Fared Better?

When Foster came up with the Yankees, he was still a wet-behind-the-ears rookie whose role on a major league roster was unclear. And he floundered for a while, putting up a .133 average and striking out more than he walked. When he arrived at Boston ten years later, he definitely had his feet under him. Although he acted as a pinch hitter for most of his 1922 season, he had contributed a hundred hits a season in his first two years and scored an average of 50 runs. His experience allowed Boston to get the better of him.

Ray Francis

In three seasons this pitcher bounced around to four different teams. Unfortunately for New York and Boston, his first year with the Washington Senators was the highlight of his career. And that was the year he went 7–18 with a 4.28 ERA. He was traded to the Detroit Tigers the next year and pitched mostly in relief on his way to a 5–8 record. Those five wins would be the last of his career. He spent 1925 with both the Yankees and Red Sox, going 0–2 with matching 7.71 ERAs.

Yankees Year

Year	Age	W	L	%	ERA	G	GS	CG	SV	IP	H	R	HR	BB	SO	ERA+	WHIP	H/9	BB/9	SO/9	SO/BB
1925	32	0	0		7.71	4	0	0	0	4.2	5	4	0	3	1	60	1.714	9.6	5.8	1.9	0.33

Red Sox Year

Year	Age	W	L	%	ERA	G	GS	CG	SV	IP	H	R	HR	BB	SO	ERA+	WHIP	H/9	BB/9	SO/9	SO/BB
1925	32	0	2	.000	7.71	6	4	0	0	28.0	44	29	3	13	4	59	2.036	14.1	4.2	1.3	0.31

Which Team Fared Better?

The teams essentially shared Francis for a year and still got only 10 games in total out of him. There are no stats to point to that would determine who got the better value; instead, a look at the midseason trade between the two teams finds the answer. The Red Sox received only Francis, who participated in six games. In return, the Yankees received Alex Ferguson and Bobby Veach. Veach gave the Yankees 116 at-bats and 15 RBIs, and Ferguson pitched in with 54.1 innings and four wins. Francis threw 28.0 innings, with the underwhelming results already mentioned. Advantage New York.

MILT GASTON

A right-handed pitcher who played for five teams in 10 seasons. He began in New York during the 1924 campaign, pitching in 29 games. He moved on for three seasons with the St. Louis Browns, one year in Washington, three years in Boston, and three years in Chicago, with the White Sox. He won 94 games in his career but lost 164. He only had two winning seasons, the first two years he played. He led the league in one category or another six times—but all were categories in which pitchers would rather not lead: losses (twice), wild pitches (twice), earned runs, and home runs allowed.

Yankees Year

Year	Age	W	L	%	ERA	G	GS	CG	SV	IP	H	R	HR	BB	SO	ERA+	WHIP	H/9	BB/9	SO/9	SO/BB
1924	28	5	3	.625	4.50	29	2	0	1	86.0	92	48	3	44	24	93	1.581	9.6	4.6	2.5	0.55

Red Sox Years

Year	Age	W	L	%	ERA	G	GS	CG	SV	IP	H	R	HR	BB	SO	ERA+	WHIP	H/9	BB/9	SO/9	SO/BB
1929	33	12	19	.367	3.73	39	28	20	2	243.2	265	121	15	81	83	114	1.420	9.8	3.0	3.1	1.02
1930	34	13	20	.394	3.92	38	34	21	2	273.0	272	138	15	98	99	117	1.355	9.0	3.2	3.3	1.01
1931	35	2	13	.133	4.46	23	18	4	0	119.0	137	76	4	41	33	96	1.496	10.4	3.1	2.5	080.
Totals		27	52	.342	3.95	100	80	45	4	635.2	674	335	34	220	215	112	1.406	9.5	3.1	3.0	0.98

Which Team Fared Better?

It would be easy to look at the win-loss record and give this one to the Yankees. After all, Gaston had one of his two winning seasons with the team, going 5–3, and he never had a winning season for the Red Sox. When you look closer, though, it becomes clear that the record doesn't begin to tell the story of how bad he was with Boston. Gaston's seasons with the Red Sox were really, really bad. He paced the circuit in losses, with 20, in 1930. The year before he almost lost 20 as well, going 12–19. In his final year with Boston he won only two, losing 13 for a .133 winning percentage. Overall, he went 27–52 for them, losing almost twice as often as he won. This time the win-loss record reflects the worth of the pitcher.

Joe Glenn

A backup catcher who posted eight seasons. Six of them were with the Yankees. Even with all that time, his best season came in 1939 as a St. Louis Brown. That year he had career highs in at-bats (286), hits (78), home runs (4), RBIs (29), and walks (29). He played one more year with the Boston Red Sox.

Yankees Years

Year	Age	G	AB	R	H	2B	3B	HR	RBI	SB	CS	BB	SO	BA	OBP	SLG	OPS	OPS+	TB	SH
1932	23	6	16	0	2	0	0	0	0	0	0	1	5	.125	.222	.125	.347	-6	2	0
1933	24	5	21	1	3	0	0	0	1	0	0	0	3	.143	.143	.143	.286	-22	3	0
1935	26	17	43	7	10	4	0	0	6	0	0	4	1	.233	.298	.326	.623	65	14	2
1936	27	44	129	21	35	7	0	1	20	1	1	20	10	.271	.373	.349	.722	82	45	0
1937	28	25	53	6	15	2	2	0	4	0	0	10	11	.263	.397	.396	.793	99	21	1
1938	29	41	123	10	32	7	2	0	25	1	0	10	14	.260	.316	.350	.665	66	43	0
Totals		138	385	45	97	20	4	1	56	2	1	45	44	.252	.333	.332	.666	69	128	3

Red Sox Year

Year	Age	G	AB	R	H	2B	3B	HR	RBI	SB	CS	BB	SO	BA	OBP	SLG	OPS	OPS+	TB	SH
1940	31	22	47	3	6	1	0	0	4	0	0	5	7	.128	.212	.149	.360	-6	7	1

Which Team Fared Better?

Glenn had some unique moments for both teams. For the Yankees in 1933 he caught the last game that Babe Ruth ever pitched in. He also caught Ted Williams the only time the Splendid Splinter pitched in a major league game, on August 24, 1940. He racked up far more years with the Yankees and won a World Series with them in 1932. He might not have had so much as an at-bat in the Series, but that doesn't change the fact that the Yankees got more out of him.

Harry Harper

A southpaw who pitched for 10 years, Harper threw his first seven seasons for the Washington Senators. He had a respectable 2.75 ERA with them during that time but the team was awful, accounting for his 48–58 record. Even with a low 1.77 ERA in 1915, he managed only a .500 record in 19 games. He spent a year with the Red Sox, then one with the Yankees, and completed his career with the Brooklyn Robins. He had a career 2.87 ERA with 66 complete games.

Red Sox Year

Year	Age	W	L	%	ERA	G	GS	CG	SV	IP	H	R	HR	BB	SO	ERA+	WHIP	H/9	BB/9	SO/9	SO/BB
1920	25	5	14	.263	3.04	27	22	11	0	162.2	163	73	9	66	71	120	1.408	9.0	3.7	3.9	1.08

Yankees Year

Year	Age	W	L	%	ERA	G	GS	CG	SV	IP	H	R	HR	BB	SO	ERA+	WHIP	H/9	BB/9	SO/9	SO/BB
1921	26	4	3	.571	3.76	8	7	4	0	52.2	52	23	3	25	22	112	1.462	8.9	4.3	3.8	0.88

Which Team Fared Better?

He had an awful 5–14 record with the Red Sox, but this was more an indicator of the quality of the team than of Harper's pitching, as Boston finished in fifth with a 72–81 record. He went 4–3 with the 1921 Yankees, but again the team was more responsible for the narrow margin between wins and losses than his pitching was. That year the Yankees won the pennant with a 98–55 record. He pitched in the 1921 World Series with the Yankees but could hardly be considered an attribute to the team. He pitched 1.1 innings and gave up three earned runs. He had a lower ERA with Boston, lower WHIP, more strikeouts, more innings, and more complete games. He contributions to a bad Boston team were more than his contributions to a great Yankee team.

JOE HARRIS

Not to be confused with Joe Harris, the pitcher who played for the Boston Americans during the 1905–1907 seasons. This Joe Harris was a first baseman who played for ten years. He started with the Yankees. Then he logged two years with Cleveland, four with the Red Sox, two with Washington, and two with Pittsburgh before finishing the 1928 season with the Brooklyn Robins. He played in two World Series, surprisingly not with the Yankees but rather with the 1925 Senators and 1927 Pirates. He became the first player ever to hit a home run in his first appearance in a World Series game.

Yankees Year

Year	Age	G	AB	R	H	2B	3B	HR	RBI	SB	CS	BB	SO	BA	OBP	SLG	OPS	OPS+	TB	SH
1914	23	2	1	0	0	0	0	0	0	0	0	3	1	.000	.800	.000	.800	143	0	1

Red Sox Years

Year	Age	G	AB	R	H	2B	3B	HR	RBI	SB	CS	BB	SO	BA	OBP	SLG	OPS	OPS+	TB	SH
1922	31	119	408	53	129	30	9	6	54	2	6	30	15	.316	.364	.478	.842	119	195	9
1923	32	142	483	82	162	28	11	13	76	7	3	52	27	.335	.406	.520	.925	142	251	13
1924	33	133	491	82	148	36	9	3	77	6	1	81	25	.301	.406	.430	.835	116	211	15
1925	34	8	19	4	3	0	1	1	2	0	0	5	5	.158	.333	.421	.754	91	8	1
Totals		402	1,401	221	441	94	30	23	209	15	10	168	72	.315	.393	.475	.868	126	665	38

Which Team Fared Better?

He got a cup of coffee with the Yankees his first year in 1914. Even though the box score shows he got a single at-bat, he walked three times, got hit by a pitch, and had a sacrifice fly for a .800 OBP. This small sample size cannot compare with the 1,401 at-bats he got with the Red Sox. Not only is this 1,400 more at-bats, he batted .300 in three seasons, had over 200 RBIs, and scored 221 runs. In 1923, with the Red Sox, he enjoyed his best season as a player, batting .335 with a .520 slugging percentage to go along with 76 RBIs, 82 runs, and 13 homers.

FRED HEIMACH

Nicknamed Lefty, as were 207 other pitchers in baseball, Heimach had 13 seasons of major league experience, pitching for four different teams. His first seven seasons were with the Philadelphia Athletics. He spent only half a season with the Red Sox before playing all of 1927 in the minors. He came back with the Yankees for two seasons, and then spent the last four years of his career with Brooklyn Dodgers. He was 62–69 in his career with a 4.46 ERA.

Red Sox Year

Year	Age	W	L	%	ERA	G	GS	CG	SV	IP	H	R	HR	BB	SO	ERA+	WHIP	H/9	BB/9	SO/9	SO/BB
1926	25	2	9	.182	5.65	20	13	6	1	102.0	119	72	5	42	17	72	1.578	10.5	3.7	1.5	0.40

Yankees Years

Year	Age	W	L	%	ERA	G	GS	CG	SV	IP	H	R	HR	BB	SO	ERA+	WHIP	H/9	BB/9	SO/9	SO/BB
1928	27	2	3	.400	3.31	13	9	5	0	68.0	66	30	3	16	25	115	1.206	8.7	2.1	3.3	1.56
1929	28	11	6	.647	4.01	35	10	3	4	134.2	141	72	5	29	26	96	1.262	9.4	1.9	1.7	0.90
Totals		13	9	.591	3.77	48	19	8	4	202.2	207	102	8	45	51	102	1.243	9.2	2.0	2.3	1.13

Which Team Fared Better?

His 2–9 season with the Red Sox seems to fit his 5.65 ERA (75 ERA+). He was as bad as that sounds, in other words, walking 42 and striking out only 17 in 102 innings and giving up 10.5 hits for every nine innings tossed. His time with the Yankees was much more productive, as he went 13–9 with a 3.77 ERA, ever-so-slightly better than the league average. He helped the Yankees get to the 1928 World Series, which they won. His best season, 1929, also benefitted New York, who got more out of him.

Fred Hofmann

With one of baseball's more colorful nicknames, Bootnose, Hofmann served in World War I in the Navy and then began his major league career with the Yankees, playing seven years for the pinstripers as a backup catcher. He spent a year in the minors before landing a job as backup catcher for the Red Sox in 1927. He played another year for them and then spent the rest of his baseball career, which lasted until 1937, in the minor leagues. He remained in baseball as a coach for the St. Louis Browns for a decade and then became a scout for them and later the Orioles when the Browns moved to Baltimore. He signed Orioles players Boog Powell and Wally Bunker, and was involved in the signing of Brooks Robinson.

Yankees Years

Year	Age	G	AB	R	H	2B	3B	HR	RBI	SB	CS	BB	SO	BA	OBP	SLG	OPS	OPS+	TB	SH
1919	25	1	1	0	0	0	0	0	0	0	0	0	0	.000	.000	.000	.000	-100	0	0
1920	26	15	24	3	7	0	0	0	1	0	0	1	2	.292	.346	.292	.638	67	7	0
1921	27	23	62	7	11	1	1	1	5	0	0	5	13	.177	.250	.274	.524	32	17	0
1922	28	37	91	13	27	5	3	2	10	0	0	9	12	.297	.360	.484	.844	116	44	1
1923	29	72	238	24	69	10	4	3	26	2	1	18	27	.290	.350	.403	.753	96	96	3
1924	30	62	166	17	29	6	1	1	11	2	1	12	15	.175	.239	.241	.480	24	40	5
1925	31	3	2	0	0	0	0	0	0	0	0	0	0	.000	.000	.000	.000	-100	0	0
Totals		213	584	64	143	22	9	7	53	4	2	45	69	.245	.308	.349	.657	70	204	9

Red Sox Years

Year	Age	G	AB	R	H	2B	3B	HR	RBI	SB	CS	BB	SO	BA	OBP	SLG	OPS	OPS+	TB	SH
1927	33	87	217	20	59	19	1	0	24	2	0	21	26	.272	.342	.369	.710	87	80	9
1928	34	78	199	14	45	8	1	0	16	0	1	11	25	.226	.270	.276	.547	46	55	2
Totals		165	416	34	104	27	2	0	40	2	1	32	51	.250	.308	.325	.633	68	135	11

Which Team Fared Better?

Having only played with the Red Sox or Yankees in his major league career, he never got much playing time until his fifth year with New York. That year he got into 72 games and got 69 hits and 26 RBIs. He also batted .290, pretty good for a backup catcher. After that his plate appearances began to dwindle to the point that in 1925 he only had 2 at-bats. He got pretty regular playing time with the Red Sox, averaging over 200 at-bats in his two years with them. His batting average, on-base percentage, slugging, and OBP were almost identical between the two teams. Considering he was a catcher, one would think his value as a second string catcher with Boston would be better than a third string catcher with the Yankees.

WAITE HOYT

Hall of Famer Waite Hoyt was a pitcher for 21 years in the majors. He began with the Giants and spent two years with Boston before logging the bulk of his career, or 10 seasons, with the Yankees. That would be a good career for most people but Hoyt played another eight seasons, going through Detroit, Philadelphia, Brooklyn, and Pittsburgh, playing for seven teams total. He finished with 237 wins and 182 losses. At the time of his retirement he was the winningest pitcher in World Series history with 6 victories to his credit.

Red Sox Years

Year	Age	W	L	%	ERA	G	GS	CG	SV	IP	H	R	HR	BB	SO	ERA+	WHIP	H/9	BB/9	SO/9	SO/BB
1919	19	4	6	.400	3.25	13	11	6	0	105.1	99	42	1	22	28		94	1.149	8.5	1.9	2.4	1.27
1920	20	6	6	.500	4.38	22	11	6	1	121.1	123	72	2	47	45	83	1.401	9.1	3.5	3.3	0.96
Totals		10	12	.455	3.85	35	22	12	1	226.2	222	114	3	69	73	87	1.284	8.8	2.7	2.9	1.06

Yankees Years

Year	Age	W	L	%	ERA	G	GS	CG	SV	IP	H	R	HR	BB	SO	ERA+	WHIP	H/9	BB/9	SO/9	SO/BB
1921	21	19	13	.594	3.09	43	32	21	3	282.1	301	121	3	81	102	136	1.353	9.6	2.6	3.3	1.26
1922	22	19	12	.613	3.43	37	31	17	0	265.0	271	114	13	76	95	117	1.309	9.2	2.6	3.2	1.25
1923	23	17	9	.654	3.02	37	28	19	1	238.2	227	97	9	66	60	131	1.228	8.6	2.5	2.3	0.91
1924	24	18	13	.581	3.79	46	32	14	4	247.0	295	117	8	76	71	111	1.502	10.7	2.8	2.6	0.93
1925	25	11	14	.440	4.00	46	30	17	6	243.0	283	124	14	78	86	107	1.486	10.5	2.9	3.2	1.10
1926	26	16	12	.571	3.85	40	28	12	4	217.2	224	112	4	62	79	100	1.314	9.3	2.6	3.3	1.27
1927	27	22	7	.759	2.63	36	32	23	1	256.1	242	90	10	54	86	148	1.155	8.5	1.9	3.0	1.59
1928	28	23	7	.767	3.36	42	31	19	8	273.0	279	118	16	60	67	113	1.242	9.2	2.0	2.2	1.12
1929	29	10	9	.526	4.24	30	25	12	2	201.2	219	115	9	69	57	91	1.428	9.8	3.1	2.5	0.83
1930	30	2	2	.500	4.53	8	7	2	0	47.2	64	27	7	9	10	96	1.531	12.1	1.7	1.9	1.11
Totals		157	98	.616	3.48	365	276	156	29	2,272.1	2,405	1,035	93	631	713	115	1.336	9.5	2.5	2.8	1.13

Which Team Fared Better?

Hoyt serves as a prime example of Boston giving its talent away and the Yankees benefitting as a result. Of his 237 wins, 157 came with New York, and he enjoyed seven seasons of 15-or-more wins there. Hoyt also pitched in twelve World Series games over seven Fall Classics for the Yankees, boasting a 1.83 ERA during these games and winning rings in 1923, 1927, and 1928. His best season as a pitcher was likewise with the 1927 Yankees, when he led the league with 22 wins, a 1.155 WHIP, a 1.59 strikeout-to-walk ratio, and a 2.63 ERA. The Yankees win this one, easily.

A consistent pitcher, Hoyt won 10 or more games 12 times, including 11 seasons in a row, and amassed 237 victories in a 21-year Hall of Fame career. During the decade of the 1920s, he was New York's winningest pitcher, going 157–98.

Hank Johnson

A pitcher who pitched in 249 games in his career, starting 116 and saving 11 games, Johnson played for 12 years. Most of his seasons, seven, were spent with the Yankees. From there he went to the Red Sox, Philadelphia Athletics, and Reds. He finished with a career 63–56 record.

Yankees Years

Year	Age	W	L	%	ERA	G	GS	CG	SV	IP	H	R	HR	BB	SO	ERA+	WHIP	H/9	BB/9	SO/9	SO/BB
1925	19	1	3	.250	6.85	24	4	2	0	67.0	88	58	3	37	25	63	1.866	11.8	5.0	3.4	0.68
1926	20	0	0		18.00	1	0	0	1	1.0	2	2	0	2	0	30	4.000	18.0	18.0	0.0	0.00
1928	22	14	9	.609	4.30	31	22	10	0	199.0	188	107	16	104	110	89	1.467	8.5	4.7	5.0	1.06
1929	23	3	3	.500	5.06	12	8	2	0	42.2	37	28	5	39	24	77	1.781	7.8	8.2	5.1	0.62
1930	24	14	11	.560	4.67	44	15	7	2	175.1	177	112	12	104	115	93	1.603	9.1	5.3	5.9	1.11
1931	25	13	8	.619	4.72	40	23	8	4	196.1	176	114	13	102	106	85	1.416	8.1	4.7	4.9	1.04
1932	26	2	2	.500	4.88	5	4	2	0	31.1	34	18	7	15	27	84	1.564	9.8	4.3	7.8	1.80
Totals		47	36	.566	4.84	157	76	31	7	712.2	702	439	56	403	407	84	1.551	8.9	5.1	5.1	1.01

Red Sox Years

Year	Age	W	L	%	ERA	G	GS	CG	SV	IP	H	R	HR	BB	SO	ERA+	WHIP	H/9	BB/9	SO/9	SO/BB
1933	27	8	6	.571	4.06	25	21	7	1	155.1	156	84	13	74	65	109	1.481	9.0	4.3	3.8	0.88
1934	28	6	8	.429	5.36	31	14	7	1	124.1	162	95	12	53	66	88	1.729	11.7	3.8	4.8	1.25
1935	29	2	1	.667	5.52	13	2	0	1	31.0	41	21	3	14	14	87	1.774	11.9	4.1	4.1	1.00
Totals		16	15	.516	4.72	69	37	14	3	310.2	359	200	28	141	145	97	1.609	10.4	4.1	4.2	1.03

Which Team Fared Better?

Johnson's best seasons came with the Yankees. He won 14 with them in 1928 and 1930 and 13 in 1931. His ERA was lower in his three years with Boston, but he was just barely above .500, with a .516 winning percentage. His WHIP, strikeout-to-walk ratio, and home runs per 9 innings were almost identical between the teams, but he helped the Yankees win a world championship in 1928, giving them the advantage.

Roy Johnson

There was a Roy Johnson who pitched for the Philadelphia Athletics and coached for some time with the Chicago Cubs. The Roy Johnson who played for both the Yankees and Red Sox was an outfielder and began as a rookie with the Detroit Tigers. He set rookie records, for most runs (128) and most doubles (45), that still stand today. After four years with the

Tigers he played another four with the Red Sox, two years with the Yankees, and two more with the Boston Bees. He was a career .296 hitter with 58 home runs and 556 RBIs.

Red Sox Years

Year	Age	G	AB	R	H	2B	3B	HR	RBI	SB	CS	BB	SO	BA	OBP	SLG	OPS	OPS+	TB	SH
1932	29	94	349	70	104	24	4	11	47	13	4	44	41	.298	.378	.484	.862	128	169	0
1933	30	133	483	88	151	30	7	10	95	13	10	55	36	.313	.387	.466	.853	123	225	5
1934	31	143	569	85	182	43	10	7	119	11	5	54	36	.320	.379	.467	.846	114	266	3
1935	32	145	553	70	174	33	9	3	66	11	12	74	34	.315	.398	.423	.822	108	234	5
Totals		515	1,954	313	611	130	30	31	327	48	31	227	147	.313	.386	.458	.844	117	894	13

Yankees Years

Year	Age	G	AB	R	H	2B	3B	HR	RBI	SB	CS	BB	SO	BA	OBP	SLG	OPS	OPS+	TB	SH
1936	33	63	147	21	39	8	2	1	19	3	1	21	14	.265	.361	.367	.728	82	54	1
1937	34	12	51	5	15	3	0	0	6	1	0	3	2	.294	.333	.353	.686	72	18	0
Totals		75	198	26	54	11	2	1	25	4	1	24	16	.273	.354	.364	.718	80	72	1

Which Team Fared Better?

In the four years he spent with the Red Sox he put up pretty good numbers. His best year of his career came while playing for Boston in 1934 where he batted .320, had 119 RBIs, seven home runs, and 85 runs. The two years previous to that he hit 11 and 10 home runs, respectively. In his final year with Boston he continued to bat at a .300 clip, an average of .315, but his production numbers began to fall. He had only three home runs and 66 RBIs even though he had more plate appearances than in his 1934 season. He was not traded directly from Boston to New York. The Red Sox traded him to Washington in December, as part of a package (with Carl Reynolds) for Heinie Manush, and a month later the Senators traded him to the Yankees. He was only a part-time outfielder with the Yankees and thus had part-time numbers. Johnson managed only one home run and 25 RBIs in nearly 200 at-bats over two seasons.

SAD SAM JONES

Jones, whose nickname did not match his personality, pitched 22 years in the big leagues, beginning with Cleveland before going to the Red Sox for six years, which were followed by five years with the Yankees. After a single season with the St. Louis Browns, he pitched four seasons for the Washington Senators before finishing out his last four years with the Chicago White Sox. He won 229 games in his career but, with 217 losses, finished only a little above .500 in winning percentage. His 22 consecutive years of pitching in one league is a major league record shared with four other pitchers.

Red Sox Years

Year	Age	W	L	%	ERA	G	GS	CG	SV	IP	H	R	HR	BB	SO	ERA+	WHIP	H/9	BB/9	SO/9	SO/BB
1916	23	0	1	.000	3.67	12	0	0	1	27.0	25	14	0	10	7	77	1.296	8.3	3.3	2.3	0.70
1917	24	0	1	.000	4.41	9	1	0	1	16.1	15	9	1	6	5	61	1.266	8.3	3.3	2.8	0.83
1918	25	16	5	.762	2.25	24	21	16	0	184.0	151	66	1	70	44	120	1.201	7.4	3.4	2.2	0.63
1919	26	12	20	.375	3.75	35	31	21	0	245.0	258	120	4	95	67	81	1.441	9.5	3.5	2.5	0.71
1920	27	13	16	.448	3.94	37	33	21	0	274.0	302	143	9	79	86	92	1.391	9.9	2.6	2.8	1.09
1921	28	23	16	.590	3.22	40	38	25	1	298.2	318	122	1	78	98	132	1.326	9.6	2.4	3.0	1.26
Totals		64	59	.520	3.39	157	124	83	4	1,045.0	1,069	474	16	338	307	102	1.346	9.2	2.9	2.6	0.91

Which Team Fared Better?

This one is a pretty tough call. He has nearly identical win-loss records with the two teams, going 64–59 for Boston and 67–56 with New York, and put up similar numbers in innings pitched and strikeouts, as well. He won twenty games with both teams once. His most productive year was with the 1921 Red Sox, for whom he won 23 games, led the league in shutouts with five, and posted career bests in innings pitched and strikeouts. But the year he is probably most remembered for came two years later in New York where he served as their ace, won 21 games, and pitched a no-hitter against the A's. He won World Series with the 1916 and 1918 Red Sox, and another with the 1923 Yankees. Jones contributed much the same level of performance to both teams, but his ERA and WHIP are a tad lower for Boston, so give that team the nod.

A 200-game winner who pitched for three world champions, Sad Sam Jones has career numbers very similar to those of Waite Hoyt, and he proved effective for both the Red Sox and Yankees. Red Sox fans may also remember him as one of the three principles in the trade that sent Tris Speaker to the Indians.

Yankees Years

Year	Age	W	L	%	ERA	G	GS	CG	SV	IP	H	R	HR	BB	SO	ERA+	WHIP	H/9	BB/9	SO/9	SO/BB
1922	29	13	13	.500	3.67	45	28	20	8	260.0	270	132	16	76	81	109	1.331	9.3	2.6	2.8	1.07
1923	30	21	8	.724	3.63	39	27	18	4	243.0	239	114	11	69	68	109	1.267	8.9	2.6	2.5	0.99
1924	31	9	6	.600	3.63	36	21	8	3	178.2	187	85	6	76	53	116	1.472	9.4	3.8	2.7	0.70
1925	32	15	21	.417	4.63	43	31	14	2	246.2	267	147	14	104	92	92	1.504	9.7	3.8	3.4	0.88
1926	33	9	8	.529	4.98	39	23	6	5	161.0	186	104	6	80	69	78	1.652	10.4	4.5	3.9	0.86
Totals		67	56	.545	4.06	202	130	66	22	1,089.1	1,149	582	53	405	363	100	1.427	9.5	3.3	3.0	0.90

Lyn Lary

A shortstop who played for 12 years, Lary lent his defensive prowess to six different teams. He began his career with the Yankees, spending six years there before being shared by the Red Sox, Senators, and Browns over two seasons. He spent the next three years with the Cleveland Indians, then played for the Indians, Dodgers, and Cardinals in 1939. He returned to the Browns for his final year. While he was valued primarily for his ability to turn the double play, he made above-average (for his position) contributions at the plate.

Yankees Years

Year	Age	G	AB	R	H	2B	3B	HR	RBI	SB	CS	BB	SO	BA	OBP	SLG	OPS	OPS+	TB	SH
1929	23	80	236	48	73	9	2	5	26	4	1	24	15	.309	.380	.428	.808	113	101	5
1930	24	117	464	93	134	20	8	3	52	14	2	45	40	.289	.357	.386	.743	91	179	19
1931	25	155	610	100	171	35	9	10	107	13	10	88	54	.280	.376	.416	.793	113	254	8

Year	Age	G	AB	R	H	2B	3B	HR	RBI	SB	CS	BB	SO	BA	OBP	SLG	OPS	OPS+	TB	SH
1932	26	91	280	56	65	14	4	3	39	9	3	52	28	.232	.358	.343	.701	86	96	4
1933	27	52	127	25	28	3	3	0	13	2	1	28	17	.220	.361	.291	.653	79	37	3
1934	28	1	0	0	0	0	0	0	0	0	0	1	0		1.000				0	0
Totals		496	1,717	322	471	81	26	21	237	42	17	238	154	.274	.368	.388	.756	100	667	39

Red Sox Year

Year	Age	G	AB	R	H	2B	3B	HR	RBI	SB	CS	BB	SO	BA	OBP	SLG	OPS	OPS+	TB	SH
1936	28	129	419	58	101	20	4	2	54	12	5	66	51	.241	.344	.322	.667	70	135	15

Which Team Fared Better?

A look at Lary's 21 home runs and 237 RBIS would suggest that the Yankees got more out of him, but his true value came in the form of a trade. Boston managed to swap Lary, with some money, to the Washington Senators for fellow shortstop Joe Cronin. Cronin would go on to become a legendary Red Sox player, spending eleven years with the club as a player before signing on as manager and then general manager for thirteen years. He is a member of the Hall of Fame and was named to the All-Century team. Lary did contribute to the Yankees, getting 107 RBIs in 1931, a record for Yankee shortstops. But when the Yankees traded him to Boston, all they got was Freddie Mueller, who never even played with the big league club.

JOE LUCEY

A shortstop and pitcher, Lucey spent only two seasons in the major leagues, one with the Yankees and the other with the Red Sox. He spent no time in the minors, debuting with New York fresh out of college ball in 1920, but after that first year it took five seasons in the minors to get back to the major leagues. He began the 1925 season with the Red Sox but halfway through the season his contract was purchased by the Buffalo Bisons of the International League, and he finished out his last year of professional baseball two years later, in Toronto.

Yankees Years

Year	Age	G	AB	R	H	2B	3B	HR	RBI	SB	CS	BB	SO	BA	OBP	SLG	OPS	OPS+	TB	SH
1920	23	3	3	0	0	0	0	0	0	0	0	0	0	.000	.000	.000	.000	-100	0	0

Red Sox Years

Year	Age	G	AB	R	H	2B	3B	HR	RBI	SB	CS	BB	SO	BA	OBP	SLG	OPS	OPS+	TB	SH
1925	28	10	15	0	2	0	0	0	0	0	0	0	4	.133	.133	.133	.367	-32	2	0

Year	Age	W	L	%	ERA	G	GS	CG	SV	IP	H	R	HR	BB	SO	ERA+	WHIP	H/9	BB/9	SO/9	SO/BB
1925	28	0	1	.000	9.00	7	2	0	0	11.0	18	20	0	14	2	52	2.909	14.7	11.5	1.6	0.14

Which Team Fared Better?

The Red Sox got two players for the price of one. Lucey played the shortstop position for three games and pitched in seven more. While he managed only two hits in his time in Boston, this was two more than he had in New York, where he went hitless in three at-bats. The Red Sox win this one, but the victory is like getting to kiss your sister.

Danny MacFayden

A bespectacled pitcher who contributed 17 years of major league service, MacFayden began with the Red Sox, for whom he pitched for seven years. He was then traded to the Yankees and stayed there for three years, made a brief stop in Cincinnati, and played for five years for the Boston Bees. After playing sporadically for the Pittsburgh Pirates and Washington Senators, he returned to Boston for the newly named Braves. His best year as a pitcher came in 1936 when he went 17–13 for the Boston Bees and the second lowest ERA in the league at 2.87, earning him some small MVP consideration. He finished with a career 132–159 record.

Red Sox Years

Year	Age	W	L	%	ERA	G	GS	CG	SV	IP	H	R	HR	BB	SO	ERA+	WHIP	H/9	BB/9	SO/9	SO/BB
1926	21	0	1	.000	4.85	3	1	1	0	13.0	10	7	0	7	1	86	1.308	6.9	4.8	0.7	0.14
1927	22	5	8	.385	4.27	34	16	6	2	160.1	176	88	9	59	42	99	1.466	9.9	3.3	2.4	0.71
1928	23	9	15	.375	4.75	33	28	9	0	195.0	215	123	12	78	61	85	1.503	9.9	3.6	2.8	0.78
1929	24	10	18	.357	3.62	32	27	14	0	221.0	225	108	8	81	61	117	1.385	9.2	3.3	2.5	0.75
1930	25	11	14	.440	4.21	36	33	18	2	269.1	293	141	9	93	76	109	1.433	9.8	3.1	2.5	0.82
1931	26	16	12	.571	4.02	35	32	17	0	230.2	263	121	4	79	74	107	1.483	10.3	3.1	2.9	0.94
1932	27	1	10	.091	5.10	12	11	6	0	77.2	91	55	3	33	29	87	1.597	10.5	3.8	3.4	0.88
Totals		52	78	.400	4.23	185	148	71	4	1,167.0	1,273	643	45	430	344	102	1.459	9.8	3.3	2.7	0.80

Yankees Years

Year	Age	W	L	%	ERA	G	GS	CG	SV	IP	H	R	HR	BB	SO	ERA+	WHIP	H/9	BB/9	SO/9	SO/BB
1932	27	7	5	.583	3.93	17	15	9	1	121.1	137	69	11	37	33	104	1.434	10.2	2.7	2.4	0.89
1933	28	3	2	.600	5.88	25	6	2	0	90.1	120	62	8	37	28	67	1.738	12.0	3.7	2.8	0.76
1934	29	4	3	.571	4.50	22	11	4	0	96.0	110	57	5	31	41	91	1.469	10.3	2.9	3.8	1.32
Totals		14	10	.583	4.68	64	32	15	1	307.2	367	188	24	105	102	86	1.534	10.7	3.1	3.0	0.97

Which Team Fared Better?

He had only one winning season while pitching for the Red Sox, although it was during a period in which the BoSox were one of the worst teams in the league. The highlight of his time with them was in 1929 when he led the league in shutouts (finishing, nevertheless, with a 9–15 record). While playing with the Yankees one sportswriter gave him the name "Dismal Danny," which says plenty about his contributions in New York. He did have a winning record at 14–10 over his time with them. He was a member of the 1932 pennant-winning Yankees but did not go on to the World Series, which they won. One reporter blamed him for the Yankees' inability to repeat the next year as league champs, citing MacFayden's 5.88 ERA as a spot starter. The criticism was a bit harsh, as MacFayden was a bigger help to the Yankees than to the Red Sox.

Norm McMillan

Remembered, when he is at all, for having the shortest home run in major league history, McMillan was a super utility man, able to play all positions with the exception of catcher, pitcher, and left field. McMillan hit his miniature home run for the Cubs in 1929. With bases loaded, he hit a ball that landed about sixty feet beyond the third base bag. When the ball hit it took a funny hop and went into the Cubs bullpen. The opposing players searched all around the bullpen but could not locate the ball, allowing McMillan to circle around all the bases for a grand slam. Later when relief pitcher Ken Penner went to put his jacket on he found the ball, which had rolled into the jacket and up the sleeve. McMillan played for four teams in five years, bouncing from the Yankees to the Red Sox and then to the Browns in consecutive years. After some time in the minors he played two more years with the Chicago Cubs. He had only two seasons in which he played 120 games or more.

Yankees Year

Year	Age	G	AB	R	H	2B	3B	HR	RBI	SB	CS	BB	SO	BA	OBP	SLG	OPS	OPS+	TB	SH
1922	26	33	78	7	20	1	2	0	11	4	1	6	10	.256	.310	.321	.630	63	25	5

Red Sox Year

Year	Age	G	AB	R	H	2B	3B	HR	RBI	SB	CS	BB	SO	BA	OBP	SLG	OPS	OPS+	TB	SH
1923	27	131	459	37	116	24	4	2	54	12	5	66	51	.241	.344	.322	.667	70	135	15

Which Team Fared Better?

He played only a partial season with the Yankees, getting 78 at-bats, most of which came early, after the Yankees' center fielder, Bob Meusel, and right fielder, Babe Ruth, were suspended the first five weeks of the seasons for illegally barnstorming in the offseason. When the five weeks were up he became a reserve outfielder and got into only 33 more games. He played in the 1922 World Series, but his Yankees lost to the Giants. McMillan did play a full season with the Red Sox, racking up nearly 500 plate appearances and knocking in 54 runs, but his value in Boston did not compare favorably with what the Yankees received in exchange for trading him. New York got Herb Pennock, the last remaining player from the 1918 World Champion Red Sox, in exchange for McMillan and a couple of other players who never amounted to much. Pennock, on the other hand, won 162 games for New York and was later elected to the Hall of Fame.

ELMER MILLER

Miller was an outfielder who broke in as a rookie with the St. Louis Cardinals in 1912. He then spent some time in the minor leagues before returning to the majors with the Yankees in 1915. Miller played in New York for four years before being demoted to the minors for another two years, then returned to play two more seasons in the big leagues. In July 1922 he was traded to the Red Sox and finished the season with them. Over the 11-year period, he played seven seasons in the majors and hit a modest .243.

Yankees Years

Year	Age	G	AB	R	H	2B	3B	HR	RBI	SB	CS	BB	SO	BA	OBP	SLG	OPS	OPS+	TB	SH
1915	24	26	83	4	12	1	0	0	3	0	0	4	14	.145	.193	.157	.350	5	13	2
1916	25	43	152	12	34	3	2	1	18	8		11	18	.224	.280	.289	.570	70	44	6
1917	26	114	379	43	95	11	3	3	35	11		40	44	.251	.336	.319	.656	99	121	21
1918	27	67	202	18	49	9	2	1	22	4		19	17	.243	.317	.322	.639	91	65	14
1921	30	56	242	41	72	9	8	4	36	2	2	19	16	.298	.356	.450	.806	103	109	6
1922	31	51	172	31	46	7	2	3	18	2	3	11	12	.267	.311	.384	.695	79	66	5
Totals		357	1,230	149	308	40	17	12	132	27	5	104	121	.250	.318	.340	.657	86	418	54

Red Sox Year

Year	Age	G	AB	R	H	2B	3B	HR	RBI	SB	CS	BB	SO	BA	OBP	SLG	OPS	OPS+	TB	SH
1922	31	44	147	16	28	2	3	4	16	3	1	5	10	.190	.222	.327	.549	42	48	3

Which Team Fared Better?

Miller was part of the 1921 pennant-winning Yankees, getting into every one of the nine games of the World Series, which was lost to the Giants. But let's put his overall value to the franchise into perspective: In the six years he played for New York, he hit 12 home runs, scored 149 runs, and knocked in 132. Babe Ruth in 1921 alone hit 59 home runs, scored 177 runs, and knocked in 168. So in the overall scheme of things, Miller was a bit player. His numbers with New York do, however, give the Yankees an advantage, as he played only half a season with the Red Sox and produced 28 hits, a number he bested in five of the seasons he was with the pinstripers. The same is true of his 16 RBIs with Boston; he bested that mark five times for New York. He did hit four home runs for the Sox, tying the career high he set with the 1921 Yankees, but this is certainly not enough to give them the advantage.

BUSTER MILLS

Mills played sporadically for seven seasons over a 13-year period. During his time in baseball he did not accumulate many at-bats in the major leagues, having only two seasons in which he played an entire slate of games, with the St. Louis Browns and the Boston Red Sox where he appeared in 123 games for each. Other than that he averaged 34 games a season playing left field. The other teams he played for were the St. Louis Cardinals, Brooklyn Dodgers, Yankees, and the Cleveland Indians.

Red Sox Year

Year	Age	G	AB	R	H	2B	3B	HR	RBI	SB	CS	BB	SO	BA	OBP	SLG	OPS	OPS+	TB	SH
1937	28	123	505	85	149	25	8	7	58	11	8	46	41	.295	.361	.418	.779	92	211	9

Yankees Year

Year	Age	G	AB	R	H	2B	3B	HR	RBI	SB	CS	BB	SO	BA	OBP	SLG	OPS	OPS+	TB	SH
1940	31	34	63	10	25	3	3	1	15	0	0	7	5	.397	.457	.587	1.044	173	37	0

Which Team Fared Better?

The Yankees used him mostly as a pinch hitter, which accounts for his limited number at-bats at 63. He played almost every day for the Red Sox collecting 149 hits and 58 RBIs. It was his post-career involvement with both clubs that would determine his overall worth however. He served as a coach for the 1954 Red Sox under Lou Boudreau. When Pinky Higgins took over as skipper in 1955 he did not bring Mills back, saying he was not good at handling third base traffic. He served several years as a scout for the Yankees so his long term value with them is far greater than the one season spent with Boston.

JOHNNY MITCHELL

What can you say about a player who hit two home runs in his five-year career with three teams? This shortstop started with the Yankees, was traded halfway through the 1922 season to the Red Sox, and finished his career with the Brooklyn Robins. In addition to his two career home runs, he drove in a total of 63 runs, scored 152 more, and had 288 hits—for an average of 12 RBIs, 30 runs, and 58 hits a season. Not exactly numbers to write home about.

Yankees Years

Year	Age	G	AB	R	H	2B	3B	HR	RBI	SB	CS	BB	SO	BA	OBP	SLG	OPS	OPS+	TB	SH
1921	26	13	42	4	11	1	0	0	2	1	0	4	4	.262	.326	.286	.612	56	12	1
1922	27	4	4	1	0	0	0	0	0	0	0	0	1	.000	.000	.000	.000	-100	0	0
Totals		17	46	5	11	1	0	0	2	1	0	4	5	.239	.300	.261	.561	43	12	1

Red Sox Years

Year	Age	G	AB	R	H	2B	3B	HR	RBI	SB	CS	BB	SO	BA	OBP	SLG	OPS	OPS+	TB	SH
1922	27	59	203	20	51	4	1	1	8	1	2	16	17	.251	.318	.296	.614	61	60	15
1923	28	92	347	40	78	15	4	0	19	7	11	34	18	.225	.296	.291	.587	55	101	3
Totals		151	550	60	129	19	5	1	27	8	13	50	35	.235	.304	.293	.597	57	161	18

Which Team Fared Better?

A backup shortstop for the Yankees during their 1921 pennant-winning season, Mitchell saw his playing time all but vanish the next year when New York added shortstop Everett Scott as their starter. Mitchell was traded to Boston mid-season and instantly made an impact, appearing in nearly every game for the rest of the year and playing what the *Sporting News* dubbed sensational defense. One of those two career home runs came as a Red Sox and against the Yankees, and it was the difference in a 4–3 win by Boston. His playing time increased over the course of a full season with the Red Sox, and he ended up with a career-high 347 at-bats. Boston got the better performance from this player.

WILCY MOORE

In his six-year career Moore bounced between the Yankees and Red Sox, the only two major league teams he played for. He broke in as a 30-year-old rookie with the Yankees and had a spectacular season. He was not able to maintain this level, however, and after a couple of years found himself back in the minors. The Red Sox picked him up in 1931 but couldn't coax a winning season out of him for their hapless team. He was traded back to the Yankees to finish his career with a 5–6 season and a 51–44 record overall.

Yankees Years

Year	Age	W	L	%	ERA	G	GS	CG	SV	IP	H	R	HR	BB	SO	ERA+	WHIP	H/9	BB/9	SO/9	SO/BB
1927	30	19	7	.731	2.28	50	12	6	13	213.0	185	68	3	59	75	171	1.146	7.8	2.5	3.2	1.27
1928	31	4	4	.500	4.18	35	2	0	3	60.1	71	44	4	31	18	91	1.691	10.6	4.6	2.7	0.58
1929	32	6	4	.600	4.13	41	0	0	9	61.0	64	36	4	19	21	94	1.361	9.4	2.8	3.1	1.11
1932	35	2	0	1.000	2.52	10	1	0	4	25.0	27	8	1	6	8	164	1.320	9.7	2.2	2.9	1.33
1933	36	5	6	.455	5.52	35	0	0	8	62.0	92	53	1	20	17	71	1.806	13.4	2.9	2.5	0.85
Totals		36	21	.632	3.31	171	15	6	37	421.1	439	209	13	135	139	118	1.362	9.4	2.9	3.0	1.03

Red Sox Years

Year	Age	W	L	%	ERA	G	GS	CG	SV	IP	H	R	HR	BB	SO	ERA+	WHIP	H/9	BB/9	SO/9	SO/BB
1931	34	11	13	.458	3.88	53	15	8	8	185.1	195	88	7	55	37	111	1.349	9.5	2.7	1.8	0.67
1932	35	4	10	.286	5.23	37	2	0	4	84.1	98	59	5	42	28	85	1.660	10.5	4.5	3.0	0.67
Totals		15	23	.395	4.31	90	17	8	12	269.2	293	147	12	97	65	101	1.446	9.8	3.2	2.2	0.67

Which Team Fared Better?

After a promising rookie season in which he led the league in ERA at 2.28 and racked up 19 wins alongside 13 saves, Moore's sinkerball lost its sink and he was never the same. He did bounce back a little in the 1933 postseason, his solid performance recalling the better days of 1927. Between that Series and the one in 1933, he compiled a 2-0 record and a 0.56 ERA. This contribution alone put him in a higher league with the Yankees.

George Murray

A journeyman minor league pitcher, Murray played parts of six seasons for four different major league teams. He came up with the Yankees and then, after a year, was part of the two-way traffic between New York and Boston, going over to the Red Sox in a trade and playing two seasons in Fenway. After following that stint with another year in the minors, he returned to the majors with the Washington Senators, hanging on with that club for parts of two seasons before returning once again to the lower levels of baseball. This time it took him longer to find his way back to the big leagues, and when at age 34 he did return, after five years away, he got into only two games for the Chicago White Sox, giving up two earned runs in 2.1 innings. He started 42 games in his career, relieving quite a bit as well, winning 19 and losing 26.

Yankees Years

Year	Age	W	L	%	ERA	G	GS	CG	SV	IP	H	R	HR	BB	SO	ERA+	WHIP	H/9	BB/9	SO/9	SO/BB
1922	23	3	2	.600	3.97	22	2	0	0	56.2	53	27	0	26	14	101	1.394	8.4	4.1	2.2	0.54

Red Sox Years

Year	Age	W	L	%	ERA	G	GS	CG	SV	IP	H	R	HR	BB	SO	ERA+	WHIP	H/9	BB/9	SO/9	SO/BB
1923	24	7	11	.389	4.91	39	18	5	0	177.2	190	111	9	87	40	83	1.559	9.6	4.4	2.0	0.46
1924	25	2	9	.182	6.72	28	7	0	0	80.1	97	68	6	32	27	65	1.606	10.9	3.6	3.0	0.84
Totals		**9**	**20**	**.310**	**5.48**	**67**	**25**	**5**	**0**	**258.0**	**287**	**179**	**15**	**119**	**67**	**76**	**1.574**	**10.0**	**4.2**	**2.3**	**0.56**

Which Team Fared Better?

His rookie season was the high point of his career. He went 3–2 with a respectable 3.97 ERA. Like many rookies he walked more batters than he struck out, but this proved to be more than a young pitcher struggling to find his way early: He walked 199 and struck out 114 over the course of his big league career. He was part of the revolving door between the Yankees and Red Sox, going over to Boston for Herb Pennock. At the time, Harry Frazee, the much-maligned Red Sox owner, quipped to the papers that he thought he got the better end of the deal in stealing Murray away from New York. Pennock went on to win 162 games for the Yankees while Murray went 9–20 with a whopping 5.48 ERA in Boston. Not for the first time, Frazee was on the wrong side of history.

Bobo Newsom

Apparently suffering from a little Rickey Henderson–itis, Bobo Newsom often referred to himself in the third person. Maybe this was because he was traded so often in his career that he lost track of who he was. Newsom's career spanned so long that he is one of two pitchers to have played against both Babe Ruth and Mickey Mantle. Over the course of his career he played for nine different teams. (Remember at that time there were only 16 teams in the entirely of major league baseball, not the 30 there are now.) His longest cumulative stay was with the Washington Senators, playing for them five times over eight seasons. His other long stays were with the St. Louis Browns (five seasons), Philadelphia Athletics (five), Brooklyn Dodgers (four), and Detroit Tigers (three). He is one of only two pitchers to have won more than 200 games and finished his career with a losing record, going 211–222. He led the league in losses four times but was a four-time All-Star, too. His best season came with the 1940 Detroit Tigers, with whom he finished the season with a 21–5 record and a 2.83 ERA.

Red Sox Year

Year	Age	W	L	%	ERA	G	GS	CG	SV	IP	H	R	HR	BB	SO	ERA+	WHIP	H/9	BB/9	SO/9	SO/BB
1937	29	13	10	.565	4.46	30	27	14	0	207.2	193	114	14	119	127	108	1.502	8.4	5.2	5.5	1.07

Yankees Year

Year	Age	W	L	%	ERA	G	GS	CG	SV	IP	H	R	HR	BB	SO	ERA+	WHIP	H/9	BB/9	SO/9	SO/BB
1947	39	7	5	.583	2.80	17	15	6	0	115.2	109	38	8	30	42	126	1.202	8.5	2.3	3.3	1.40

Which Team Fared Better?

Newsom had losing seasons for four teams, but the Red Sox and Yankees were not among them. He was with neither team for more than a season, though. A much lower ERA with the Yankees (2.80, compared with 4.46 with Boston) strongly suggests that he was sharper for that club, despite having been 10 years older than he had been with the Red Sox. Edge: Yankees.

LEFTY O'DOUL

You would think someone with the name Lefty would be a left-handed pitcher, and he was for parts of four years at the beginning of his career, before he hurt his arm. But O'Doul is remembered as an outfielder, playing mostly in left field for five teams over his 11-year career. He spent three seasons each with the New York Giants, the Brooklyn Dodgers, and the Yankees, enjoyed two big offensive years with the Philadelphia Phillies, and stuck around for one season with the Red Sox. After his playing career ended, he managed in the Pacific Coast League for more than twenty years, setting the league record for career wins. He was also instrumental in promoting baseball in Japan, participating in goodwill tours before and after World War II. He is credited with naming the Tokyo team the Giants, for his long association with the major league club of that name. Because of his contributions to the game he was elected to the Baseball Hall of Fame in 2002.

Yankees Years

Year	Age	G	AB	R	H	2B	3B	HR	RBI	SB	CS	BB	SO	BA	OBP	SLG	OPS	OPS+	TB	SH
1919	22	19	16	2	4	0	0	0	1	1		1	2	.250	.294	.250	.544	53	4	0
1920	23	13	12	2	2	1	0	0	1	0	0	1	1	.167	.231	.250	.481	25	3	0
1922	25	8	9	0	3	1	0	0	4	0	0	0	2	.333	.333	.444	.778	99	4	0
Totals		40	37	4	9	2	0	0	6	1	0	2	5	.243	.282	.297	.579	55	11	0

Red Sox Year

Year	Age	G	AB	R	H	2B	3B	HR	RBI	SB	CS	BB	SO	BA	OBP	SLG	OPS	OPS+	TB	SH
1923	26	36	35	2	5	0	0	0	4	0	0	2	3	.143	.189	.143	.332	-12	5	2

Which Team Fared Better?

His three years with the Yankees and one with the Red Sox came before he had established himself as an elite hitter—he would put together big years at the plate after leaving Boston—and he was little used as either a pitcher or outfielder for either team. (He did throw 53 innings with Boston but was ineffective.) Probably his biggest contribution to either team was acting as manager of the San Francisco Seals and developing a young Joe DiMaggio, who went on to greatness with the Yankees, giving them the edge.

Steve O'Neill

O'Neill was a catcher who spent the bulk of his 17-year career with the Cleveland Indians, with whom he won a World Series in 1920. He also played for the Red Sox, Yankees, and St. Louis Browns. O'Neill had three brothers who also spent some time in the major leagues (Jack, Jim, and Mike), although Steve had the most successful career of the four, racking up 1,297 hits in his career and knocking in 537 runs. He served as a manager in the big leagues for four different teams, including the Red Sox, Cleveland Indians, Philadelphia Phillies, and Detroit Tigers, whom he guided to a World Series win in 1945.

Red Sox Year

Year	Age	G	AB	R	H	2B	3B	HR	RBI	SB	CS	BB	SO	BA	OBP	SLG	OPS	OPS+	TB	SH
1924	32	106	307	29	73	15	1	0	38	0	2	63	23	.238	.371	.293	.664	73	90	5

Yankees Year

Year	Age	G	AB	R	H	2B	3B	HR	RBI	SB	CS	BB	SO	BA	OBP	SLG	OPS	OPS+	TB	SH
1925	33	35	91	7	26	5	0	1	13	0	0	10	3	.286	.363	.374	.736	89	34	2

Which Team Fared Better?

The two years spent with the Red Sox and Yankees came after his heyday as a player. He got into 106 games for the Red Sox but posted a .238 batting average. He fared much better average-wise with the Yankees, hitting .286, but he appeared in only 35 games, so it was a small sample size. This is almost a push, then. But because there are no ties in baseball the win goes to the Yankees, who managed to wring more out of him (89 OPS+ to 73 with the Sox) on the offensive side.

Ben Paschal

After cups of coffee with the Cleveland Indians in 1915 and Boston Red Sox in 1920, then a couple of years off for service in World War I, Paschal finally caught with the Yankees in 1924, in part because of Ruth's famed "Belly Ache Heard Round the World." (Heading north after spring training, the Yankees found themselves in need of outfield insurance when Ruth fell ill in Asheville, North Carolina.) He played six years for New York, acting as the fourth outfielder to the big three of Babe Ruth, Bob Meusel, and Earle Combs.

Red Sox Year

Year	Age	G	AB	R	H	2B	3B	HR	RBI	SB	CS	BB	SO	BA	OBP	SLG	OPS	OPS+	TB	SH
1920	24	9	28	5	10	0	0	0	5	1	0	5	2	.357	.455	.357	.812	121	10	0

Yankees Years

Year	Age	G	AB	R	H	2B	3B	HR	RBI	SB	CS	BB	SO	BA	OBP	SLG	OPS	OPS+	TB	SH
1924	28	4	12	2	3	1	0	0	3	0	0	1	0	.250	.308	.333	.641	65	4	0
1925	29	89	247	49	89	16	5	12	56	14	9	22	29	.360	.417	.611	1.028	160	151	4
1926	30	96	258	46	74	12	3	7	31	7	6	26	35	.287	.354	.438	.792	107	113	11
1927	31	50	82	16	26	9	2	2	16	0	2	4	10	.317	.349	.549	.898	132	45	1
1928	32	65	79	12	25	6	1	1	15	1	0	8	11	.316	.379	.456	.835	120	36	3
1929	33	42	72	13	15	3	0	2	11	1	2	6	3	.208	.269	.333	.603	58	24	3
Totals		346	750	138	232	47	11	24	132	23	19	67	88	.309	.368	.497	.866	124	373	22

Which Team Fared Better?

Not only did he log considerably more playing time with the Yankees, amassing 846 plate appearances as opposed to 32 with Boston, he contributed offensively to some of the best Yankees lineups of all time. Although he was still a part-time player for New York, he averaged a 124 OPS+ for them, and in 1925 hit 12 homers and drove in 55 runs in only 247 at-bats, good for a 160 OPS+. He saw only eight at-bats between the 1926 and 1928 fall classics, but he did manage to drive in a run in each Series. He hit well for the Red Sox in 1920, but in very limited time. Advantage: Yankees.

HERB PENNOCK

Considered one of the greatest left-handed pitchers of all time, Pennock spent the bulk of his playing time with the Red Sox (eight years) and Yankees (11 years). Over the course of his 22-year career he went 241–162 with a 3.60 ERA and a WHIP of 1.348. He went to the World Series five times, once with the Athletics and the other four times with the Yankees, posting a 5–0 record with a minuscule 1.95 ERA. He was voted into the Hall of Fame in 1944, just weeks after dying from a cerebral hemorrhage.

Red Sox Years

Year	Age	W	L	%	ERA	G	GS	CG	SV	IP	H	R	HR	BB	SO	ERA+	WHIP	H/9	BB/9	SO/9	SO/BB
1915	21	0	0		9.64	5	1	0	0	14.0	23	16	0	10	7	30	2.357	14.8	6.4	4.5	0.70
1916	22	0	2	.000	3.04	9	2	0	1	26.2	23	11	0	8	12	93	1.163	7.8	2.7	4.1	1.50
1917	23	5	5	.500	3.31	24	5	4	1	100.2	90	49	2	23	35	79	1.123	8.0	2.1	3.1	1.52
1919	25	16	8	.667	2.71	32	26	16	0	219.0	223	78	2	48	70	112	1.237	9.2	2.0	2.9	1.46
1920	26	16	13	.552	3.68	37	31	19	2	242.1	244	108	9	61	68	99	1.259	9.1	2.3	2.5	1.11
1921	27	13	14	.481	4.04	32	31	16	1	222.2	269	121	7	59	91	105	1.469	10.8	2.4	3.7	1.54
1922	28	10	17	.370	4.32	32	26	15	1	202.0	230	108	7	74	59	94	1.505	10.2	3.3	2.6	0.80
1934	40	2	0	1.000	3.05	30	2	1	2	62.0	68	31	2	16	16	156	1.355	9.9	2.3	2.3	1.00
Totals		62	59	.512	3.67	201	124	71	8	1,089.1	1,169	522	29	299	358	100	1.348	9.7	2.5	3.0	1.20

Yankees Years

Year	Age	W	L	%	ERA	G	GS	CG	SV	IP	H	R	HR	BB	SO	ERA+	WHIP	H/9	BB/9	SO/9	SO/BB
1923	29	19	6	.760	3.13	35	27	21	3	238.1	235	86	11	68	93	126	1.3271	8.9	2.6	3.5	1.37
1924	30	21	9	.700	2.83	40	34	25	3	286.1	302	104	13	64	101	148	1.278	9.5	2.0	3.2	1.58
1925	31	16	17	.485	2.96	47	31	21	2	277.0	267	117	11	71	88	144	1.220	8.7	2.3	2.9	1.24
1926	32	23	11	.676	3.62	40	33	19	3	266.1	294	133	11	43	78	107	1.265	9.9	1.5	2.6	1.81
1927	33	19	8	.704	3.00	34	26	18	2	209.2	225	89	5	48	51	130	1.302	9.7	2.1	2.2	1.06
1928	34	17	6	.739	2.56	28	24	19	3	211.0	215	71	2	40	53	149	1.209	9.2	1.7	2.3	1.33
1929	35	9	11	.450	4.92	27	23	8	2	157.1	205	101	11	28	49	79	1.481	11.7	1.6	2.8	1.75
1930	36	11	7	.611	4.32	25	19	11	0	156.1	194	95	8	20	46	100	1.369	11.2	1.2	2.6	2.30
1931	37	11	6	.647	4.28	25	25	12	0	189.1	247	96	7	30	65	93	1.463	11.7	1.4	3.1	2.17
1932	38	9	5	.643	4.60	22	21	9	0	146.2	191	94	8	38	54	89	1.561	11.7	2.3	3.3	1.42

Year	Age	W	L	%	ERA	G	GS	CG	SV	IP	H	R	HR	BB	SO	ERA+	WHIP	H/9	BB/9	SO/9	SO/BB
1933	39	7	4	.636	5.54	23	5	2	4	65.0	96	46	4	21	22	71	1.800	13.3	2.9	3.0	1.05
Totals		162	90	.643	3.54	346	269	165	23	2,203.1	2,471	1,032	91	471	700	114	1.335	10.1	1.9	2.9	1.49

Which Team Fared Better?

When the Red Sox acquired Pennock from the A's, it took him a few years to become a regular starter. Once he did, he won 16 games for them twice but finished at .500 or below in five of the seasons he was there. The trade of Herb Pennock to the Yankees in 1923 was almost as devastating to the Fenway faithful as the sale of Babe Ruth. When he came to the Yankees he was finally playing for a team that could support his great pitching. He had a winning record nine of the 11 seasons he played for them, accruing 162 wins against only 90 losses. He also helped them to win three World Series in 1923, 1927, and 1932. The only argument that could be made that the Red Sox fared better is that they got Pennock for the bargain basement price of $2,500 from the A's. The Yankees, on the other hand, had to give over three players and $50,000 for the services of Pennock. That means the Red Sox paid about $40 for each win Pennock gave them while the Yankees paid about $309. Of course spending money has never bothered New York, and they would gladly have paid triple that for the three rings Pennock helped them to acquire.

In his day, Pennock was considered by some, including Connie Mack, to be the best left-handed pitcher of all time. Eleven of his 22 seasons were spent with New York, with whom he won four World Series rings (in 1923, 1927, 1928, and 1932) and had a .643 winning percentage. With Boston, he was reliable, if less spectacular, winning 62 games over eight seasons.

BILL PIERCY

A pitcher with six years in the majors, Piercy played for three different teams. He started with the New York Yankees and then was traded over to Boston for Bullet Joe Bush, Sad Sam Jones, and Everett Scott. His career numbers are an unimpressive 27–43 with 268 walks and only 165 strikeouts.

Yankees Years

Year	Age	W	L	%	ERA	G	GS	CG	SV	IP	H	R	HR	BB	SO	ERA+	WHIP	H/9	BB/9	SO/9	SO/BB
1917	21	0	1	.000	3.00	1	1	1	0	9.0	9	3	0	2	4	95	1.222	9.0	2.0	4.0	2.00
1921	25	5	4	.556	2.98	14	10	5	0	81.2	82	40	4	28	35	142	1.347	9.0	3.1	3.9	1.25
Totals		5	5	.500	2.98	15	11	6	0	90.2	91	43	4	30	39	137	1.335	9.0	3.0	3.9	1.30

Red Sox Years

Year	Age	W	L	%	ERA	G	GS	CG	SV	IP	H	R	HR	BB	SO	ERA+	WHIP	H/9	BB/9	SO/9	SO/BB
1922	26	3	9	.250	4.67	29	12	7	0	121.1	140	77	2	62	24	87	1.665	10.4	4.6	1.8	0.39
1923	27	8	17	.320	3.41	30	24	11	0	187.1	193	105	5	73	51	119	1.420	9.3	3.5	2.5	0.70
1924	28	5	7	.417	5.95	23	18	3	0	121.0	156	87	4	66	20	73	1.835	11.6	4.9	1.5	0.30
Totals		16	33	.327	4.48	82	54	21	0	429.2	489	269	11	201	95	93	1.606	10.2	4.2	2.0	0.47

Which Team Fared Better?

He went only 5–5 for the Yankees, coming up to pitch one game when he was 21 and returning when he was 25, when he went 5–4. He did post a fairly low 2.98 ERA during that time. He came to a Boston team that scored 598 runs (1922), 584 (1923), and 738 (1924). This is in comparison with the Yankees, who scored 758 (1922), 823 (1923), and 798 (1924). This shows that if Piercy had stayed in New York he would have received much more run support and likely would have done at least a little better than the 16–33 record he put up in three years with the Red Sox. Regardless, his ERA (4.48 for the Sox, 2.98 for New York) and WHIP (1.606 for the Sox, 1.335 for New York) show that the Yankees got the better of him.

GEORGE PIPGRAS

A hundred game winner over the course of his 11-year career, Pipgras was a right-handed pitcher who only played for the Yankees and the Red Sox. He spent the first nine seasons with the Yankees, who then traded him halfway through the 1933 season. He finished that season with the Red Sox and played two more before he was released. He returned to baseball in 1938 as an umpire, and held the position for nearly a decade.

Yankees Years

Year	Age	W	L	%	ERA	G	GS	CG	SV	IP	H	R	HR	BB	SO	ERA+	WHIP	H/9	BB/9	SO/9	SO/BB
1923	23	1	3	.250	5.94	8	2	2	0	33.1	34	22	2	25	12	67	1.770	9.2	6.8	3.2	0.48
1924	24	0	1	.000	9.98	9	1	0	1	15.1	20	18	0	18	4	43	2.478	11.7	10.6	2.3	0.22
1927	27	10	3	.769	4.11	29	21	9	0	166.1	148	81	2	77	81	95	1.353	8.0	4.2	4.4	1.05
1928	28	24	13	.649	3.38	46	38	22	3	300.2	314	132	4	103	139	112	1.387	9.4	3.1	4.2	1.35
1929	29	18	12	.600	4.23	39	33	13	0	225.1	229	132	16	95	125	91	1.438	9.1	3.8	5.0	1.32
1930	30	15	15	.500	4.11	44	30	15	5	221.0	230	133	9	70	111	105	1.357	9.4	2.9	4.5	1.59
1931	31	7	6	.538	3.79	36	14	6	4	137.2	134	73	8	58	59	105	1.395	8.8	3.8	3.9	1.02
1932	32	16	9	.640	4.19	32	27	14	0	219.0	235	120	15	87	111	97	1.470	9.7	3.6	4.6	1.28
1933	33	2	2	.500	3.27	4	4	3	0	33.0	32	13	1	12	14	120	1.333	8.7	3.3	3.8	1.17
Totals		93	64	.592	4.04	247	170	84	16	1,351.2	1,376	724	57	545	656	99	1.421	9.2	3.6	4.4	1.20

Red Sox Years

Year	Age	W	L	%	ERA	G	GS	CG	SV	IP	H	R	HR	BB	SO	ERA+	WHIP	H/9	BB/9	SO/9	SO/BB
1933	33	9	8	.529	4.07	22	17	9	1	128.1	140	65	5	45	56	109	1.442	9.8	3.2	3.9	1.24
1934	34	0	0		8.10	2	1	0	0	3.1	4	3	1	3	0	64	2.100	10.8	8.1	0.0	0.00
1935	35	0	1	.000	14.40	5	1	0	0	5.0	9	9	3	5	2	35	2.800	16.2	9.0	3.6	0.40
Totals		9	9	.500	4.54	29	19	9	1	136.2	153	77	9	53	58	98	1.507	10.1	3.5	3.8	1.09

Which Team Fared Better?

His best years as a pitcher came with the Yankees. The funny thing is the Red Sox had him in their system when he was coming up through the minors and traded him to the Yankees at the beginning of the 1923 season. Pipgras went on to have a stellar career with the

Yankees, falling seven games short of winning 100 games. His best year was in 1928 when he led the league in wins at 24, innings pitched at 300.2, and batters faced at 1,298. By the time the Red Sox finally got him back he was in his mid-thirties and he was not as effective a pitcher. He broke even at a 9 and 9 record with Boston. He only pitched in seven games over the last two years with Boston. He won three World Series rings with the 1927, 1928, and 1932 Yankees.

Del Pratt

When Pratt began his career with the St. Louis Browns he was the model of consistency as a hitter over his six years with them. During that time he averaged every year 156 games played, 31 steals, 80 RBIs, 70 runs scored, 160 hits, and 30 doubles. He was traded to the Yankees where he played for three years before spending a couple of years in Boston and then in Detroit. He finished his career four hits shy of 2,000, had 968 RBIs, and a respectable .292 batting average. His best years were with the Browns where in the 1916 seasons he led the league in RBIs.

Yankees Years

Year	Age	G	AB	R	H	2B	3B	HR	RBI	SB	CS	BB	SO	BA	OBP	SLG	OPS	OPS+	TB	SH
1918	30	126	477	65	131	19	7	2	55	12		35	26	.275	.327	.356	.683	104	170	23
1919	31	140	527	69	154	27	7	4	56	22		36	24	.292	.342	.393	.735	106	207	16
1920	32	154	574	84	180	37	8	4	97	12	10	50	24	.314	.372	.427	.798	108	245	27
Totals		420	1,578	218	465	83	22	10	208	46	10	121	74	.295	.348	.394	.743	106	622	66

Red Sox Years

Year	Age	G	AB	R	H	2B	3B	HR	RBI	SB	CS	BB	SO	BA	OBP	SLG	OPS	OPS+	TB	SH
1921	33	135	521	80	169	36	10	5	102	8	10	44	10	.324	.378	.461	.839	116	240	8
1922	34	154	607	73	183	44	7	6	86	7	10	53	20	.301	.361	.427	.788	106	259	9
Totals		289	1,128	153	352	80	17	11	188	15	20	97	30	.312	.369	.442	.811	110	499	17

Which Team Fared Better?

Pratt continued his consistency with the Yankees and Red Sox. With that in mind, let us average out his numbers to see who fared better. He played an average of 140 games in New York, 145 in Boston. He averaged 155 hits with the Yankees, 176 with the Red Sox. His batting average was a .295 with New York and .312 with Boston. 73 runs scored with Yankees, 77 with the Red Sox, and 28 pinstriper doubles compared to 40 BoSox doubles. The only category the Yankees averaged better was in stolen bases where he had 15 for New York and 7 for Boston. The Red Sox got the better of his consistent career.

Pratt spent 12 years as a utility infielder, logging time at third, second, and shortstop. He played only two years with the Red Sox but served as their captain for one of them (1922). He was with New York for three seasons, providing the sort of solid all-around play that the league had come to expect from the infielder.

JACK QUINN

Quinn was born in Slovakia with the birth name Joannes Pajoks. After his family immigrated to America he was signed to a baseball contract at age 14 when he caught a foul ball in the stands and threw it back to the catcher, hitting him square in the mitt. The visiting coach was impressed enough to sign him. Quinn went on to have a 23 year major league career, playing for eight different teams. He was with the Yankees the longest at 7 years, the Philadelphia Athletics for 6, and the Red Sox for 4. The remaining teams, Brooklyn, Boston Braves, Cincinnati, White Sox, and Baltimore he all spent two years or less with. He finished his career with a 247–218 record and a 3.29 ERA. Because he pitched until he was 50, he held several age related records for awhile. He was the oldest pitcher to win a game until Jamie Moyer broke that in 2012. He was the oldest man to hit a home run until Julio Franco supplanted him in 2006. He is still the oldest player to start a World Series game and start an Opening Day game. He won two World Series with the 1929 and 1930 Philadelphia Athletics.

Yankees Years

Year	Age	W	L	%	ERA	G	GS	CG	SV	IP	H	R	HR	BB	SO	ERA+	WHIP	H/9	BB/9	SO/9	SO/BB
1909	25	9	5	.643	1.97	23	11	8	1	118.2	110	45	1	24	36	130	1.129	8.3	1.8	2.7	1.50
1910	26	18	12	.600	2.37	35	31	20	0	235.2	214	88	2	58	82	112	1.154	8.2	2.2	3.1	1.41
1911	27	8	10	.444	3.76	40	16	7	2	174.2	203	111	2	41	71	95	1.397	10.5	2.1	3.7	1.73
1912	28	5	7	.417	5.79	18	11	7	0	102.2	139	89	4	23	47	63	1.578	12.2	2.0	4.1	2.04
1919	35	15	14	.517	2.61	38	31	18	0	266.0	242	96	8	65	97	123	1.154	8.2	2.2	3.3	1.49
1920	36	18	10	.643	3.20	41	32	17	3	253.1	271	110	8	48	101	120	1.259	9.6	1.7	3.6	2.10
1921	37	8	7	.533	3.78	33	13	6	0	119.0	158	61	2	32	44	111	1.597	11.9	2.4	3.3	1.38
Totals		81	65	.555	3.15	228	145	83	6	1,270.0	1,337	600	27	291	478	106	1.282	9.5	2.1	3.4	1.64

Red Sox Years

Year	Age	W	L	%	ERA	G	GS	CG	SV	IP	H	R	HR	BB	SO	ERA+	WHIP	H/9	BB/9	SO/9	SO/BB
1922	38	13	16	.448	3.48	40	32	16	0	256.0	263	119	9	59	67	117	1.258	9.2	2.1	2.4	1.14
1923	39	13	17	.433	3.89	42	28	16	7	243.0	302	125	6	53	71	105	1.461	11.2	2.0	2.6	1.34
1924	40	12	13	.480	3.27	44	25	13	7	228.2	241	109	10	52	64	134	1.281	9.5	2.0	2.5	1.23
1925	41	7	8	.467	4.37	19	15	8	0	105.0	140	68	3	26	24	104	1.581	12.0	2.2	2.1	0.92
Totals		45	54	.455	3.65	145	100	53	14	832.2	946	421	28	190	226	115	1.364	10.2	2.1	2.4	1.19

Which Team Fared Better?

He had two stints with the Yankees for a total of seven seasons. His best season with them came in 1920 when he produced a line of 18 wins, 101 strikeouts, and 1.259 WHIP. Overall he finished with an 81 and 65 record with New York and helped them to a pennant in 1921. For the Red Sox he never had a winning season, he closest being 1924 when he went 12 and 13. Overall he was 45 and 54 with Boston. His best single season came as a member of the 1928 A's when he won 18 games and an ERA of 2.90. He was 44 years-old at the time. The most telling statistic for this savvy spitballer is his WHIP. For New York it was a 1.282 but with the Red Sox it was 1.364 giving the Yankees the better of this ageless wonder.

GORDON RHODES

A right-handed pitcher who had eight years of playing experience in the major leagues for three different teams. He spent four years each with the Yankees and Red Sox before finishing his last year with the Philadelphia Athletics. He only had one winning season to his name and compiled 74 losses compared to 43 wins. He also had an unremarkable 4.85 ERA.

Yankees Years

Year	Age	W	L	%	ERA	G	GS	CG	SV	IP	H	R	HR	BB	SO	ERA+	WHIP	H/9	BB/9	SO/9	SO/BB
1929	21	0	4	.000	4.85	10	4	0	0	42.2	57	32	3	16	13	80	1.711	12.0	3.4	2.7	0.81
1930	22	0	0		9.00	3	0	0	0	2.0	3	3	0	4	1	56	3.500	13.5	18.0	4.5	0.25
1931	23	6	3	.667	3.41	18	11	4	0	87.0	82	49	3	52	36	117	1.540	8.5	5.4	3.7	0.69
1932	24	1	2	.333	7.88	10	2	1	0	24.0	25	22	0	21	15	53	1.917	9.4	7.9	5.6	0.71
Totals		7	9	.438	4.57	41	17	5	0	155.2	167	106	6	93	65	88	1.670	9.7	5.4	3.8	0.70

Red Sox Years

Year	Age	W	L	%	ERA	G	GS	CG	SV	IP	H	R	HR	BB	SO	ERA+	WHIP	H/9	BB/9	SO/9	SO/BB
1932	24	1	8	.111	5.11	12	11	4	0	79.1	79	46	5	31	22	87	1.387	9.0	3.5	2.5	0.71
1933	25	12	15	.444	4.03	34	29	14	0	232.0	242	126	13	93	85	109	1.444	9.4	3.6	3.3	0.91
1934	26	12	12	.500	4.56	44	31	10	2	219.0	247	133	10	98	79	104	1.575	10.2	4.0	3.2	0.81
1935	27	2	10	.167	5.41	34	19	1	2	146.1	195	103	14	60	44	87	1.743	12.0	3.7	2.7	0.73
Totals		27	45	.375	4.63	124	90	29	4	676.2	763	408	42	282	230	99	1.544	10.1	3.8	3.1	0.82

Which Team Fared Better?

Rhodes's value was not in his pitching (7 and 9 for Yankees, 27 and 45 for the Red Sox) but in his potential as trade chip, as the Yankees would use Rhodes to get back Wilcy Moore. Moore went 7 and 6 in his return to New York. The Red Sox used Rhodes and a minor leaguer to get Hall of Famer Jimmy Foxx and Johnny Marcum. Marcum gave Rhodes like support in pitching but Jimmy Foxx contributed mightily. Even though he was past his Philadelphia Athletic prime, he was a six-time All-Star with the Red Sox, getting 1,041 hits, 222 home runs, and 788 RBIs in his seven years. He led the league in 1938 in average, OBP, slugging, and OPS as well as total bases. Rhodes legacy lies with the Red Sox but only because he gave them Jimmy Foxx.

BRAGGO ROTH

An outfielder who played for six teams over his eight years of big league time. He began his career with the Chicago White Sox, with whom he played two seasons before being traded to the Cleveland Indians for Shoeless Joe Jackson. He played four years in Cleveland then bounced around from the Philadelphia Athletics to the Red Sox to the Washington Senators to the Yankees in three years' time. He led the league in home runs in 1915 with a whopping seven, but that was the Deadball Era.

Red Sox Year

Year	Age	G	AB	R	H	2B	3B	HR	RBI	SB	CS	BB	SO	BA	OBP	SLG	OPS	OPS+	TB	SH
1919	26	63	227	32	58	9	4	0	23	9		24	32	.256	.337	.330	.668	92	75	5

Yankees Year

Year	Age	G	AB	R	H	2B	3B	HR	RBI	SB	CS	BB	SO	BA	OBP	SLG	OPS	OPS+	TB	SH
1921	28	43	152	29	43	9	2	2	10	1	2	19	20	.283	.370	.408	.778	97	62	3

Which Team Fared Better?

He did not play a full season with either team. Although he had a lower average .256 vs. .283 in Boston than New York as well as a lower OBP .337 vs. .370, he produced more RBIs (23 vs. 10), stolen bases (9 vs. 1), and hits (58 vs. 43). Neither team is the one he will most be remembered for playing for but the Red Sox edge out the Yankees ever so slightly based on his production with the club. RBIs win games after all.

MUDDY RUEL

A catcher for 19 seasons in the majors, he was known as one of the best defensive backstops in the league. He began with the St. Louis Browns before moving on to the New York Yankees. He was the catcher for New York the day Carl Mays hit Ray Chapman in the head, resulting in Chapman dying two days later. From there he went to the Red Sox, played eight seasons with the Washington Senators, and went back to the Red Sox before finishing his playing days going from the Tigers to the Browns to the White Sox. He accumulated 1,242 hits in his career, knocked in 536 runs, and had a .275 average, not bad for a catcher. He coached for about a decade and even managed the St. Louis Browns before finishing his time in baseball as the general manager of the Detroit Tigers.

Yankees Years

Year	Age	G	AB	R	H	2B	3B	HR	RBI	SB	CS	BB	SO	BA	OBP	SLG	OPS	OPS+	TB	SH
1917	21	6	17	1	2	0	0	0	1	1		2	2	.118	.211	.118	.328	-0	2	1
1918	22	3	6	0	2	0	0	0	0	1		2	1	.333	.500	.333	.833	149	2	0
1919	23	79	233	18	56	6	0	0	31	4		34	26	.240	.340	.266	.606	71	62	5
1920	24	82	261	30	70	14	1	1	15	4	2	15	18	.268	.310	.341	.651	70	89	7
Totals		170	517	49	130	20	1	1	47	10	2	53	47	.251	.323	.300	.623	70	155	13

Red Sox Years

Year	Age	G	AB	R	H	2B	3B	HR	RBI	SB	CS	BB	SO	BA	OBP	SLG	OPS	OPS+	TB	SH
1921	25	113	358	41	99	21	1	1	45	2	7	41	15	.277	.353	.349	.702	82	125	12
1922	26	116	361	34	92	15	1	0	28	4	2	41	26	.255	.333	.302	.634	67	109	11
1931	35	33	83	6	25	5	0	0	6	0	0	9	6	.301	.370	.361	.731	98	30	1
Totals		262	802	81	216	41	2	1	79	6	9	91	47	.269	.345	.329	.674	77	264	24

Which Team Fared Better?

His best years were spent with the Senators, getting MVP consideration three of the seasons he was there. He was with the Yankees before they became the powerhouse of the 1920s, playing in only 9 games his first two seasons of the five years he wore pinstripes. He got over 275 at-bats each of his last two seasons with them but only had a total of 47 RBIs, 130 hits, and 49 runs scored. In the three seasons he played for the Red Sox, he outdistanced all of those numbers with 79 RBIs, 216 hits, and 81 runs. Of course when he came to the Red Sox they had previously dominated the 1910s with the four World Series titles, but were lousy by the time he arrived. If Ruel had only flip flopped the years he spent with each team he would have been on championship clubs but then they claim baseball is all about timing.

RED RUFFING

Ruffing has quite the baseball resume. He was a six-time All-Star while with the Yankees, won six World Series championships, again all with New York, and was elected to Cooperstown at the Baseball Hall of Fame in 1967. He played all but one of his years with either Boston or New York, spending his final year with the White Sox. He finished his pitching career with 273 wins, 225 losses. He had 1987 strikeouts and an ERA of 3.80.

Red Sox Years

Year	Age	W	L	%	ERA	G	GS	CG	SV	IP	H	R	HR	BB	SO	ERA+	WHIP	H/9	BB/9	SO/9	SO/BB
1924	19	0	0		6.65	8	2	0	0	23.0	29	17	0	9	10	66	1.652	11.3	3.5	3.9	1.11
1925	20	9	18	.333	5.01	37	27	13	1	217.1	253	135	10	75	64	90	1.509	10.5	3.1	2.7	0.85
1926	21	6	15	.286	4.39	37	22	6	2	166.0	169	96	4	68	58	93	1.428	9.2	3.7	3.1	0.85
1927	22	5	13	.278	4.66	26	18	10	2	158.1	160	94	7	87	77	91	1.560	9.1	4.9	4.4	0.89
1928	23	10	25	.286	3.89	42	34	25	2	289.1	303	147	8	96	118	104	1.379	9.4	3.0	3.7	1.23
1929	24	9	22	.290	4.86	35	32	18	2	244.1	280	162	17	118	109	87	1.629	10.3	4.3	4.0	0.92
1930	25	0	3	.000	6.38	4	3	1	0	24.0	32	19	1	6	14	73	1.583	12.0	2.3	5.3	2.33
Totals		39	96	.289	4.61	189	138	73	9	1,122.1	1,226	670	47	459	450	92	1.501	9.8	3.7	3.6	0.98

Yankees Years

Year	Age	W	L	%	ERA	G	GS	CG	SV	IP	H	R	HR	BB	SO	ERA+	WHIP	H/9	BB/9	SO/9	SO/BB
1930	25	15	5	.750	4.14	34	25	12	1	197.2	200	106	10	62	117	105	1.325	9.1	2.8	5.3	1.89
1931	26	16	14	.533	4.41	37	30	19	2	237.0	240	130	11	87	132	91	1.380	9.1	3.3	5.0	1.52
1932	27	18	7	.720	3.09	35	29	22	2	259.0	219	102	16	115	190	132	1.290	7.6	4.0	6.6	1.65
1933	28	9	14	.391	3.91	35	28	18	3	235.0	230	118	7	93	122	100	1.374	8.8	3.6	4.7	1.31
1934	29	19	11	.633	3.93	36	31	19	1	256.1	232	134	18	104	149	104	1.311	8.1	3.7	5.2	1.43
1935	30	16	11	.593	3.12	30	29	19	0	222.0	201	88	17	76	81	130	1.248	8.1	3.1	3.3	1.07
1936	31	20	12	.625	3.65	33	33	25	0	271.0	274	133	22	90	102	120	1.343	9.1	3.0	3.4	1.13
1937	32	20	7	.741	2.98	31	31	22	0	256.1	242	101	17	68	131	150	1.209	8.5	2.4	4.6	1.93
1938	33	21	7	.750	3.31	31	31	22	0	247.1	246	104	16	82	127	138	1.326	9.0	3.0	4.6	1.55
1939	34	21	7	.750	2.93	28	28	22	0	233.1	211	88	15	75	95	148	1.226	8.1	2.9	3.7	1.27
1940	35	15	12	.556	3.38	30	30	20	0	226.0	218	98	24	76	97	119	1.301	8.7	3.0	3.9	1.28
1941	36	15	6	.714	3.54	23	23	13	0	185.2	177	87	13	54	60	112	1.244	8.6	2.6	2.9	1.11
1942	37	14	7	.667	3.21	24	24	16	0	193.2	183	72	10	41	80	107	1.157	8.5	1.9	3.7	1.95
1945	40	7	3	.700	2.89	11	11	8	0	87.1	85	32	2	20	24	121	1.202	8.8	2.1	2.5	1.20
1946	41	5	1	.833	1.77	8	8	4	0	61.0	37	13	2	23	19	195	0.984	5.5	3.4	2.8	0.83
Totals		231	124	.651	3.47	426	391	261	9	3,168.2	2,995	1,406	200	1,066	1,526	119	1.282	8.5	3.0	4.3	1.43

Which Team Fared Better?

His time spent between the Red Sox and Yankees are like mirror images of one another. Everything he did while a Yankee looked normal while his years with the Red Sox were backwards. He went 36 and 96 in his seven years with the Red Sox, leading the league in losses twice with over 20. He went 231 and 124 with the Yankees, winning twenty games four times in his fifteen years. While he never had a winning season with the Red Sox, he had fourteen of them with New York. He had more walks than strikeouts with Boston, 459 walks to 450 strikeouts. He reversed this with the Yankees, 1,066 walks, 1,526 strikeouts. The Yankees win this one by a landslide.

BABE RUTH

The Great Bambino, the Sultan of Swat, the King of Crash, the Colossus of Clout, but most people know him simply as The Babe. Arguably the best player to ever play the game of baseball, Ruth changed the sport forever. Baseball hadn't been known for its offense in the Deadball Era but when owners saw the sort of crowds they would get to see Babe Ruth hit a home run, they changed the ball so it would carry better and the modern game of baseball was invented. He began his time in the league as a pitcher for the Red Sox, playing for six years and winning three World Series championships. By the time he was traded to the Yankees in one of the most controversial trades in baseball history, he had decided he wanted to be a hitter instead of a pitcher, playing right field for the Yankees and winning four championships with them. He played one final year with the Boston Braves but hung it up after playing in only 28 games. We could write a book about Ruth's accomplishments, and many good ones have been written, but here is a highlight of some of the major league records he holds:

- 1st on all-time slugging percentage with 0.690
- 1st on all-time OPS with 1.164
- 1st on all-time OPS+ with 206
- 2nd on all-time on-base percentage list with .474
- 2nd on all-time RBI list with 2,213
- 3rd on all-time home run list with 714
- 3rd on all-time bases on balls list with 2,062
- 4th on all-time runs list with 2,174
- 6th on all-time total bases list with 5,793

Red Sox Years

Year	Age	W	L	%	ERA	G	GS	CG	SV	IP	H	R	HR	BB	SO	ERA+	WHIP	H/9	BB/9	SO/9	SO/BB
1914	19	2	1	.667	3.91	4	3	1	0	23.0	21	12	1	7	3	71	1.217	8.2	2.7	1.2	0.43
1915	20	18	8	.692	.244	32	28	16	0	217.2	166	80	3	85	112	114	1.153	6.9	3.5	4.6	1.32
1916	21	23	12	.657	1.75	44	40	23	1	323.2	230	83	0	118	170	158	1.075	6.4	3.3	4.7	1.44
1917	22	24	13	.649	2.01	41	38	35	2	326.1	244	93	2	108	128	128	1.079	6.7	3.0	3.5	1.19
1918	23	13	7	.650	2.22	.20	19	18	0	166.1	125	51	1	49	40	122	1.046	6.8	2.7	2.2	0.82
1919	24	9	5	.643	2.97	17	15	12	1	133.1	148	59	2	58	30	102	1.545	10.0	3.9	2.0	0.52
Totals		89	46	.659	2.19	158	143	105	4	1,190.1	934	378	9	425	483	125	1.142	7.1	3.2	3.7	1.14

Year	Age	G	AB	R	H	2B	3B	HR	RBI	SB	CS	BB	SO	BA	OBP	SLG	OPS	OPS+	TB	SH
1914	19	5	10	1	2	1	0	0	0	0	0	0	4	.200	.200	.300	.500	49	3	0
1915	20	42	92	16	29	10	1	4	20	0	0	9	23	.315	.376	.576	.952	188	53	2
1916	21	67	136	18	37	5	3	3	16	0		10	23	.272	.322	.419	.741	121	57	4
1917	22	52	123	14	40	6	3	2	14	0		12	18	.325	.365	.472	.857	162	58	7
1918	23	95	317	50	95	26	11	11	61	6		58	58	.300	.411	.555	.966	192	176	3
1919	24	130	432	103	139	34	12	29	113	7		101	58	.322	.456	.657	1.114	217	284	3
Totals		391	1,110	202	342	82	30	49	224	13	0	190	184	.308	.413	.568	.981	190	631	19

Yankees Years

Year	Age	G	AB	R	H	2B	3B	HR	RBI	SB	CS	BB	SO	BA	OBP	SLG	OPS	OPS+	TB	SH
1920	25	142	458	158	172	36	9	54	135	14	14	150	80	.376	.532	.847	1.379	255	388	5
1921	26	182	540	177	204	44	16	59	168	17	13	145	81	.378	.512	.846	1.359	238	457	4
1922	27	110	406	94	128	24	8	35	96	2	5	84	80	.315	.434	.672	1.106	182	273	4
1923	28	152	522	151	205	45	13	41	130	17	21	170	93	.393	.545	.764	1.309	239	399	3
1924	29	153	529	143	200	39	7	46	124	9	13	142	81	.378	.513	.739	1.252	220	391	6
1925	30	98	359	61	104	12	2	25	67	2	4	59	68	.290	.393	.543	.936	137	195	6
1926	31	152	495	139	184	30	5	47	153	11	9	144	76	.372	.516	.737	1.253	225	365	10
1927	32	151	540	158	192	29	8	60	165	7	6	137	89	.356	.486	.772	1.258	225	417	14
1928	33	154	536	163	173	29	8	54	146	4	5	137	87	.323	.463	.709	1.172	206	380	8
1929	34	135	499	121	172	26	6	46	154	5	3	72	60	.345	.430	.697	1.128	193	348	13
1930	35	145	518	150	186	28	9	49	153	10	10	136	61	.359	.493	.732	1.225	211	379	21
1931	36	145	534	149	199	31	3	46	162	5	4	128	51	.373	.495	.700	1.195	218	374	0
1932	37	133	457	120	156	13	5	41	137	2	2	130	62	.341	.489	.661	1.150	201	302	0
1933	38	137	459	97	138	21	3	34	104	4	5	114	90	.301	.442	.582	1.023	176	267	0
1934	39	125	365	78	105	17	4	22	84	1	3	104	63	.288	.448	.537	.985	160	196	0
Totals		2,084	7,217	1,959	2,518	424	106	659	1,978	110	117	1,852	1,122	.349	.484	.711	1.195	209	5,131	94

Year	Age	W	L	%	ERA	G	GS	CG	SV	IP	H	R	HR	BB	SO	ERA+	WHIP	H/9	BB/9	SO/9	SO/BB
1920	25	1	0	1.000	4.50	1	1	0	0	4.0	3	4	0	2	0	94	1.250	6.8	4.5	0.0	0.00
1921	26	2	0	1.000	9.00	2	1	0	0	9.0	14	10	1	9	2	49	2.556	14.0	9.0	2.0	0.22
1930	35	1	0	1.000	3.00	1	1	1	0	9.0	11	3	0	2	3	150	1.444	11.0	2.0	3.0	1.50
1933	38	1	0	1.000	5.00	1	1	1	0	9.0	12	5	0	3	0	81	1.667	12.0	3.0	0.0	0.00
Totals		5	0	1.000	5.52	5	4	2	0	31.0	40	22	1	16	5	78	1.806	11.6	4.6	1.5	0.31

Which Team Fared Better?

The career of Babe Ruth is the tale of two players. In his time with the Red Sox he was known primarily as a pitcher and a pretty darn good one. He went 89 and 46 with a 2.19 ERA and a 1.142 WHIP. He was a perfect 3–0 pitching in the World Series. If Ruth had remained exclusively a pitcher and averaged merely 14 wins a season, which is what he did while pitching with Boston, he would have finished with 313 wins in his career. But Ruth decided pitching was boring and instead broke all sorts of records as a hitter. He slugged 659 home runs, 1,978 RBIs, 1959 runs, and posted a .711 slugging percentage. Let us pretend he decided much earlier in his career to be a hitter and he averaged 29 home runs a season in those six years, he would have finished his career with 833 home runs, a record even Steroid Era champ Barry Bonds would have never broken. It is nearly impossible to compare his time with the two teams because he was a completely different player with each of them. Boston got the better pitcher and New York got the better hitter. But New York wins the war because the trade of Ruth sent repercussions throughout Boston that lasted for 86 years. That was how long it took them to win World Series after trading the Hall of Famer.

BOB SEEDS

Known as Suitcase Bob because of his very large, suitcase-like feet, Seeds played outfield for nine seasons in the majors, most of them with Cleveland. He finished his last three years with the New York Giants and played with the Red Sox, Yankees, and White Sox. Seeds was not a regular, everyday player, and he never got into more than 118 games in a season, playing in a total of 615. His three best years came as a member of the Giants, for whom he knocked in 94 runs and hit 18 home runs.

Red Sox Years

Year	Age	G	AB	R	H	2B	3B	HR	RBI	SB	CS	BB	SO	BA	OBP	SLG	OPS	OPS+	TB	SH
1933	26	82	230	26	56	13	4	0	23	1	3	21	20	.243	.310	.335	.644	69	77	3
1934	27	8	6	0	1	0	0	0	1	0	0	0	1	.167	.167	.167	.333	-15	1	0
Totals		90	236	26	57	13	4	0	24	1	3	21	21	.242	.306	.331	.637	67	78	3

Yankees Year

Year	Age	G	AB	R	H	2B	3B	HR	RBI	SB	CS	BB	SO	BA	OBP	SLG	OPS	OPS+	TB	SH
1936	29	13	42	12	11	1	0	4	10	3	1	5	3	.262	.340	.571	.912	124	224	0

Which Team Fared Better?

Neither team gave Seeds a lot of playing time. In 236 at-bats with Boston, he had 24 RBIs and no home runs. In just 42 at-bats with the Yankees he drove in 10 runs (on just 11 hits) and hit four home runs. That means he knocked in a run every 10 at-bats with Boston while with the Yankees he did so nearly every four at-bats. The Yankees got a more efficient Seeds.

Howie Shanks

A Washington Senator for 11 seasons, this outfielder came to the Red Sox and Yankees in the final three years of his playing career. He had 1,440 hits in his career and 620 RBIs. Obviously his best years came with Washington, where he played in 100 or more games in all but one of his seasons. His playing time diminished in his final two seasons, and he became a part-time player.

Red Sox Years

Year	Age	G	AB	R	H	2B	3B	HR	RBI	SB	CS	BB	SO	BA	OBP	SLG	OPS	OPS+	TB	SH
1923	32	131	464	38	118	19	5	3	57	6	6	19	37	.254	.285	.336	.621	63	156	15
1924	33	72	193	22	50	16	3	0	25	1	0	21	15	.259	.332	.373	.705	82	72	9
Totals		203	657	60	168	35	8	3	82	7	6	40	49	.256	.299	.347	.646	69	228	24

Yankees Year

Year	Age	G	AB	R	H	2B	3B	HR	RBI	SB	CS	BB	SO	BA	OBP	SLG	OPS	OPS+	TB	SH
1923	34	66	155	15	40	3	1	1	18	1	0	20	15	.258	.343	.310	.653	68	48	9

Which Team Fared Better?

His average and OPS with the two teams are nearly the same, his on-base percentage is considerably better for New York, and his slugging percentage for Boston. In the end the Red Sox win this one based on volume of performance. He saw more playing time with the Red Sox even if you only compare his first season with them to his one season with the Yankees. The increased playing time led to significantly more hits, RBIs, and runs scored with Boston.

Ben Shields

Over the course of four seasons with three teams, Shields was a middle reliever in a time that when middle relievers were used infrequently. (Starters usually completed their games.) He pitched a total of 41.1 innings over those four seasons, and although he finished with a 4–0 record, his career ERA was an abysmal 8.27. In addition to the Yankees and Red Sox, he played for the Philadelphia Phillies.

Yankees Years

Year	Age	W	L	%	ERA	G	GS	CG	SV	IP	H	R	HR	BB	SO	ERA+	WHIP	H/9	BB/9	SO/9	SO/BB
1924	21	0	0		27.00	2	0	0	0	2.0	6	6	0	2	3	18	4.000	27.0	9.0	13.5	1.50
1925	22	3	0	1.000	4.88	4	2	2	0	24.0	24	13	2	12	5	89	1.500	9.0	4.5	1.9	0.42
Totals		3	0	1.000	6.58	6	2	2	0	26.0	30	19	2	14	8	67	1.692	10.4	4.8	2.8	0.57

Red Sox Year

Year	Age	W	L	%	ERA	G	GS	CG	SV	IP	H	R	HR	BB	SO	ERA+	WHIP	H/9	BB/9	SO/9	SO/BB
1930	27	0	0		9.00	3	0	0	0	10.0	16	11	0	6	1	53	2.200	14.4	5.4	0.9	0.17

Which Team Fared Better?

Neither team really got much out of Shields. He pitched 26 innings for the Yankees over two seasons, getting into six games. He pitched in three games for Boston, accumulating 10 innings of work. Although he produced no significant work for either club, the Yankees would have to win this one based on the fact that he gave them three wins and the Red Sox none.

Camp Skinner

Playing for just two seasons and for only two teams, Skinner was a reserve outfielder who batted left-handed. He appeared in only 34 games in that time and had a career .196 batting average. Skinner was no Babe Ruth.

Yankees Year

Year	Age	G	AB	R	H	2B	3B	HR	RBI	SB	CS	BB	SO	BA	OBP	SLG	OPS	OPS+	TB	SH
1922	25	27	33	1	6	0	0	0	2	1	0	0	4	.182	.206	.182	.388	1	6	0

Red Sox Year

Year	Age	G	AB	R	H	2B	3B	HR	RBI	SB	CS	BB	SO	BA	OBP	SLG	OPS	OPS+	TB	SH
1923	26	7	13	1	3	2	0	0	1	0	0	0	0	.231	.231	.385	.615	60	5	0

Which Team Fared Better?

There is very little to go on here. Amassing a total of 46 at-bats between both ballclubs, Skinner might nevertheless have helped the Yankees more, getting twice as many hits for them (6) as for the Red Sox (3). A better argument in favor of New York can be made by noting that Skinner was one of the players in the package sent to Boston for Herb Pennock, who brought the Yankees 162 victories as a pitcher.

Elmer Smith

Playing for five different teams in his 10-year career, Smith was an outfielder who was born in Ohio and spent time with both of that state's major league teams, playing a year for Cincinnati and seven for Cleveland. He also made stops with the Senators, Yankees, and Red Sox. Smith played in two World Series, winning in 1920 with the Indians and losing with the Yankees in 1922 against the Giants. He finished with a .276 average, producing 881 hits, 70 home runs, 541 RBIs, and scoring 469 runs.

Red Sox Year

Year	Age	G	AB	R	H	2B	3B	HR	RBI	SB	CS	BB	SO	BA	OBP	SLG	OPS	OPS+	TB	SH
1922	29	73	231	43	66	13	6	6	32	0	3	25	21	.286	.358	.472	.830	116	109	6

Yankees Years

Year	Age	G	AB	R	H	2B	3B	HR	RBI	SB	CS	BB	SO	BA	OBP	SLG	OPS	OPS+	TB	SH
1922	29	21	27	1	5	0	0	1	5	0	0	3	5	.185	.267	.296	.563	45	8	1
1923	30	70	183	30	56	6	2	7	35	3	1	21	21	.306	.377	.475	.853	122	87	4
Totals		91	210	31	61	6	2	8	40	3	1	24	26	.290	.363	.452	.816	112	95	5

Which Team Fared Better?

He played in a similar number of games for each team, getting into 73 for Boston and 91 for the Yankees, but had more at-bats for the Red Sox. His average is roughly the same, too, at .286 for the Red Sox and .290 for New York. The same is true of his total hits (66 for Sox, 61 for Yankees) and RBIs (32 for Sox, 40 for Yankees). He did play for the Yankees on two pennant-winning teams, but that is not the reason they get the nod. New York managed to trade him in 1924 and get rookie Earle Combs in return. Combs would spend the entirety of his Hall of Fame career, 12 seasons, with the Yankees, finishing with a .325 average, 1,866 hits, 632 RBIs, and a .397 OBP.

HANK THORMAHLEN

A left-handed pitcher, Thormahlen played six years for three teams. His longest stop was with the Yankees, with whom he pitched for four seasons. He spent a season with the Red Sox before riding out his days with the Brooklyn Robins. Although he won only 29 games in the big leagues, he was a 159-game winner in the minors.

Yankees Years

Year	Age	W	L	%	ERA	G	GS	CG	SV	IP	H	R	HR	BB	SO	ERA+	WHIP	H/9	BB/9	SO/9	SO/BB
1917	20	0	1	.000	2.25	1	1	0	0	8.0	9	3	0	4	5	128	1.625	10.1	4.5	5.6	1.25
1918	21	7	3	.700	2.48	16	12	5	0	112.2	85	39	1	52	22	114	1.216	6.8	4.2	1.8	0.42
1919	22	12	8	.600	2.62	30	25	13	1	188.2	155	69	10	61	62	122	1.145	7.4	2.9	3.0	1.02
1920	23	9	6	.600	4.14	29	15	6	1	143.1	178	86	5	43	35	93	1.542	11.2	2.7	2.2	0.81
Totals		28	18	.609	3.06	76	53	24	2	452.2	427	197	16	160	124	108	1.297	8.5	3.2	2.5	0.78

Red Sox Year

Year	Age	W	L	%	ERA	G	GS	CG	SV	IP	H	R	HR	BB	SO	ERA+	WHIP	H/9	BB/9	SO/9	SO/BB
1921	24	1	7	.125	4.48	23	9	3	1	96.1	101	56	3	34	17	95	1.401	9.4	3.2	1.6	0.50

Which Team Fared Better?

The Yankees rode him for 28 of his 29 career wins, his best year in the majors probably being 1919 when he went 12–8, pitched 188.2 innings, and had a 2.62 ERA. Not only was he part of the trade that gave the Yankees the Red Sox players they needed to win their first World Series (Waite Hoyt, Harry Harper, Wally Schang and Mike McNally), but when he got to the Red Sox, Thormahlen pitched abysmally, going 1–7 with a 4.48 ERA and giving up more hits than innings pitched.

BOBBY VEACH

Veach was a 14-year major leaguer, spending most of those seasons with the Detroit Tigers. He spent his final two years bouncing around between the Red Sox, Yankees, and Senators. He put together a decent career as a left fielder, leading the league in RBIs in 1915, 1917, and 1918 as well as being the leader in hits in 1919. He was the first Detroit Tiger ever to hit for the cycle, and his 3,754 putouts are among the all-time leaders for left field. In an eight-year stretch with the Tigers, he led all major league players in RBIs and extra base hits, outstripping players such as Ty Cobb, Babe Ruth, Tris Speaker, and George Sisler, all of whom were inducted into the Hall of Fame. He was also a great defensive outfielder and was the third man in the Detroit outfield that also included Ty Cobb and Sam Crawford. The trio is thought by some to be the best outfield ever. He did appear in a World Series with the 1925 Washington Senators.

Red Sox Years

Year	Age	G	AB	R	H	2B	3B	HR	RBI	SB	CS	BB	SO	BA	OBP	SLG	OPS	OPS+	TB	SH
1924	36	142	519	77	153	35	9	5	99	5	5	47	18	.295	.359	.426	.785	103	221	28
1925	37	1	5	0	1	0	0	0	2	0	0	1	1	.200	.333	.200	.533	38	1	0
Totals		143	524	77	154	35	9	5	101	5	5	48	19	.294	.359	.424	.782	102	222	28

Yankees Year

Year	Age	G	AB	R	H	2B	3B	HR	RBI	SB	CS	BB	SO	BA	OBP	SLG	OPS	OPS+	TB	SH
1925	37	56	116	13	41	10	2	0	15	1	4	8	0	.353	.400	.474	.874	123	55	2

Which Team Fared Better?

When Veach went to the Red Sox in 1924, he had a little gas left in the tank. He managed 99 RBIs, 153 hits, 77 runs, and walked 47 times. A year later he split time as a bench player with three different teams, getting only five at-bats with the Red Sox and 116 with the Yankees. The Tigers really got the best of Veach, but Boston did better with him than did New York.

SAMMY VICK

Vick was an outfielder who became the regular right fielder for the Yankees in 1919 after being drafted into the military during the 1918 season limited him to two games. He played one more year with the Yankees but lost his starting position to Babe Ruth, who came over from the Red Sox. So in 1921 he went to the Red Sox, serving mostly as a pinch hitter and defensive replacement in later innings. Those are the only two teams he played for in his five-year major league career. Vick played another eight years in the minor leagues.

Yankees Years

Year	Age	G	AB	R	H	2B	3B	HR	RBI	SB	CS	BB	SO	BA	OBP	SLG	OPS	OPS+	TB	SH
1917	22	10	36	4	10	3	0	0	2	2		1	6	.278	.297	.361	.658	100	13	1
1918	23	2	3	1	2	0	0	0	1	0		0	0	.667	.667	.667	1.333	298	2	0
1919	24	106	407	59	101	15	9	2	27	9		35	55	.248	.308	.344	.652	83	140	7
1920	25	51	118	21	26	7	1	0	11	1	1	14	20	.220	.313	.297	.610	60	35	1
Totals		169	564	85	139	25	10	2	41	12	1	50	81	.246	.310	.337	.647	79	190	9

Red Sox Year

Year	Age	G	AB	R	H	2B	3B	HR	RBI	SB	CS	BB	SO	BA	OBP	SLG	OPS	OPS+	TB	SH
1921	26	44	77	5	20	3	1	0	9	0	1	1	10	.260	.269	.325	.594	53	25	2

Which Team Fared Better?

The only team he had any regular playing time with was the Yankees, and only for one year. That season, he batted .248 with 101 hits, 27 RBIs, and 59 runs. He was replaced in 1920 by Babe Ruth, whose 172 hits, 54 home runs, 135 RBIs, and 158 runs scored that season were more than Vick managed in his career. Despite this, the Yankees got more out of him given that the Red Sox used him in only 44 games. Even if you take his lone Boston season and compare it with his final season with the Yankees, when he was a part-time player, New York comes out on top with a .313 average compared to .260, 11 RBIs to nine, and 21 runs to five. Throw on top of that the fact that the Yankees used Vick and three others to bring future Hall of Famer Waite Hoyt to New York and it becomes a landslide.

ROXY WALTERS

A player who caught for 11 seasons in the majors, recording time with the Yankees, Red Sox, and Cleveland Indians, Walters was known more for his defense than his hitting. He finished four seasons with a sub–.200 batting average and two more right at the .200 mark. Over his eleven seasons he produced a .222 batting average, 317 hits, 119 runs, 116 RBIs, and a .259 slugging percentage with no home runs.

Yankees Years

Year	Age	G	AB	R	H	2B	3B	HR	RBI	SB	CS	BB	SO	BA	OBP	SLG	OPS	OPS+	TB	SH
1915	22	3	0	1	0	0	0	0	0	0	0	0	0	.333	.333	.333	.667	99	1	0
1916	23	66	203	13	54	9	3	0	23	2		14	42	.266	.320	.340	.660	96	69	6
1917	24	61	171	16	45	2	0	0	14	2		9	22	.263	.304	.275	.579	76	47	6
1918	25	64	191	18	38	5	1	0	12	3		9	18	.199	.239	.236	.474	42	45	4
Totals		193	568	47	138	16	4	0	49	7	0	32	82	.243	.288	.285	.573	72	162	16

Red Sox Years

Year	Age	G	AB	R	H	2B	3B	HR	RBI	SB	CS	BB	SO	BA	OBP	SLG	OPS	OPS+	TB	SH
1919	26	48	135	7	26	2	0	0	9	1		7	15	.193	.259	.207	.466	34	28	7
1920	27	88	258	25	51	11	1	0	28	2	2	30	21	.198	.303	.248	.551	50	64	11
1921	28	54	169	17	34	4	1	0	14	3	0	10	11	.201	.254	.237	.491	27	40	5
1922	29	38	98	4	19	2	0	0	6	0	0	6	8	.194	.240	.214	.455	20	21	5
1923	30	40	104	9	26	4	0	0	5	0	2	2	6	.250	.264	.288	.553	45	30	11
Totals		268	764	62	156	23	2	0	62	6	4	55	61	.204	.272	.240	.511	38	183	39

Which Team Fared Better?

He spent the bulk of his career with the Yankees and Red Sox but saw infrequent playing time with each team. Rather than looking at his entire time with either, let us take a look at

two comparable seasons. In 1917 for the Yankees he had 171 at-bats; in 1921 for the Red Sox, he had 169, pretty darn close. For the Yankees that year his offensive numbers shake out like this: 14 RBIs, 45 hits, .263 average, and 16 runs scored. With the Red Sox he had 14 RBIs, 34 hits, .201 average, and 17 runs scored. The Yankees win this war of mediocrity.

At a glance, what stands out about Roxy Walters's batting line is that he hit no home runs in his 11 seasons in the big leagues. But this was at time (1915–1925) when catchers were generally valued more for their defense than for their skills at the plate. He had a .973 fielding percentage behind the plate, and he finished in the top five for caught-stealing percentage three times. He spent five seasons in Boston and four in the Bronx.

PEE WEE WANNIGER

With only two seasons in the majors with three teams, Wanniger is a minor footnote in the rivalry. He does have the distinction of replacing Everett Scott at shortstop, who at that time had the longest streak of consecutively played games in baseball at 1,307. Then the roles became reversed as Lou Gehrig came in as a pinch-hitter for Wanniger and played 2,130 in a row, the new major league record until Cal Ripken broke it in 1995. In addition to the BoSox and Yankees he played for the Cincinnati Reds for half a season.

Yankees Year

Year	Age	G	AB	R	H	2B	3B	HR	RBI	SB	CS	BB	SO	BA	OBP	SLG	OPS	OPS+	TB	SH
1925	22	117	403	35	95	13	6	1	22	3	5	11	34	.236	.256	.305	.561	43	123	13

Red Sox Year

Year	Age	G	AB	R	H	2B	3B	HR	RBI	SB	CS	BB	SO	BA	OBP	SLG	OPS	OPS+	TB	SH
1927	24	18	60	4	12	0	0	0	1	2	4	6	2	.200	.284	.200	.484	29	12	0

Which Team Fared Better?

The Yankees definitely got the better of Wanniger, who had nearly six times the at-bats for them. In those 403 at-bats he produced 95 hits, 13 doubles, scored 35 runs, and had 22 RBIs. In his 60 at-bats with the Red Sox he had 12 hits, all singles; scored only four runs; and had a single RBI. To sum up the vast difference between the two teams one has only to look at the total bases: New York 123, Boston 12.

BILL WERBER

Fleet of foot, Werber led the league in stolen bases three times and scored 100 or more runs in a season three times in his 11-year career. He came up with the Yankees, playing third, and then went to Boston for four years before spending some time with the Athletics, the Reds, and finally the Giants. He finished his career with 215 stolen bases and scored 875 runs.

Yankees Years

Year	Age	G	AB	R	H	2B	3B	HR	RBI	SB	CS	BB	SO	BA	OBP	SLG	OPS	OPS+	TB	SH
1930	22	4	14	5	4	0	0	0	2	0	0	3	1	.286	.412	.286	.697	83	4	0
1933	25	3	2	0	0	0	0	0	0	0	0	0	0	.000	.000	.000	.000	-100	0	0
Totals		7	16	5	4	0	0	0	2	0	0	3	1	.250	.368	.250	.618	64	4	0

Red Sox Years

Year	Age	G	AB	R	H	2B	3B	HR	RBI	SB	CS	BB	SO	BA	OBP	SLG	OPS	OPS+	TB	SH
1933	25	108	425	64	110	30	6	3	39	15	5	33	39	.259	.312	.379	.691	81	161	13
1934	26	152	623	129	200	41	10	11	67	40	15	77	37	.321	.397	.472	.868	120	294	15
1935	27	124	462	84	118	30	3	14	61	29	7	69	41	.255	.357	.424	.781	97	196	14
1936	28	145	535	89	147	29	6	10	67	23	13	89	37	.275	.383	.407	.790	90	218	11
Totals		529	2,045	366	575	130	25	38	234	107	40	268	154	.281	.367	.425	.792	99	869	53

Which Team Fared Better?

His best overall season was 1934, spent with the Red Sox. That year he had 200 hits, batted .321, led the league in stolen bases with 40, had 77 walks, 11 home runs, and an OBP of nearly .400. When he was playing with the Yankees, he was still trying to establish himself as a major leaguer, and he saw only 16 at-bats over two seasons, producing only 4 hits. With the Red Sox he received much more playing time, getting 2,045 at-bats and 575 hits. There were actually four teams Werber fared better with than with the Yankees, but he played his very best with the Red Sox.

3. The Trade That Almost Happened
The Integration Era (1942–1960)

Nineteen forty-seven was one of the most significant years in baseball history. Although it was never an official rule, for decades there had been a gentlemen's agreement among owners not to allow blacks to play for their teams. Branch Rickey decided that there was an untapped resource out there and convinced Jackie Robinson to be the first to take the step that would integrate baseball. On April 15th of that year, Robinson stood in at first base for the Brooklyn Dodgers, the first black player to play major league baseball since the 1880s. Less than three months later, on July 5, Larry Doby became the first African American to play in the American League.

Both the Yankees and the Red Sox were slow to jump on this new trend. The Yankees did not have their first black player until eight years later, when Elston Howard became their backup catcher and sometime outfielder. Boston, a town notorious for its treatment of African Americans, was the last team in baseball to integrate. They did so 12 years after Robinson, bringing in Pumpsie Green in July of 1958. If the late move to integrate made the Red Sox more competitive—they finished second or third seven times during this period—it did not allow them to overtake the Yankees, who won eight World Series titles.

The reason for the good fortunes of both clubs, however, could be found in two other players. Joe DiMaggio, the Yankee Clipper, was the stalwart for the pinstripers. He was league MVP in 1947 and runner-up the following year. Even playing only half a season in 1949, he still came in 12th in the MVP balloting. Boston's Ted Williams was the MVP in 1946 and 1949, coming in second in 1947 and 1957. Without these two greats, the teams would not have enjoyed the success they had during this time. But here's an interesting question: Would they have seen the same success had the players switched teams?

The 1947 season almost became important for another reason. That was the year Tom Yawkey, owner of the Red Sox, and Dan Topping, who owned the Yankees, met in Toots Shors' famous New York saloon and worked out a oral agreement to swap Williams and DiMaggio. The next day, before they could put anything in writing, Yawkey decided that a straight-up trade was not fair for his team. He wanted another player thrown into the deal, a rookie left fielder who had not done much for the Yankees as of yet. This left fielder was Yogi Berra, who would go on to win 10 championships with the Yankees and be elected to the Baseball Hall of Fame. Topping thought this deal was too rich for his blood and decided to pass on Williams.

Putting aside the notion of having both DiMaggio and Berra in Boston, one wonders how the careers of these two legends might have changed if DiMaggio played for the Red Sox and Williams for the Yankees. The obvious benefit to both of their careers is that Yankee Stadium had that short porch in right field, a left-handed power hitter's delight. And at Fenway, home of the Red Sox, there is the Green Monster, a mere 310 feet from home plate. Imagine how much wall ball DiMaggio, a hard-hitting right-handed batter, would have played had he spent most of his games at Fenway Park.

Using statistics, we can speculate about the how much the two sluggers might have added to their numbers playing in parks more friendly to the side of the plate they stood on. Here are DiMaggio's and Williams's numbers as they stand.

Joe DiMaggio

G	AB	R	H	2B	3B	HR	RBI	SB	CS	BB	SO	BA	OBP	SLG	OPS	OPS+	TB	SH
1,736	6,821	1,390	2,214	389	131	361	1,537	30	9	790	369	.325	.398	.579	.977	155	3,948	14

Ted Williams

G	AB	R	H	2B	3B	HR	RBI	SB	CS	BB	SO	BA	OBP	SLG	OPS	OPS+	TB	SH
2,292	7,706	1,798	2,564	525	71	521	1,839	24	17	2,021	709	.344	.482	.634	1.116	190	4,884	5

Williams did play six seasons longer than DiMaggio, and both of them had the prime years of their careers interrupted by military service. Comparing their home run totals, we find that DiMaggio hit 361 while Williams hit 521. Out of those 361 homers DiMaggio hit, 148 of them, 41 percent, came at Yankee Stadium. He had 3,360 at-bats there over the course of his career, meaning he averaged a home run every 22–23 at-bats. On the road he had 3,461 at-bats and hit 213 home runs, for an average of a home run every 16 at-bats. It was clear DiMaggio was a more powerful hitter away from Yankee Stadium. None of the eight World Series home runs DiMaggio hit came at home. Similarly, of Williams's 521 home runs, 248 were launched at Fenway, 273 on the road. With 3,887 at-bats at home, that works out to a home run every 15–16 times to the plate. His away ratio was every 14 at-bats. Clearly, both of these players were better home-run hitters outside of their home park. So what would have happened if DiMaggio had played in Fenway and Williams at Yankee Stadium?

With the short porch in right field at the Stadium, it is safe to assume that Williams's non-Fenway home-run rate (again, one for every 14 at-bats) would probably be even better. Let us say that he would hit a home run every 13 at-bats, which seems a conservative estimate. From 1947 through the rest of his career, Williams hit 356 home runs; if we assume half of those were on the road and half at home (even though he was slightly better away), he would have hit 178 at his home park. In Yankee Stadium, using our one-homer-per-13-at-bats figure, that number would increase to 195, or nearly 20 more home runs over the rest of his career, putting him around 540. Williams is currently tied for 18th on the all-time career home runs. Playing in Yankee Stadium in the latter half of his career could have moved him up to 16th on the list, putting him ahead of Mickey Mantle.

In 476 at-bats at Fenway Park, DiMaggio hit 29 home runs. That is one for every 16 at-bats. If we take his total at-bats from 1947 until the end of his career, that would be 2,340 at-bats. If we assume he would continue homering at that pace at Fenway—for the sake of our thought experiment, we'll ignore the fact that he would have been aging through the last part of his career—that means DiMaggio would have hit 146 home runs during this time rather than the 117 he actually did. That is an even bigger increase than Williams. What major leaguer wouldn't want 30 home runs tacked on to his career totals? When you look at doubles, something a wall 310 feet away to a right-handed hitter would give a boost to, DiMaggio hit

126 doubles post–1946. Surely that number, too, would have increased if half of his games were played at Fenway.

Another interesting what-if to consider is that if DiMaggio had gone to the Red Sox, he would have played the outfield with his brother, Dom DiMaggio, who was a Boston stalwart for 11 seasons. Might that fact have inspired him to extend his career another year or two? Might he have enjoyed an even stronger finish to that career? There is the brother factor to consider—in this case, whether home run output increases when playing on the same team as your brother because of the good-natured rivalry. After Justin Upton was traded to the Atlanta Braves in 2013 and played in the same outfield as his brother, Melvin (then called "B.J."), he averaged 27 home runs a year. In his five full seasons with the Arizona Diamondbacks he averaged only 21. Roberto Alomar likewise had his highest home-run total in 1999, while playing with his brother Sandy on the Cleveland Indians. Hank Aaron's top two seasons of home runs, 47 in 1971 and 45 in 1962, came while playing with his brother Tommie. Playing in the same outfield with brother Who knows? Dom might have inspired Joe to hit a few more.

Also intriguing is that Williams finally would have gotten the World Series ring that eluded him his entire career. From 1947 to 1960 the Yankees won eight world championships, five in a row from 1949–1953. Surely Williams would have propelled the Yankees to similar greatness and maybe even won a few more. But alas, he will go down in history as one of the greatest players never to have won a World Series ring.

Had the trade actually taken place, there is no denying that the home parks these two gentlemen played in hurt their overall careers and they would have been better off in a park built to their strengths. Even nowadays right-handers love to play wall ball at Fenway Park while left-handers wonder what playing most of their games at Yankee Stadium might do for their career home run numbers.

Players Who Spent Time with Both Teams, 1942–1960

Lou Berberet

Known as a defensive catcher who once went three seasons without an error, Berberet played for four teams over his seven seasons on a big league roster. After serving time with the military in Korea, he started with the Yankees but had only 10 at-bats over two seasons. Then he went to the Washington Senators, where he racked up the bulk of his career at-bats before being traded to Boston mid-way through the 1958 season. He finished out his last two years for the Detroit Tigers, compiling a .230 lifetime batting average with 31 home runs and 153 RBIs. He is one of only four catchers to play an entire season with a 1.000 fielding percentage.

Yankees Years

Year	Age	G	AB	R	H	2B	3B	HR	RBI	SB	CS	BB	SO	BA	OBP	SLG	OPS	OPS+	TB	SH
1954	24	5	5	1	2	0	0	0	3	0	0	1	1	.400	.500	.400	.900	153	2	0
1955	25	2	5	1	2	0	0	0	2	0	0	1	0	.400	.500	.400	.900	146	2	0
Totals		7	10	2	4	0	0	0	5	0	0	2	1	.400	.500	.400	.900	150	4	0

Red Sox Year

Year	Age	G	AB	R	H	2B	3B	HR	RBI	SB	CS	BB	SO	BA	OBP	SLG	OPS	OPS+	TB	SH
1958	28	57	167	11	35	5	3	2	18	0	2	31	32	.210	.337	.311	.648	76	52	1

Which Team Fared Better?

He was just getting his feet wet as a major league player in his time spent with the Yankees. Accumulating five at-bats in each of the two seasons he played with them, he managed 5 RBIs, but that presents too small a sample size from which to draw any meaningful conclusions about how he might have performed over the course of a full season. He played for a shorter period with Boston but saw more playing time, making it into 57 games and batting 167 times after being acquired from the Senators. He batted only .210, but what he provided for the Red Sox was a reliable defensive back-up to their regular catcher, Sammy White. That gives them the edge.

HAL BROWN

A knuckleballer with great control, Brown spent 14 years playing for five different teams, including a career-high eight seasons with Baltimore. He came up with the Chicago White Sox before going to Boston for three years. After his long stop with Baltimore, he went to the Yankees briefly before ending his career with the Houston Colt .45s. In his career he had 85 wins and 92 losses with a 3.81 ERA. His finest season came as an Oriole in 1960. He went 12–5 and led the league in both WHIP with a 1.113 and walks per nine innings at 1.25. His career walks per nine innings was a solid 2.1, which is quite good considering how difficult it is to control a knuckleball. Consider the BB/9 for other notable knuckleballers: Phil Niekro, 3.0; Hoyt Wilhelm, 3.1; Tim Wakefield, 3.4; and Charlie Hough, 3.9.

Red Sox Years

Year	Age	W	L	%	ERA	G	GS	CG	SV	IP	H	R	HR	BB	SO	ERA+	WHIP	H/9	BB/9	SO/9	SO/BB
1953	28	11	6	.647	4.65	30	25	6	0	166.1	177	94	16	57	62	89	1.407	9.6	3.1	3.4	1.09
1954	29	1	8	.111	4.12	40	5	1	0	118.0	126	64	6	41	66	101	1.415	9.6	3.1	5.0	1.61
1955	30	1	0	1.000	2.25	2	0	0	0	4.0	2	1	0	2	2	209	1.000	4.5	4.5	4.5	1.00
Totals		13	14	.481	4.40	72	30	7	0	288.1	305	159	22	100	130	95	1.405	9.5	3.1	4.1	1.30

Yankees Year

Year	Age	W	L	%	ERA	G	GS	CG	SV	IP	H	R	HR	BB	SO	ERA+	WHIP	H/9	BB/9	SO/9	SO/BB
1962	37	0	1	.000	6.75	2	1	0	0	6.2	9	10	3	2	2	59	1.650	12.2	2.7	2.7	1.00

Which Team Fared Better?

While with Boston, Brown served as both a starter and a reliever. In 1953 he was mostly a starter, compiling an 11–6 record but with a 4.65 ERA (league average was 3.99). His ERA in 1954 was better as a reliever at 4.12 (league average, 3.72), but he had a 1–8 record. His best ERA was 2.25, for the 1955 season, but he pitched in only two games, as a reliever. Despite his inconsistencies with the Red Sox, he simply did not spend much time with the Yankees. Appearing in only two games, he gave up nine hits, 10 runs, and five earned runs. Not a good line. The Red Sox win by default.

TEX CLEVENGER

This bushy-eye-browed pitcher made his debut with the Red Sox as a 21-year-old. After spending the following season, 1955, in the minors again, he was traded to Washington. He spent five years there, compiling a 29–31 record. He was taken by the Los Angeles Angels in the expansion draft of 1960 but soon thereafter was traded to the Bronx, where he spent his last two seasons.

Red Sox Year

Year	Age	W	L	%	ERA	G	GS	CG	SV	IP	H	R	HR	BB	SO	ERA+	WHIP	H/9	BB/9	SO/9	SO/BB
1954	21	2	4	.333	4.79	23	8	1	0	67.2	67	42	9	29	43	87	1.419	8.9	3.9	5.7	1.48

Yankees Years

Year	Age	W	L	%	ERA	G	GS	CG	SV	IP	H	R	HR	BB	SO	ERA+	WHIP	H/9	BB/9	SO/9	SO/BB
1961	28	1	1	.500	4.83	21	0	0	0	31.2	35	20	3	21	14	78	1.768	9.9	6.0	4.0	0.67
1962	29	2	0	1.000	2.84	21	0	0	0	38.0	36	14	3	17	11	134	1.395	8.5	4.0	2.6	0.65
Totals		3	1	.750	3.75	42	0	0	0	69.2	71	34	6	38	25	101	1.565	9.2	4.9	3.2	0.66

Which Team Fared Better?

The Red Sox used Clevenger as a starter and managed to get 67.2 innings from him in one season. The Yankees used him as a reliever and got 69.2 innings in two seasons. He faced a similar number of batters with both teams. His ERA with the Yankees (3.75) was lower than it was for the Red Sox (4.79); his WHIP with the Red Sox was a little lower (1.419) than it was with the Yankees (1.565). Had Clevenger carried more of an innings load as a Red Sox starter, that fact might have outweighed any modest improvement in his performance with the Yankees. But since the Bronx team got more innings and even a slightly better ERA+ out of him, they receive the nod.

RANDY GUMPERT

Starting his career playing three seasons for the Philadelphia Athletics, Gumpert then spent some time in the Yankees minor league system before joining the Coast Guard during World War II. After a seven-year absence from the majors, he played for the Yankees for three seasons before being traded to the Chicago White Sox. He played four years with the White Sox, and he was one of their All-Stars in 1951. He split time between the Red Sox and the Washington Senators in his final season.

Yankees Years

Year	Age	W	L	%	ERA	G	GS	CG	SV	IP	H	R	HR	BB	SO	ERA+	WHIP	H/9	BB/9	SO/9	SO/BB
1946	28	11	3	.786	2.31	33	12	4	1	132.2	113	44	8	32	63	149	1.093	7.7	2.2	4.3	1.97
1947	29	4	1	.800	5.43	24	6	2	0	56.1	71	36	4	28	25	65	1.757	11.3	4.5	4.0	0.89
1948	30	1	0	1.000	2.88	15	0	0	0	25.0	27	10	0	6	12	143	1.320	9.7	2.2	4.3	2.00
Totals		16	4	.800	3.20	72	18	6	1	214.0	211	90	12	66	100	111	1.294	8.9	2.8	4.2	1.52

Red Sox Year

Year	Age	W	L	%	ERA	G	GS	CG	SV	IP	H	R	HR	BB	SO	ERA+	WHIP	H/9	BB/9	SO/9	SO/BB
1952	34	1	0	1.000	4.12	10	1	0	1	19.2	15	11	1	5	6	97	1.017	6.9	2.3	2.7	1.20

Which Team Fared Better?

This one is a no-brainer. Gumpert had a 16–4 record with the Yankees over three seasons and pitched only 19 innings for the Red Sox in his half-season at Fenway. Making the decision easier, or at least more poetic, is the fact that as a pitcher for the White Sox, he threw Mickey Mantle his first career home run ball. He also managed for the Yankees minor league teams and served over twenty years as a scout for them.

KEN HOLCOMBE

Holcombe played in the majors intermittently, coming up with the Yankees in 1945, then disappearing until 1948, when he popped up with the Cincinnati Reds. He was shipped back to the minors again in 1949 before turning up in 1950 with the Chicago White Sox. The four-year stretch that followed was his longest stint in the majors, as he played for the White Sox, Browns, and the Red Sox before a chronic bursitis problem forced him to retire. He finished with an unimpressive 18–32 career record but did turn in a solid season in 1951, throwing 12 complete games and posting a respectable 3.78 ERA (107 ERA+).

Yankees Year

Year	Age	W	L	%	ERA	G	GS	CG	SV	IP	H	R	HR	BB	SO	ERA+	WHIP	H/9	BB/9	SO/9	SO/BB
1945	26	3	3	.500	1.79	23	2	0	0	55.1	43	19	2	27	20	195	1.265	7.0	4.4	3.3	0.74

Red Sox Year

Year	Age	W	L	%	ERA	G	GS	CG	SV	IP	H	R	HR	BB	SO	ERA+	WHIP	H/9	BB/9	SO/9	SO/BB
1953	34	1	0	1.000	6.00	3	0	0	1	6.0	9	4	0	3	1	74	2.000	13.5	4.5	1.5	0.33

Which Team Fared Better?

Although he went back and forth between starting and relieving, he served mostly as a reliever for both teams. He had a pretty decent rookie season with the Yankees, posting a 1.79 ERA in 55.1 innings of work. His WHIP was a better-than-league-average 1.265, although he did walk more than he struck out. He appeared in only three games for the Red Sox, and by that time he was 34, not the ideal age for a pitcher. He gave up nine hits and four runs in just six innings of work. The Yankees have this one.

ELSTON HOWARD

Both the Yankees and the Red Sox were late to the game in signing black players for their teams. Elston Howard was the first African American to play for the Yankees—and what a first he was. Howard played 13 years for New York, earning nine All-Star nods, claiming the league MVP Award in 1963, and catching in ten World Series. He was the backbone for the club during a good decade stretch and was shocked when the Yankees traded him to the Red Sox in 1967. He even considered retirement rather than playing for the enemy. He would ultimately suit up for Boston, playing his last year and a half with the Red Sox, but never recaptured his offensive stroke there. Howard nevertheless buoyed the pitching staff with his defensive skills and helped the Sox capture the 1967 pennant.

Yankees Years

Year	Age	G	AB	R	H	2B	3B	HR	RBI	SB	CS	BB	SO	BA	OBP	SLG	OPS	OPS+	TB	SH
1955	26	97	279	33	81	8	7	10	43	0	0	20	36	.290	.336	.477	.812	118	133	1
1956	27	98	290	35	76	8	3	5	34	0	1	21	30	.262	.312	.362	.674	80	105	2
1957	28	110	356	33	90	13	4	8	44	2	5	16	43	.253	.283	.379	.663	81	135	6
1958	29	103	376	45	118	19	5	11	66	1	1	22	60	.314	.348	.479	.827	130	180	4
1959	30	125	443	59	121	24	6	18	73	0	1	20	57	.273	.306	.476	.783	116	211	4
1960	31	107	323	29	79	11	3	6	39	3	0	28	43	.245	.298	.353	.651	80	114	2
1961	32	129	446	64	155	17	5	21	77	0	3	28	65	.348	.387	.549	.936	153	245	1
1962	33	136	494	63	138	23	5	21	91	1	1	31	76	.279	.318	.474	.791	112	234	3
1963	34	135	487	75	140	21	6	28	85	0	0	35	68	.287	.342	.526	.869	141	257	1
1964	35	150	550	63	172	27	3	15	84	1	1	48	73	.313	.371	.455	.825	127	250	0
1965	36	110	391	38	91	15	1	9	45	0	0	24	65	.233	.278	.345	.623	77	135	1
1966	37	126	410	38	105	19	2	6	35	0	0	37	65	.256	.317	.356	.673	98	146	0
1967	38	66	199	13	39	6	0	3	17	0	0	12	36	.196	.247	.271	.518	57	54	1
Totals		1,492	5,044	588	1,405	211	50	161	733	8	13	342	717	.279	.324	.436	.760	110	2,199	26

Red Sox Years

Year	Age	G	AB	R	H	2B	3B	HR	RBI	SB	CS	BB	SO	BA	OBP	SLG	OPS	OPS+	TB	SH
1967	38	42	116	9	17	3	0	1	11	0	0	9	24	.147	.211	.198	.409	17	23	1
1968	39	71	203	22	49	4	0	5	18	1	1	22	45	.241	.317	.335	.652	93	68	2
Totals		113	319	31	66	7	0	6	29	1	1	31	69	.207	.279	.285	.564	65	91	3

Which Team Fared Better?

Talk about a no-brainer. Elston had over 5,000 at-bats with the Yankees, gathering 733 RBIs, 1,405 hits, and 161 home runs. He was a legendary catcher on a team full of legendary catchers, including Dickey, Berra, Munson, and Posada. After his playing days, he spent another ten years with the team as their first-base coach. The Yankees retired his number 32 in 1984. By the time he went to the Red Sox he was nearly 40 and certainly not the same player who won four World Series with the Yankees. Boston managed to squeeze 319 at-bats out of him, but he batted .207, a far cry from the .279 mark he had with the Yankees. Although the rivalry was not as intense in those days, it must have been difficult for Elston to go and play for the Red Sox. He was, however, a consummate professional, even though his contributions to Boston paled alongside those made to the Yankees.

The only two teams Elston Howard played for were the Yankees and Red Sox, but he will forever be remembered as a Yankee. Many baseball pundits rate Howard in the top five catchers in Yankees history—quite an accomplishment considering how many great catchers the Yankees have produced. He is widely regarded as one of the best catchers not in the Hall of Fame (courtesy Arnie Lee photography).

JACKIE JENSEN

A neat thing about researching players from the past is that occasionally you run across the equivalent of a shiny penny that has fallen to the back of the drawer. Jackie Jensen was a right fielder for eleven years in the major leagues and compiled pretty good numbers, including 1,463 hits, 199 home runs, 929 RBIs, and 143 stolen bases. This guy would have been great to have on a fantasy league if such things existed back then. He was a three-time All-Star, league MVP, Gold Glove winner, World Series champion, and three-time league leader in RBIs. His career came to an end because of a fear of flying. As the league expanded to the West Coast, air travel became a necessity for teams, and Jensen would have panic attacks at the airport. He decided not to play in 1960 for this reason but was eventually coaxed back for 1961, which was a sub-par season by his standards. He decided to retire for good rather than to endure the stress. One wonders what might have happened with his career had he been able to continue playing past age 34.

Yankees Years

Year	Age	G	AB	R	H	2B	3B	HR	RBI	SB	CS	BB	SO	BA	OBP	SLG	OPS	OPS+	TB	SH
1950	23	45	70	13	12	2	2	1	5	4	0	7	8	.171	.247	.300	.547	41	21	1
1951	24	56	168	30	50	8	1	8	25	8	2	18	18	.298	.369	.500	.869	137	84	1
1952	25	7	19	3	2	1	1	0	2	1	0	4	4	.105	.261	.263	.524	50	5	0
Totals		108	257	46	64	11	4	9	32	13	2	29	30	.249	.328	.428	.756	104	110	2

Red Sox Years

Year	Age	G	AB	R	H	2B	3B	HR	RBI	SB	CS	BB	SO	BA	OBP	SLG	OPS	OPS+	TB	SH
1954	27	152	580	92	160	25	7	25	117	22	7	79	52	.276	.359	.472	.831	117	274	1
1955	28	152	574	95	158	27	6	26	116	16	7	89	63	.275	.369	.479	.848	119	275	3
1956	29	151	578	80	182	23	11	20	97	11	3	89	43	.315	.405	.497	.901	127	287	1
1957	30	145	544	82	153	29	2	23	103	8	5	75	66	.281	.367	.469	.836	122	255	1
1958	31	154	548	83	157	31	0	35	122	9	4	99	65	.286	.396	.535	.931	148	293	1
1959	32	148	535	101	148	31	0	28	112	20	5	88	67	.277	.372	.492	.863	132	263	1
1961	34	137	498	64	131	21	2	13	66	9	8	66	69	.263	.350	.392	.742	98	195	2
Totals		1,039	3,857	597	1,089	187	28	170	733	95	39	585	425	.282	.374	.478	.852	123	1,842	10

Which Team Fared Better?

The Yankees didn't quite know what they had, using Jensen only occasionally (257 at-bats in three seasons, 108 games), mostly as a backup to DiMaggio. When Mickey Mantle came along, they figured they no longer needed him. By the time Jensen got to Boston, after a nearly two-years stop in Washington, he was a genuine star. With the Red Sox, he led the league in RBIs and sacrifice flies three times, in stolen bases once, and in triples once. He was in the top 20 for MVP balloting five of the seven years he played in Beantown, winning it in 1958. He did not contribute much to the actual rivalry, however—if only because the Red Sox never finishing high enough to pose much of a threat. Nevertheless, Jensen remains one of those unheralded players whose accomplishments should not be lost in time.

JACK KRAMER

No, this isn't the Jack Kramer who was the number one player in the world in tennis. This Jack Kramer was instead a pitcher for 12 seasons, playing for the St. Louis Browns for a majority of his career but spending time as well with the New York Giants, Red Sox, and Yankees. He was an All-Star twice for the lowly Browns, despite 13–11 and 11–16 records those two seasons. (They were the Browns, after all; a winning record was no doubt hard to maintain.) Over the course of his career he had a 95–103 record with a 4.24 ERA, and his best season might have been 1944, when the Browns surprised everyone by winning the pennant and Kramer went 17–13 with an impressive 2.49 ERA, 1.198 WHIP, and 18 complete games. He finished 16th in the MVP balloting that year.

Red Sox Years

Year	Age	W	L	%	ERA	G	GS	CG	SV	IP	H	R	HR	BB	SO	ERA+	WHIP	H/9	BB/9	SO/9	SO/BB
1948	30	18	5	.783	4.35	29	29	14	0	205.0	233	104	12	64	72	101	1.449	10.2	2.8	3.2	1.13
1949	31	6	8	.429	5.16	21	18	7	1	111.2	126	70	8	49	24	85	1.567	10.2	3.9	1.9	0.49
Totals		24	13	.649	4.63	50	47	21	1	316.2	359	174	20	113	96	94	1.491	10.2	3.2	2.7	0.85

Yankees Year

Year	Age	W	L	%	ERA	G	GS	CG	SV	IP	H	R	HR	BB	SO	ERA+	WHIP	H/9	BB/9	SO/9	SO/BB
1951	33	1	3	.250	4.65	19	3	0	0	40.2	46	27	1	21	15	83	1.648	10.2	4.6	3.3	0.71

Which Team Fared Better?

One of Kramer's better seasons came while playing for Boston. In the 1948 season he went 18–5, with five of his wins coming against the Yankees, and led the league in winning percentage. Over two seasons for the Red Sox he had 24 wins and 13 losses, making a solid contribution to two second-place teams. He played with the Yankees his final season, going 1–3 as a starter and reliever. The Yankees did not think him valuable enough to keep around for the World Series, which they won over the New York Giants, the other team Kramer played for that season.

MICKEY McDERMOTT

In 12 years as a major league pitcher, McDermott assembled a 69–69 record for six teams. He spent the most time with the Red Sox, for whom he played six years. He also played for the Washington Senators, Kansas City Athletics (twice), St. Louis Cardinals, and the Detroit Tigers. He acted as both a starter and a reliever and won a World Series ring with the 1956 Yankees. A colorful character, he was also lucky, apparently: In 1991, he won $7 million dollars in the Arizona lottery. A little more than a decade later, mere months before his death in August 2003, he published a memoir about his career and issues with drinking. The title? *A Funny Thing Happened on the Way to Cooperstown*.

Red Sox Years

Year	Age	W	L	%	ERA	G	GS	CG	SV	IP	H	R	HR	BB	SO	ERA+	WHIP	H/9	BB/9	SO/9	SO/BB
1948	19	0	0		6.17	7	0	0	0	23.1	16	18	2	35	17	72	2.186	6.2	13.5	6.6	0.49
1949	20	5	4	.556	4.05	12	12	6	0	80.0	63	37	5	52	50	108	1.438	7.1	5.9	5.6	0.96
1950	21	7	3	.700	5.19	38	15	4	5	130.0	119	80	8	124	96	95	1.869	8.2	8.6	6.6	0.77
1951	22	8	8	.500	3.35	34	19	9	3	172.0	141	72	9	92	127	133	1.355	7.4	4.8	6.6	1.38
1952	23	10	9	.526	3.72	30	21	7	0	162.0	139	70	14	92	117	106	1.426	7.7	5.1	6.5	1.27
1953	24	18	10	.643	3.01	32	30	8	0	206.1	169	82	9	109	92	138	1.347	7.4	4.8	4.0	0.84
Totals		48	34	.585	3.80	153	97	34	8	773.2	647	359	47	504	499	114	1.488	7.5	5.9	5.8	0.99

Yankees Year

Year	Age	W	L	%	ERA	G	GS	CG	SV	IP	H	R	HR	BB	SO	ERA+	WHIP	H/9	BB/9	SO/9	SO/BB
1956	27	2	6	.250	4.24	23	9	1	0	87.0	85	46	10	47	38	92	1.517	8.8	4.9	3.9	0.81

Which Team Fared Better?

In six seasons with Boston, McDermott won 48 and lost 34, by far the best record he compiled for any team. His best year was 1953, when he went 18–10 for the Red Sox and pitched a career-high 206.1 innings. He also had a career-low ERA that season at 3.01, good for sixth in the league. In addition, Boston was able to trade McDermott to the Senators for Jackie Jensen, who turned out to be a good player for the Red Sox. In his lone season for the Yankees, McDermott went 2–6 with a 4.24 ERA. He did win a World Series with the Yankees but pitched in only one game, going three innings. Boston got more out of him.

JIM McDONALD

A right-handed pitcher who played for nine years and four different teams, McDonald bookended his career with the Sox, starting with the Red Sox and finishing with the White Sox. In between he also played for the Yankees, St. Louis Browns, and Baltimore Orioles. He was used primarily as the long reliever, meaning he would get a spot start here and there, but also served as a middle reliever in the bullpen. He did win a world championship in 1953 with the Yankees, winning his one start against Brooklyn.

Red Sox Year

Year	Age	W	L	%	ERA	G	GS	CG	SV	IP	H	R	HR	BB	SO	ERA+	WHIP	H/9	BB/9	SO/9	SO/BB
1950	23	1	0	1.000	3.79	9	0	0	0	19.0	23	9	1	10	5	133	1.737	10.9	4.7	2.4	0.50

Yankees Years

Year	Age	W	L	%	ERA	G	GS	CG	SV	IP	H	R	HR	BB	SO	ERA+	WHIP	H/9	BB/9	SO/9	SO/BB
1952	25	3	4	.429	3.50	26	5	1	0	69.1	71	31	1	40	20	95	1.601	9.2	5.2	2.6	0.50
1953	26	9	7	.563	3.82	27	18	6	0	129.2	128	64	4	39	43	97	1.288	8.9	2.7	3.0	1.10
1954	27	4	1	.800	3.17	16	10	3	0	71.0	54	28	3	45	20	110	1.394	6.8	5.7	2.5	0.44
Totals		**16**	**12**	**.571**	**3.57**	**69**	**33**	**10**	**0**	**270.0**	**253**	**123**	**8**	**124**	**83**	**99**	**1.396**	**8.4**	**4.1**	**2.8**	**0.67**

Which Team Fared Better?

The Yankees and Red Sox were the only two teams McDonald had winning records with, but they are vastly different winning records. He appeared in only nine games for the Red Sox, none of which he started. In his 19 innings pitched for them he had a 3.79 ERA. He appeared in 69 games for the Yankees, going 16–12 over three seasons. Half of those games were starts and he had a 3.57 ERA. His WHIP was significantly better for the Yankees (1.396) than with Boston (1.737). McDonald was also part of a 17-player trade before the 1955 season that brought the Yankees seven players, one of whom was Don Larsen, who went 45–24 for the Yankees and threw a perfect game in the 1956 World Series. To quote Yankees radio broadcaster John Sterling, "Ballgame! Yankees win! Thhhhheeeeee Yankees *win*!"

JOHNNY MURPHY

Playing for only two teams in his career, Murphy was a relief pitcher who led the league in saves four years out of the 13 he pitched and led the league in wins by a relief pitcher seven times. He spent 12 years playing for the Yankees, for whom he was a three-time All-Star. He also won seven World Series with New York. He finished his career with a 93–53 record and a 3.50 ERA (117 ERA+). He stayed in baseball after retiring and was the general manager of the 1969 New York Mets.

Yankees Years

Year	Age	W	L	%	ERA	G	GS	CG	SV	IP	H	R	HR	BB	SO	ERA+	WHIP	H/9	BB/9	SO/9	SO/BB
1932	23	0	0		16.20	2	0	0	0	3.1	7	6	0	3	2	28	3.000	18.9	8.1	5.4	0.67
1934	25	14	10	.583	3.12	40	20	10	4	207.2	193	79	11	76	70	131	1.295	8.4	3.3	3.0	0.92
1935	26	10	5	.667	4.08	40	8	4	5	117.0	110	67	7	55	28	100	1.410	8.5	4.2	2.2	0.51
1936	27	9	3	.750	3.38	27	5	2	5	88.0	90	38	5	36	34	138	1.432	9.2	3.7	3.5	0.94
1937	28	13	4	.765	4.17	39	4	0	10	110.0	121	59	7	50	36	108	1.555	9.9	4.1	2.9	0.72
1938	29	8	2	.800	4.24	32	2	1	11	91.1	90	47	5	41	43	108	1.434	8.9	4.0	4.2	1.05
1939	30	3	6	.333	4.40	38	0	0	19	61.1	57	33	2	28	30	99	1.386	8.4	4.1	4.4	1.07
1940	31	8	4	.667	3.69	35	1	0	9	63.1	58	27	5	15	23	110	1.153	8.2	2.1	3.3	1.53
1941	32	8	3	.727	1.98	35	0	0	15	77.1	68	20	1	40	29	200	1.397	7.9	4.7	3.4	0.73
1942	33	4	10	.286	3.41	31	0	0	11	58.0	66	27	2	23	24	101	1.534	10.2	3.6	3.7	1.04
1943	34	12	4	.750	2.51	37	0	0	8	68.0	44	22	2	30	31	129	1.088	5.8	4.0	4.1	1.03
1946	37	4	2	.667	3.40	27	0	0	7	45.0	40	22	4	19	19	102	1.311	8.0	3.8	3.8	1.00
Totals		93	53	.637	3.54	383	40	17	104	990.1	944	447	51	416	369	116	1.373	8.6	3.8	3.4	0.89

Red Sox Year

Year	Age	W	L	%	ERA	G	GS	CG	SV	IP	H	R	HR	BB	SO	ERA+	WHIP	H/9	BB/9	SO/9	SO/BB
1947	38	0	0		2.80	32	0	0	3	54.2	41	17	1	28	9	139	1.262	6.8	4.6	1.5	0.32

Which Team Fared Better?

Aside from two years spent in the military, Murphy was a steady reliever for the Yankees. Even though he appeared in 32 games for the Red Sox, he did not record a win or a loss, meaning his career numbers in those categories were amassed with the Yankees. His contributions after his career were in favor of the Red Sox, as he spent 13 seasons running the scouting and farm system for the BoSox. But our concern here is with the playing days, and the Yankees got far more out of him.

GUS NIARHOS

A catcher who played for nine years, he was a starter for the 1948 Yankees before a fella named Yogi Berra took over the catching duties. After that his playing time diminished, and he appeared in only one game in the 1950 season before being shipped off to the Chicago White Sox. After two years with the Pale Hose he spent two years with the Red Sox and another two years with the Philadelphia Phillies, his last team. Niarhos's career high in games played was 83, and he accumulated only 315 games played over the course of his career. He was a .252 hitter who had one career home run and only 59 RBIs. That means he averaged 7 RBIs a season.

Yankees Years

Year	Age	G	AB	R	H	2B	3B	HR	RBI	SB	CS	BB	SO	BA	OBP	SLG	OPS	OPS+	TB	SH
1946	25	37	40	11	9	1	1	0	2	1	0	11	2	.225	.392	.300	.692	94	12	0
1948	27	83	228	41	61	12	2	0	19	1	3	52	15	.268	.404	.338	.741	99	77	5
1949	28	32	43	7	12	2	1	0	6	0	0	13	8	.279	.456	.372	.828	120	16	0
1950	29	1	0	0	0	0	0	0	0	0	0	0	0						0	0
Totals		153	311	59	82	15	4	0	27	2	3	76	25	.264	.410	.338	.747	102	105	5

Red Sox Years

Year	Age	G	AB	R	H	2B	3B	HR	RBI	SB	CS	BB	SO	BA	OBP	SLG	OPS	OPS+	TB	SH
1952	31	29	58	4	6	0	0	0	4	0	0	12	9	.103	.268	.103	.371	3	6	1
1953	32	16	35	6	7	1	1	0	2	0	1	4	4	.200	.300	.286	.586	56	10	1
Totals		45	93	10	13	1	1	0	6	0	1	16	13	.140	.279	.172	.451	23	16	2

Which Team Fared Better?

The Yankees gave Niarhos far more plate appearances, 393, than did the Red Sox, who sent him to the plate 113 times over two seasons. His best year as a major leaguer came in 1948 while with New York: He got into 83 games, had 61 hits, scored 41 runs and knocked in 19, and walked 52 times. All of those totals were career bests. In 1949 he won a World Series with the Yankees, although he appeared in a single game and never got to bat. Despite this, the Yankees fared better.

BOB PORTERFIELD

This one-time All-Star played 12 seasons in the majors, spending time with the Yankees, Washington Senators, Red Sox, Pittsburgh Pirates, and the Chicago Cubs. He finished his pitching career with an 87 and 97 record, having his best season with the Senators where he led the league in wins with 22 as opposed to 10 losses. He also led the league in shutouts (9) and complete games (24) that season.

Yankees Years

Year	Age	W	L	%	ERA	G	GS	CG	SV	IP	H	R	HR	BB	SO	ERA+	WHIP	H/9	BB/9	SO/9	SO/BB
1948	24	5	3	.625	4.50	16	12	2	0	78.0	85	42	5	34	30	91	1.526	9.8	3.9	3.5	0.88
1949	25	2	5	.286	4.06	12	8	3	0	57.2	53	26	3	29	25	100	1.422	8.3	4.5	3.9	0.86
1950	26	1	1	.500	8.69	10	2	0	1	19.2	28	19	2	8	9	50	1.831	12.8	3.7	4.1	1.13
1951	27	0	0		15.00	2	0	0	0	3.0	5	6	0	3	2	29	2.667	15.0	9.0	6.0	0.67
Totals		8	9	.471	5.06	40	22	5	1	158.1	171	93	10	74	66	81	1.547	9.7	4.2	3.8	0.89

Red Sox Years

Year	Age	W	L	%	ERA	G	GS	CG	SV	IP	H	R	HR	BB	SO	ERA+	WHIP	H/9	BB/9	SO/9	SO/BB
1956	32	3	12	.200	5.14	25	18	4	0	126.0	127	82	21	64	53	90	1.516	9.1	4.6	3.8	0.83
1957	33	4	4	.500	4.05	28	9	3	1	102.1	107	54	8	30	28	99	1.339	9.4	2.6	2.5	0.93
1958	34	0	0		4.50	2	0	0	0	4.0	3	2	1	0	1	97	0.750	6.8	3.0	2.3	
Totals		7	16	.304	4.65	55	27	7	1	232.1	237	138	30	94	82	93	1.425	9.2	3.6	3.2	0.87

Which Team Fared Better?

Even though he was with the Yankees for four seasons, none of them was a full season (the most games he got into was 16 during his rookie season). He got into more games in three seasons with the Red Sox, 55, and pitched 74 more innings. Neither of his records was that impressive, 8–9 with New York, 7 and 16 with Boston, so we look at the ERA and WHIP to determine the winner here. He had a 5.06 ERA with the Yankees and a 1.547 WHIP, while posting a 4.65 ERA and 1.425 WHIP, giving the Red Sox the edge in this one.

BILL RENNA

In six years of major league ball, Renna played outfield for four different teams and came off the bench as a pinch hitter occasionally. After his rookie season with the Yankees he played his only full season with the Philadelphia Athletics before going to the Kansas City Athletics and Red Sox for two years each. His most productive season was the one full season he got in 1954, reaching career highs in games (123), home runs (13), RBIs (53), runs scored (52), doubles (15), and leading all right fielders with five double plays.

Yankees Years

Year	Age	G	AB	R	H	2B	3B	HR	RBI	SB	CS	BB	SO	BA	OBP	SLG	OPS	OPS+	TB	SH
1953	28	61	121	19	38	6	3	2	13	0	1	13	31	.314	.385	.463	.848	132	56	2

Red Sox Years

Year	Age	G	AB	R	H	2B	3B	HR	RBI	SB	CS	BB	SO	BA	OBP	SLG	OPS	OPS+	TB	SH
1958	33	39	56	5	15	5	0	4	18	0	0	6	14	.268	.339	.571	.910	140	32	0
1959	34	14	22	2	2	0	0	0	2	0	0	5	9	.091	.259	.091	.350	-1	2	0
Totals		53	78	7	17	5	0	4	20	0	0	11	23	.218	.315	.436	.751	100	34	0

Which Team Fared Better?

Renna had a pretty good rookie season with the Yankees, appearing in 61 games and managing a .314 average. The Yankees traded back for him in 1956 but he never reached the majors before being shipped off to Boston before the start of the 1957 season. He served mostly as a pinch hitter for the Red Sox, driving in an impressive 18 runs in 15 pinch hit appearances in 1958. Even though he had more at-bats with the Yankees (121), Renna made better use of his 78 at-bats with the Red Sox. He got 13 RBIs out of 38 hits for the Yankees but got 20 RBIs out of only 17 hits for Boston. Add to that his .571 slugging in the 1958 season for Boston and they got the better of Renna.

AARON ROBINSON

With 61 home runs, 272 RBIs, a .260 average, and 208 runs, catcher Aaron Robinson played for eight seasons with four different teams. When he started with the Yankees, Bill Dickey, the Hall of Famer, was just finishing his tenure as catcher. Yogi Berra, a future Hall of Famer, had not yet begun his time behind the dish, so Robinson acted as a stopgap between the two during the 1946 season. He found his role diminished as Berra began to establish himself as the starting catcher, and Robinson moved on to the Chicago White Sox. His most productive years came while playing for the Detroit Tigers, nearly equaling the numbers he put up with the Yankees in four years' time in only two and a half seasons. He became an August pickup with Boston in 1951, finishing out the last couple of months of the season.

Yankees Years

Year	Age	G	AB	R	H	2B	3B	HR	RBI	SB	CS	BB	SO	BA	OBP	SLG	OPS	OPS+	TB	SH
1943	28	1	1	0	0	0	0	0	0	0	0	0	1	.000	.000	.000	.000	-100	0	0
1945	30	50	160	19	45	6	1	8	24	0	0	21	23	.281	.368	.481	.849	142	77	1
1946	31	100	330	32	98	17	2	16	64	0	1	48	39	.297	.388	.506	.894	147	167	2
1947	32	82	252	23	68	11	5	5	36	0	1	40	26	.270	.370	.413	.783	118	104	0
Totals		233	743	74	211	34	8	29	124	0	2	109	89	.284	.377	.468	.845	136	348	3

Red Sox Years

Year	Age	G	AB	R	H	2B	3B	HR	RBI	SB	CS	BB	SO	BA	OBP	SLG	OPS	OPS+	TB	SH
1951	36	26	74	9	15	1	1	2	7	0	0	17	10	.203	.352	.324	.676	76	24	0

Which Team Fared Better?

His finest single season came while with the Yankees. Even though he was an All-Star for New York in 1947, this was based mostly on his good work during the 1946 season, batting .297, knocking in 64, and having a slugging percentage of .506. Even if you take his worst season with the Yankees, 1945 (.281 average, 24 RBIs, and 19 runs), this is way better than the numbers he put up in a few months for Boston (.203 average, 7 RBIs, 9 runs). He also has a world championship with the 1947 Yankees to boot.

BUDDY ROSAR

Apparently the Integration Era Yankees were very good at cultivating catchers because Rosar is one in a long line of pretty good major league catchers that started with the pinstripers; Robinson, Berberet, Niarhos, Berra, Howard. He started his career in 1939 with the Yankees, playing for four years before moving on the Cleveland Indians, Philadelphia Athletics, and Red Sox, spanning a 13-year career. He was a five-time All-Star, once as a Yankee and an Indian, and three years in a row for the Athletics. He maintained a career .261 batting average, had 836 hits, 367 RBIs, 315 walks as compared to 161 strikeouts, and scored 335 runs. His best year was with the 1946 Athletics where he hit .283 as well as posting career-highs with 120 hits and 48 RBIs. Defensively he led American League catchers in assists, runners caught stealing, and had a perfect fielding percentage, setting a record for errorless games by a catcher with a 1.000 fielding percentage in 117 games. He continued this streak into the next year, setting at the time a major league record of 147 games without an error.

Yankees Years

Year	Age	G	AB	R	H	2B	3B	HR	RBI	SB	CS	BB	SO	BA	OBP	SLG	OPS	OPS+	TB	SH
1939	24	43	105	18	29	5	1	0	12	4	0	13	10	.276	.356	.343	.699	80	36	3
1940	25	73	228	34	68	11	3	4	37	7	1	19	11	.298	.357	.425	.783	105	97	5
1941	26	67	209	25	60	17	2	1	36	0	0	22	10	.287	.355	.402	.757	101	84	2
1942	27	69	209	18	48	10	0	2	34	1	2	17	20	.230	.288	.306	.594	68	64	0
Totals		252	751	95	205	43	6	7	119	12	3	71	51	.273	.337	.374	.712	91	281	10

Red Sox Years

Year	Age	G	AB	R	H	2B	3B	HR	RBI	SB	CS	BB	SO	BA	OBP	SLG	OPS	OPS+	TB	SH
1950	35	27	84	13	25	2	0	1	12	0	0	7	4	.298	.352	.357	.709	75	30	0
1951	36	58	170	11	39	7	0	1	13	0	0	19	14	.229	.307	.288	.595	55	49	2
Totals		85	254	24	64	9	0	2	25	0	0	26	18	.252	.321	.311	.632	62	79	2

Which Team Fared Better?

He started as the backup catcher to Hall of Famer Bill Dickey but put up better numbers than the starter. Because Rosar went home to be with his wife when she was going to have a baby against the wishes of Yankee manager Joe McCarthy, he was relegated to third string catcher in his final year with the Yankees before being traded to the Indians. While with the Red Sox he served as the third string catcher the entire time, putting up third string catcher numbers of .252 average, 25 RBIs, 64 hits, and 24 runs. Any one of the three seasons he played more than 60 games with the Yankees compare to his two seasons with the Red Sox, so when you put the three of them together New York certainly got the better of him.

RAY SCARBOROUGH

Signed by the Senators, this pitcher spent 7 seasons in Washington before being traded to the Chicago White Sox. From there he went to Boston for two years, then New York for another two, finishing his career with the Detroit Tigers. He was an All-Star with the Senators in 1950 and won a World Series ring with the 1952 Yankees. He ended his career with an 80–85 record, 4.13 ERA, and 564 strikeouts.

Red Sox Years

Year	Age	W	L	%	ERA	G	GS	CG	SV	IP	H	R	HR	BB	SO	ERA+	WHIP	H/9	BB/9	SO/9	SO/BB
1951	33	12	9	.571	5.09	37	22	8	0	184.0	201	106	21	61	71	88	1.424	9.8	3.0	3.5	1.16
1952	34	1	5	.167	4.81	28	8	1	4	76.2	79	47	8	35	29	82	1.487	9.3	4.1	3.4	0.83
Totals		13	14	.481	5.01	65	30	9	4	260.2	280	153	29	96	100	86	1.442	9.7	3.3	3.5	1.04

Yankees Years

Year	Age	W	L	%	ERA	G	GS	CG	SV	IP	H	R	HR	BB	SO	ERA+	WHIP	H/9	BB/9	SO/9	SO/BB
1952	34	5	1	.833	2.91	9	4	1	0	34.0	27	11	4	15	13	115	1.235	7.1	4.0	3.4	0.87
1953	35	2	2	.500	3.29	25	1	0	2	54.2	52	23	4	26	20	112	1.427	8.6	4.3	3.3	0.77
Totals		7	3	.700	3.15	34	5	1	2	88.2	79	34	8	41	33	113	1.353	8.0	4.2	3.3	0.80

Which Team Fared Better?

The only team he had a career winning record with was the Yankees, for whom he went 7–3. His best season was in 1948 while starting for the Senators. That year he went 15–8 with a 2.82 ERA. His second best season was with the Yankees in 1952. Coming over to the team in August from the Red Sox, he went 5–1 down the stretch with a 2.91 ERA. He did go 12–9 with the 1951 Red Sox, but his ERA was a 5.09 and he gave up 21 home runs. In his second year with Boston his won-lost record caught up with his 4.81 ERA, as he went 1–5 before the August trade. He definitely contributed more to New York.

JOHNNY SCHMITZ

Called Bear Tracks because of the way he shuffled his size 14 feet to the pitcher's mound, Schmitz lasted 13 season in the major leagues, spending most of his time with the Cubs. He played eleven years with Chicago, missing three seasons due to time served in World War II. From 1951 to 1953 he bounced around six teams, going from the Cubs to the Brooklyn Dodgers to the Yankees, then to Cincinnati, back to the Yankees, and finally ending up with the Washington Senators where he stuck for three seasons. He split his final season in 1956 between the Red Sox and the Baltimore Orioles. He was twice named to the All-Star team, in 1946 and 1948 representing the Cubs. He had 746 strikeouts over the course of his career with a 3.55 ERA and 93 and 114 record.

Yankees Years

Year	Age	W	L	%	ERA	G	GS	CG	SV	IP	H	R	HR	BB	SO	ERA+	WHIP	H/9	BB/9	SO/9	SO/BB
1952	31	1	1	.500	3.60	5	2	1	1	15.0	15	7	0	9	3	95	1.600	9.0	5.4	1.8	0.33
1953	32	0	0		2.08	3	0	0	0	4.1	2	1	1	3	0	194	1.154	4.2	6.2	0.0	0.00
Totals		1	1	.500	3.26	8	2	1	1	19.1	17	8	1	12	3	109	1.500	7.9	5.6	1.4	0.25

Red Sox Years

Year	Age	W	L	%	ERA	G	GS	CG	SV	IP	H	R	HR	BB	SO	ERA+	WHIP	H/9	BB/9	SO/9	SO/BB
1956	35	0	0		0.00	2	0	0	0	4.1	5	2	0	4	0		2.077	8.8	4.9	3.9	0.81

Which Team Fared Better?

Combined the two teams only got 10 games out of Schmitz. He spent most of his good years playing with the Chicago Cubs where he was in the top 30 for MVP voting three years. He played for the Yankees in 1952 until being traded to the Reds. The Yankees purchased him in the offseason and then put him on waivers in May of 1953. One wonders why the Yankees parted ways with him considering he had a 2.08 ERA in only 4.1 innings pitched in relief. He matched that inning total in his lone year with Boston, posting a 0.00 ERA in two games. Again, one wonders why the Red Sox lost patience with him and allowed Baltimore to purchase his contract. Regardless, the Yankees win this one based on the 15 additional innings he pitched for the Yankees in 1952, posting a solid reliever ERA of 3.60.

Tom Sturdivant

In ten years' time he pitched for seven different teams. He acted as both a starter and reliever, pitching in 335 games in his career and compiling a 59 and 51 record. He began his career with the Yankees, playing five years with them before bouncing around from the Kansas City Athletics to the Red Sox to the Washington Senators before settling in Pittsburgh for three seasons. He then spent half a season with the Detroit Tigers before going back to Kansas City. He finished his career in New York, only this time playing for the expansion Mets.

Yankees Years

Year	Age	W	L	%	ERA	G	GS	CG	SV	IP	H	R	HR	BB	SO	ERA+	WHIP	H/9	BB/9	SO/9	SO/BB
1955	25	1	3	.250	3.16	33	1	0	0	68.1	48	24	6	42	48	120	1.317	6.3	5.5	6.3	1.14
1956	26	16	8	.667	3.30	32	17	6	5	158.1	134	63	15	52	110	118	1.175	7.6	3.0	6.3	2.12
1957	27	16	6	.727	2.54	28	28	7	0	201.2	170	65	14	80	118	142	1.240	7.6	3.6	5.3	1.48
1958	28	3	6	.333	4.20	15	10	0	0	70.2	77	37	6	38	41	85	1.627	9.8	4.8	5.2	1.08
1959	29	0	2	.000	4.97	7	3	0	0	25.1	20	16	4	9	16	74	1.145	7.1	3.2	5.7	1.78
Totals		36	25	.590	3.19	115	59	13	5	524.1	449	205	45	221	333	116	1.278	7.7	3.8	5.7	1.51

Red Sox Years

Year	Age	W	L	%	ERA	G	GS	CG	SV	IP	H	R	HR	BB	SO	ERA+	WHIP	H/9	BB/9	SO/9	SO/BB
1960	30	3	3	.500	4.97	40	3	0	1	101.1	106	58	16	45	67	81	1.490	9.4	4.0	6.0	1.49

Which Team Fared Better?

His best year in the majors was in 1957 when he went 16 and 6 for the Yankees, leading the league in winning percentage and having career bests in innings pitched (201.2), strikeouts (118), ERA (2.54), and ERA+ (142). In four of the five years he pitched for the Yankees, he had a much lower ERA than his 4.97 with the 1960 Red Sox. His worst season in New York matched this. He also won a World Series with the Yankees in 1956, throwing a complete game for the victory in game four versus Brooklyn. His 36 and 25 record with the Yankees definitely gives them the victory here.

Jake Wade

A pitcher who played eight seasons, Jake was one of three brothers who played professional ball. His oldest brother Winfred spent some time in the minors and his younger brother Ben played five years in the majors. Jake played for six different teams, beginning with the Detroit Tigers before moving on to the Red Sox and St. Louis Browns. Then after two years in the minor leagues he managed to work his way back due to the depletion of players because of World War II. He played with the Chicago White Sox for three years before missing 1945 due to his own military service. He returned in 1946 to finish out his career with the Yankees and then the Washington Senators. Given that his most productive season, 1937, was a losing one at 7 and 10 with a 5.39 ERA, it is understandable why Wade bounced up and down between the majors and minors.

Red Sox Year

Year	Age	W	L	%	ERA	G	GS	CG	SV	IP	H	R	HR	BB	SO	ERA+	WHIP	H/9	BB/9	SO/9	SO/BB
1939	27	1	4	.200	6.23	20	6	1	0	47.2	68	43	1	37	21	76	2.203	12.8	7.0	4.0	0.57

Yankees Year

Year	Age	W	L	%	ERA	G	GS	CG	SV	IP	H	R	HR	BB	SO	ERA+	WHIP	H/9	BB/9	SO/9	SO/BB
1946	34	2	1	.667	2.29	13	1	0	1	35.1	33	9	2	14	22	152	1.330	8.4	3.6	5.6	1.57

Which Team Fared Better?

In his time with the Red Sox he was much more green, pitching in 20 games with a 1–4 record and 6.23 ERA. Probably the most damaging statistic in his time spent in Boston was the 105 runners he put on base in just 47.2 innings of work. He had the distinction of walking in two runs in a July 29th game. The Yankees benefitted from an older and wiser Wade when he played for them seven years later. The Wade of the Yankees years was a more seasoned pitcher. In 13 games he was 2–1 with a 2.29 ERA. His WHIP was 1.330 and he had 22 strikeouts as opposed to 14 walks.

Bill Wight

Although he did not have a very distinguished career record of 77–99, Wight did pitch for 12 seasons in the major leagues, logging time with eight different teams. Wight began his tenure in baseball with the Yankees, getting only 49.1 innings in two seasons. He began to get regular playing time as a starter for the Chicago White Sox, pitching in 99 games for them over three seasons. He continued to start for the Red Sox and the Detroit Tigers before the

Cleveland Indians made him a reliever. For the remainder of his career he did a little bit of starting and relieving, playing three seasons with the Baltimore Orioles before finishing out the 1958 season splitting time with the Cincinnati Reds and St. Louis Cardinals. He went on to become a scout for the Houston Colt .45s, signing Hall of Famer second baseman Joe Morgan.

Yankees Years

Year	Age	W	L	%	ERA	G	GS	CG	SV	IP	H	R	HR	BB	SO	ERA+	WHIP	H/9	BB/9	SO/9	SO/BB
1946	24	2	2	.500	4.46	14	4	1	0	40.1	44	22	1	30	11	78	1.835	9.8	6.7	2.5	0.37
1947	25	1	0	1.000	1.00	1	1	1	0	9.0	8	3	0	2	3	369	1.111	8.0	2.0	3.0	1.50
Totals		3	2	.600	3.83	15	5	2	0	49.1	52	25	1	32	14	92	1.703	9.5	5.8	2.6	0.44

Red Sox Years

Year	Age	W	L	%	ERA	G	GS	CG	SV	IP	H	R	HR	BB	SO	ERA+	WHIP	H/9	BB/9	SO/9	SO/BB
1951	29	7	7	.500	5.10	34	17	4	0	118.1	128	77	5	63	38	88	1.614	9.7	4.8	2.9	0.60
1952	30	2	1	.667	2.96	10	2	0	0	24.1	14	11	3	14	5	135	1.151	5.2	5.2	1.8	0.36
Totals		9	8	.529	4.73	44	19	4	0	142.2	142	88	8	77	43	93	1.535	9.0	4.9	2.7	0.56

Which Team Fared Better?

He had almost 100 more innings of work with the Red Sox but his ERA was lower while pitching for New York. Both records were only one game above .500 and his other statistics are pretty even. The Yankees did manage to use Wight in a trade for Eddie Lopat from the White Sox. Lopat would go on to have a 113 and 59 record with New York over 8 seasons. Boston traded Wight and received some aging Detroit Tigers in Dizzy Trout and Hoot Evers but also got George Kell, who was an All-Star both years he played with the Red Sox. Unfortunately his two years of productive hitting do not compare with 7 seasons of winning baseball not to mention the five straight World Series Lopat helped the Yankees gain from 1949 to 1953. This gives the Yankees the win.

ARCHIE WILSON

Wilson only logged 14 at-bats in the two years he played in the major leagues as an outfielder. He began with the Yankees and a month into his second season with them was traded to the Washington Senators. He stuck with Washington for a little over a month before being moved to the Red Sox. After that he spent another ten years in the minors where he played mostly for Toronto.

Yankees Years

Year	Age	G	AB	R	H	2B	3B	HR	RBI	SB	CS	BB	SO	BA	OBP	SLG	OPS	OPS+	TB	SH
1951	27	4	4	0	0	0	0	0	0	0	0	0	0	.000	.000	.000	.200	-42	0	0
1952	28	3	2	0	1	0	0	0	1	0	0	0	0	.500	.500	.500	1.000	186	1	0
Totals		7	6	0	1	0	0	0	1	0	0	0	0	.167	.286	.167	.452	28	1	0

Red Sox Year

Year	Age	G	AB	R	H	2B	3B	HR	RBI	SB	CS	BB	SO	BA	OBP	SLG	OPS	OPS+	TB	SH
1952	28	18	38	1	10	3	0	0	2	0	0	2	3	.263	.300	.342	.642	73	13	1

Which Team Fared Better?

There is almost nothing to go on for either team. In one and a half seasons with the Yankees he only had 7 plate appearances and although he had 41 plate appearances with the Red Sox, he only collected 10 hits and 2 RBIs. This one will not be decided on the play of Wilson but rather what he brought back in trades. The Yankees traded Wilson along with Jackie Jensen, Spec Shea, and Jerry Snyder to the Senators and in return received Irv Noren and Tom Upton. Noren played five seasons for the Yankees, hitting 31 home runs and 198 RBIs. He was an All-Star with them in 1954 and helped them to win two World Series. Upton never made it to the big league club with the Yankees so his contributions are nil. Boston simply sold him to the Toronto club, not getting any players in return meaning the Yankees got the most out of trading him.

Bill Zuber

A pitcher with 11 years of experience in the major leagues, Zuber played for four teams in his career. He began with the Cleveland Indians, appearing in no more than 17 games in each of the four seasons he was there. Then he moved to the Washington Senators for two years where he began to get a little more work as a starter. He took this experience with him to the Yankees for four seasons, becoming an occasional starter. He finished his career with Boston after being purchased in June. He played for nearly two seasons there before returning to the minors for a season and then retiring.

Yankees Years

Year	Age	W	L	%	ERA	G	GS	CG	SV	IP	H	R	HR	BB	SO	ERA+	WHIP	H/9	BB/9	SO/9	SO/BB
1943	30	8	4	.667	3.89	20	13	7	1	118.0	100	54	3	74	57	83	1.475	7.6	5.6	4.3	0.77
1944	31	5	7	.417	4.21	22	13	2	0	107.0	101	54	5	54	59	84	1.449	8.5	4.5	5.0	1.09
1945	32	5	11	.313	3.19	21	14	7	1	127.0	121	50	2	56	50	109	1.394	8.6	4.0	3.5	0.89
1946	33	0	1	.000	12.71	3	0	0	0	5.2	10	9	2	3	3	29	2.294	15.9	4.8	4.8	1.00
Totals		18	23	.439	3.88	66	40	16	2	357.2	332	167	12	187	169	88	1.451	8.4	4.7	4.3	0.90

Red Sox Years

Year	Age	W	L	%	ERA	G	GS	CG	SV	IP	H	R	HR	BB	SO	ERA+	WHIP	H/9	BB/9	SO/9	SO/BB
1946	33	5	1	.833	2.54	15	7	2	0	56.2	37	20	4	39	29	144	1.341	5.9	6.2	4.6	0.74
1947	34	1	0	1.000	5.33	20	1	0	0	50.2	60	32	4	31	23	73	1.796	10.7	5.5	4.1	0.74
Totals		6	1	.857	3.86	35	8	2	0	107.1	97	52	8	70	52	98	1.556	8.1	5.9	4.4	0.74

Which Team Fared Better?

He pitched for two seasons longer with the Yankees than he did with the Red Sox, and as a result all of his numbers are doubled or more with New York. He pitched in 66 games compared to 35 in Boston, 169 strikeouts compared to 52, 167 runs allowed compared to 52. The ERAs are almost identical, a 3.88 with the Yankees and a 3.86 with Boston. His record was 6–1 with the Red Sox and 18–23 with the Yankees, but his true value can be determined by his contributions to the pennant drive of both teams. For the 1943 Yankees he went 8–4 with 7 complete games in their run to the World Series although he did not appear in a post season game. He helped the 1946 Red Sox win their first pennant since they had last won the World Series in 1918. Even though they lost in the Series to the St. Louis Cardinals, he contributed 2 innings of work. This one would have to go to the Red Sox because it had been so long since they had won a pennant. Since 1918 the Yankees had won 14 pennants, meaning that as unfair as this seems, getting to the postseason was probably not as meaningful because they were there nearly every year.

4. Managing for the Enemy
The Expansion Era (1961–1973)

It is one thing to play for both the Red Sox and the Yankees, but could you imagine managing for both teams? As the manager, you are the general of your troops going to war on a daily basis with other teams. And one of those teams is your most hated rival. It is your job to instill in your players a hatred for that other squad. Then, because either you were let go of your managing position or you wanted a change of scenery, suddenly you find yourself as general for the other side, trying to get your players to rally against the very squad you had just been supporting. Could you imagine Billy Martin coaching for the Red Sox or Joe Cronin heading the Yankees? These were guys so intense they got into fistfights with their own players. And yet this has happened a few times in the long tenure of the Red Sox and Yankees.

Ralph Houk was born and bred for the side of the Yankees. He was a player for the team from 1947 to 1954, although in that eight years he only amassed 91 games as the third string catcher behind the prolific Yogi Berra. His last years as a player saw him acting as the bullpen coach for New York and when he finally retired, he became the triple A manager for the Yankees. After three years he was promoted to the big leagues and acted as the first base coach, taking over as manager when the current one was sidelined with illness. Houk ushered in the Expansion Era, taking over for the legendary Casey Stengel, who had been there for 11 years, after the Yankees lost the 1960 World Series to the Pittsburgh Pirates. After leading the Yankees to three straight World Series, winning two of them, from there Houk moved to the front office, becoming the general manager of the Yankees for another three years before firing Johnny Keane and naming himself as manager. This time he was not as successful, the Yankees finishing in last place for the first time since 1912. He spent six years managing before resigning in 1973.

After this Houk spent a couple of years managing the Detroit Tigers (1974–1978) before retiring again. It seemed as though he was done with baseball but at the age of 61 and only two years of retirement, he was itching to manage again. Ironically it was the Red Sox who came calling. He closed out the Expansion Era by taking over the Boston team in 1981 and developing players such as Roger Clemens and Wade Boggs, both of whom went on to play for the Yankees as well. He retired for good in 1984, leaving a core of a ballclub that would go on to the 1986 World Series.

The man whom Houk replaced in Boston was none other than Don Zimmer. Zimmer was the Boston skipper from 1976 to 1980. Zimmer had some success with the Red Sox, leading them to 90 win seasons in all three full years he managed. He also was the manager of the Red Sox during one of the greatest collapses in major league history. After leading the division in 1978 by as many as 14 games, the Yankees were able to gain ground, finally catching them after a four game sweep known as the Boston Massacre. The Red Sox then lost the pennant in a one game playoff with the Yankees where Bucky Dent hit his claim to fame home run. Zimmer was not popular when he was the Red Sox manager. He released the beloved Red Sox player Rico Petrocelli and fought with his starting pitcher Bill Lee. Zimmer once said "When I was manager there, 36,000 people a night, every night, booed me — everybody except my wife." Zimmer managed again in Texas for the Rangers and for the Chicago Cubs, eventually returning to Boston as a coach in 1992. In 1996 he went to work for Joe Torre, manager of the Yankees, as the bench coach during the stretch where the Yankees won four World Series. The event that he is most remembered for his time with the Yankees was during a particularly heated game in the 2003 League Championship series between the Yankees and Red Sox. Pedro Martinez and the Yankees had no love lost between them. Known as a headhunter, Martinez had already thrown behind Yankee Karem Garcia's head in the fourth inning. When tempers flared, Martinez made a gesture to his head as if that was where the next one was coming. When Yankee pitcher Roger Clemens threw a pitch that came high and tight to Red Sox Manny Ramirez in the top of the inning, the benches cleared. In the melee, Don Zimmer went after Martinez. Martinez grabbed Zimmer by the back of the head and threw the 72 year-old to the ground. Zimmer later apologized for his behavior in the skirmish but Red Sox fans were wondering where was this apology when Zimmer pitched rookie Bobby Sprowl over Bill Lee, who had won 12 out of 17 decisions against the Yankees, in the last game of the Boston Massacre.

Probably one of the most surprising managers to commandeer both the Yankees and the Red Sox was Joe McCarthy. McCarthy managed the New York Yankees for fifteen years, from 1931 to 1946. During this time he won seven world championships including four in a row. He is the all-time winningest manager in Yankee history with 1,460 wins, as well as the highest winning percentage, being the victor in over sixty percent of the games he managed. He is synonymous with the Yankees and yet in 1946 he resigned from the team due to a personality conflict with new general manager Larry MacPhail. He took two years off and decided he would head the Boston Red Sox in 1948. He was able to get them to the top of the division, but lost the pennant to Cleveland in a one game playoff. He finished second again the following year, losing the pennant to the dreaded Yankees the final week of the season. In July of 1950 McCarthy had had enough of finishing behind the Yankees (the Yankees would again go to the World Series and win that year while the Red Sox finished in third place). He resigned citing health reasons and never managed again. He was eventually inducted into the Baseball Hall of Fame in 1957 but it was not for his work with the Red Sox.

Frank Chance of the Tinkers to Evers to Chance fame is the third person to manage for both teams. His tenure with both clubs was very short. He managed the Yankees for two years, from 1913–1914, finishing second to last in the league both seasons. He acted as player/manager although he only played 12 games in a season during this time. He resigned with three weeks to go in the 1914 season because he felt the Yankee front office did not provide him with enough talent. His time with the Red Sox was even shorter. He managed the 1923 Boston team to a 61 and 91 record, dead last in the league. He was not brought back for the next season.

The question is with the intensity of the rivalry as it currently stands, will there ever be another manager who heads both teams? Could you imagine Joe Torre taking over for the Red Sox or Terry Francona acting as the skipper of the Yankees? Those two men will forever be linked to Boston and New York, even though Torre finished his managerial career with the Los Angeles Dodgers (taking over for former Red Sox manager Grady Little) and Francona was through with Boston after the 2011 season. (After a year away from the dugout, he was hired in 2013 to manage the Indians, with whom he remains.) I am sure there were those who never could have imagined Joe McCarthy managing for anyone else, much less the Boston Red Sox, and yet he did. Only time will tell.

Players Who Spent Time with Both Teams, 1961–1976

KEN BRETT

Selected as the fourth overall pick by the Boston Red Sox in the 1966 draft, Ken Brett was one of four brothers who played professional baseball. His youngest brother is George Brett, the Hall of Famer with the Kansas City Royals. Ken pitched for 14 years in the majors, spending the first four with Boston before bouncing to Milwaukee and Philadelphia, then settling in for two seasons in Pittsburgh where he was an All-Star in 1974. Then he went to the Yankees, White Sox, Angels, Twins, and Dodgers before finishing up his career with his famous younger brother in Kansas City. He pitched over 1,500 innings in his career, compiling a record of 83–85 and a 3.93 ERA. He was also one of the better-hitting pitchers of his era.

In 1967, he became the youngest pitcher ever to appear in a World Series game when at the age of 19 years and one month he pitched the final inning of Game Four.

Red Sox Years

Year	Age	W	L	%	ERA	G	GS	CG	SV	IP	H	R	HR	BB	SO	ERA+	WHIP	H/9	BB/9	SO/9	SO/BB
1967	18	0	0		4.50	1	0	0	0	2.0	3	1	0	0	2	95	1.500	13.5	0.0	9.0	
1969	20	2	3	.400	5.26	8	8	0	0	39.1	41	24	6	22	23	74	1.602	9.4	5.0	5.3	1.05
1970	21	8	9	.471	4.07	41	14	1	2	139.1	118	71	17	79	155	98	1.414	7.6	5.1	10.0	1.96
1971	22	0	3	.000	5.34	29	2	0	1	59.0	57	38	7	35	57	70	1.559	8.7	5.3	8.7	1.63
Totals		10	15	.400	4.58	79	24	1	3	239.2	219	134	30	136	237	85	1.481	8.2	5.1	8.9	1.74

Yankees Year

Year	Age	W	L	%	ERA	G	GS	CG	SV	IP	H	R	HR	BB	SO	ERA+	WHIP	H/9	BB/9	SO/9	SO/BB
1976	27	0	0		0.00	2	0	0	1	2.1	2	0	0	0	1		0.857	7.7	0.0	3.9	

Which Team Fared Better?

Even though other teams coveted him as a center fielder before the draft, the Red Sox saw his potential as a pitcher. It took him only 15 months to crack the major league roster, and he helped that 1967 Red Sox team clinch the division title. After a six-month stint in the Army that began that offseason, he injured his elbow on the comeback trail, and spent much of 1968 and part of 1969 trying to get back to the big leagues for good. It looked as if he had in 1970, when he pitched 139.1 innings in 41 games, but a year later he bounced between the big league team and its minor league affiliate before being traded to the Brewers. His best run as a pitcher came in Pittsburgh where he got into 50 games and posted a 22–14 record, career bests. He was the winning pitcher for the National League All-Star team in 1974.

JUAN BENIQUEZ

In 17 years as a major leaguer, Beniquez played in more than 1,500 games for eight teams, all in the American League: Boston, Texas, New York, Seattle, California, Baltimore, Kansas

City, and Toronto. He spent the most time with the Angels, batting .293 in five seasons with a .739 OPS (105 OPS+). He received MVP consideration with them in 1984. He was also a Gold Glove winner while playing center field for the Rangers in 1977.

Red Sox Years

Year	Age	G	AB	R	H	2B	3B	HR	RBI	SB	CS	BB	SO	BA	OBP	SLG	OPS	OPS+	TB	SH
1971	21	13	57	8	17	2	0	0	4	3	1	3	4	2.98	.333	.333	.667	84	19	3
1972	22	33	99	10	24	4	1	1	8	2	0	7	11	.242	.287	.333	.620	80	33	0
1974	24	106	389	60	104	14	3	5	33	19	11	25	61	.267	.313	.357	.670	87	139	7
1975	25	78	254	43	74	14	4	2	17	7	10	25	26	.291	.358	.402	.760	108	102	6
Totals		233	799	121	219	34	8	8	62	31	22	60	102	.274	.326	.367	.692	93	293	16

Yankees Year

Year	Age	G	AB	R	H	2B	3B	HR	RBI	SB	CS	BB	SO	BA	OBP	SLG	OPS	OPS+	TB	SH
1979	29	62	142	19	36	6	1	4	17	3	3	9	17	.254	.299	.394	.694	88	56	1

Which Team Fared Better?

At the end of his four seasons with Boston, Beniquez went to the 1975 World Series with the team, getting into three games in what many consider to be the greatest Fall Classic ever. He spent a single season, 1979, with the Yankees, and that year they finished in fourth. He batted .254 and knocked in only 17 runs, good for a -.2 WAR. With Boston, which gets the nod, he contributed a 2.3 WAR.

DANNY CATER

Cater carved himself out a respectable major league career, playing for six teams in 12 years of service. He began with the Philadelphia Phillies in 1964 but did not get regular playing time until he went to the Chicago White Sox a year later. From 1965 to 1972, a period that includes his two Yankees seasons, he averaged 500 plate appearances a season. Known as a professional hitter who was difficult to strikeout, he had 1,229 hits, 519 RBIs, and 1,676 total bases. His career highlight was when he finished second to Carl Yastrzemski in the batting title in 1968 at .290; in a season dominated by pitching, Yaz was the only qualifying player in the American League to top .300.

Yankees Years

Year	Age	G	AB	R	H	2B	3B	HR	RBI	SB	CS	BB	SO	BA	OBP	SLG	OPS	OPS+	TB	SH
1970	30	155	582	64	175	26	5	6	76	4	2	34	44	.301	.340	.393	.734	107	229	1
1971	31	121	428	39	118	16	5	4	50	0	3	19	25	.276	.308	.364	.672	95	156	4
Totals		276	1,010	103	293	42	10	10	126	4	5	53	69	.290	.326	.381	.708	102	385	2

Red Sox Years

Year	Age	G	AB	R	H	2B	3B	HR	RBI	SB	CS	BB	SO	BA	OBP	SLG	OPS	OPS+	TB	SH
1972	32	92	317	32	75	17	1	8	39	0	1	15	33	.237	.270	.372	.642	85	118	1
1973	33	63	195	30	61	12	0	1	24	0	0	10	22	.313	.348	.390	.738	103	76	1
1974	34	56	126	14	31	5	0	5	20	1	0	10	13	.246	.309	.405	.714	98	51	1
Totals		211	638	76	167	34	1	14	83	1	1	35	68	.262	.301	.384	.685	93	245	3

Which Team Fared Better?

Because Cater was a regular with the Yankees, he accumulated more plate appearances, hits, RBIs, and runs scored in two seasons than he did in the three he played for the Red Sox. Perhaps his largest contribution to the Yankees, however, came in the form of a trade: Cater was shipped to Boston in return for Sparky Lyle. Lyle went on to play seven seasons with New York, saving 141 games for the pinstripers.

LOU CLINTON

A right fielder who played for five teams over eight years, Clinton came up with Boston, spending five seasons with them before being traded to the Los Angeles Angels. In 1965 he was waived by the Angels and claimed off by the Kansas City Athletics, who in turn let him go on waivers, this time to the Cleveland Indians. He ended his career playing two seasons with the Yankees. He got into 110 or more games only three times in his career, twice with Boston, and in the first of those seasons he put up a 133 OPS+ and 2.4 WAR.

Red Sox Years

Year	Age	G	AB	R	H	2B	3B	HR	RBI	SB	CS	BB	SO	BA	OBP	SLG	OPS	OPS+	TB	SH
1960	22	96	298	37	68	17	5	6	37	4	3	20	66	.228	.278	.379	.657	74	113	5
1961	23	17	51	4	13	2	1	0	3	0	0	2	10	.255	.283	.333	.616	64	17	1
1962	24	114	398	63	117	24	10	18	75	2	1	34	79	.294	.349	.540	.890	133	215	1
1963	25	148	560	71	130	23	7	22	77	0	0	49	118	.232	.294	.416	.710	95	233	0
1964	26	37	120	15	31	4	3	3	6	1	0	9	33	.258	.310	.417	.727	96	50	1
Totals		412	1,427	190	359	70	26	49	198	7	4	114	306	.252	.307	.440	.747	100	628	8

Yankees Years

Year	Age	G	AB	R	H	2B	3B	HR	RBI	SB	CS	BB	SO	BA	OBP	SLG	OPS	OPS+	TB	SH
1966	28	80	159	18	35	10	2	5	21	0	0	16	27	.220	.288	.403	.691	101	64	2
1967	29	6	4	1	2	1	0	0	2	0	0	1	1	.500	.600	.750	1.350	306	3	0
Totals		86	163	19	37	11	2	5	23	0	0	17	28	.227	.297	.411	.708	106	67	2

Which Team Fared Better?

Clinton played in more games with the Red Sox than with all of his other stops combined. His 1962 and 1963 seasons with Boston brought the most playing time he ever received, and he capitalized, averaging .263, 76 RBIs, 20 home runs, a .478 slugging percentage, and 124 hits. He did not come close to those numbers while playing for the Yankees. In his only full year with New York, in 1966, he got in 80 games, batted .220, and had 21 RBIs.

BILLY GARDNER

A light-hitting infielder, Gardner played for five teams in the ten years he called major league baseball his profession. The majority of his playing time came with the Orioles; he spent four seasons in Baltimore, accumulating 2,337 plate appearances, more than the combined total for his other six seasons. His best season was also in Baltimore, where in 1957 he led the league in at-bats, plate appearances, and doubles on his way to a 12th-place finish in the MVP balloting. He spent two years each with the New York Giants, Minnesota Twins, Yankees, and Red Sox. He later managed for the Minnesota Twins and the Kansas City Royals, accumulating a 330–417 record.

Yankees Years

Year	Age	G	AB	R	H	2B	3B	HR	RBI	SB	CS	BB	SO	BA	OBP	SLG	OPS	OPS+	TB	SH
1961	33	41	99	11	21	5	0	1	2	0	0	6	18	.212	.278	.293	.571	57	29	1
1962	34	4	1	1	0	0	0	0	0	0	0	0	1	.000	.000	.000	.000	-100	0	0
Totals		45	100	12	21	5	0	1	2	0	0	6	19	.210	.275	.290	.565	55	29	1

Red Sox Years

Year	Age	G	AB	R	H	2B	3B	HR	RBI	SB	CS	BB	SO	BA	OBP	SLG	OPS	OPS+	TB	SH
1962	34	53	199	22	54	9	2	0	12	0	1	10	39	.271	.310	.337	.646	72	67	2
1963	35	36	84	4	16	2	1	0	1	0	0	4	19	.190	.236	.238	.474	32	20	0
Totals		89	283	26	70	11	3	0	13	0	1	14	58	.247	.288	.307	.595	61	87	2

Which Team Fared Better?

Gardner did not put in substantial time with either team, playing in 45 games for the Yankees and 89 for the Red Sox. With the Yankees he only hit .210 with two RBIs, numbers more likely to come from a pitcher than an infielder. He batted an abysmal .190 for the 1963 Red Sox, driving in only one run in 84 at-bats. The lone bright spot in his career with either team was the 1962 season with Boston, with whom he batted .271, knocked in 12, and scored 22 runs. More significant than anything he did as a player were the eight seasons he spent coaching and managing in the Red Sox farm system.

DERON JOHNSON

Hitting 245 home runs in his career, good enough for 215th on the all-time home run list, Johnson was a hard hitter who knocked in nearly 1,000 runs in his career. He played for eight teams over the course of 16 years, his most productive stint coming with the Cincinnati Reds. In the 1965 season he knocked in a league-leading 130 RBIs, popped 32 home runs, and finished fourth in the MVP balloting. Pete Rose said he never saw anyone hit the ball harder than Johnson. Johnson won a World Series in 1973 in his second stop with the Oakland Athletics. He also played for the Atlanta Braves, Philadelphia Phillies, Milwaukee Brewers, and Chicago White Sox. After retiring, he served 13 seasons as a coach in the major leagues.

Yankees Years

Year	Age	G	AB	R	H	2B	3B	HR	RBI	SB	CS	BB	SO	BA	OBP	SLG	OPS	OPS+	TB	SH
1960	21	6	4	0	2	1	0	0	0	0	0	0	0	.500	.500	.750	1.250	242	3	0
1961	22	13	19	1	2	0	0	0	2	0	0	2	5	.105	.182	.105	.287	-19	2	0
Totals		19	23	1	4	1	0	0	2	0	0	2	5	.174	.231	.217	.448	24	5	0

Red Sox Years

Year	Age	G	AB	R	H	2B	3B	HR	RBI	SB	CS	BB	SO	BA	OBP	SLG	OPS	OPS+	TB	SH
1974	35	11	25	0	3	0	0	0	2	0	0	0	6	.120	.115	.120	.235	-34	3	1
1975	36	3	10	2	6	0	0	1	3	0	0	2	0	.600	.667	.900	1.567	325	9	0
1976	37	15	38	3	5	1	1	0	0	0	0	5	11	.132	.233	.211	.443	24	8	0
Totals		29	73	5	14	1	1	1	5	0	0	7	17	.192	.259	.274	.533	49	20	1

Which Team Fared Better?

Johnson's 16-year career was bookended by New York, where he played his first two seasons, and Boston, his home for the final three campaigns of his career. Neither one provided him with much playing time: He got into only 19 games for the Yankees and 29 for the Red Sox. When he was in the lineup, he provided little offensive help, putting up a 49 OPS+ with Boston and a 24 OPS+ with New York. It is difficult to say that either team fared well with Johnson, but since there are no ties in baseball (unless it is an All-Star game), the Red Sox get the nod as the beneficiaries of his only home run and four more runs scored.

JOHN KENNEDY

No, the 35th president of the United States did not play professional baseball. This John Kennedy did, however, share a birthday with the more famous one, and like JFK, he was a Senator for a time, beginning his career playing for the Washington club. The major leagues' John Kennedy then went to the Los Angeles Dodgers and helped them get to the World Series both years he played for them. After a year with the Yankees he played for the Seattle Pilots the lone season they existed before moving with them to Milwaukee. He finished out his last five years playing in Boston.

Yankees Year

Year	Age	G	AB	R	H	2B	3B	HR	RBI	SB	CS	BB	SO	BA	OBP	SLG	OPS	OPS+	TB	SH
1967	26	78	179	22	35	4	0	1	17	2	1	17	35	.196	.265	.235	.500	52	42	8

Red Sox Years

Year	Age	G	AB	R	H	2B	3B	HR	RBI	SB	CS	BB	SO	BA	OBP	SLG	OPS	OPS+	TB	SH
1970	29	43	129	15	33	7	1	4	17	0	0	6	14	.256	.292	.419	.711	88	54	1
1971	30	74	272	41	75	12	5	5	22	1	1	14	42	.276	.320	.412	.731	100	112	5
1972	31	71	212	22	52	11	1	2	22	0	1	18	40	.245	.311	.335	.646	88	71	2
1973	32	67	155	17	28	9	1	1	16	0	0	12	45	.181	.246	.271	.517	42	42	3
1974	33	10	15	3	2	0	0	1	1	0	0	1	6	.133	.188	.333	.521	43	5	0
Totals		265	783	98	190	39	8	13	78	1	2	51	147	.243	.295	.363	.658	82	284	11

Which Team Fared Better?

Kennedy was a regular in only one season, making 521 plate appearances with the 1964 Senators. In no other year did he top 300. He played in 78 games for the Yankees, but batted only .196 with one home run and a slugging percentage of .235, which is probably why they sold him to the Seattle Pilots. He fared a little better with the Red Sox, carrying a .243 average, 13 home runs, and a .363 slugging percentage over four and a half seasons.

ANDY KOSCO

In his first three years, spent with the Minnesota Twins, Kosco saw little playing time. It was not until he went to the Yankees, in 1968, that he began to get regular time on the field. This continued for one more year with the Los Angeles Dodgers before his playing time diminished; he would average roughly 64 games a season for the remainder of his career while playing with the Milwaukee Brewers, California Angels, Red Sox, and Cincinnati Reds. He finished with a total of 658 games over 10 years, batting .236, knocking in 267 runs, and hitting 73 homers.

Yankees Year

Year	Age	G	AB	R	H	2B	3B	HR	RBI	SB	CS	BB	SO	BA	OBP	SLG	OPS	OPS+	TB	SH
1968	26	131	466	47	112	19	1	15	59	2	2	16	71	.240	.268	.382	.650	100	178	3

Red Sox Year

Year	Age	G	AB	R	H	2B	3B	HR	RBI	SB	CS	BB	SO	BA	OBP	SLG	OPS	OPS+	TB	SH
1972	30	17	47	5	10	2	1	3	6	0	0	2	9	.213	.260	.489	.749	114	23	0

Which Team Fared Better?

He spent only one year with the Yankees and only a couple of months with the Red Sox, whom he joined as part of a trade-deadline deal. His time with the Yankees was more significant, as he tallied 15 home runs, 59 RBIs, and 47 runs scored. Because he played for Boston a couple of months, he played in only 17 games, hitting three home runs, driving in six runs, and scoring five. He was disappointed when New York traded him, saying, "I loved being a Yankee," and while his rate of production might have been higher in his short stint with Boston, he contributed more in the Bronx than in Beantown.

SPARKY LYLE

Pitching in an impressive 899 games while forging an ERA of only 2.88, Lyle was one of the premier closers of the 1970s. During that decade he piled up 190 of his 238 career saves. He began with the Red Sox in 1967, developing into a good relief pitcher who was given the closer's role. Then he was traded to New York where he spent seven years, helping them win two World Series in 1977 and 1978. He spent his last four years with three different teams, going from the Texas Rangers to the Philadelphia Phillies and finally to the Chicago White Sox. He was a three-time All-Star and won the Cy Young Award in 1977

Red Sox Years

Year	Age	W	L	%	ERA	G	GS	CG	SV	IP	H	R	HR	BB	SO	ERA+	WHIP	H/9	BB/9	SO/9	SO/BB
1967	22	1	2	.333	2.28	27	0	0	5	43.1	33	13	3	14	42	156	1.085	6.9	2.9	8.7	3.00
1968	23	6	1	.857	2.74	49	0	0	11	65.2	67	25	6	14	52	117	1.234	9.2	1.9	7.1	3.71
1969	24	8	3	.727	2.54	71	0	0	17	102.2	91	33	8	48	93	152	1.354	8.0	4.2	8.2	1.94
1970	25	1	7	.125	3.88	63	0	0	20	67.1	62	37	5	34	51	103	1.426	8.3	4.5	6.8	1.50
1971	26	6	4	.600	2.75	50	0	0	16	52.1	41	16	5	23	37	136	1.223	7.1	4.0	6.4	1.61
Totals		22	17	.564	2.85	260	0	0	69	331.1	294	124	27	133	275	130	1.289	8.0	3.6	7.5	2.07

Yankees Years

Year	Age	W	L	%	ERA	G	GS	CG	SV	IP	H	R	HR	BB	SO	ERA+	WHIP	H/9	BB/9	SO/9	SO/BB
1972	27	9	5	.643	1.92	59	0	0	35	107.2	84	25	3	29	75	154	1.050	7.0	2.4	6.3	2.59
1973	28	5	9	.357	2.51	51	0	0	27	82.1	66	30	4	18	63	147	1.020	7.0	2.0	6.9	3.50
1974	29	9	3	.750	1.66	66	0	0	15	114.0	93	30	6	43	89	215	1.193	7.3	3.4	7.0	2.07
1975	30	5	7	.417	3.12	49	0	0	6	89.1	94	34	1	36	65	119	1.455	9.5	3.6	6.5	1.81
1976	31	7	8	.467	2.26	64	0	0	23	103.2	82	33	5	42	61	154	1.196	7.1	3.6	5.3	1.45
1977	32	13	5	.722	2.17	72	0	0	26	137.0	131	41	7	33	68	183	1.197	8.6	2.2	4.5	2.06
1978	33	9	3	.750	3.47	59	0	0	9	111.2	116	46	6	33	33	105	1.334	9.3	2.7	2.7	1.00
Totals		57	40	.588	2.41	420	0	0	141	745.2	666	239	32	234	454	148	1.207	8.0	2.8	5.5	1.94

Which Team Fared Better?

People are quick to point to the selling of Babe Ruth as the biggest player-transaction mistake the Red Sox ever made, and for very good reason; but there are those who would argue the trading of Sparky Lyle before the 1972 season was worse. One reason it could be considered worse is that after selling Babe Ruth and a slew of other players, the Red Sox were essentially toothless for many years, finishing in fifth place or worse 14 years in a row. What that means is the presence of Babe Ruth, no matter how good he was, would not have elevated those teams to winning seasons or championships. When Sparky Lyle was traded in 1972, the Red Sox were a pretty good club. In the years Lyle played for the Yankees, the Red Sox finished second four times, third twice, and won the pennant in 1975 only to lose in the World Series. If Sparky Lyle had been on those teams contributing the saves he instead racked up for the New York Yankees, the Red Sox could have finished in first more often. And imagine if he had been pitching in Game Seven of the 1975 World Series when Boston was up 3-2 on Cincinnati going into the seventh; might the Sox would have won? Or if he had been pitching for them in 1978 when New York caught Boston after being behind by 14 games and then won a one-game playoff. Things might have been very different. Not only did the Yankees enjoy more than twice as many saves (141 to 69) and slightly sharper pitching (a 2.41 ERA and 1.207 WHIP as compared with 2.85 and 1.289), they also prevented Lyle's helping the Red Sox from 1972–1978, when Boston really could have used his help.

Lynn McGlothen

McGlothen was drafted by the Red Sox out of Grambling State University in 1968. It took him a few years to crack the major league roster but he would stick around for 11 seasons and had a fairly successful stint with the St. Louis Cardinals, for whom he was an All-Star in 1974 and won 16, 15, and 13 games over a three-year span. He went to San Francisco for a couple of years before spending three and a half, his longest hitch with any team, with the Cubs. He was then traded across town to the White Sox for half a season on the South Side before moving on again, this time to the Bronx, where he finished his playing career. He finished with nearly 1,000 strikeouts and a 3.98 ERA.

Red Sox Years

Year	Age	W	L	%	ERA	G	GS	CG	SV	IP	H	R	HR	BB	SO	ERA+	WHIP	H/9	BB/9	SO/9	SO/BB
1972	22	8	7	.533	3.41	22	22	4	0	145.0	135	66	9	59	112	95	1.338	8.4	3.7	7.0	1.90
1973	23	1	2	.333	8.22	6	3	0	0	23.0	39	23	6	8	16	50	2.043	15.3	3.1	6.3	2.00
Totals		9	9	.500	4.07	28	25	4	0	168.0	174	89	15	67	128	82	1.435	9.3	3.6	6.9	1.91

Yankees Year

Year	Age	W	L	%	ERA	G	GS	CG	SV	IP	H	R	HR	BB	SO	ERA+	WHIP	H/9	BB/9	SO/9	SO/BB
1982	32	0	0		10.80	4	0	0	0	5.0	9	6	1	2	2	40	2.200	16.2	3.6	3.6	1.00

Which Team Fared Better?

The Red Sox got him at the beginning of his career when he was still figuring out how to pitch; the Yankees had him at the end, when he had been fighting injuries for several years. Neither was a good scenario. He did go 9–9 for Boston and pitched 168.0 innings, striking out 128 while walking 76. In four games with the Yankees, he pitched five innings, giving up six runs. Although neither team benefitted as much as St. Louis did from his talents, the Red Sox got the better end of the stick.

Bill Monbouquette

Winning 114 games and losing 112 in his 11-year career, Monbouquette was a pitcher for four different teams. He spent a majority of his career with the Red Sox, for whom he threw a no-hitter in 1962. After eight years, the Sox traded him to Detroit in 1966, and he lasted a couple of seasons with Detroit before being released and signed by the Yankees. He finished out his pitching career with the San Francisco Giants, then spent time in the majors as a pitching coach with the New York Mets.

Red Sox Years

Year	Age	W	L	%	ERA	G	GS	CG	SV	IP	H	R	HR	BB	SO	ERA+	WHIP	H/9	BB/9	SO/9	SO/BB
1958	21	3	4	.49	3.31	10	8	3	0	54.1	52	25	4	20	30	121	1.325	8.6	3.3	5.0	1.50
1959	22	7	7	.500	4.15	34	17	4	0	151.2	165	86	15	33	87	97	1.305	9.8	2.0	5.2	2.64
1960	23	14	11	.560	3.64	35	30	12	0	215.0	217	91	18	68	134	111	1.326	9.1	2.8	5.6	1.97
1961	24	14	14	.500	3.39	32	32	12	0	236.1	233	106	24	100	161	122	1.409	8.9	3.8	6.1	1.61
1962	25	15	13	.536	3.33	35	35	11	0	235.1	227	100	22	65	153	124	1.241	8.7	2.5	5.9	2.35
1963	26	20	10	.667	3.81	37	36	13	0	266.2	258	119	31	42	174	99	1.125	8.7	1.4	5.9	4.14
1964	27	13	14	.481	4.04	36	35	7	1	234.0	258	114	34	40	120	96	1.274	9.9	1.5	4.6	3.00
1965	28	10	18	.357	3.70	35	35	10	0	228.2	239	114	32	40	110	101	1.220	9.4	1.6	4.3	2.75
Totals		96	91	.513	3.69	254	228	72	1	1,622.0	1,649	755	180	408	969	107	1.268	9.1	2.3	5.4	2.38

Yankees Years

Year	Age	W	L	%	ERA	G	GS	CG	SV	IP	H	R	HR	BB	SO	ERA+	WHIP	H/9	BB/9	SO/9	SO/BB
1967	30	6	5	.545	2.36	33	10	2	1	133.1	122	39	6	17	53	132	1.043	8.2	1.1	3.6	3.12
1968	31	5	7	.417	4.43	17	11	2	0	89.1	92	47	7	13	32	65	1.175	9.3	1.3	3.2	2.46
Totals		11	12	.478	3.19	50	21	4	1	222.2	214	86	13	30	85	95	1.096	8.6	1.2	3.4	2.83

Which Team Fared Better?

He was a 20-game winner with the 1963 Sox and appeared as an All-Star for them in 1960, 1962, and 1963. They got 200 innings or more out of him six of the eight seasons he was there, while he barely reached that total over two seasons with the Yankees. While he did have a lower ERA (3.19) and WHIP (1.096) with the Yankees, he was primarily a number one or two pitcher for Boston and contributed mightily to a weak pitching staff. With the Yankees he was a fifth starter at best, and was sometimes used a reliever. He was more valuable to the Red Sox, and the team inducted him into their Hall of Fame in the year 2000.

JERRY MOSES

A catcher who at 18 years old was the youngest player in Boston Red Sox history to hit a home run, Moses played for nine seasons in the big leagues. After a very brief stint with the Red Sox in 1965, he spent a few years in the minors before returning to Boston for three more seasons. He was then traded in four straight years from the California Angels to the Cleveland Indians then the Yankees, and finally the Detroit Tigers. He split his last seasons between the San Diego Padres and Chicago White Sox. In all, he appeared in 386 games, batting .251 with 109 runs batted in.

Red Sox Years

Year	Age	G	AB	R	H	2B	3B	HR	RBI	SB	CS	BB	SO	BA	OBP	SLG	OPS	OPS+	TB	SH
1965	18	4	4	1	1	0	0	1	1	0	0	0	2	.250	.250	1.000	1.250	230	4	0
1968	21	6	18	2	6	0	0	2	4	0	1	1	4	.333	.368	.667	1.035	200	12	0
1969	22	53	135	13	41	9	1	4	17	0	1	5	23	.304	.326	.474	.800	117	64	0
1970	23	92	315	26	83	18	1	6	35	1	1	21	45	.263	.313	.384	.697	86	121	1
Totals		155	472	42	131	27	2	13	57	1	3	27	74	.278	.318	.426	.744	100	201	1

Yankees Year

Year	Age	G	AB	R	H	2B	3B	HR	RBI	SB	CS	BB	SO	BA	OBP	SLG	OPS	OPS+	TB	SH
1973	26	21	59	5	15	2	0	0	3	0	0	2	6	.254	.270	.288	.558	60	17	1

Which Team Fared Better?

When you look at the numbers, it seems obvious this one belongs to the Red Sox. He played in 155 games for Boston, only 21 with the Yankees. His numbers are also better with Boston, as he batted .278 compared with .254 for New York, drove in 57 runs as opposed to three, and scored 42 runs compared with five. The Yankees surge ahead, however, when it's considered what they managed to get out of Moses in a trade. Moses was part of a blockbuster trade that saw the Red Sox send Tony Conigliaro and Ray Jarvis to the California Angels in return for Doug Griffen, Jarvis Tatum, and Ken Tatum; the trade ended up a bust for both teams. When the Yankees traded for Moses, then with the Cleveland Indians, they also managed to get Graig Nettles, who became a five-time All-Star with New York and helped them to win two world championships.

DICK SCHOFIELD

In an impressive 19-year major league career, Schofield had tenures of eight years with both the St. Louis Cardinals and Pittsburgh Pirates and still managed to play for five more teams. Those five are the San Francisco Giants, Yankees, Los Angeles Dodgers, Red Sox, and Milwaukee Brewers. He greatly helped the pennant run of the 1960 Pittsburgh Pirates when he took over for team captain Dick Groat and batted .403 down the stretch. He also contributed to their winning the World Series that year. Never driving in more than 36 runs in a season (he had 221 for his career), Schofield was a shortstop at a time when men at that position were expected to be contribute almost entirely with the glove.

Yankees Year

Year	Age	G	AB	R	H	2B	3B	HR	RBI	SB	CS	BB	SO	BA	OBP	SLG	OPS	OPS+	TB	SH
1966	31	25	58	5	9	2	0	0	2	0	0	9	8	.155	.265	.190	.454	37	11	1

Red Sox Years

Year	Age	G	AB	R	H	2B	3B	HR	RBI	SB	CS	BB	SO	BA	OBP	SLG	OPS	OPS+	TB	SH
1969	34	94	226	30	58	9	3	2	20	0	2	29	44	.257	.349	.350	.698	92	79	0
1970	35	76	139	16	26	1	2	1	14	0	1	21	26	.187	.294	.245	.539	46	34	0
Totals		170	365	46	84	10	5	3	34	0	3	50	70	.230	.328	.310	.637	74	113	0

Which Team Fared Better?

Because his contributions were not primarily offensive, it is difficult to compare Schofield's performance for the two teams looking only at his batting. It would be more appropriate to look at his contributions defensively. Playing exclusively at shortstop, he had a poor .909 fielding percentage for the Yankees, albeit in only 19 games and while boasting an above-average range factor (5.06 to the league's 4.79). For the Red Sox he played five different positions in 1969, including shortstop, second base, third base, right field, and left field, his lowest fielding position at any of those being .926. He also only committed seven errors in 67 games. For what he had to contribute, namely his glove, the Red Sox made out better.

Rollie Sheldon

Sheldon spent five seasons in the major leagues, three and a half of those spent with the Yankees. He was eventually traded to the Kansas City Royals, who in turn traded him to Boston after only a year. He finished his career in Boston as a reliever and spot starter. He pitched 724.2 innings, compiling a record of 38–36 with a 4.09 ERA.

Yankees Years

Year	Age	W	L	%	ERA	G	GS	CG	SV	IP	H	R	HR	BB	SO	ERA+	WHIP	H/9	BB/9	SO/9	SO/BB
1961	24	11	5	.688	3.60	35	21	6	0	162.2	149	70	17	55	84	103	1.254	8.2	3.0	4.6	1.53
1962	25	7	8	.467	5.49	34	16	2	1	118.0	136	78	12	28	54	69	1.390	10.4	2.1	4.1	1.93
1964	27	5	2	.714	3.61	19	12	3	1	102.1	92	43	18	18	57	101	1.075	8.1	1.6	5.0	3.17
1965	28	0	0		1.42	3	0	0	0	6.1	5	1	0	1	7	256	0.947	7.1	1.4	9.9	7.00
Totals		23	15	.605	4.14	91	49	11	2	389.1	382	192	47	102	202	90	1.243	8.8	2.4	4.7	1.98

Red Sox Year

Year	Age	W	L	%	ERA	G	GS	CG	SV	IP	H	R	HR	BB	SO	ERA+	WHIP	H/9	BB/9	SO/9	SO/BB
1966	29	1	6	.143	4.97	23	10	1	0	79.2	106	49	15	23	38	77	1.619	12.0	2.6	4.3	1.65

Which Team Fared Better?

Unfortunately for Sheldon he peaked after his rookie season, in which he went 11–5 with a 3.60 ERA. The Yankees benefitted from this greatly, and even though he never repeated this success, he did have a 23–15 record with the Yankees over three and a half seasons. By the time he arrived with the Red Sox he had run out of gas, pitching in 79.2 innings yet giving up 106 hits with an ERA of nearly five.

Bill Short

Short was quite the minor league player—he was inducted into the International League Hall of Fame in 2009—but he never managed to stick in the big leagues. He played on and off for six seasons, pitching in more than 10 games only once, with the 1968 New York Mets, for whom he threw in 34 games but only amassed 29.2 innings. He mostly bounced from the majors to the minors, appearing with six teams in those six seasons. In addition to the Yankees, with whom he began his big league career, and the Red Sox, he pitched for the Orioles, Pirates, Mets, and Reds.

Yankees Year

Year	Age	W	L	%	ERA	G	GS	CG	SV	IP	H	R	HR	BB	SO	ERA+	WHIP	H/9	BB/9	SO/9	SO/BB
1960	22	3	5	.375	4.79	10	10	2	0	47.0	49	25	5	30	14	76	1.681	9.4	5.7	2.7	0.47

Red Sox Year

Year	Age	W	L	%	ERA	G	GS	CG	SV	IP	H	R	HR	BB	SO	ERA+	WHIP	H/9	BB/9	SO/9	SO/BB
1966	28	0	0		4.32	8	0	0	0	8.1	10	6	1	2	2	93	1.440	10.8	2.2	2.2	1.00

Which Team Fared Better?

The Yankees win this one but are not really popping the champagne bottles open and dousing one another. He appeared in only 47.0 innings for New York, going 3–5 with a 4.79

ERA. Although he had an ERA of 4.32 and a better WHIP (1.440) with Boston, his 8.1 innings of pitching do not constitute enough of a contribution to give the BoSox the advantage.

Norm Siebern

Siebern crafted himself a nifty career in baseball, playing 12 seasons for six teams. Career highlights include making the All-Star team three times, twice with the Kansas City Athletics and once with the Baltimore Orioles. He even received MVP consideration from 1961 to 1963 while playing with KC. His finest season was 1962, with the Athletics, when he hit 25 home runs and 117 RBIs to go with a .308 batting average. He had more than 1,200 hits in his major league career and swatted 132 home runs while driving in 636 runs. In addition to the aforementioned teams, he played for the California Angels and San Francisco Giants.

Yankees Years

Year	Age	G	AB	R	H	2B	3B	HR	RBI	SB	CS	BB	SO	BA	OBP	SLG	OPS	OPS+	TB	SH
1956	22	54	162	27	33	1	4	4	21	1	1	19	38	.204	.286	.333	.619	66	54	2
1958	24	134	460	79	138	19	5	14	55	5	8	66	87	.300	.388	.454	.842	136	209	4
1959	25	120	380	52	103	17	0	11	53	3	1	41	71	.271	.341	.403	.744	108	153	3
Totals		308	1,002	158	274	37	9	29	129	9	10	126	196	.273	.354	.415	.769	113	416	9

Red Sox Years

Year	Age	G	AB	R	H	2B	3B	HR	RBI	SB	CS	BB	SO	BA	OBP	SLG	OPS	OPS+	TB	SH
1967	33	33	44	2	9	0	2	0	7	0	0	6	8	.205	.300	.295	.595	71	13	0
1968	34	27	30	0	2	0	0	0	0	0	0	0	5	.067	.067	.067	.133	-61	2	0
Totals		60	74	2	11	0	2	0	7	0	0	6	13	.149	.213	.203	.415	21	15	0

Which Team Fared Better?

Siebern was awarded the Gold Glove in the second year they were handing them out while playing left field with the Yankees. He was a full time player for two of the seasons he was with New York but for Boston he was used more sparingly, averaging 40 plate appearances in the two seasons he was with them. He also won two World Series with the Yankees in 1956 and 1958. Probably more important than the 274 hits, 29 home runs, and 129 RBIs he had with New York, was being part of the trade that brought Roger Maris to the Yankees. In seven years with the pinstripers Maris clubbed 275 home runs including his record breaking 1961 season, as well as being named the MVP of the league twice.

Lee Thomas

An outfielder and sometime first baseman, Thomas played eight years for six teams. After being drafted by the New York Yankees, he spent the majority of his career with the Los Angeles Angels, for whom he was an All-Star in 1962, hitting 26 home runs and knocking in 104 while batting .290. He enjoyed his last regular playing time with the Red Sox before becoming a part-time player and pinch hitter with the Atlanta Braves, Chicago Cubs, and Houston Astros. After leaving major league baseball, he spent another year playing in Japan for the Nankai Hawks. He would become a front-office man in the St. Louis Cardinals organization and was eventually named general manager of the Philadelphia Phillies, helping to build the 1993 pennant-winning team.

Yankees Year

Year	Age	G	AB	R	H	2B	3B	HR	RBI	SB	CS	BB	SO	BA	OBP	SLG	OPS	OPS+	TB	SH
1961	25	2	2	0	1	0	0	0	0	0	0	0	0	.500	.500	.500	1.000	175	1	0

Red Sox Years

Year	Age	G	AB	R	H	2B	3B	HR	RBI	SB	CS	BB	SO	BA	OBP	SLG	OPS	OPS+	TB	SH
1964	28	107	401	44	103	19	2	13	42	2	1	34	29	.257	.319	.411	.730	98	165	0
1965	29	151	521	74	141	27	4	22	75	6	2	72	42	.271	.361	.464	.826	128	242	5
Totals		258	922	118	244	46	6	35	117	8	3	106	71	.265	.343	.441	.785	115	407	5

Which Team Fared Better?

The Yankees had a powerful lineup already in 1961. The outfield composed of Yogi Berra, Mickey Mantle, and Roger Maris made it difficult for Thomas to crack the lineup, so after appearing in two games he was sent to the expansion Los Angeles Angels. He was an everyday player with the Red Sox, accumulating 117 RBIs, 35 home runs, and scoring 118 runs in two seasons. The one hit he had with the Yankees does not stack up.

Luis Tiant

The fiery Cuban pitcher with an odd delivery played 19 years. The two teams he spent the most time with were the Red Sox (eight years) and Cleveland Indians (six years). He also spent some time with the Yankees, Minnesota Twins, Pittsburgh Pirates, and the California Angels. During his career he won 229 games, losing only 172, and had 2,416 strikeouts to go with his 3.30 ERA. He was a 20-game winner four times in his career and an All-Star twice.

Red Sox Years

Year	Age	W	L	%	ERA	G	GS	CG	SV	IP	H	R	HR	BB	SO	ERA+	WHIP	H/9	BB/9	SO/9	SO/BB
1971	30	1	7	.125	4.85	21	10	1	0	72.1	73	42	8	32	59	77	1.452	9.1	4.0	7.3	1.84
1972	31	15	6	.714	1.91	43	19	12	3	179.0	128	45	7	65	123	169	1.078	6.4	3.3	6.2	1.89
1973	32	20	13	.606	3.34	35	35	23	0	272.0	217	105	32	78	206	120	1.085	7.2	2.6	6.8	2.64
1974	33	22	13	.629	2.92	38	38	25	0	311.1	281	106	21	82	176	133	1.166	8.1	2.4	5.1	2.15
1975	34	18	14	.563	4.02	35	35	18	0	260.0	262	126	25	72	142	103	1.285	9.1	2.5	4.9	1.97
1976	35	21	12	.636	3.06	38	38	19	0	279.0	274	107	25	64	131	129	1.211	8.8	2.1	4.2	2.05
1977	36	12	8	.600	4.53	32	32	3	0	188.2	210	98	26	51	124	100	1.383	10.0	2.4	5.9	2.43
1978	37	13	8	.619	3.31	32	31	12	0	212.1	185	80	26	57	114	126	1.140	7.8	2.4	4.8	2.00
Totals		122	81	.601	3.36	274	238	113	3	1,774.2	1,630	709	170	501	1,075	118	1.201	8.3	2.5	5.5	2.15

Yankees Years

Year	Age	W	L	%	ERA	G	GS	CG	SV	IP	H	R	HR	BB	SO	ERA+	WHIP	H/9	BB/9	SO/9	SO/BB
1979	38	13	8	.619	3.91	30	30	5	0	195.2	190	94	22	53	104	104	1.242	8.7	2.4	4.8	1.96
1980	39	8	9	.471	4.89	25	25	3	0	136.1	139	79	10	50	84	81	1.386	9.2	3.3	5.5	1.68
Totals		21	17	.553	4.31	55	55	8	0	332.0	329	173	32	103	188	93	1.301	8.9	2.8	5.1	1.83

Which Team Fared Better?

After helping Boston win the World Series in 2004, Pedro Martinez met with Yankees owner George Steinbrenner, and they talked at length about the possibility of Martinez joining the Yanks. In the end he ended up going to the other New York team, the Mets, but it would have been hard for those in Red Sox Nation to see Martinez in the Bronx. That was how it must have been when Luis Tiant went to the Yankees for the 1979 season after spending eight years with the Red Sox. The Yankees had just broken Boston's spirit the season before, charging back from a 14-game deficit at the All-Star break to tie Boston at season's end, and then beat them in a one-game playoff. Then, as if rubbing salt in the wound, the Yankees signed Tiant as a free agent. Despite this, Tiant will be best remembered in baseball lore as a Red Sox starter who pitched brilliantly in the 1975 World Series against the Cincinnati Reds, winning two games. He won 122 games with Boston and only 21 with New York. He is a member of the Boston Red Sox Hall of Fame.

The Cuban whose bizarre delivery and ball movement buckled many a hitter's knees, Tiant spent 10 years of his career between the Yankees and Red Sox. Most of these seasons came in Boston, where he pitched in 274 games, winning 122 of those. He was selected to the Red Sox Hall of Fame in 1997 (courtesy David Shankbone).

Bob Tillman

A catcher who logged 9 seasons behind the plate, he spent the first five and a half of them with the Red Sox before moving on with the Yankees for the remainder of the sixth year. He then played his final three years with the Atlanta Braves. In his career he played in 775 games and had 2,329 at-bats, 189 runs, 540 hits, 68 doubles, 10 triples, 79 home runs, 282 RBI, 1 stolen base, 228 walks, and a .232 batting average.

Red Sox Years

Year	Age	G	AB	R	H	2B	3B	HR	RBI	SB	CS	BB	SO	BA	OBP	SLG	OPS	OPS+	TB	SH
1962	25	81	249	28	57	6	4	14	38	0	0	19	65	.229	.283	.454	.737	93	113	0
1963	26	96	307	24	69	10	2	8	32	0	0	34	64	.225	.304	.349	.653	81	107	1
1964	27	131	425	43	118	18	1	17	61	0	0	49	74	.278	.352	.445	.796	116	189	4
1965	28	111	368	20	79	10	3	6	35	0	0	40	69	.215	.288	.307	.595	66	113	0
1966	29	78	204	12	47	8	0	3	24	0	0	22	35	.230	.303	.314	.616	70	64	1
1967	30	30	64	4	12	1	0	1	4	0	0	3	18	.188	.224	.250	.474	35	16	0
Totals		527	1,617	131	382	53	10	49	194	0	0	167	325	.236	.307	.372	.679	86	602	6

Yankees Year

Year	Age	G	AB	R	H	2B	3B	HR	RBI	SB	CS	BB	SO	BA	OBP	SLG	OPS	OPS+	TB	SH
1967	30	22	63	5	16	1	0	2	9	0	0	7	17	.254	.324	.365	.689	108	23	0

Which Team Fared Better?

Like most catchers Tillman was not a great hitter which accounts for his .236 batting average with the Red Sox. His .254 with the Yankees was better than most of his seasons in Boston but this is a pretty small sample size, comprising of only 63 at-bats compared with

1,617 with the Red Sox. If you look at just 1967 where he played for both teams and had a similar amount of at-bats, the Yankees made out better because he had 9 RBIs compared to 4, 2 home runs compared to 1, and 16 hits compared to 12. But you cannot overlook the other five years Tillman played for the Red Sox averaging nearly 100 games during those seasons, contributing much more to Boston than he was able to in only two months with the Yankees.

BOB TURLEY

A pitcher who spent 12 years building a 101–85 record, Bob Turley began his career with the St. Louis Browns. In 1954, after two seasons, he moved along with the franchise to Baltimore, where the team became the Orioles and he became an All-Star, leading the league in strikeouts. That November Turley became part of the largest trade in MLB history when the Orioles and Yankees swapped 17 players. He spent eight seasons in the Bronx, enjoying his best season in 1958 when he made the All-Star team, won 21 games, led the league in complete games at 19, and won the Cy Young Award. He split his final season between the Los Angeles Angels and the Red Sox.

Yankees Years

Year	Age	W	L	%	ERA	G	GS	CG	SV	IP	H	R	HR	BB	SO	ERA+	WHIP	H/9	BB/9	SO/9	SO/BB
1955	24	17	13	.567	3.06	36	34	13	1	246.2	168	92	16	177	210	123	1.399	6.1	6.5	7.7	1.19
1956	25	8	4	.667	5.05	27	21	5	1	132.0	138	76	13	103	91	77	1.826	9.4	7.0	6.2	0.88
1957	26	13	6	.684	2.71	32	23	9	3	176.1	120	59	17	85	152	133	1.163	6.1	4.3	7.8	1.79
1958	27	21	7	.750	2.97	33	31	19	1	245.1	178	82	24	128	168	119	1.247	6.5	4.7	6.2	1.31
1959	28	8	11	.421	4.32	33	22	7	0	154.1	141	80	15	83	111	84	1.451	8.2	4.8	6.5	1.34
1960	29	9	3	.750	3.27	34	24	4	5	173.1	138	67	14	87	110	110	1.298	7.2	4.5	4.5	1.00
1961	30	3	5	.375	5.75	15	12	1	0	72.0	74	47	11	51	48	65	1.736	9.3	6.4	6.0	0.94
1962	31	3	3	.500	4.57	24	8	0	1	69.0	68	45	8	47	42	83	1.667	8.9	6.1	5.5	0.89
Totals		82	52	.612	3.62	234	175	58	12	1,269.0	1,025	548	118	761	909	102	1.407	7.3	5.4	6.4	1.19

Red Sox Year

Year	Age	W	L	%	ERA	G	GS	CG	SV	IP	H	R	HR	BB	SO	ERA+	WHIP	H/9	BB/9	SO/9	SO/BB
1963	32	1	4	.200	6.10	11	7	0	0	41.1	42	28	6	28	35	63	1.694	9.1	6.1	7.6	1.25

Which Team Fared Better?

For the Yankees, Turley played eight seasons, pitching in 234 games and finishing 30 games above .500 despite a roughly league-average ERA+. He was an All-Star in 1955 and 1958, and went on to win the Cy Young Award and World Series MVP in the latter season. How did he do for the Red Sox? In one season, he pitched in 11 games, winning once, with an ERA of 6.10. He was released that October. It seems obvious who got more out of him.

GARY WASLEWSKI

Bouncing around quite a bit, Waslewski pitched for five different teams in his six-year career. His first two seasons were spent with the Red Sox, who traded him to the St. Louis Cardinals, who in turn sent him on to the Montreal Expos. The Expos then moved him on to the Yankees, with whom he spent nearly two years before being released and picked up by Oakland, where he finished out his career. Waslewski was a relief pitcher primarily and finished his career with an 11–26 record.

Red Sox Years

Year	Age	W	L	%	ERA	G	GS	CG	SV	IP	H	R	HR	BB	SO	ERA+	WHIP	H/9	BB/9	SO/9	SO/BB
1967	25	2	2	.500	3.21	12	8	0	0	42.0	34	18	3	20	20	111	1.286	7.3	4.3	4.3	1.00
1968	26	4	7	.364	3.67	34	11	2	2	105.1	108	50	9	40	59	87	1.405	9.2	3.4	5.0	1.48
Totals		6	9	.400	3.54	46	19	2	2	147.1	142	68	12	60	79	93	1.371	8.7	3.7	4.8	1.32

Yankees Years

Year	Age	W	L	%	ERA	G	GS	CG	SV	IP	H	R	HR	BB	SO	ERA+	WHIP	H/9	BB/9	SO/9	SO/BB
1970	28	2	2	.500	3.11	26	5	0	0	55.0	42	20	4	27	27	115	1.255	6.9	4.4.	4.4	1.00
1971	29	0	1	.000	3.28	24	0	0	1	35.2	28	15	2	16	17	101	1.234	7.1	4.0	4.3	1.06
Totals		2	3	.400	3.18	50	5	0	1	90.2	70	35	6	43	44	109	1.246	6.9	4.3	4.4	1.02

Which Team Fared Better?

This one is fairly close. He appeared in nearly the same number of games, 46 for Boston and 50 for the Yankees. His winning percentage was the same for the two teams at .400, but his ERA and WHIP were slightly better with New York. The only thing the Red Sox have over the Yankees is the fact that because Waslewski was used more as a starter he was able to eat up nearly 60 more innings, 147.1 to 90.2 for New York. But that meant giving up more hits and runs than he did with the Yankees, too. The Yankees eek this one out.

STAN WILLIAMS

Williams logged 28 years in the major leagues, 14 as a player and another 14 as a pitching coach. He is probably best remembered for his time with the Los Angeles Dodgers, the team that drafted him. He played five years for them, won a World Series with them in 1959, and was an All-Star with them in 1960. He was traded to the Yankees and pitched in the Bronx for two seasons before moving on to Cleveland for four. He spent his last three years with the Minnesota Twins, St. Louis Cardinals, and Boston. He won 109 games in his career, racking up 1,305 strikeouts. He acted as a pitching coach for both the Red Sox and Yankees, as well as for the Seattle Mariners, Chicago White Sox, and the Cincinnati Reds.

Yankees Years

Year	Age	W	L	%	ERA	G	GS	CG	SV	IP	H	R	HR	BB	SO	ERA+	WHIP	H/9	BB/9	SO/9	SO/BB
1963	26	9	8	.529	3.21	29	21	6	0	146.0	137	59	7	57	98	110	1.329	8.4	3.5	6.0	1.72
1964	27	1	5	.167	3.84	21	10	1	0	82.0	76	39	7	38	54	95	1.390	8.3	4.2	5.9	1.42
Totals		10	13	.435	3.43	50	31	7	0	228.0	213	98	14	95	152	104	1.351	8.4	3.8	6.0	1.60

Red Sox Year

Year	Age	W	L	%	ERA	G	GS	CG	SV	IP	H	R	HR	BB	SO	ERA+	WHIP	H/9	BB/9	SO/9	SO/BB
1972	35	0	0		6.23	3	0	0	0	4.1	5	3	0	1	3	57	1.385	10.4	2.1	6.2	3.00

Which Team Fared Better?

There is no doubt that Williams fared much better with the Yankees than the Red Sox. The mere fact that he pitched 228.0 innings for New York and only 4.1 for Boston puts him way over the edge. But Williams contributed to both of these teams long after he stopped pitching for them. He was the pitching coach for the Red Sox during the 1975 and 1976 seasons, then filled the same position for the Yankees from 1980 to 1982 and from 1987 to 1988. During that time the pitching staffs had the following records:

Red Sox	Record	Rank
1975	95–65	2nd
1976	83–79	6th

Yankees	Record	Rank
1980	103–59	1st
1981	59–48	4th
1982	79–83	8th
1987	89–73	4th
1988	85–76	7th

Those Boston teams averaged 89 wins a season; if the strike-shortened 1981 season is discounted, the Yankees averaged the same victory total. (Interestingly, New York was on pace for precisely 89 wins in 1981.) In 1975, however, he guided Boston's staff to the pennant and nearly to the championship, as the Sox lost an all-time great World Series in seven games. His 1980 New York team also made the playoffs, but they were swept in the American League Championship Series by the Royals. Nod to Boston.

John Wyatt

Starting his professional baseball career in the Negro Leagues with the Indianapolis Clowns, Wyatt was 26 by the time he joined up with the Kansas City Athletics. He was with them for six seasons, earning an All-Star nod in 1964. He then went to the Red Sox, staying for two and a half years and winning Game Six of the World Series for them in 1967. In 1968 he bounced from Boston to the Yankees and then to the Detroit Tigers. Wyatt finished his career, in a sense, where he started, going back to the A's, who by then had moved to Oakland. Pitching mostly in relief during his career, he accumulated 103 saves in 435 games pitched with 540 strikeouts.

Red Sox Years

Year	Age	W	L	%	ERA	G	GS	CG	SV	IP	H	R	HR	BB	SO	ERA+	WHIP	H/9	BB/9	SO/9	SO/BB
1966	31	3	4	.429	3.14	42	0	0	8	71.2	59	27	3	27	63	122	1.200	7.4	3.4	7.9	2.33
1967	32	10	7	.588	2.60	60	0	0	20	93.1	71	30	6	39	68	136	1.179	6.8	3.8	6.6	1.74
1968	33	1	2	.333	4.22	8	0	0	0	10.2	9	7	2	6	11	79	1.406	7.6	5.1	9.3	1.83
Totals		14	13	.519	2.92	110	0	0	28	175.2	139	64	11	72	142	125	1.201	7.1	3.7	7.3	1.97

Yankees Year

Year	Age	W	L	%	ERA	G	GS	CG	SV	IP	H	R	HR	BB	SO	ERA+	WHIP	H/9	BB/9	SO/9	SO/BB
1968	33	0	2	.000	2.16	7	0	0	0	8.1	7	3	1	9	6	141	1.920	7.6	9.7	6.5	0.67

Which Team Fared Better?

He pitched in 110 games for the Red Sox and only seven for New York. His ERA for both was pretty impressive—2.92 for Boston, 2.16 for the Yankees. He certainly pitched better for the Yankees in 1968 than he did for the BoSox, but in his 1967 season with Boston he won 10 games, saved 20, and posted a 2.60 ERA. He also contributed to their World Series run. Boston wins this one.

5. The Shot Heard Round the Nation
The Free Agency Era (1974–1993)

The 1770 Boston Massacre was a pivotal moment in the relationship between the British Commonwealth and the American colonies. British troops and American drunkards exchanged heated words with each other over an outstanding bill, and as tempers flared, the colonists began to throw stones and bottles at the soldiers. Fearing for their lives, or perhaps just realizing they had guns, the military men opened fire, shooting into the crowd and killing five colonists. Up until this point, the relationship between England and America had been contentious, with the British taxing the populous on everything from playing cards to sugar and the Colonists tarring and feathering those who tried to collect the taxes. The Boston Massacre, however, was the straw that broke the camel's back. The British, who had been the protectors of the colonists from the American Indians and the French, were now seen as a threat. It was this event that sent the two sides hurtling down the road toward war.

History often repeats itself, and it did again on September 7, 1978. This was the beginning of a four-game series between the Yankees and the Red Sox. Just a couple of months earlier, the Red Sox enjoyed a comfortable 14-game lead in the division. But the Yankees, who endured several injuries early in the season but were now nearing full strength, were closing ground and putting the pressure on the Boston club. New York was only four games back at the beginning of the late-season series. If they swept, they would be tied with Boston. But sweeping a four-game series was next to impossible, especially at Fenway Park, right?

The Yankees did not think so. Outfielder Mickey Rivers was quoted as saying, "We're not thinking of a split. We're thinking of all four." And the Yankees did in fact sweep the Red Sox, pummeling them 15–3, 13–2, 7–0, and 7–4. It was another Boston Massacre.

The rivalry between the two had been lopsided at the beginning, with Boston claiming five World Series championships during the Deadball Era. Then it went in favor of the Yankees for several years as they dominated baseball, winning 20 World Series between 1923 and 1962. Although there had been a healthy rivalry between the Yankees and Red Sox during the 1950s, there had always been a certain gentleman's level of respect. Ted Williams did not hate the Yankees. Joe DiMaggio's brother played for the Red Sox. These 1970s Red Sox hated the Yankees. Carlton Fisk, the Boston catcher, and Thurman Munson, the Yankees backstop, particularly disliked each other. They had gotten into a fistfight in 1976 when Munson came barreling into Fisk during a failed squeeze play. There had been a lot of bad blood during this time and it came to a head at the end of the 1978 season.

After the Massacre, the Yankees captured the lead in the AL East and had a one-game advantage on Boston with seven games to go. The Yankees went 6–1 during that stretch, but the Red Sox went 7–0. This put the two of them in a mathematical tie. To break it they would have a one-game playoff, game 163, to see who was moving on to the postseason. Boston was again the home team, and this time they put up more of a fight, going into the seventh inning with a 2–0 lead. That was the inning the not-so-mighty Bucky Dent strode to the plate with two Yankees on base. To this point Dent had hit four home runs for the year, and during his at-bat he had fouled a pitch off of his foot so hard the trainer had to give him medical attention, treating his leg with icy spray. And yet he was able to loft a Mike Torrez pitch over the Green Monster to give the Yankees a 3–2 lead. Reggie Jackson added another home run in the eighth, making it 5–2. The Red Sox fought back, scoring two in the bottom of the eighth, and they were poised to tie the game an inning later. With men on first and third, Carl Yastrzemski, who had already hit a home run in the game, strode to the plate. A base hit here would tie the game, and an extra-base hit might win it, giving Boston the pennant. If Red Sox fans could have picked anyone to be up at bat in this situation, most would have chosen Yastrzemski, who had come through for them so many other times. But it wasn't meant to be: The future Hall of Famer popped out to the Yankees third baseman Graig Nettles, ending the game. The Yankees went on to win the 1978 World Series while the Red Sox and their fans coped with another inexplicable loss.

If the four-game series was the Boston Massacre, this one-game playoff was like the Battle of Lexington and Concord, in which the British came to seize the arsenals of the colonists, only to find resistance. If the Patriots fought valiantly in those battles, the British military still won out in the end, as the Yankees did some 200 years later. The Red Sox would have to wait for their Yorktown equivalent, a postseason defeat of the Yankees, until 2004, when they pulled off perhaps the greatest comeback in playoffs history.

Players Who Spent Time with Both Teams, 1972–1993

Don Baylor

Baylor has spent a lot of time in the major leagues in one capacity or another. He played for 19 years, retiring in 1988, then was the hitting coach of the Milwaukee Brewers and St. Louis Cardinals before taking over as the manager of the Rockies in 1993. After five years with Colorado, he was let go when the team went on a bad run. He was then hired as the hitting coach for the Atlanta Braves before getting another chance at managing, this time with the Chicago Cubs. That stint lasted for only two years before he ended up as bench coach for the New York Mets. Then he bounced around as the hitting coach for the Seattle Mariners, the Colorado Rockies, the Arizona Diamondbacks, and his current team the Anaheim Angels, putting his time in the majors at over 40 years. As a player he spent most of his time with the California Angels and Baltimore Orioles, playing six years for each team. He also had stops in Oakland and Minnesota. He was an All-Star with the 1979 Angels where he was also named the league MVP. He was a three-time Silver Slugger Winner and won a World Series with the Minnesota Twins in 1987. He finished his career as a player with over 2,000 hits and nearly 350 home runs. He also has the dubious distinction of being hit by a pitch 267 times, 4th most in major league history.

Yankees Years

Year	Age	G	AB	R	H	2B	3B	HR	RBI	SB	CS	BB	SO	BA	OBP	SLG	OPS	OPS+	TB	SH
1983	34	144	534	82	162	33	3	21	85	17	7	40	53	.303	.361	.494	.856	138	264	2
1984	35	134	493	84	129	29	1	27	89	1	1	38	68	.262	.341	.489	.830	131	241	1

Year	Age	G	AB	R	H	2B	3B	HR	RBI	SB	CS	BB	SO	BA	OBP	SLG	OPS	OPS+	TB	SH
1985	36	142	477	70	110	24	1	23	91	0	4	52	90	.231	.330	.430	.760	109	205	1
Totals		420	1,504	236	401	86	5	71	265	18	12	130	211	.267	.345	.472	.817	126	710	4

Red Sox Years

Year	Age	G	AB	R	H	2B	3B	HR	RBI	SB	CS	BB	SO	BA	OBP	SLG	OPS	OPS+	TB	SH
1986	37	160	585	93	139	23	1	31	94	3	5	62	111	.238	.344	.439	.783	112	257	0
1987	38	108	339	64	81	8	0	16	57	5	2	40	47	.239	.355	.404	.759	100	137	0
Totals		268	924	157	220	31	1	47	151	8	7	102	158	.238	.348	.426	.774	107	394	0

Which Team Fared Better?

Baylor played three years for the Yankees and two for the Red Sox. His numbers during these stints were pretty similar. If you were to take the average of his seasons with each team, this gives a better picture of who made out better.

	Yankees	Red Sox
Hits	134	110
Batting Avg.	.267	.238
RBIs	88	76
Home runs	24	24
Runs	79	79
OBP	.345	.348
Slugging	.472	.426

It is fairly close but the Yankees just get the edge with a higher batting average and slugging percentage.

DOUG BIRD

Bird pitched for a total of 11 seasons in the majors, most of that time spent with the Kansas City Royals, for whom he went 49 and 36. His last four years he bounced around to four different teams, starting with the Philadelphia Phillies, then moving on to the Yankees, the Cubs, and finally the Red Sox. He served as both a starter and a reliever, winning 73 games in his career while losing 60 and also earning 60 saves.

Yankees Years

Year	Age	W	L	%	ERA	G	GS	CG	SV	IP	H	R	HR	BB	SO	ERA+	WHIP	H/9	BB/9	SO/9	SO/BB
1980	30	3	0	1.000	2.66	22	1	0	1	50.2	47	16	3	14	17	148	1.204	8.3	2.5	3.0	1.21
1981	31	5	1	.833	2.70	17	4	0	0	53.1	58	19	5	16	28	133	1.388	9.8	2.7	4.7	1.75
Totals		8	1	.889	2.68	39	5	0	1	104.0	105	35	8	30	45	140	1.298	9.1	2.6	3.9	1.50

Red Sox Year

Year	Age	W	L	%	ERA	G	GS	CG	SV	IP	H	R	HR	BB	SO	ERA+	WHIP	H/9	BB/9	SO/9	SO/BB
1983	33	1	4	.200	6.65	22	6	0	1	67.2	91	52	14	16	33	66	1.581	12.1	2.1	4.4	2.06

Which Team Fared Better?

He pitched so badly for the Red Sox, going 1–4 with a 6.65 ERA, that most any performance he might have turned in for the Yankees, so long as it was sufficient to keep him in the major leagues, would look good in comparison. But he did pitch well for New York, losing only once in nine decisions and finishing with a 2.68 ERA. One of the most telling stats in his time with each team is the number of hits allowed per nine innings. He pitched 67.2 innings for the Red Sox and gave up 91 hits for 12.1 hits per nine innings; for the Yankees he pitched 104.0 innings, giving up 105 hits. While not great, it is a much lower 9.1 hits per nine innings.

WADE BOGGS

A member of the Baseball Hall of Fame, Boggs was one of the best hitters of his time. He played for 18 seasons and posted a .328 career average, putting him in the top 30 of all time. In addition to Boston and New York, he played with division foe Tampa Bay. He was a 12-time All-Star, 8-time Silver Slugger winner at third base, and a five-time league batting champion.

Red Sox Years

Year	Age	G	AB	R	H	2B	3B	HR	RBI	SB	CS	BB	SO	BA	OBP	SLG	OPS	OPS+	TB	SH
1982	24	104	338	51	118	14	1	5	44	1	0	35	21	.349	.406	.441	.847	128	149	4
1983	25	153	582	100	210	44	7	5	74	3	3	92	36	.361	.444	.486	.931	150	283	3
1984	26	158	625	109	203	31	4	6	55	3	2	89	44	.325	.407	.416	.823	125	260	8
1985	27	161	653	107	240	42	3	8	78	2	1	96	61	.368	.450	.478	.928	151	312	3
1986	28	149	580	107	204	47	2	8	71	0	4	105	44	.357	.453	.486	.939	157	282	4
1987	29	147	551	108	200	40	6	24	89	1	3	105	48	.363	.461	.588	1.049	174	324	1
1988	30	155	584	128	214	45	6	5	58	2	3	125	34	.366	.476	.490	.965	168	286	0
1989	31	156	621	113	205	51	7	3	54	2	6	107	51	.330	.430	.449	.879	142	279	0
1990	32	155	619	89	187	44	5	6	63	0	0	87	68	.302	.386	.418	.804	122	259	0
1991	33	144	546	93	181	42	2	8	51	1	2	89	32	.332	.421	.460	.881	140	251	0
1992	34	143	514	62	133	22	4	7	50	1	3	74	31	.259	.353	.358	.711	96	184	0
Totals		1,625	6,213	1,067	2,098	422	47	85	687	16	27	1,004	470	.338	.428	.462	.890	142	2,869	23

Yankees Years

Year	Age	G	AB	R	H	2B	3B	HR	RBI	SB	CS	BB	SO	BA	OBP	SLG	OPS	OPS+	TB	SH
1993	35	143	560	83	169	26	1	2	59	0	1	74	49	.302	.378	.363	.740	104	203	1
1994	36	97	366	61	125	19	1	11	55	2	1	61	29	.342	.433	.489	.922	142	179	2
1995	37	126	460	76	149	22	4	5	63	1	1	74	50	.324	.412	.422	.834	119	194	0
1996	38	132	501	80	156	29	2	2	41	1	2	67	32	.311	.389	.389	.778	98	195	1
1997	39	104	353	55	103	23	1	4	28	0	1	48	38	.292	.373	.397	.769	102	140	2
Totals		602	2,240	355	702	119	9	24	246	4	6	324	198	.313	.396	.407	.803	112	911	6

Which Team Fared Better?

Wade Boggs is the reason for a book like this; it isn't obvious whether it was Boston or New York that got more out of him. While he spent more time with the Red Sox, 11 seasons, and went with them to the 1986 World Series (which they lost to the New York Mets), he *won* a Series title with the Yankees in the fourth of his five seasons in the Bronx. He was an All-Star eight of the 11 years he was with Boston, but was an All-Star all five years he was with New York. He won more Silver Sluggers with the Red Sox—six, as compared to two with the pinstripers—but won his only two Gold Gloves with the Yankees. Yet it has to be said that while his offensive value with the Yankees was high (a triple slash of .313/.396/.407), it was considerably higher with the Red Sox (.338/.428/.462). When the Baseball Hall of Fame decided, in 2005, that Boggs's Cooperstown plaque should show him wearing a Red Sox cap, they made the right call.

RICK CERONE

Drafted by the Cleveland Indians in the first round of the 1975 draft, Cerone played for 18 seasons in baseball, mostly as a catcher. His longest time with any team was with the Yankees, with whom he played three different times over a total of seven seasons. He also played with the Toronto Blue Jays, New York Mets, Montreal Expos, Atlanta Braves, and Milwaukee Brewers in addition to the Red Sox. He fell just two hits shy of 1,000 in his career.

Yankees Years

Year	Age	G	AB	R	H	2B	3B	HR	RBI	SB	CS	BB	SO	BA	OBP	SLG	OPS	OPS+	TB	SH
1980	26	147	519	70	144	30	4	14	85	1	3	32	56	.277	.321	.432	.753	107	224	8
1981	27	71	234	23	57	13	2	2	21	0	2	12	24	.244	.276	.342	.618	79	80	4
1982	28	89	300	29	68	10	0	5	28	0	2	19	27	.227	.271	.310	.581	61	93	4
1983	29	80	246	18	54	7	0	2	22	0	0	15	29	.220	.267	.272	.540	52	67	4
1984	30	38	120	8	25	3	0	2	13	1	0	9	15	.208	.269	.283	.553	56	34	2
1987	33	113	284	28	69	12	1	4	23	0	1	30	46	.243	.320	.335	.654	75	95	5
1990	36	49	139	12	42	6	0	2	11	0	0	5	13	.302	.324	.388	.713	99	54	1
Totals		587	1,842	188	459	81	7	31	203	2	8	122	210	.249	.297	.351	.648	80	647	28

Red Sox Years

Year	Age	G	AB	R	H	2B	3B	HR	RBI	SB	CS	BB	SO	BA	OBP	SLG	OPS	OPS+	TB	SH
1988	34	84	264	31	71	13	1	3	27	0	0	20	32	.269	.326	.360	.686	90	95	1
1989	35	102	296	28	72	16	1	4	48	0	0	34	40	.243	.320	.345	.665	83	102	4
Totals		186	560	59	143	29	2	7	75	0	0	54	72	.255	.323	.352	.675	86	197	5

Which Team Fared Better?

Numbers aside, Cerone meant much more to the Yankees because of the big shoes he was assigned to fill. In August 1979, Thurman Munson, the captain of the Yankees and their starting catcher for the previous 10 years, died in a tragic plane crash. Cerone took over the full-time catching duties the following season, playing in 147 games and knocking in 85 runs. He also gave one of the best defensive performances of the year, leading the league with a 51.8 percent caught-stealing rate, throwing out 57 baserunners. His performance earned him the seventh-place finish in the MVP race, and he managed to direct the Yankees to the playoffs. Even though his production fell off the next couple of seasons and he became a backup catcher, he gave his best offensive season to New York, and his solid play that year made the transition to a new full-time catcher easier for the team and its fans.

JACK CLARK

Jack the Ripper played 18 seasons in the majors, 10 of those spent with the San Francisco Giants. Known for his outspokenness, and as a feared hitter, Clark won the Silver Slugger Award twice, was an All-Star four times, and finished in the top 20 for MVP six times. He wasn't opposed to taking a walk, either, leading the league three times in his career. This resulted in a solid .379 on-base percentage. He finished his career as a .267 hitter with 340 home runs and 1,180 RBIs. He also scored 1,118 runs, hit 332 doubles, stole 77 bases, and had 1,826 hits. Some of the other teams he played for were the St. Louis Cardinals, the San Diego Padres, and of course the Yankees and Red Sox.

Yankees Year

Year	Age	G	AB	R	H	2B	3B	HR	RBI	SB	CS	BB	SO	BA	OBP	SLG	OPS	OPS+	TB	SH
1988	32	150	496	81	120	14	0	27	93	3	2	113	141	.242	.381	.433	.815	130	215	0

Red Sox Years

Year	Age	G	AB	R	H	2B	3B	HR	RBI	SB	CS	BB	SO	BA	OBP	SLG	OPS	OPS+	TB	SH
1991	35	140	481	75	120	18	1	28	87	0	2	96	133	.249	.374	.466	.840	127	224	0
1992	36	81	257	32	54	11	0	5	33	1	1	56	87	.210	.350	.311	.661	83	80	0
Totals		221	738	107	174	29	1	33	120	1	3	152	220	.236	.366	.412	.778	112	304	0

Which Team Fared Better?

Clark's brashness did not allow him to finish out his contracts with either team. He signed a two-year deal with the Yankees but requested a trade after not getting along with manager Lou Piniella. He had signed a three-year contract with Boston but after a lackluster 1992 season the Red Sox released him. He served as the designated hitter for both teams, knocking in 93 for the Yankees in his lone season and 87 in his best year with Boston. The Red Sox take the advantage because although his 1988 season with the Yankees and the 1991 year with Boston are very close, he had an additional half-season with the Sox that gives him more production with them.

MIKE EASLER

Easler had a 14-year career, playing for six teams. Most of that time was spent with the Pittsburgh Pirates, with whom he won a World Series in 1979 and was an All-Star in 1981. He also played for the Houston Astros, California Angels, Philadelphia Phillies, and the Yankees and BoSox. During his career he had 1,087 hits, 118 home runs, 465 runs, and 522 RBIs. After his major league career he played in Japan for two years. He has been a hitting coach for three different teams, the Red Sox (1993–1994), St. Louis Cardinals (1999–2001), and the Los Angeles Dodgers (2008).

Red Sox Years

Year	Age	G	AB	R	H	2B	3B	HR	RBI	SB	CS	BB	SO	BA	OBP	SLG	OPS	OPS+	TB	SH
1984	33	156	601	87	188	31	5	27	91	1	1	58	134	.313	.376	.516	.892	140	310	1
1985	34	155	568	71	149	29	4	16	74	0	1	53	129	.262	.325	.412	.737	98	234	0
Totals		311	1,169	158	337	60	9	43	165	1	2	111	263	.288	.351	.465	.816	119	544	1

Yankees Years

Year	Age	G	AB	R	H	2B	3B	HR	RBI	SB	CS	BB	SO	BA	OBP	SLG	OPS	OPS+	TB	SH
1986	35	146	490	64	148	26	2	14	78	3	2	49	87	.302	.362	.449	.811	121	220	2
1987	36	65	167	13	47	6	0	4	21	1	0	14	32	.281	.337	.389	.726	93	65	0
Totals		211	657	77	195	32	2	18	99	4	1	63	119	.297	.356	.434	.790	114	285	2

Which Team Fared Better?

The Red Sox definitely got more at-bats in the two years Easler played for them, nearly doubling the number he got with the Yankees. The question is whether those Boston at-bats were of the same quality as those he gave the Yankees. The answer is yes. In 1984 Easler had a very solid year for the Red Sox, hitting 27 home runs and knocking in 91, both career highs for him. He batted a respectable .313 and had a slugging percentage of .516, good for seventh in the league. He had a solid first year with the Yankees as well but only had 14 home runs with 78 RBIs to go with his .302 average. Not only did Easler give the Red Sox better years than he gave the Yankees, he gave his best year to them in the course of his 14 years playing.

STEVE FARR

Farr was mostly a closer in his career, playing 11 seasons for 4 different teams. He gave most of his time to Kansas City, where he played for six years and won a world championship in 1985. He was with the Yankees for three seasons, Cleveland for two, and Boston for one. Farr accumulated 132 saves in his career, his best total coming while with New York, for whom he had 30. He started only 28 games in his career but finished 313, and he struck out batters exactly twice as often (668) as he walked them (334).

Yankees Years

Year	Age	W	L	%	ERA	G	GS	CG	SV	IP	H	R	HR	BB	SO	ERA+	WHIP	H/9	BB/9	SO/9	SO/BB
1991	34	5	5	.500	2.19	60	0	0	23	70.0	57	19	4	20	60	191	1.100	7.3	2.6	7.7	3.00
1992	35	2	2	.500	1.56	50	0	0	30	52.0	34	10	2	19	37	253	1.019	5.9	3.3	6.4	1.95
1993	36	2	2	.500	4.21	49	0	0	25	47.0	44	22	8	28	39	100	1.532	8.4	5.4	7.5	1.39
Totals		9	9	.500	2.56	159	0	0	78	169.0	135	51	14	67	136	161	1.195	7.2	3.6	7.2	2.03

Red Sox Year

Year	Age	W	L	%	ERA	G	GS	CG	SV	IP	H	R	HR	BB	SO	ERA+	WHIP	H/9	BB/9	SO/9	SO/BB
1994	37	1	0	1.000	6.23	11	0	0	0	13.0	24	9	2	3	8	82	2.077	16.6	2.1	5.5	2.67

Which Team Fared Better?

It has been famously said that numbers do not lie. A 6.23 ERA tells a cringe-inducing story about Farr's time with the Red Sox, and specifically about why he pitched only 13 innings with the team. With the Yankees he pitched 169.30 innings, and in 1992 he saved 30 games and posted a 1.56 ERA, both career highs. More importantly, he filled the role of the closer for New York until it could be taken over by John Wetteland for two years and then by Mariano Rivera, who stayed for 17 years. He gave them 78 saves in three seasons, not exactly Rivera-like numbers, but pretty good.

GREG HARRIS

Greg A. Harris (there was another pitcher named Greg W. Harris, whose career overlapped) pitched in professional ball for 15 years, sporting eight different uniforms. He staked his claim to fame in a game during the 1995 season when he switch-pitched. In other words, he faced a batter as a right-handed pitcher, then when the next batter came up, he pitched as a left-hander. Harris began his career with the New York Mets before spending two seasons with the Cincinnati Reds. He split 1984 between the Montreal Expos and San Diego, helping the Padres to the World Series. He then spent three years with the Texas Rangers and another two with the Philadelphia Phillies before his longest tenure of six years with the Red Sox. When he was released by Boston the Yankees picked him up and then he finished his career with Montreal. A lifetime 74–90 with a 3.69 ERA and 1,141 strikeouts, he appeared in 703 games, 98 of them as a starter.

Red Sox Years

Year	Age	W	L	%	ERA	G	GS	CG	SV	IP	H	R	HR	BB	SO	ERA+	WHIP	H/9	BB/9	SO/9	SO/BB
1989	33	2	2	.500	2.57	15	0	0	0	28.0	21	12	1	15	25	163	1.286	6.8	4.8	8.0	1.67
1990	34	13	9	.591	4.00	34	30	1	0	184.1	186	90	13	77	117	102	1.427	9.1	3.8	5.7	1.52
1991	35	11	12	.478	3.85	53	21	1	2	173.0	157	79	13	69	127	112	1.306	8.2	3.6	6.6	1.84
1992	36	4	9	.308	2.51	70	2	1	4	107.2	82	38	6	60	73	168	1.319	6.9	5.0	6.1	1.22
1993	37	6	7	.462	3.77	80	0	0	8	112.1	95	55	7	60	103	124	1.380	7.6	4.8	8.3	1.72
1994	38	3	4	.429	8.28	35	0	0	2	45.2	60	44	8	23	44	61	1.818	11.8	4.5	8.7	1.91
Totals		39	43	.476	3.91	287	53	3	16	651.0	601	318	48	304	489	111	1.390	8.3	4.2	6.8	1.61

Yankees Year

Year	Age	W	L	%	ERA	G	GS	CG	SV	IP	H	R	HR	BB	SO	ERA+	WHIP	H/9	BB/9	SO/9	SO/BB
1994	38	0	1	.000	5.40	3	0	0	0	5.0	4	5	1	3	4	90	1.400	7.2	5.4	7.2	1.33

Which Team Fared Better?

Harris had some good years for the Red Sox, posting a 2.57 ERA the first year he played for them and a 2.51 a couple of years later. He served as a starter for them during the 1990–1991 season, winning 24 games over the course of those two years. Even though he had an overall record of 39–43 with them, he provided some valuable relief work. The Yankees used him for only three games for a grand total of five innings in which he gave up five runs, walked three, and struck out four. This was sadly better than earlier that year with Boston where he posted a dismal 8.28 ERA. Overall, the Red Sox made out better.

RICKEY HENDERSON

Considered by many to be the greatest leadoff hitter in history, Henderson played for 25 seasons and never officially retired from the game. During that time he established four major league records: He has the most steals in history with 1,406 (the number two person, Lou Brock, has 938), the most runs scored at 2,295, the most home runs by a leadoff hitter with 81, and the most steals in a single season in 1982 when he swiped 130 bases. Henderson was also a 10-time All-Star, 12-time stolen base champion, three-time Silver Slugger Award winner, a two-time World Series champion (one Series title with the Oakland A's, a second with the Toronto Blue Jays), and an American League MVP in 1990. Henderson spent 14 seasons with the Oakland A's, the team that has retired his number 24. In addition, he played for the Yankees, San Diego Padres, New York Mets, Boston, LA Dodgers, Anaheim Angels, and the Seattle Mariners. He is also a member of the 3,000-hit club with 3,055 and had nearly 300 home runs.

Yankees Years

Year	Age	G	AB	R	H	2B	3B	HR	RBI	SB	CS	BB	SO	BA	OBP	SLG	OPS	OPS+	TB	SH
1985	26	143	547	146	172	28	5	24	72	80	10	99	65	.314	.419	.516	.934	157	282	0
1986	27	153	608	130	160	31	5	28	74	87	18	89	81	.263	.358	.469	.827	125	285	0
1987	28	95	358	78	104	17	3	17	37	41	8	80	52	.291	.423	.497	.920	145	178	0
1988	29	140	554	118	169	30	2	6	50	93	13	82	54	.305	.394	.399	.793	124	221	2
1989	30	65	235	41	58	13	1	3	22	25	8	56	29	.247	.392	.349	.741	112	82	0
Totals		596	2,302	513	663	119	16	78	255	326	57	406	281	.288	.395	.455	.850	135	1,048	2

Red Sox Year

Year	Age	G	AB	R	H	2B	3B	HR	RBI	SB	CS	BB	SO	BA	OBP	SLG	OPS	OPS+	TB	SH
2002	43	72	179	40	40	6	1	5	16	8	2	38	47	.223	.369	.352	.721	92	63	0

Which Team Fared Better?

Henderson will best be remembered for his time with the Oakland A's, but he did spent five good seasons with the Yankees. During the first two years, he put up career-average statistics—which for most players would be career-best numbers—topping 80 steals, 70 RBIs, and 135 runs scored per season. He was in his late-twenties while playing for the Yankees, and was an All-Star with them for four seasons. By the time he went to Boston he was 43 years of age. When Henderson joined the Red Sox he had more career stolen bases than Boston had in its franchise history. Despite his having become the oldest center fielder in major league history, however, the season was not a memorable one. He hit an anemic .223 (even if he did get on base at a very respectable .369 clip), drove in 16 runs, and stole only eight bases. The Yankees definitely fared better.

BUTCH HOBSON

Known as a tough player with a football mentality, Hobson played third base with reckless abandon. After having a promising third season with Boston, launching 30 home runs, Hobson went on to hit only 98 in his eight-year career. In his time in the majors he played mostly for Boston before being traded to the California Angels and then to the New York Yankees.

Red Sox Years

Year	Age	G	AB	R	H	2B	3B	HR	RBI	SB	CS	BB	SO	BA	OBP	SLG	OPS	OPS+	TB	SH
1975	23	2	4	0	1	0	0	0	0	0	0	0	2	.250	.250	.250	.500	37	1	0
1976	24	76	269	34	63	7	5	8	34	0	1	15	62	.234	.272	.387	.658	82	104	5
1977	25	159	593	77	157	33	5	30	112	5	4	27	162	.265	.300	.489	.789	101	290	10
1978	26	147	512	65	128	26	2	17	80	1	0	50	122	.250	.312	.408	.720	92	209	4
1979	27	146	528	74	138	26	7	28	93	3	2	30	78	.261	.298	.496	.794	106	262	6
1980	28	93	324	35	74	6	0	11	39	1	1	25	69	.228	.281	.349	.630	68	113	0
Totals		623	2,230	285	561	98	19	94	358	10	8	147	495	.252	.296	.439	.735	93	979	25

Yankees Year

Year	Age	G	AB	R	H	2B	3B	HR	RBI	SB	CS	BB	SO	BA	OBP	SLG	OPS	OPS+	TB	SH
1982	30	30	58	2	10	2	0	0	3	0	0	1	14	.172	.183	.207	.390	8	12	0

Which Team Fared Better?

He gave Boston three pretty good seasons from 1977–1979, his best being 1977, when he had 30 home runs, 112 RBIs, and 77 runs scored, all career bests. Injuries and a lead glove caused his playing time to diminish in 1980, and the Red Sox traded him to the Angels in exchange for Carney Lansford, who led the league in batting average in his first year with the Red Sox. His time with the Yankees was limited to 30 games, and he batted a meager .172. He did go on to have a managing career with the Red Sox as well, serving as the skipper for New Britain (AA) and Pawtucket (AAA) before being hired to take over the major league club. In his time leading the big league Red Sox, from 1992 to 1994, he had a 207–232 record. After being fired he managed an independent team (1995) and the Phillies' AAA affiliate (1996) before making his way back, in 1999, to Boston's farm system, managing Sarasota (A+).

TIM LOLLAR

In his seven years in baseball, Lollar only had one winning season as a starter, going 16–9 with a 3.13 ERA in 232.2 innings pitched while playing for the San Diego Padres in 1982.

He did pitch with the Padres when they went to the 1984 World Series but was not very effective in the postseason, getting lit up to the tune of a 10.50 ERA in two games pitched. He spent a brief time with the Yankees at the beginning of his career and after the Padres bounced from the Chicago White Sox to the Red Sox. Probably known less for his pitching and more for his hitting as a pitcher, he hit eight home runs during his four years in the National League.

Yankees Year

Year	Age	W	L	%	ERA	G	GS	CG	SV	IP	H	R	HR	BB	SO	ERA+	WHIP	H/9	BB/9	SO/9	SO/BB
1980	24	1	0	1.000	3.34	14	1	0	2	32.1	33	14	3	20	13	119	1.639	9.2	5.6	3.6	0.65

Red Sox Years

Year	Age	W	L	%	ERA	G	GS	CG	SV	IP	H	R	HR	BB	SO	ERA+	WHIP	H/9	BB/9	SO/9	SO/BB
1985	29	5	5	.500	4.57	16	10	1	1	67.0	57	37	9	40	44	94	1.448	7.7	5.4	5.9	1.10
1986	30	2	0	1.000	6.91	32	1	0	0	43.0	51	35	7	34	28	61	1.977	10.7	7.1	5.9	0.82
Totals		7	5	.583	5.48	48	11	1	1	110.0	108	72	16	74	72	78	1.655	8.8	6.1	5.9	0.97

Which Team Fared Better?

The Padres made out better than either the Yankees or Red Sox but since this isn't a book about them, it has to be determined which of the two teams Lollar benefitted most. He played in three times as many games with the Red Sox and posted seven wins with them, but his ERA with New York was nearly half (3.34) of what it was with Boston (5.48). His WHIP is almost identical for the two teams, as is his hits per nine innings, but his walk-to-strikeout ratio was a little worse with the Red Sox. He nevertheless struck out far more batters with the BoSox. It is nearly a coin flip, then, and the tiebreaker comes in the form of salary. Lollar broke in with the Yankees, who paid only around $30,000 for his 32 innings pitched. Boston, on the other hand, had to pay half a million dollars for his mediocrity, giving the Yankees the best value.

Bob Melvin

When all is said and done and Bob Melvin's entry in baseball's history books has been written, he will probably be best remembered as a manager rather than for his playing time. For the record, he played in 10 seasons in the major leagues, finishing with a .233 batting average and 35 home runs. He began with the Detroit Tigers, went to the San Francisco Giants, then moved on to the Baltimore Orioles and Kansas City Royals before going through Boston and New York and finishing his career with the Chicago White Sox. He was a backup catcher, topping out at 93 games played in a season, something he accomplished with the Orioles. After his playing days, he was named Manager of the Year for the National League in 2007 while leading the Arizona Diamondbacks and then again for the American League in 2012, when he was with the Oakland Athletics. He also managed the Seattle Mariners early in his career.

Red Sox Year

Year	Age	G	AB	R	H	2B	3B	HR	RBI	SB	CS	BB	SO	BA	OBP	SLG	OPS	OPS+	TB	SH
1993	31	77	176	13	39	7	0	3	23	0	0	7	44	.222	.251	.313	.564	48	55	3

Yankees Year

Year	Age	G	AB	R	H	2B	3B	HR	RBI	SB	CS	BB	SO	BA	OBP	SLG	OPS	OPS+	TB	SH
1994	32	9	14	2	4	0	0	1	3	0	0	0	3	.286	.286	.500	.786	102	7	0

Which Team Fared Better?

Melvin had backup-catcher-like numbers while playing in Boston, appearing in 77 games, batting .222, and knocking in 23 runs. His role when he went to the Yankees was even smaller, as he appeared in only nine games. He hit .286 in his handful of at-bats and had three RBIs. Given his limited amount of playing time, Boston fared a bit better.

ROB MURPHY

A left-handed relief pitcher, Murphy spent 11 seasons in the majors. Like many left-handed relievers, he moved around, never staying with one team for too long. He played for eight teams, including Cincinnati (his original team), Boston, Seattle, Houston, St. Louis, New York, Los Angeles, and Florida. Murphy amassed a 32–38 record with a 3.64 ERA and 30 saves. At retirement, he had appeared in 597 games, ranked 18th in the history of baseball for left-handed relief pitchers.

Red Sox Years

Year	Age	W	L	%	ERA	G	GS	CG	SV	IP	H	R	HR	BB	SO	ERA+	WHIP	H/9	BB/9	SO/9	SO/BB
1989	29	5	7	.417	2.74	74	0	0	9	105.0	97	38	7	41	107	151	1.314	8.3	3.5	9.2	2.61
1990	30	0	6	.000	6.32	68	0	0	7	57.0	85	46	10	32	54	65	2.053	13.4	5.1	8.5	1.69
Totals		5	13	.278	4.00	142	0	0	16	162.0	182	84	17	73	161	103	1.574	10.1	4.1	8.9	2.21

Yankees Year

Year	Age	W	L	%	ERA	G	GS	CG	SV	IP	H	R	HR	BB	SO	ERA+	WHIP	H/9	BB/9	SO/9	SO/BB
1994	34	0	0		16.20	3	0	0	0	1.2	3	3	2	0	0	34	1.800	16.2	0.0	0.0	

Which Team Fared Better?

His first year with Boston was probably his best as a pitcher. He had a career-high 105 innings pitched and managed nine saves even though Lee Smith was the primary closer. He appeared in 74 games, a team record for a left-handed reliever at that time, and the Boston area baseball writers named him the Fireman of the Year, an award given to the reliever believed to be the team's best. He did not fare as well his second year with Boston, but even his 6.32 ERA and six losses look good compared with the 16.20 ERA he had while pitching just 1.2 innings for the Yankees in 1994. He gave up two home runs and three earned runs in just three games.

OTIS NIXON

The quick-footed Nixon was a center fielder for 17 years in the majors, playing for nine different teams. His longest tenure, four years, was spent with Atlanta, the team he will probably best be remembered for playing with. He went to the World Series with them twice, losing to the Blue Jays in 1992 and the Yankees in 1999. He would have gone a third time in 1991 but was arrested on drug charges. He logged multiple years with Cleveland, Montreal, and Toronto, and spent one season apiece with Minnesota, Boston, Los Angeles, Texas, and

New York. Over his career he was a .270 hitter with 11 home runs, 318 RBI, 878 runs, 1,379 hits, 142 doubles, 27 triples, and an impressive 620 stolen bases in 1,709 games. He is ranked 16th in major league history in career stolen bases.

Yankees Year

Year	Age	G	AB	R	H	2B	3B	HR	RBI	SB	CS	BB	SO	BA	OBP	SLG	OPS	OPS+	TB	SH
1983	24	13	14	2	2	0	0	0	0	2	0	1	5	.143	.200	.143	.343	-2	2	0

Red Sox Year

Year	Age	G	AB	R	H	2B	3B	HR	RBI	SB	CS	BB	SO	BA	OBP	SLG	OPS	OPS+	TB	SH
1994	35	103	398	60	109	15	1	0	25	42	10	55	65	.274	.360	.317	.677	75	126	6

Which Team Fared Better?

Nixon came up with the Yankees, and like most rookies just getting their beaks wet, he saw limited playing time, appearing in only 13 games. In those games he had only 14 at-bats, meaning he was used mostly in a pinch-hitting role. Eleven years later, when he played with the Red Sox, he had developed into a fairly reliable player who was never going to be an offensive threat but would play a serviceable center field and steal a few bases. He played nearly a full season with Boston, appearing in 103 games, stealing 42 bases, and forging a .989 fielding percentage—exactly what he was advertised as being able to do. Because the Red Sox got a player who had established himself as a major leaguer, they got the better of him.

MIKE O'BERRY

A backup catcher who managed to eke out a seven-year career, he averaged about 28 games a season. During this time he posted a .191 batting average, three home runs, and 27 RBIs. Those are hardly Hall of Fame caliber numbers, but, then, he was used more as a defensive backup; if he happened to make contact at the plate, well, that was more than what was expected of him. He began his career with the Red Sox before being traded after a year to the Chicago Cubs, who then traded him after a year to the Cincinnati Reds. The Reds held on to him for two years before shipping him off to the California Angels. He finished with the Yankees and Montreal Expos.

Red Sox Year

Year	Age	G	AB	R	H	2B	3B	HR	RBI	SB	CS	BB	SO	BA	OBP	SLG	OPS	OPS+	TB	SH
1979	25	43	59	8	10	1	0	1	4	0	0	5	16	.169	.242	.237	.480	28	14	2

Yankees Year

Year	Age	G	AB	R	H	2B	3B	HR	RBI	SB	CS	BB	SO	BA	OBP	SLG	OPS	OPS+	TB	SH
1984	30	13	32	3	8	2	0	0	5	0	0	2	2	.250	.294	.313	.607	72	10	0

Which Team Fared Better?

O'Berry got into 43 games for Boston in 1979, filling in for Carlton Fisk, who had injured his ribcage the year before and was limited to only 91 games that year. His .169 average and four RBIs do not speak of the value he provided behind the plate for the Red Sox. When he played for the Yankees, he found himself the third-string catcher behind Rick Cerone and starter Butch Wynegar. He appeared in only 13 games, but in half the plate appearances, he had one more RBI than he did while with Boston, and he almost had as many hits. He was not as valuable defensively—even if measured only by the number of innings logged as Fisk's relief—but his batting average, on-base percentage, and slugging percentage were all higher while playing with the Yankees, giving them the better of him.

Bob Ojeda

When all is said and done, Bob Ojeda will probably be remembered for two things in his career, one of them positive, the other tragic. The positive was Ojeda's being the anchor for the 1986 New York Mets, going 18–5 that year and going 2–0 in the postseason, helping the Mets win the World Series against a Boston team that had them on the ropes. The tragic came when he was a pitcher with the Cleveland Indians. He and two other pitchers, Steve Olin and Tim Crews, were out for a boat ride when they ran into a pier. Only Ojeda survived. As a pitcher he spent 15 years playing major league ball, starting with the Red Sox and then going over to the Mets. He pitched for the Los Angeles Dodgers before going to Cleveland for one season and finishing his career with the Yankees. He had a 115–98 record and a 3.65 ERA.

Red Sox Years

Year	Age	W	L	%	ERA	G	GS	CG	SV	IP	H	R	HR	BB	SO	ERA+	WHIP	H/9	BB/9	SO/9	SO/BB
1980	22	1	1	.500	6.92	7	7	0	0	26.0	39	20	2	14	12	62	2.038	13.5	4.8	4.2	0.86
1981	23	6	2	.750	3.12	10	10	2	0	66.1	50	25	6	25	28	125	1.131	6.8	3.4	3.8	1.12
1982	24	4	6	.400	5.63	22	14	0	0	78.1	95	53	13	29	52	77	1.583	10.9	3.3	6.0	1.79
1983	25	12	7	.632	4.04	29	29	5	0	173.2	173	85	15	73	94	108	1.417	9.0.	3.8	4.9	1.29
1984	26	12	12	.500	3.99	33	32	8	0	216.2	211	106	17	96	137	104	1.417	8.8	4.0	5.7	1.43
1985	27	9	11	.450	4.00	39	22	5	1	157.2	166	74	11	48	102	107	1.357	9.5	2.7	5.8	2.13
Totals		44	39	.530	4.21	140	113	20	1	718.2	734	363	64	285	425	101	1.418	9.2	3.6	5.3	1.49

Yankees Year

Year	Age	W	L	%	ERA	G	GS	CG	SV	IP	H	R	HR	BB	SO	ERA+	WHIP	H/9	BB/9	SO/9	SO/BB
1994	36	0	0		24.00	2	2	0	0	3.0	11	8	1	6	3	21	5.667	33.0	18.0	9.0	0.50

Which Team Fared Better?

Ojeda started slow with the Red Sox but eventually was a 12-game winner for them twice, in 1983 and 1984. He compiled a 44–39 record, being relegated to the bullpen in his final season. Where Ojeda hurt Boston was when they traded him to the New York Mets, getting Calvin Schiraldi in return. Ojeda won Game Three of the World Series after the Mets had dropped the first two while Schiraldi was the loser in Games Six and Seven, giving the Mets the Series victory over the Red Sox and continuing the supposed Curse of the Bambino. Despite this, Ojeda did more for the Red Sox in his six seasons with them than he did for the Yankees in his limited time in the Bronx. Ojeda had suffered severe head lacerations in the boating accident and never fully recovered as a player. He had a 24.00 ERA in just two games, giving up eight runs and 11 hits in just three innings of work.

Spike Owen

A shortstop who spent 13 years in the league, Owen was never a Gold Glover and yet led the league in fielding percentage in 1990 and 1991, and in 1989 set a record for shortstops for errorless games at 61. He began his career with the Seattle Mariners, who eventually named him captain, then was traded to the Red Sox. Boston then traded him to the Montreal Expos where he enjoyed his best year offensively, having career highs in average (.269), stolen bases (7), home runs (7), and slugging percentage (.381). He also carried a .348 on-base percentage and hit .319 with runners in scoring position. He went to New York for a single season before spending his last two with the California Angels. He played in over 1,500 games and raked 1,211 hits including 215 doubles and 59 triples.

Red Sox Years

Year	Age	G	AB	R	H	2B	3B	HR	RBI	SB	CS	BB	SO	BA	OBP	SLG	OPS	OPS+	TB	SH
1986	25	42	126	21	23	2	1	1	10	3	1	17	9	.183	.283	.238	.521	44	30	2
1987	26	132	437	50	113	17	7	2	48	11	8	53	43	.259	.337	.343	.681	80	150	9
1988	27	89	257	40	64	14	1	5	18	0	1	27	27	.249	.324	.370	.694	91	95	7
Totals		263	820	111	200	33	9	8	76	14	10	97	79	.244	.325	.335	.660	78	275	18

Yankees Year

Year	Age	G	AB	R	H	2B	3B	HR	RBI	SB	CS	BB	SO	BA	OBP	SLG	OPS	OPS+	TB	SH
1993	32	103	334	41	78	16	2	2	20	3	2	29	30	.234	.294	.311	.605	66	104	2

Which Team Fared Better?

This is another case where a player spent much more time with one team than the other, making him more valuable over a longer period of time. Despite this Owen was of value to the Red Sox in other ways. During the 1986 postseason, Owen batted .429 in the ALCS and .300 in the World Series. In 1992 the Yankees signed Owen to a three year contract but the only category he led middle infielders in his one year with them was salary; they paid him $2.25 million. They quickly got rid of him by trading him to the California Angels, eating some of his salary in the process. In contrast the Red Sox never paid him more than $525,000. It all worked out for the Yankees, who had an up-and-coming shortstop named Derek Jeter who would soon take over the shortstop position for the next 20 years.

Jeff Reardon

Reardon was one of the pioneers of the advent of the closer in baseball. The role of a late inning relief specialist who finished games began to take shape in the 1980s and 1990s, right smack dab in the middle of Reardon's career. He led the league only once in saves with 41 but was often near the top of the league in the category many other times. In his career he had 367 saves, which at one time led major league baseball. He has since been passed many times, putting him at number seven on the career saves list. He was a four time All-Star, twice with the Montreal Expos and then with the Minnesota Twins and Red Sox. He won a World Series with the Twins in 1997 and was named the Rolaids Relief Man in 1985. In addition to the teams already mentioned, he played for the New York Mets, Cincinnati Reds, and Atlanta Braves in his 16 years career.

Red Sox Years

Year	Age	W	L	%	ERA	G	GS	CG	SV	IP	H	R	HR	BB	SO	ERA+	WHIP	H/9	BB/9	SO/9	SO/BB
1990	34	5	3	.625	3.16	47	0	0	21	51.1	39	19	5	19	33	130	1.130	6.8	3.3	5.8	1.74
1991	35	1	4	.200	3.03	57	0	0	40	59.1	54	21	9	16	44	143	1.180	8.2	2.4	6.7	2.75
1992	36	2	2	.500	4.25	46	0	0	27	42.1	53	20	6	7	32	99	1.417	11.3	1.5	6.8	4.57
Totals		8	9	.471	3.41	150	0	0	88	153.0	146	60	20	42	109	124	1.229	8.6	2.5	6.4	2.60

Yankees Year

Year	Age	W	L	%	ERA	G	GS	CG	SV	IP	H	R	HR	BB	SO	ERA+	WHIP	H/9	BB/9	SO/9	SO/BB
1994	38	1	0	1.000	8.38	11	0	0	2	9.2	17	9	3	3	4	56	2.069	15.8	2.8	3.7	1.33

Which Team Fared Better?

The value comes in how each of the teams used Reardon. The Red Sox utilized him as their primary closer, saving 88 games over three seasons. When Reardon was with the Yankees, Steve Howe was the primary closer, so Reardon only got 2 saves and pitched in only 9.2 innings as compared with 153.0 with Boston. Realizing there was not enough room in the Yankee bullpen for him, Reardon retired in May of that season, spending only a month with the Yankees and not really providing them much value.

GEORGE SCOTT

A first baseman who averaged nearly 20 home runs a year during his 14-year career as well as knocking in over 100 runs twice, Scott was a three-time All-Star, in 1966 and 1977 with Boston and also with the 1975 Milwaukee Brewers. He won the Gold Glove Award for defense at first base 8 times including 6 years in a row from 1971–1976. He received some MVP consideration for 7 of the seasons he played and was the home run and RBI champ in the American League in 1975. He spent most of his career with either the Red Sox or Milwaukee Brewers, but also played a year for the Yankees and the Kansas City Royals.

Red Sox Years

Year	Age	G	AB	R	H	2B	3B	HR	RBI	SB	CS	BB	SO	BA	OBP	SLG	OPS	OPS+	TB	SH
1966	22	162	601	73	147	18	7	27	90	4	0	65	152	.245	.324	.433	.757	107	260	2
1967	23	159	565	74	171	21	7	19	82	10	8	63	119	.303	.373	.465	.839	138	263	3
1968	24	124	350	23	60	14	0	3	25	3	5	26	88	.171	.236	.237	.473	40	83	1
1969	25	152	549	63	139	14	5	16	52	4	3	61	74	.253	.331	.384	.716	95	211	1
1970	26	127	480	50	142	24	5	16	63	4	11	44	95	.296	.355	.467	.821	118	224	0
1971	27	146	537	72	141	16	4	24	78	0	3	41	102	.263	.317	.441	.758	107	237	0
1977	33	157	584	103	157	26	5	33	95	1	1	57	112	.269	.337	.500	.837	114	292	1
1978	34	120	412	51	96	16	4	12	54	1	1	44	86	.233	.305	.379	.684	83	156	7
1979	35	45	156	18	35	9	1	4	23	0	0	17	22	.224	.299	.372	.671	76	58	1
Totals		1,192	4,234	527	1,088	158	38	154	562	27	32	418	850	.257	.326	.421	.747	103	1,784	16

Yankees Year

Year	Age	G	AB	R	H	2B	3B	HR	RBI	SB	CS	BB	SO	BA	OBP	SLG	OPS	OPS+	TB	SH
1979	35	16	44	9	14	3	1	1	6	1	0	2	7	.318	.340	.500	.840	126	22	0

Which Team Fared Better?

Scott had two different stints with the Red Sox, playing with them for six years before returning six year later and playing another three seasons. He is enshrined in the Boston Red

Sox Hall of Fame. He is also Boston's all-time leader at first base with 988 games played, including 944 starts and hit 154 of his 271 career home runs with the Red Sox. His resume with the Yankees was not as impressive, appearing in 16 games and only hitting 6 RBIs and 1 home run.

LEE SMITH

At one time Smith was the most dominant closer in baseball, leading the league in saves four different seasons as well as being the career saves leader for ten years until Trevor Hoffman passed him (then Mariano Rivera passed Hoffman). He was a 7-time All-Star, twice with the Chicago Cubs, three times with the St. Louis Cardinals, and then with the California Angels and Baltimore Orioles. He was also named the Rolaids Relief Man for three years and received consideration for the Cy Young Award on four different occasions. He finished his career with 478 saves in 1,022 games pitched. In his 18 years he only went to the postseason twice, once with the Chicago Cubs and another with the Red Sox, but lost in the League Championship Series both times. He also played for the Montreal Expos and Cincinnati Reds. He has gotten some votes for election into the Hall of Fame but the closest he has come to meeting the 75 percent needed for induction was in 2010 when he got 47.3 percent of the vote.

Red Sox Years

Year	Age	W	L	%	ERA	G	GS	CG	SV	IP	H	R	HR	BB	SO	ERA+	WHIP	H/9	BB/9	SO/9	SO/BB
1988	30	4	5	.444	2.80	64	0	0	29	83.2	72	34	7	37	96	148	1.303	7.7	4.0	10.3	2.59
1989	31	6	1	.857	3.57	64	0	0	25	70.2	53	30	6	33	96	116	1.217	6.8	4.2	12.2	2.91
1990	32	2	1	.667	1.88	11	0	0	4	14.1	13	4	0	9	17	222	1.535	8.2	5.7	10.7	1.89
Totals		12	7	.632	3.04	139	0	0	58	168.2	138	68	13	79	209	137	1.287	7.4	4.2	11.2	2.65

Yankees Year

Year	Age	W	L	%	ERA	G	GS	CG	SV	IP	H	R	HR	BB	SO	ERA+	WHIP	H/9	BB/9	SO/9	SO/BB
1993	35	0	0		0.00	8	0	0	3	8.0	4	0	0	5	11		1.125	4.5	5.6	12.4	2.20

Which Team Fared Better?

Lee spent eight years with the Cubs before being traded to the Red Sox. He spent three seasons there, compiling 58 saves. When Boston acquired Jeff Reardon they had one closer too many and thus traded Smith to the Cardinals. He had one year in Boson in which he was really good, with a 2.80 ERA and 29 saves over 83.2 innings, and another that was OK, having 25 saves and a 6-1 record but a 3.57 in 70.2 innings pitched. When the Yankees acquired Smith they were just 1 1/2 games behind the Toronto Blue Jays with a month to go. While Smith pitched admirably for New York, appearing in 8 games and not giving up a single run, the Yanks could not catch the Blue Jays, who went on to win their second World Series in as many years. If Lee had been able to provide the spark for the Yankees to have overtaken Toronto in the standings he might have been more valuable to them, but he did help the Red Sox catch the Detroit Tigers during the 1988 pennant chase, giving them the advantage.

FRANK TANANA

Pitching for an impressive 21 years, Tanana won 240 games and lost 236. He started his career with a blazing fastball that at times topped out at 100 MPH, but an injury forced him to become a junk baller in order to continue his career. He started for 6 different teams in his career, spending 8 years with both the Detroit Tigers and the California Angels as well as spending four years with the Texas Rangers and a year apiece with the New York Mets, Yankees, and Red Sox. He was an All-Star during a three year stretch from 1976–1978 while with the Angels. His best year on the mound came in 1977 when he led the league in ERA (2.54) and shutouts (7), as well as having a 15–9 record. He had 2,773 strikeouts and a 3.66 ERA over the course of his career.

Red Sox Year

Year	Age	W	L	%	ERA	G	GS	CG	SV	IP	H	R	HR	BB	SO	ERA+	WHIP	H/9	BB/9	SO/9	SO/BB
1981	27	4	10	.286	4.01	24	23	5	0	141.1	142	70	17	43	78	97	1.309	9.0	2.7	5.0	1.81

Yankees Year

Year	Age	W	L	%	ERA	G	GS	CG	SV	IP	H	R	HR	BB	SO	ERA+	WHIP	H/9	BB/9	SO/9	SO/BB
1993	39	0	2	.000	3.20	3	3	0	0	19.2	18	10	2	7	12	132	1.271	8.2	3.2	5.5	1.71

Which Team Fared Better?

Neither team got the Tanana who pitched so well for the California Angels. Instead they got the Tanana who pitched so poorly for the Texas Rangers. He went 4–10 with the Red Sox and a 4.01 ERA over 141.1 innings. His ERA with the Yankees was lower at 3.20 but they had acquired him to help down the stretch in a September trade and he ended up losing 2 of his 3 starts. Neither team fared all that well but he probably hurt the Yankees more by not helping them in the pennant run while the Red Sox finished fifth in their division, so no matter how well he pitched they more than likely were not going to finish much better.

MIKE TORREZ

Over an 18-year career, Torrez was never a great pitcher but was usually a pretty good one. He finished with 185 wins and 160 losses and a 3.96 ERA. He was a 20 game winner once with the Baltimore Orioles and had a winning record with every team he pitched except the New York Mets. He also pitched for the St. Louis Cardinals, Montreal Expos, Oakland Athletics, as well as the Yankees and Red Sox. He threw nearly as many walks (1,371) as he did strikeouts (1,404), leading the league in walks on three separate occasions, but his most notable accomplishment as a pitcher was as an innings eater, pitching 200 or more innings 9 times in his career.

Yankees Year

Year	Age	W	L	%	ERA	G	GS	CG	SV	IP	H	R	HR	BB	SO	ERA+	WHIP	H/9	BB/9	SO/9	SO/BB
1977	30	14	12	.538	3.82	31	31	15	0	217.0	212	99	20	75	90	104	1.323	8.8	3.1	3.7	1.20

Red Sox Years

Year	Age	W	L	%	ERA	G	GS	CG	SV	IP	H	R	HR	BB	SO	ERA+	WHIP	H/9	BB/9	SO/9	SO/BB
1978	31	16	13	.552	3.96	36	36	15	0	250.0	272	122	19	99	120	105	1.484	9.8	3.6	4.3	1.21
1979	32	16	13	.552	4.49	36	36	12	0	252.1	254	144	20	121	125	99	1.486	9.1	4.3	4.5	1.03
1980	33	9	16	.360	5.08	36	32	6	0	207.1	256	124	18	75	97	84	1.596	11.1	3.3	4.2	1.29
1981	34	10	3	.769	3.68	22	22	2	0	127.1	130	61	10	51	54	106	1.421	9.2	3.6	3.8	1.06
1982	35	9	9	.500	5.23	31	31	1	0	175.2	196	107	20	74	84	83	1.537	10.0	3.8	4.3	1.14
Totals		60	54	.526	4.51	161	157	36	0	1,012.2	1,108	558	87	420	480	94	1.509	9.8	3.7	4.3	1.14

Which Team Fared Better?

This is one of those cases of if you cannot beat him, then sign him. Torrez won two games for the Yankees in the 1977 World Series, so Boston signed him to a half a million dollar contract the following year, making him one of the highest paid pitchers at that time. Although he won 16 games each of the first two years with the Red Sox, overall he ended up 60 and 54 with a 4.51 ERA, not exactly highest paid pitcher in the league statistics. Torrez was not terribly effective when he pitched against the Yankees, going 1 and 11 in his career versus the Bronx Bombers. Most importantly, Torrez was the pitcher who gave up the home run to Bucky Dent in the 1978 one game playoff between the Yankees and the Red Sox that allowed New York to go on to win the World Series. Some would say this alone is enough to warrant saying the Yankees got the better of him.

Bob Watson

Watson spent 14 of his 19 seasons playing first base or left field for the Houston Astros. He was twice named to the All-Star squad with them, in 1973 and 1975, and twice knocked in over 100 runs. His best season was in 1977 when he set career highs in home runs (22) and RBIs (110), and slugged nearly .500. Toward the end of his career he played with Boston, the Yankees, and the Atlanta Braves. He finished with a .295 batting average and close to 1,000 RBIs. He was the first player to hit for the cycle in both the National League (Astros) and American League (Red Sox). His post playing career involved him being the general manager for both the Houston Astros and New York Yankees and later became major league baseball's vice president in charge of discipline and vice president of rules and on-field operations.

Red Sox Year

Year	Age	G	AB	R	H	2B	3B	HR	RBI	SB	CS	BB	SO	BA	OBP	SLG	OPS	OPS+	TB	SH
1979	33	84	312	48	105	19	4	13	53	3	2	29	33	.337	.401	.548	.949	148	171	0

Yankees Years

Year	Age	G	AB	R	H	2B	3B	HR	RBI	SB	CS	BB	SO	BA	OBP	SLG	OPS	OPS+	TB	SH
1980	34	130	469	62	144	25	3	13	68	2	1	48	56	.307	.368	.456	.825	127	214	1
1981	35	59	156	15	33	3	3	6	12	0	0	24	17	.212	.317	.385	.701	104	60	0
1982	36	7	17	3	4	3	0	0	3	0	0	3	0	.235	.350	.412	.762	111	7	0
Totals		196	642	80	181	31	6	19	83	2	1	75	73	.282	.355	.438	.793	121	281	1

Which Team Fared Better?

He was traded in June to the Red Sox so he did not play a full season with them. He did bat .337 with 53 RBIs and 13 home runs in his 84 games played. He signed as a free-agent with the Yankees and became their regular first baseman for the 1980 season where he hit 13 home runs and knocked in 68 to go with a .307 batting average. All of his post season at-bats came with the Yankees where he batted .371 with 9 RBIs and 23 hits. Even though he did not play as much in the 1981 season, he was a large contributor in the World Series against the Los Angeles Dodgers, batting .317 with 7 RBIs in the 6 games played. He was traded less than a month into the 1982 season but overall he gave much more to the Yankees than the Red Sox.

6. The Lightning (A-)Rod
The Steroid Era (1994–2005)

It is always fun to play the "what if" game, especially in a sport like baseball where one turn of events can cause a long chain reaction. For instance, what if fan Steve Bartman had not interfered with left fielder Moises Alou going for a fly ball in the stands on October 14, 2003? Would Alou have caught the ball and would the Cubs then have won that game against the Florida Marlins, winning the NLCS, and go on to win their first World Series in nearly 100 years? Instead what really happened is that Bartman, instinctually trying to catch the foul ball, prevented Alou from snagging it, allowing Luis Castillo another chance. The following chain of events was what followed.

Castillo actually draws a walk instead of being an out. Ivan Rodriguez, the Marlins catcher, then singles to drive in the first run, Cubs 3, Marlins 1. It seems as though the Cubbies are going to get out of the inning as Miguel Cabrera hits what looks like a double play ball to shortstop Alex Gonzalez, but it is misplayed, leaving the bases loaded. Then Dereck Lee steps to the plate, the giant first baseman and soon-to-be-Cub, who doubles for the Marlins, tying the score at 3–3. After Mike Lowell is intentionally walked, wily veteran Jeff Conine hits a sacrifice fly to give the Marlins a 4–3 edge. After another intentional walk, Mike Mordecai officially puts a dagger through the hopes of the faithful Cubs fans by clearing the bases with a double, giving the Florida team an insurmountable 7–3 lead. But the Marlins were not done there. Juan Pierre, who had been the first Marlin to score in the inning, comes back up and hits a single to make it 8–3. The inning mercifully ends where it almost began, with Luis Castillo coming to bat and this time has his pop up caught by the second baseman, far away from any interfering Steve Bartman.

This brought the series to a deciding game seven of the National League Championship Series, which Florida won, dashing the dreams of Cubs fans everywhere and forever vilifying Steve Bartman. The Florida Marlins would go on to beat the New York Yankees 4 games to 2 to win their second World Series, just as many as the Chicago Cubs have. Of course the Cubs have had over 130 years to win those two World Series while the Marlins did it in just 10.

Another big "what if" would be what if Alex Rodriguez had been traded from the Texas Rangers to the Red Sox in 2004 rather than to the Yankees? It very nearly happened. It was one of those situations that if things had gone a little differently, it might have changed the fate of both teams. Alex Rodriguez had been signed by the Rangers as a free agent in 2000 for the unheard sum of $252 million dollars for ten years. This was over a decade ago and yet it is still the second highest contract ever signed by a player in a professional sport (eclipsed only by the one A-Rod signed with the Yankees in 2007 for $275 million). The Rangers thought they were getting the best player in baseball and for all intents and purposes, they did. Alex Rodriguez performed quite well for the Rangers:

Year	Games	Runs	Hits	HR	RBIs	BA	OBP	SLG	MVP Voting
2001	162	133	201	52	135	.318	.399	.622	6th
2002	162	125	187	57	142	.300	.392	.623	2nd
2003	161	124	181	47	118	.298	.396	.600	1st

As great as Rodriguez played for the Rangers, going to the All-Star game all three years, winning a Gold Glove two of the three years, being a Silver Slugger (best hitter at his position) all three years, and the MVP on the league in 2003, the Rangers could finish no better than dead last all three years he was with the team. This was virtually the exact same amount of wins and losses that the Rangers had the year before A-Rod joined the team and previous to them paying him more than the GDP of most small countries. This was no fault of Rodriguez. This is what happens when a mid-market team puts all their eggs in one basket, or $25 million a year in payroll to one player. There was just not much money left to put supporting players around him. One man does not make a team and the Rangers were figuring this out the hard and expensive way. They had to figure out a way to move Rodriquez.

Alex Rodriguez himself figured out if he were going to win a World Series he was going to have to go to a team that had deeper pockets, one of the large market teams such as the Dodgers, Yankees, or Red Sox. This way they could afford to pay him his outrageous salary as well as afford other good players to support him. The Rangers began to shop Rodriguez around to see if anyone was willing to take the bait. One such bite was the Red Sox general manager Theo Epstein. He had an issue of his own; Manny Ramirez (known for Manny being Manny) had worn out his welcome in Boston to the point they had put the high priced talent on irrevocable waivers only weeks before, hoping someone would take the troubled slugger off their plate. Although Texas had asked for Nomar Garciaparra, exchanging shortstop for shortstop, Epstein dangled his problem in front of Texas and they accepted, but not a straight contract for contract. Boston wanted to reduce Rodriguez's $25 million-a-year contract down $4 million in order to stay under the luxury tax. Rodriguez agreed to the pay cut. The Rangers also did not want to trade one bloated contract for another. They wanted some freedom financially to go out and get some pitching to help prevent their team from finishing last in the division. They asked Boston to absorb some of Ramirez's contract, $15 million to be exact. This was ridiculous from the perspective of the Red Sox. Regardless of the $4 million less, they would essentially be paying $36 million for Rodriguez's services. Understandably they were hesitant. Rodriguez wanted so badly to go to Boston he supposedly called the owner of the Rangers, Tom Hicks, and offered to pay the $15 million the owner was seeking for Ramirez's contract. All that was needed now was the approval of the union.

While the Red Sox were waiting on the player's union to decide whether the trade could go through or not, they made another trade. This one was getting rid of Nomar Garciaparra, after all, they now had a shortstop and no longer needed him, to the White Sox for Magglio Ordonez, an outfielder they could certainly use. It was contingent on the Rodriguez deal going through. This would have been the lineup for the 2004 Red Sox had both deals gone through:

1. Johnny Damon — Center Field
2. Kevin Millar — 1st Base
3. Alex Rodriguez — Shortstop
4. David Ortiz — Designated Hitter
5. Magglio Ordonez — Right Field
6. Bill Mueller — 3rd Base
7. Mark Bellhorn — 2nd Base
8. Jason Varitek — Catcher
9. Trot Nixon — Left Field

When Theo Epstein told first-year manager Terry Francona of this possible lineup at the winter meetings, Francona was said to have jumped up on the bed and performed a happy dance. Who wouldn't want a lineup like that?

The union crushed the dreams of Francona and many other Red Sox Nation fans when they decided against the trade. They could not allow a player to take less than the initial contract he signed. This would be setting a bad precedent for players. What if teams started asking their players to restructure their contracts to take less? This would negate much of the work the union had done for players during the free agency years. Thus the deal was off, declared dead on December 23. No Rodriguez going to Boston. Tom Hicks, the Texas owner, said they were going to hold on to A-Rod.

This statement was true for less than two months. On February 15, the New York Yankees successfully traded for the slugger when they suddenly had an opening at third. They sent their second baseman, Alfonzo Soriano, to Texas with a player to be named later, Joaquin Arias. Rodriguez agreed to move from shortstop to third. Ironically enough, the Rangers had to promise to pay $67 million of the remaining $179 million owed to Rodriguez in order for the deal to go through. As of 2014, with A-Rod being banned from baseball for the entire season due to his link to performance-enhancing drugs and an anti-aging clinic in Florida, the Rangers are still on the hook for millions. They will not have his money paid off until the year 2025. It is the gift that keeps on giving.

Unfortunately for the Yankees, A-Rod has become a symbol of everything that is wrong with baseball. He is said to have a gigantic ego and brags about his having the two richest contracts ever in baseball history. He has generally put up good numbers in the regular season—witness his MVP in pinstripes in 2007—but he is infamous for performing poorly in the postseason. In his lone World Series appearance here is his stat line:

AB	R	H	HR	RBI	SO	BA	OBP	SLG	HBP
20	5	5	1	6	8	.250	.423	.550	3

While these are decent statistics, they are hardly what you expect to get from someone being paid $25 million dollars a year. They are certainly not the numbers of David Ortiz, who in his three World Series appearances has monster numbers:

AB	R	H	HR	RBI	SO	BA	OBP	SLG	HBP
44	14	20	3	14	5	.455	.576	.795	0

Those are numbers any team would pay $25 million dollars to have. A-Rod always seems to attract controversy, whether it be his deteriorating friendship with teammates such as Derek Jeter, his announcing that he was opting out of his contract during Game Six of a World Series he was not playing in, or his marriage falling apart because he was allegedly dating Madonna. And let us not forget about his links to performance-enhancing drugs. He has become a poster child for the Steroid Era. First there was his admission that he took PEDs as a Texas Ranger. He held a press conference in which his Yankee teammates showed their support and he swore he would never do it again. Then as a Yankee he was linked to the Biogenesis clinic in Florida where he supposedly not only took PEDs but then tried to cover it up by purchasing his medical records from the clinic. Then, to top things off, he sued major league baseball. He has gone from being the indisputable best player in baseball to one of the game's most reviled athletes.

Given this information, here is another what-if game that would be fun to play out. What if on January 16, 2004, Aaron Boone decided, "Hey, it might be a bad idea to play a game of pickup basketball." Here is the chain of events that unfolds as a result.

The Yankees honor the contract that Boone signed to remain their third baseman. When the Texas Rangers are looking to unload the bloated $179 million still left on the contract of Alex Rodriguez, they do not have the Yankees as an option because they already have a third baseman they are paying nearly six million dollars for. Instead, the deal with the Red Sox is reconfigured and A-Rod goes to play shortstop for them, taking over for Nomar Garciaparra and sending Manny Ramirez to the Rangers. Because they no longer have Nomar, the Red Sox are not able to make the huge four-team deal that sent him and Matt Murton to the Cubs and brought in Orlando Cabrera from the Montreal Expos and Doug Mientkiewicz from the Minnesota Twins. The Red Sox end up not winning the 2004 World Series because although they have A-Rod and his monster regular-season statistics, his postseason numbers are a .263 batting average, 13 home runs, and 41 RBIs in 75 postseason games. This is compared to the now-traded-away Manny Ramirez, who has a .285 average, 29 home runs, and 78 RBIs in 111 postseason appearances. They also would have missed Ramirez's 10 RBIs in the American League Championship Series against the Cleveland Indians. The Red Sox, now saddled with the large A-Rod's huge contract, are not able to make the free agent acquisitions or trades they make over the next ten years—including Josh Beckett and Mike Lowell, Daisuke Matsuzaka, Coco Crisp, Mike Napoli, Shane Victorino, or Jonny Gomes—that give them another two World Series wins. The Yankees, now free to spend money on someone other than just a third baseman, are able to win more than just the 2009 World Series they earned during Rodriguez's tenure with them. But no, Aaron Boone did decide to play basketball on that fateful day. As a result, he tore a ligament in his knee and was unable to play the entire 2004 season. The Yankees had major league baseball void Boone's contract since it stipulates players should not do stupid things, like play pickup basketball, that could jeopardize their ability to play baseball. This series of events opened up third base for the Yankees, who set their sights on Alex Rodriguez, and brought him to New York, along with all the controversy that surrounds him.

Players Who Spent Time with Both Teams, 1994–2005

Scott Bankhead

A former first-round pick by the Kansas City Royals, Bankhead pitched for five teams total in his career. The last three years were with the Sox and Yankees. He signed as a free agent with Boston for the 1993 and 1994 seasons. In September of 1994 the Yankees purchased his contract from the Sox but he did not play that year due to the work stoppage caused by the players' strike. He did re-sign with the Yankees in 1995 but was released in July.

Red Sox Years

Year	Age	W	L	%	ERA	G	GS	CG	SV	IP	H	R	HR	BB	SO	ERA+	WHIP	H/9	BB/9	SO/9	SO/BB
1993	29	2	1	.667	3.50	40	0	0	0	64.1	59	28	7	29	47	133	1.368	8.3	4.1	6.6	1.62
1994	30	3	2	.600	4.54	27	0	0	0	37.2	34	21	5	12	25	111	1.221	8.1	2.9	6.0	2.08
Totals		5	3	.625	3.88	67	0	0	0	102.0	93	49	12	41	72	124	1.314	8.2	3.6	6.4	1.76

Yankees Year

Year	Age	W	L	%	ERA	G	GS	CG	SV	IP	H	R	HR	BB	SO	ERA+	WHIP	H/9	BB/9	SO/9	SO/BB
1995	31	1	1	.500	6.00	20	1	0	0	39.0	44	26	9	16	20	78	1.538	10.2	3.7	4.6	1.25

Which Team Fared Better?

Neither team benefitted that greatly from having Bankhead in the bullpen. The edge would have to go to Red Sox just because his ERA was better although nearly 30 walks in just 64 innings pitched is nothing to write home about. He was a fairly cheap acquisition for both teams. Boston signed him as free agent for $1.1 million and the Yankees took him off their hands for about half of that.

WILLIE BANKS

Banks pitched for 8 different teams over his 11-year career. He began his career as a starter, winning a World Series ring pitching with the Minnesota Twins in 1991, but eventually became a bullpen guy. He spent two years with both the Yankees and Sox, although his New York days were cut short when he was traded to the Arizona Diamondbacks in June. After two years not pitching in the majors, the Red Sox signed him in August of 2001 to finish out the year with them as well as the 2002 season.

Yankees Years

Year	Age	W	L	%	ERA	G	GS	CG	SV	IP	H	R	HR	BB	SO	ERA+	WHIP	H/9	BB/9	SO/9	SO/BB
1993	28	3	0	1.000	1.93	5	1	0	0	14.0	9	3	0	6	8	238	1.071	5.8	3.9	5.1	1.33
1994	29	1	1	.500	10.05	9	0	0	0	14.1	20	16	4	12	8	45	2.233	12.6	7.5	5.0	0.67
Totals		4	1	.800	6.04	14	1	0	0	28.1	29	19	4	18	16	76	1.659	9.2	5.7	5.1	0.89

Red Sox Years

Year	Age	W	L	%	ERA	G	GS	CG	SV	IP	H	R	HR	BB	SO	ERA+	WHIP	H/9	BB/9	SO/9	SO/BB
2001	32	0	0		0.84	5	0	0	0	10.2	5	4	0	4	10	548	0.844	4.2	3.4	8.4	2.50
2002	33	2	1	.667	3.23	29	0	0	1	39.0	32	15	5	14	26	142	1.179	7.4	3.2	6.0	1.86
Totals		2	1	.667	2.72	34	0	0	1	49.2	37	19	5	18	36	169	1.107	6.7	3.3	6.5	2.00

Which Team Fared Better?

New York did not think enough of his services to let him finish the season and lower his 10.05 ERA. In 14 innings pitching with them in 1998 he gave up 16 run, not to mention 12 walks. Although his years with the Red Sox were not stellar either, he gave up only 14 runs in 39 innings, posting a respectable 3.23 ERA, making the Sox the ones who received the better service. He was signed a free agent by the Yankees for a paltry sum of $342,500 and they were able to parlay him into two minor leaguers in Joe Lisio and Scott Brow although neither ever made it to the bigs. Boston signed him as a free agent for $450,000 so the impact on payroll was minimal.

DARREN BRAGG

Bragg played for 11 seasons in the major leagues, his longest tenure being with the Red Sox. He also played for Seattle, St. Louis, Colorado, the Mets, the Braves, San Diego, and Cincinnati. He spent only one season with the Yankees. He was a journeyman whose services were just enough to get him signed by a team but never great enough to have him remain for very long. He would provide the proverbial "professional at-bat", but was not a real power threat.

Red Sox Years

Year	Age	G	AB	R	H	2B	3B	HR	RBI	SB	CS	BB	SO	BA	OBP	SLG	OPS	OPS+	TB	SH
1996	26	58	222	38	56	14	1	3	22	6	4	36	39	.252	.357	.365	.722	83	81	1
1997	27	153	513	65	132	35	2	9	57	10	6	61	102	.257	.337	.386	.723	87	198	5
1998	28	129	409	51	114	29	3	8	57	5	3	42	99	.279	.351	.423	.774	99	173	4
Totals		340	1,144	154	302	78	6	20	136	21	13	139	240	.264	.346	.395	.741	91	452	10

Yankees Year

Year	Age	G	AB	R	H	2B	3B	HR	RBI	SB	CS	BB	SO	BA	OBP	SLG	OPS	OPS+	TB	SH
2001	31	5	4	1	1	1	0	0	0	0	0	0	1	.250	.250	.500	.750	91	2	0

Which Team Fared Better?

This one is an easy call in that the Red Sox were the team he was with when he hit his stride as a player. After a trade from Seattle, he played his way into the everyday lineup and stayed there for the entire 1997 season. The one thing that might make it a loss for Boston is the fact they traded away Jamie Moyer. With Seattle, Moyer went on to play 11 seasons and garner 145 wins. Of course some would argue Moyer would not have been as successful in tiny Fenway as he was in cavernous Safeco Field where he pitched a majority of his Seattle games. The edge still goes to Boston because by the time Bragg got to the Yankees off waivers, he was relegated to a utility outfielder that was good for a pinch hitting appearance every once in a while. He got into five games with the Yankees and only had a single hit for them.

JOSE CANSECO

There are volumes of books that could be written on Jose Canseco considering his involvement in steroids, but not really much to say about his time spent with the Yankees or Red Sox. A majority of his great years were with the Oakland A's and to a lesser extent the Toronto Blue Jays. He spent 17 years in the majors playing for 7 different teams. He also played for the Texas Rangers, Tampa Bay Devil Rays, and the Chicago White Sox. His legacy will not be the 482 home runs he hit but that fact that he spoke so openly about his steroid use and influencing others to use it as well, earning him the nickname "The Chemist."

Red Sox Years

Year	Age	G	AB	R	H	2B	3B	HR	RBI	SB	CS	BB	SO	BA	OBP	SLG	OPS	OPS+	TB	SH
1995	30	102	396	64	121	25	1	24	81	4	0	42	93	.306	.378	.556	.933	137	220	0
1996	31	96	360	68	104	22	1	28	82	3	1	63	82	.289	.400	.589	.989	146	212	0
Totals		198	756	132	225	47	2	52	163	7	1	105	175	.298	.389	.571	.960	141	432	0

Yankees Year

Year	Age	G	AB	R	H	2B	3B	HR	RBI	SB	CS	BB	SO	BA	OBP	SLG	OPS	OPS+	TB	SH
2000	35	37	111	16	27	3	0	6	19	0	0	23	37	.243	.365	.432	.797	103	48	0

Which Team Fared Better?

While the Red Sox did not get Canseco in his prime, he did club an average of 26 home runs and knock in 81 runs during his two year stint with them. This came at a price of $5.5 million a year, which was his highest salary for any team he played for. His time with New York was more of a chess move than it was trying to help the team. At the time New York picked him up, they already had four outfielders and a designated hitter. Why would they need another? Brian Cashman, the general manager, explained he was simply trying to prevent division rivals, the Toronto Blue Jays, from picking up the slugger. Canseco was miserable during his time with the Yankees. He claimed it to be "the worst time of my life" because he had such an insignificant role. How insignificant, during the three series of postseason play with the pinstripes that year he had one at-bat. Although the Yankees won the World Series that year and Canseco received a ring, he was merely a hood ornament on a finely tuned car that was winning its third World Series in a row.

Tony Clark

This is another player with a lot of time in the big leagues, fifteen years, with a majority of it spent with a team other than the Red Sox and Yankees. If Tony Clark were ever to go into the Hall of Fame, and that is not going to happen as a player, he would go in as a Detroit Tiger, having spent seven years playing first base for that club. He went to Boston for a year following that stint and then to the Yankees a couple of years later for a single season. Neither tenure was very memorable.

Red Sox Year

Year	Age	G	AB	R	H	2B	3B	HR	RBI	SB	CS	BB	SO	BA	OBP	SLG	OPS	OPS+	TB	SH
2002	30	90	275	25	57	12	1	3	29	0	0	21	57	.207	.265	.291	.556	47	80	0

Yankees Year

Year	Age	G	AB	R	H	2B	3B	HR	RBI	SB	CS	BB	SO	BA	OBP	SLG	OPS	OPS+	TB	SH
2004	32	106	253	37	56	12	0	16	49	0	0	26	92	.221	.297	.458	.755	95	116	0

Which Team Fared Better?

After being an All-Star with the Detroit Tigers, Clark came to the Red Sox and underperformed. He had a career low slugging percentage of .291 and batted an anemic .207. By the time the Yankees signed him in 2004, he had been relegated to a bench role rather than the starter he had once been. He filled in for an injured Jason Giambi and although his numbers were not stellar, they were certainly better than his days with Boston. It also fit better with the role the team expected him to play. Boston thought it was getting a top of the line free agent first baseman while the Yankees were simply looking for a backup. His highlight for the year with New York was hitting three home runs in one game, tying his entire season total while playing for Boston.

Roger Clemens

Along with Canseco, Barry Bonds, and now A-Rod, Clemens' legacy will be greatly tainted by his alleged use of performance enhancing drugs. He played his first twelve years with Boston, winning three Cy Young Awards as the league's best pitcher as well as the most valuable player award in 1986, striking out 20 batters in a single game that season. After spending a couple of years in Toronto, winning Cy Young Awards both years, he went to play for the Yankees. He spent six years with the Yankees, five of them between 1999–2003. During that time he won two World Series championships and another Cy Young Award. He left for Houston for a few years before finishing his career in New York in 2007.

Red Sox Years

Year	Age	W	L	%	ERA	G	GS	CG	SV	IP	H	R	HR	BB	SO	ERA+	WHIP	H/9	BB/9	SO/9	SO/BB
1984	21	9	4	.692	4.32	21	20	5	0	133.1	146	67	13	29	126	97	1.313	9.9	2.0	8.5	4.34
1985	22	7	5	.583	3.29	15	15	3	0	98.1	83	38	5	37	74	130	1.220	7.6	3.4	6.8	2.00
1986	23	24	4	.857	2.48	33	33	10	0	254.0	179	77	21	67	238	169	0.969	6.3	2.4	8.4	3.55
1987	24	20	9	.690	2.97	36	36	18	0	281.2	248	100	19	83	256	154	1.175	7.9	2.7	8.2	3.08
1988	25	18	12	.600	2.93	35	35	14	0	264.0	217	93	17	62	291	141	1.057	7.4	2.1	9.9	4.69
1989	26	17	11	.607	3.13	35	35	8	0	253.1	215	101	20	93	230	132	1.216	7.6	3.3	8.2	2.47
1990	27	21	6	.778	1.93	31	31	7	0	228.1	193	59	7	54	209	211	1.082	7.6	2.1	8.2	3.87
1991	28	18	10	.643	2.62	35	35	13	0	271.1	219	93	15	65	241	165	1.047	7.3	2.2	8.0	3.71
1992	29	18	11	.621	2.41	32	32	11	0	246.2	203	80	11	62	208	174	1.074	7.4	2.3	7.6	3.35
1993	30	11	14	.440	4.46	29	29	2	0	191.2	175	99	17	67	160	104	1.263	8.2	3.1	7.5	2.39
1994	31	9	7	.563	2.85	24	24	3	0	170.2	124	62	15	71	168	176	1.143	6.5	3.7	8.9	2.37
1995	32	10	5	.667	4.18	23	23	0	0	140.0	141	70	15	60	132	117	1.436	9.1	3.9	8.5	2.20
1996	33	10	13	.435	3.63	34	34	6	0	242.2	216	106	19	106	257	139	1.327	8.0	3.9	9.5	2.42
Totals		191	111	.634	3.06	383	382	100	0	2,776.0	2,359	1045	194	856	2,590	144	1.158	7.6	2.8	8.4	3.03

Yankees Years

Year	Age	W	L	%	ERA	G	GS	CG	SV	IP	H	R	HR	BB	SO	ERA+	WHIP	H/9	BB/9	SO/9	SO/BB
1999	36	14	10	.583	4.60	30	30	1	0	187.2	185	101	20	90	163	102	1.465	8.9	4.3	7.8	1.81
2000	37	13	8	.619	3.70	32	32	1	0	204.1	184	96	26	84	188	131	1.312	8.1	3.7	8.3	2.24
2001	38	20	3	.870	3.51	33	33	0	0	220.1	205	94	19	72	213	128	1.257	8.4	2.9	8.7	2.96
2002	39	13	6	.684	4.35	29	29	0	0	180.0	172	94	18	63	192	102	1.306	8.6	3.2	9.6	3.05
2003	40	17	9	6.54	3.91	33	33	1	0	211.2	199	99	24	58	190	113	1.214	8.5	2.5	8.1	3.28
2007	44	6	6	.500	4.18	18	17	0	0	99.0	99	52	9	31	68	108	1.313	9.0	2.8	6.2	2.19
Totals		83	42	.664	4.01	175	174	3	0	1,103.0	1,044	536	116	398	1,014	114	1.307	8.5	3.2	8.3	2.55

Which Team Fared Better?

This is an extremely close call. If voters ever get past the steroids accusations and elect Clemens to the Hall of Fame, it will be very interesting to see which cap he dons. Although he spent twice as much time with the Red Sox, who drafted and developed him, he did not leave on good terms. Plus he won his championships with New York. His time with the Yankees will be tainted by the steroid rumors, which gives the edge to the Red Sox. Besides that, the Red Sox were able to get more bang for their dollar. Boston paid him $5.5 million a year for his last two seasons with them, in both of which he won 10 games. The year he won 24 games he was only making $650,000. The Yankees on the other hand paid him an average of $10 million for the first five years he was with then and brought Clemens back as a 44 year-old for half of the season, paying him $17 mil-

A winner of 354 games in his career, it would seem obvious that Clemens is a first-ballot Hall of Famer. Unfortunately, his tie to steroids has tarnished an otherwise spectacular career. He was an 11-time All-Star, a four-time AL wins leader, a seven-time ERA champ, and five-time strikeout king. Oh, and he won the Cy Young Award an astonishing seven times. He was even selected to be a member of the Major League Baseball All-Century Team. His two World Series rings came with the Yankees, but he spent almost twice as many years pitching for Boston (courtesy KeithAllisonPhoto.com).

lion. He only won six games for them that year meaning they paid about $2.8 million per win.

Michael Coleman

Coleman played for only two teams in the major leagues, the Yankees and Red Sox. He was drafted by the Red Sox and got a couple of cups of coffee, but nothing of significance. He was eventually traded to New York and played in only twelve games before being granted free agency. He never again appeared in the big leagues.

Red Sox Years

Year	Age	G	AB	R	H	2B	3B	HR	RBI	SB	CS	BB	SO	BA	OBP	SLG	OPS	OPS+	TB	SH
1997	21	8	24	2	4	1	0	0	2	1	0	0	11	.167	.167	.208	.375	-3	5	1
1999	23	2	5	1	1	0	0	0	0	0	0	1	0	.200	.333	.200	.533	39	1	0
Total		10	29	3	5	1	0	0	2	1	0	1	11	.172	.200	.207	.407	5	6	1

Yankees Years

Year	Age	G	AB	R	H	2B	3B	HR	RBI	SB	CS	BB	SO	BA	OBP	SLG	OPS	OPS+	TB	SH
2001	25	12	38	5	8	0	0	1	7	0	1	0	15	.211	.205	.289	.495	28	11	0

Which Team Fared Better?

Even though Boston drafted and developed him, the Yankees got more consistent (yet limited) production out of Coleman. Most of his value was in the form of trade bait. During the 2001 offseason Coleman was traded by Boston to the Cincinnati Reds and received Chris Stynes in return. Before he ever put on a Cincinnati uniform, the Yankees traded their highly touted prospect Wily Mo Pena for Coleman. Pena never amounted to much, so the Yankees did not give up a lot but Chris Stynes had a solid year for Boston, batting .280 with 8 home runs and 33 RBIs, meaning they made out better in the exchange of players than the Yankees did. With that in mind, the Red Sox win.

David Cone

During his 17-year career, Cone won five World Series rings, four of them with the Yankees. Although drafted by the Kansas City Royals, he did not come into his own as a major league pitcher until being traded to the New York Mets. By the time he was traded to the Yankees mid-season from the Toronto Blue Jays, he was a veteran pitcher who stabilized the rotation. In his tenure with the Yankees he even pitched a perfect game, although after that game his effectiveness began to wane. In 2001 he was signed by the Red Sox and put up decent numbers but nothing to justify resigning him.

Yankees Years

Year	Age	W	L	%	ERA	G	GS	CG	SV	IP	H	R	HR	BB	SO	ERA+	WHIP	H/9	BB/9	SO/9	SO/BB
1995	32	9	2	.818	3.82	13	13	1	0	99.0	82	42	12	47	89	122	1.303	7.5	4.3	8.1	1.89
1996	33	7	2	.778	2.88	11	11	1	0	72.0	50	25	3	34	71	175	1.167	6.3	4.3	8.9	2.09
1997	34	12	6	.667	2.82	29	29	1	0	195.0	155	67	17	86	222	159	1.236	7.2	4.0	10.2	2.58
1998	35	20	7	.741	3.55	31	31	3	0	207.2	186	89	20	59	209	125	1.180	8.1	2.6	9.1	3.54
1999	36	12	9	.571	3.44	31	31	1	0	193.1	164	84	21	90	177	136	1.314	7.6	4.2	8.2	1.97
2000	37	4	14	.222	6.91	30	29	0	0	155.0	192	124	25	82	120	70	1.768	11.1	4.8	7.0	1.46
Totals		64	40	.615	3.91	145	144	7	0	922.0	829	431	98	398	888	118	1.331	8.1	3.9	8.7	2.23

Red Sox Year

Year	Age	W	L	%	ERA	G	GS	CG	SV	IP	H	R	HR	BB	SO	ERA+	WHIP	H/9	BB/9	SO/9	SO/BB
2001	38	9	7	.563	4.31	25	25	0	0	135.2	148	74	17	57	115	104	1.511	9.8	3.8	7.6	2.02

Which Team Fared Better?

Even if you take out the four World Series rings Cone won with the Yankees, he most certainly was a better pitcher with them. He was a 20 game winner in 1998 and represented the Yankees at the All-Star game twice. He really only had one bad year with the Yankees in 2000 when he went 4–14 with a 6.91 ERA. His results with the Red Sox were mixed. Although he had a winning record with them, 9–7, his ERA was one the highest of his career, 4.31. Post-retirement Cone continued to keep his affiliation with the Yankees, working for the YES network on and off for several years.

ALAN EMBREE

Known as a quintessential left-handed specialist, Embree made a career out of working out of the bullpen, accumulating 774.0 innings of work. He started only 4 games (all in the first year he played) but finished 217. During his 16-year career he played for 10 different teams. He is probably best known for his relief work for the Boston Red Sox against the New York Yankees in the 2004 ALCS in which he recorded the final out of the series that Boston won. The Red Sox then went on to win their first World Series in over 80 years. Embree was released by the Red Sox in 2005 and picked up by the Yankees, with whom he finished out the year. He did return to the Red Sox on a minor league deal in 2010. He was called up to the big club in April but never faced a batter before being designated for assignment. He also played for the Cleveland Indians, Atlanta Braves, Arizona Diamondbacks, San Francisco Giants, Chicago White Sox, the Oakland A's, and the Colorado Rockies.

Red Sox Years

Year	Age	W	L	%	ERA	G	GS	CG	SV	IP	H	R	HR	BB	SO	ERA+	WHIP	H/9	BB/9	SO/9	SO/BB
2002	32	1	2	.333	2.97	32	0	0	2	33.1	24	12	4	11	43	155	1.050	6.5	3.0	11.6	3.91
2003	33	4	1	.800	4.25	65	0	0	1	55.0	49	26	5	16	45	110	1.182	8.0	2.6	7.4	2.81
2004	34	2	2	.500	4.13	71	0	0	0	52.1	49	28	7	11	37	118	1.146	8.4	1.9	6.4	3.36
2005	35	1	4	.200	7.65	43	0	0	1	37.2	42	33	8	11	30	60	1.407	10.0	2.6	7.2	2.73
Totals		8	9	.471	4.69	211	0	0	4	178.1	164	99	24	49	155	100	1.194	8.3	2.5	7.8	3.16

Yankees Year

Year	Age	W	L	%	ERA	G	GS	CG	SV	IP	H	R	HR	BB	SO	ERA+	WHIP	H/9	BB/9	SO/9	SO/BB
2005	35	1	1	.500	7.53	24	0	0	0	14.1	20	14	2	3	8	58	1.605	12.6	1.9	5.0	2.67

Which Team Fared Better?

Boston definitely gets the edge here not only because of Embree being a major cog in the bullpen of the Sox in their 2004 World Series win, but because he did not even play an entire season with the Yankees. Boston figured out he didn't have it anymore and the Yankees thought a change of scenery would reignite his lefty arm. Unfortunately for them it did not. Embree along with Mike Timlin acted as the lefty, righty duo that Boston turned to late in games. Between the two of them they appeared in over 140 games, setting up Keith Foulke, the closer. This is probably the role Embree will best be remembered for.

Todd Erdos

Erdos had a modest five season career in the major leagues, three years with the Yankees and one with Boston. He also spent two different stints with the San Diego Padres. He was a middle reliever who never amassed 100 innings in the big leagues and finished his career playing in the minor leagues.

Yankees Years

Year	Age	W	L	%	ERA	G	GS	CG	SV	IP	H	R	HR	BB	SO	ERA+	WHIP	H/9	BB/9	SO/9	SO/BB
1998	24	0	0		9.00	2	0	0	0	2.0	5	2	0	1	0	58	3.000	22.5	4.5	0.0	0.00
1999	25	0	0		3.68	4	0	0	0	7.0	5	4	2	4	4	127	1.286	6.4	5.1	5.1	1.00
2000	26	0	0		5.04	14	0	0	1	25.0	31	14	2	11	18	97	1.680	11..2	4.0	6.5	1.64
Totals		0	0		5.03	20	0	0	1	34.0	41	20	4	16	22	98	1.676	10.9	4.2	5.8	1.38

Red Sox Year

Year	Age	W	L	%	ERA	G	GS	CG	SV	IP	H	R	HR	BB	SO	ERA+	WHIP	H/9	BB/9	SO/9	SO/BB
2001	27	0	0		4.96	10	0	0	0	16.1	15	9	2	8	7	92	1.408	8.3	4.4	3.9	0.88

Which Team Fared Better?

Erdos did receive two World Series rings with the Yankees although if you asked most baseball fans they probably would not remember him having played for them and he was not on the postseason roster either year. The nod would have to go to New York however just from the sheer fact that he pitched twice as many innings and was with them for the better part of three seasons instead of the single season he was with Boston. The Yankees did have to give up Andy Fox for Erdos, who after leaving the Yankees had decent seasons with Arizona and Florida.

John Flaherty

Flaherty was drafted by the Red Sox as a catcher in 1988, eventually making it to the big club in 1992. He played two more years for Boston before being traded to the Detroit Tigers. He then went to the San Diego Padres for a couple of seasons and the Tampa Bay Devil Rays for 5 until going to the Yankees where he played his last three years. He did re-sign with the Red Sox in 2006 and went to Spring Training to act as Tim Wakefield's knuckleball designated catcher, but retired before the season began.

Red Sox Years

Year	Age	G	AB	R	H	2B	3B	HR	RBI	SB	CS	BB	SO	BA	OBP	SLG	OPS	OPS+	TB	SH
1992	24	35	66	3	13	2	0	0	2	0	0	3	7	.197	.229	.227	.456	26	15	1
1993	25	13	25	3	3	2	0	0	2	0	0	2	6	.120	.214	.200	.414	10	5	1
Totals		48	91	6	16	4	0	0	4	0	0	5	13	.176	.224	.220	.444	21	20	2

Yankees Years

Year	Age	G	AB	R	H	2B	3B	HR	RBI	SB	CS	BB	SO	BA	OBP	SLG	OPS	OPS+	TB	SH
2003	35	40	105	16	28	8	0	4	14	0	0	4	19	.267	.297	.457	.754	97	48	5
2004	36	47	127	11	32	9	0	6	16	0	2	5	25	.252	.286	.465	.750	93	59	2
2005	37	47	127	10	21	5	0	2	11	0	0	6	26	.165	.206	.252	.458	23	32	2
Totals		134	359	37	81	22	0	12	41	0	2	15	70	.226	.261	.387	.648	69	139	9

Which Team Fared Better?

Flaherty was drafted by the Red Sox in the 25th round and took a few years to make his way out of the minors. He never got more than 35 games with them in a season. By the time Flaherty got to the Yankees, his role as a backup catcher was well established as he spelled Yankee stalwart Jorge Posada throughout the year. Because he knew his role he was able to get consistent at-bats and production. The edge also goes to the Yankees as he did more damage to Boston as an opponent than he did to the Yankees. As a Tampa Bay Devil Ray he broke up a no-hit bid by Red Sox starter Pedro Martinez with a hit in the ninth inning. When he played for the Yankees he hit a game-winning pinch-hit ground-rule double in the 13th inning to beat Boston.

Tony Fossas

Fossas spent a lot of time in the minor leagues before making his major league debut at age 31 with the Texas Rangers. You would think his career would not have lasted much longer but being a left-handed reliever, the shelf-life for such a player is far longer than any other spot in baseball. Fossas was able to make a career out of being a LOOGY, which stands for **Lefty One Out GuY**, getting ten more years out of his career. Like most LOOGYs he pitched for many teams, the longest tenure being with the Red Sox from 1991 to 1994. He also played for the Texas Rangers, Milwaukee Brewers, St. Louis Cardinals, Seattle Mariners, and the Chicago Cubs before finishing his last season with the Yankees in 1999.

Red Sox Years

Year	Age	W	L	%	ERA	G	GS	CG	SV	IP	H	R	HR	BB	SO	ERA+	WHIP	H/9	BB/9	SO/9	SO/BB
1991	33	3	2	.600	3.47	64	0	0	1	57.0	49	27	3	28	29	125	1.351	7.7	4.4	4.6	1.04
1992	34	1	2	.333	2.43	60	0	0	2	29.2	31	9	1	14	19	175	1.517	9.4	4.2	5.8	1.36
1993	35	1	1	.500	5.18	71	0	0	0	40.0	38	28	4	15	39	90	1.325	8.6	3.4	8.8	2.60
1994	36	2	0	1.000	4.76	44	0	0	1	34.0	35	18	6	15	31	106	1.471	9.3	4.0	8.2	2.07
Totals		7	5	.583	3.98	239	0	0	4	160.2	153	82	14	72	118	114	1.400	8.6	4.0	6.6	1.64

Yankees Year

Year	Age	W	L	%	ERA	G	GS	CG	SV	IP	H	R	HR	BB	SO	ERA+	WHIP	H/9	BB/9	SO/9	SO/BB
1999	41	0	0		36.00	5	0	0	0	1.0	6	4	1	1	0	17	7.000	54.0	9.0	0.0	0.00

Which Team Fared Better?

Because he was a left-handed specialist, Fossas rarely pitched an entire inning. When he played for Boston he appeared in 239 games but only logged 160 innings pitched. His best year as a pitcher was with Boston in 1992 when he finished with a 2.42 ERA and appeared in 60 games. By the time he got to New York in 1999 he was 41 and was not as effective at getting lefties out. His 36.00 ERA in 5 games for New York showed his deterioration. Boston got the better of Fossas. On an interesting note, Fossas was released in the offseason by Boston in 1992 but was resigned back with them as a free agent within the month. The Yankees did the same thing with him in 1999. Apparently the clubs changed their minds.

Tom Gordon

Otherwise known as "Flash", Gordon began his career as a starter for the Kansas City Royals but made a household name for himself as a reliever for Boston. When the Red Sox converted him to their closer, it clicked for Gordon, setting the club record for most saves in a season (46). He continued closing well until Tommy John surgery forced him to take a year off. He reemerged as a set-up guy, performing these duties for the Chicago Cubs, Houston Astros, and Chicago White Sox before finding a groove as set-up man for Yankee closer Mariano Rivera from 2004 to 2005. He was also an All-Star with the Philadelphia Phillies in 2006 and finished his career at age 41 with the Arizona Diamondbacks. Overall he had a 138–126 record and 158 saves.

Red Sox Years

Year	Age	W	L	%	ERA	G	GS	CG	SV	IP	H	R	HR	BB	SO	ERA+	WHIP	H/9	BB/9	SO/9	SO/BB
1996	28	12	9	.571	5.59	34	34	4	0	215.2	249	143	28	105	171	90	1.641	10.4	4.4	7.1	1.63
1997	29	6	10	.375	3.74	42	25	2	11	182.2	155	85	10	78	159	125	1.276	7.6	3.8	7.8	2.04
1998	30	7	4	.636	2.72	73	0	0	46	79.1	55	24	2	25	78	173	1.008	6.2	2.8	8.8	3.12
1999	31	0	2	.000	5.60	21	0	0	11	17.2	17	11	2	12	24	91	1.642	8.7	6.1	12.2	2.00
Totals		25	25	.500	4.45	170	59	6	68	495.1	476	263	42	220	432	109	1.405	8.6	4.0	7.8	1.96

Yankees Years

Year	Age	W	L	%	ERA	G	GS	CG	SV	IP	H	R	HR	BB	SO	ERA+	WHIP	H/9	BB/9	SO/9	SO/BB
2004	36	9	4	.692	2.21	80	0	0	4	89.2	56	23	5	23	96	204	0.881	5.6	2.3	9.6	4.17
2005	37	5	4	.556	2.57	79	0	0	2	80.2	59	25	8	29	69	166	1.091	6.6	3.2	7.7	2.38
Totals		14	8	.636	2.38	159	0	0	6	170.1	115	48	13	52	165	185	0.980	6.1	2.7	8.7	3.17

Which Team Fared Better?

In the roles each team designated for Gordon, he performed admirably. As the Red Sox closer he became an All-Star, winning the Rolaids Relief Man Award in 1998. As a set-up man for the Yankees he kept his ERA in the low two range, keeping teams as bay until Rivera could be brought in the ninth for the kill. The edge would have to go to Boston however only because in today's market, closers are a much more precious commodity than a set-up man. Although he got his nickname "Flash" while starting for Kansas City, he earned the moniker while pitching in Boston.

Chris Hammond

Hammond began as a starter in the Cincinnati Reds organization in 1990. By the time he got to the Red Sox in 1997 from the Florida Marlins, they had designs on him being a reliever. He retired from baseball in 1998 but made an attempt at a comeback in 2001. Being a left-handed relief pitcher made this possible and he played for the Atlanta Braves, Oakland A's, San Diego Padres and then the Yankees during the 2003 season. He eventually retired a second and final time in 2006 back with Cincinnati.

Red Sox Year

Year	Age	W	L	%	ERA	G	GS	CG	SV	IP	H	R	HR	BB	SO	ERA+	WHIP	H/9	BB/9	SO/9	SO/BB
1997	31	3	4	.429	5.92	29	8	0	1	65.1	81	45	5	27	48	79	1.653	11.2	3.7	6.6	1.78

Yankees Year

Year	Age	W	L	%	ERA	G	GS	CG	SV	IP	H	R	HR	BB	SO	ERA+	WHIP	H/9	BB/9	SO/9	SO/BB
2003	37	3	2	.600	2.86	62	0	0	1	63.0	65	23	5	11	45	155	1.206	9.3	1.6	6.4	4.09

Which Team Fared Better?

While Hammond thought he was going to Boston as a starter, the club had other ideas. Hammond even said in a Yankee magazine interview in 2002 that he felt the Red Sox offered this promise of being a starter to get him to sign but never intended to honor it. This made his time in Boston an unpleasant one as evidenced by his 5.92 ERA. When he got to New York he had accepted his role as a left-handed specialist and was quite successful at it, posting a 2.86 ERA. While pitching almost an equal amount of innings for each team, his ERA with the Yankees was three runs lower and he gave up 16 fewer hits. The Yankees definitely used him best.

JIM LEYRITZ

Leyritz was an undrafted free agent who signed with the Yankees and moved his way up their system as a catcher. He arrived in the bigs in 1990 and spent seven years with them. After stints with the Anaheim Angels and the Texas Rangers in 1997, he was traded to Boston in 1998. He was only there for half of the year before being traded away to the San Diego Padres. He did play for the Yankees again, mostly as a pinch hitter, being traded to them at the deadline in 1999 and then the Yanks doing the same at the 2000 deadline, sending him to the Los Angeles Dodgers.

Yankees Years

Year	Age	G	AB	R	H	2B	3B	HR	RBI	SB	CS	BB	SO	BA	OBP	SLG	OPS	OPS+	TB	SH
1990	26	92	303	28	78	13	1	5	25	2	3	27	51	.257	.331	.356	.688	93	108	1
1991	27	32	77	8	14	3	0	0	4	0	1	13	15	.182	.300	.221	.521	47	17	1
1992	28	63	144	17	37	6	0	7	26	0	1	14	22	.257	.341	.444	.786	120	64	0
1993	29	95	259	43	80	14	0	14	53	0	0	37	59	.309	.410	.525	.935	154	136	0
1994	30	75	249	47	66	12	0	17	58	0	0	35	61	.265	.365	.518	.883	129	129	0
1995	31	77	264	37	71	12	0	7	37	1	1	37	73	.269	.374	.394	.768	102	104	0
1996	32	88	265	23	70	10	0	7	40	2	0	30	68	.264	.355	.381	.736	86	101	2
1999	35	31	66	8	15	4	1	0	5	0	0	13	17	.227	.354	.318	.673	76	21	0
2000	36	24	55	2	12	0	0	1	4	0	0	7	14	.218	.317	.273	.590	53	15	0
Totals		577	1,682	213	443	74	2	58	252	5	6	213	380	.263	.359	.413	.772	106	695	4

Red Sox Year

Year	Age	G	AB	R	H	2B	3B	HR	RBI	SB	CS	BB	SO	BA	OBP	SLG	OPS	OPS+	TB	SH
1998	34	52	129	17	37	6	0	8	24	0	0	21	34	.287	.385	.519	.904	131	67	0

Which Team Fared Better?

Although never more than a backup catcher during the regular season, Leyritz made his claim to fame by some clutch performances in the postseason for the Yankees. In 1995 while playing against the Seattle Mariners in the ALDS, he hit a two-run home run in the 15th inning to win the game. In 1996 against the Atlanta Braves in the World Series, the Yankees were down by three runs and Leyritz hit a three-run home run in the 8th allowing them to tie it and eventually win in ten innings. In 1999 after coming back to the Yankees, he hit a home run in game four of the World Series against the Braves, putting the series out of reach. Yankees win big time even if they only count his October at-bats.

Derek Lowe

Lowe was a sinkerball pitcher in the major leagues who played for seven different teams. He was used as both a starter and a closer. Lowe acted as both reliever and starter for Boston during his 8 year tenure with them, leaving for free agency after winning a championship in 2004. He spent 4 years with the Los Angeles Dodgers and 3 years with the Atlanta Braves. He came to the Yankees in 2012 in August after being released by the Cleveland Indians, finishing out the year with them. He ended his career with the Texas Rangers, a 176–157 record and 86 saves.

Red Sox Years

Year	Age	W	L	%	ERA	G	GS	CG	SV	IP	H	R	HR	BB	SO	ERA+	WHIP	H/9	BB/9	SO/9	SO/BB
1997	24	0	2	.000	3.38	8	0	0	0	16.0	15	6	0	3	13	141	1.125	8.4	1.7	7.3	4.33
1998	25	3	9	.250	4.02	63	10	0	4	123.0	126	65	5	42	77	117	1.366	9.2	3.1	5.6	1.83
1999	26	6	3	.667	2.63	74	0	0	15	109.1	84	65	7	25	80	191	0.997	6.9	2.1	6.6	3.20
2000	27	4	4	.500	2.56	74	0	0	42	91.1	90	27	6	22	79	199	1.226	8.9	2.2	7.8	3.59
2001	28	5	10	.333	3.53	67	3	0	24	91.2	103	39	7	29	82	127	1.440	10.1	2.8	8.1	2.83
2002	29	21	8	.724	2.58	32	32	1	0	219.2	166	65	12	48	127	177	0.974	6.8	2.0	5.2	2.65
2003	30	17	7	.708	4.47	33	33	1	0	203.1	216	113	17	72	110	105	1.416	9.6	3.2	4.9	1.53
2004	31	14	12	.538	5.42	33	33	0	0	182.2	224	138	15	71	105	89	1.615	11.0	3.5	5.2	1.48
Totals		70	55	.560	3.72	384	111	2	85	1,037.0	1024	488	69	312	673	127	1.288	8.9	2.7	5.8	2.16

Yankees Year

Year	Age	W	L	%	ERA	G	GS	CG	SV	IP	H	R	HR	BB	SO	ERA+	WHIP	H/9	BB/9	SO/9	SO/BB
2012	39	1	1	.500	3.04	17	0	0	1	23.2	24	9	2	6	14	141	1.268	9.1	2.3	5.3	2.33

Which Team Fared Better?

Lowe spent eight years with the Boston Red Sox. In 2000 he had 42 saves, which led the league and a 2.56 ERA. He converted into a starter for Boston and won 21 games in 2002, throwing a no hitter as well. Lowe will probably be best remembered as the person on the mound when the Red Sox won the championship in 2004. In fact, he was the winning pitcher of the final game of all three series, the American League Division, the American League Championship, and the World Series. Further padding his resume with the BoSox, he was part of one of the most lopsided trades in baseball history when the Mariners sent Lowe and catcher Jason Varitek to Boston for the middle reliever Heathcliff Slocumb. Slocumb did not provide much for the Mariners, only spending one and a half years there, while Varitek and Lowe went on to play a combined 23 years with the Red Sox. Lowe's time

Derek Lowe was a utility pitcher for the Red Sox, serving as middle relief, as a closer, and even as the ace. The high point of his career was winning the 2004 World Series championship with the Red Sox, which he used as a springboard to a lucrative contract with the Los Angeles Dodgers. He was a durable pitcher, going 12 straight years without going on the disabled list (courtesy KeithAllisonPhoto.com).

spent with the Yankees was during the curtain call of his career, when he had little left to offer. He had been relegated to the bullpen again and only got into 17 games. He retired the following year two months into the season for Texas after being designated for assignment.

Jeff Manto

Manto is the purest definition of a journeyman. He was originally drafted by the Yankees in 1982 in the 35th round but did not sign. The following year he was drafted by the California Angels in the 14th round and signed. He played ten years in the majors and played for eight different teams, having stints with the Cleveland Indians on three separate occasions as well as for the Philadelphia Phillies, Baltimore Orioles, the Detroit Tigers, and the Colorado Rockies. He even spent a little time playing in Japan. He did not even spend an entire season with Boston or New York. He played a little over three months with Boston before being traded to Seattle at the trade deadline in 1996 and then in 1999 the Yankees claimed him off waivers from the Indians and he spent just a little more than a month with the club before being released and going back to the Indians.

Red Sox Year

Year	Age	G	AB	R	H	2B	3B	HR	RBI	SB	CS	BB	SO	BA	OBP	SLG	OPS	OPS+	TB	SH
1996	31	12	18	3	2	0	0	0	2	0	0	5	6	.111	.304	.111	.415	11	2	0

Yankees Year

Year	Age	G	AB	R	H	2B	3B	HR	RBI	SB	CS	BB	SO	BA	OBP	SLG	OPS	OPS+	TB	SH
1999	34	6	8	0	1	0	0	0	0	0	0	2	4	1.25	.300	.125	425	16	1	0

Which Team Fared Better?

Neither team benefitted very much from Manto being a part of the roster. He had 18 at-bats with Boston and only 8 with New York, garnering a total of three hits between the teams. If he were a game of blackjack this would probably be a push. Digging a little deeper, Boston probably got a little more in the trade of Manto, receiving infielder Arquimedez Pozo, who contributed 11 RBIs after arriving at Fenway. Because the Yankees simply released him, they got nothing in return.

Josias Manzanillo

Known more for events that happened to him rather than his pitching, Manzanillo is that trivia answer to the question, "which pitcher did Manny Ramirez hit with a line drive in the nuts and ruptured his testicles?" He also was named in the Mitchell Report, the report that listed all the players who had tested positive for PEDs in 2007. Famous Mets clubhouse attendant Kirk Radomski, a major witness in the report, claimed to have injected Manzanillo with steroids. In addition he pitched for the Milwaukee Brewers, Seattle Mariners, Pittsburgh Pirates, Cincinnati Reds, and the Florida Marlins. In his 11 years he appeared in 267 games but only had a 13–15 record.

Red Sox Year

Year	Age	W	L	%	ERA	G	GS	CG	SV	IP	H	R	HR	BB	SO	ERA+	WHIP	H/9	BB/9	SO/9	SO/BB
1991	23	0	0		18.00	1	0	0	0	1.0	2	2	0	3	1	32	5.000	18.0	27.0	9.0	0.33

Yankees Year

Year	Age	W	L	%	ERA	G	GS	CG	SV	IP	H	R	HR	BB	SO	ERA+	WHIP	H/9	BB/9	SO/9	SO/BB
1995	27	0	0		2.08	11	0	0	0	17.1	19	4	1	9	11	227	1.615	9.9	4.7	5.7	1.22

Which Team Fared Better?

His time with the Yankees and Red Sox was not as memorable, spending a single year with both, Manzanillo only pitched a single inning for Boston and gave up two runs. He at least pitched in 17 innings for the Yankees with a respectable 2.08 ERA, giving the edge to New York. Neither team paid very much for him as Boston drafted him as an amateur free agent and New York picked him up on waivers. Boston did sign him again in January of 2005 but he never played for them in the majors again. Edge goes to the Yankees.

Ramiro Mendoza

This is one of those rare players during this era where over a lengthy 10-year career the only two teams Mendoza played for were the Yankees and the Red Sox. A majority of that time was spent with New York as he pitched with them for seven years, then he went to Boston for two years, and then finished up his career with the Yankees. A middle reliever, what is really impressive is that in that ten year span, Mendoza won five World Series rings for two different teams, 4 with the Yankees and the 2004 crown with Boston. For a while he was the only player in the last 75 years to win a ring with both New York and Boston, until Johnny Damon and Eric Hinske were added in 2009 when the Yankees won.

Yankees Years

Year	Age	W	L	%	ERA	G	GS	CG	SV	IP	H	R	HR	BB	SO	ERA+	WHIP	H/9	BB/9	SO/9	SO/BB
1996	24	4	5	.444	6.79	12	11	0	0	53.0	80	43	5	10	34	74	1.698	13.6	1.7	5.8	3.40
1997	25	8	6	.571	4.24	39	15	0	2	133.2	157	67	15	28	82	106	1.384	10.6	1.9	5.5	2.93
1998	26	10	2	.833	3.25	41	14	1	1	130.1	131	50	9	30	56	137	1.235	9.0	2.1	3.9	1.87
1999	27	9	9	.500	4.29	53	6	0	3	123.2	141	68	13	27	80	109	1.358	10.3	2.0	5.8	2.96
2000	28	7	4	.636	4.25	14	9	1	0	65.2	66	32	9	20	30	114	1.310	9.0	2.7	4.1	1.50
2001	29	8	4	.667	3.75	56	2	0	6	100.2	89	44	9	23	70	120	1.113	8.0	2.1	6.3	3.04
2002	30	8	4	.667	3.44	62	0	0	4	91.2	102	43	8	16	61	129	1.287	10.0	1.6	6.0	3.81
2005	33	0	0		18.00	1	0	0	0	1.0	2	2	1	0	1	32	2.000	18.0	0.0	9.0	
Totals		54	34	.614	4.10	278	57	2	16	699.2	768	349	69	154	414	112	1.318	9.9	2.0	5.3	2.696

Red Sox Years

Year	Age	W	L	%	ERA	G	GS	CG	SV	IP	H	R	HR	BB	SO	ERA+	WHIP	H/9	BB/9	SO/9	SO/BB
2003	31	3	5	.375	6.75	37	5	0	0	66.2	98	51	10	20	36	69	1.770	13.2	2.7	4.9	1.80
2004	32	2	1	.667	3.52	27	0	0	0	30.2	25	12	3	7	13	138	1.043	7.3	2.1	3.8	1.86
Totals		5	6	.455	5.73	64	5	0	0	97.1	123	63	13	27	49	83	1.541	11.4	2.5	4.5	1.81

Which Team Fared Better?

By sheer volume the Yankees win this one. Eight years with one team as a middle reliever is quite an accomplishment and Mendoza was the setup mainstay for the Yankees through their magical run of 1996, 1998–2000. Winning the first World Series with a team that had been on a nearly 90-year drought is pretty special as well although Embree and Timlin were the setup men that season for Boston. In terms of dollar value, the Yankees paid him a total of $5 million in the first six years he played for them. Boston, who had him for only two years, paid him a total of $6.5 million. Yankees definitely got more for their money.

Doug Mientkiewicz

Mientkiewicz had a twelve year major league career, 7 of it spent with the Minnesota Twins. He did not even play a full season with the Red Sox or the Yankees. He came over in a trade deadline deal in 2004 and finished out the season with Boston. When he played for the Yankees he suffered a concussion in a collision with Boston runner Mike Lowell and missed three months of the season. He never spent more than a single season with his other teams, the New York Mets, Kansas City Royals, Pittsburgh Pirates, and Los Angeles Dodgers. He was a career .271 hitter with nearly 900 hits and a .360 on-base percentage.

Red Sox Year

Year	Age	G	AB	R	H	2B	3B	HR	RBI	SB	CS	BB	SO	BA	OBP	SLG	OPS	OPS+	TB	SH
2004	30	49	107	13	23	6	1	1	10	0	1	10	18	.215	.286	.318	.603	54	34	0

Yankees Year

Year	Age	G	AB	R	H	2B	3B	HR	RBI	SB	CS	BB	SO	BA	OBP	SLG	OPS	OPS+	TB	SH
2007	33	72	166	26	46	12	0	5	24	0	0	16	23	.277	.349	.440	.789	106	73	6

Which Team Fared Better?

Looking at his legacy with these teams, Mientkiewicz was a member of the 2004 World Series winning Boston Red Sox, the one that killed the curse and got the 86-year-old drought off their back. He caught the final out of the game to seal the championship. Even though his numbers are better, with the Yankees his time was not very memorable. Unfortunately part of the Red Sox memory is tainted as Mientkiewicz kept the ball he caught as the last out. When Red Sox management asked for this ball, Mientkiewicz refused to part with it, claiming it was his. Eventually the dispute went to court and the ball was turned over to the Baseball Hall of Fame. He was also part of the legendary trade that broke the curse. In July of 2004, Red Sox general manager Theo Epstein managed a four team trade sending Nomar Garciaparra and Matt Murton to the Cubs. The Montreal Expos gave Boston Orlando Cabrera. The Cubs then sent some players to the Twins, who parted with Mientkiewicz. Both he and Cabrera were important players in the playoffs and World Series for Boston so the edge goes to them.

Mike Myers

Yet another in a long line of left-handed relievers to have played for both teams. He spent thirteen years in the bigs, kind of short for a lefty reliever, playing for nine different teams including the Detroit Tigers, Milwaukee Brewers, Colorado Rockies, Arizona Diamondbacks, and the Seattle Mariners before spending a year and a half with both the Red Sox and Yankees. He finished his career with the Chicago White Sox, pitching 541.2 innings and appearing in 883 games.

Boston Years

Year	Age	W	L	%	ERA	G	GS	CG	SV	IP	H	R	HR	BB	SO	ERA+	WHIP	H/9	BB/9	SO/9	SO/BB
2004	35	1	0	1.000	4.20	25	0	0	0	15.0	16	7	2	6	9	117	1.467	9.6	3.6	5.4	1.50
2005	36	3	1	.750	3.13	65	0	0	0	37.1	30	14	3	13	21	146	1.152	7.2	3.1	5.1	1.62
Totals		**4**	**1**	**.800**	**3.44**	**90**	**0**	**0**	**0**	**52.1**	**46**	**21**	**5**	**19**	**30**	**136**	**1.242**	**7.9**	**3.3**	**5.2**	**1.58**

Yankees Years

Year	Age	W	L	%	ERA	G	GS	CG	SV	IP	H	R	HR	BB	SO	ERA+	WHIP	H/9	BB/9	SO/9	SO/BB
2006	37	1	2	.333	3.23	62	0	0	0	30.2	29	14	3	10	22	142	1.272	8.5	2.9	6.5	2.20
2007	38	3	0	1.000	2.66	55	0	0	0	40.2	38	14	3	16	21	171	1.328	8.4	3.5	4.6	1.31
Totals		4	2	.667	2.90	117	0	0	0	71.1	67	28	6	26	43	157	1.304	8.5	3.3	5.4	1.65

Which Team Fared Better?

Like most LOOGYs, Myers came in and did his job effectively for both teams. He probably did it a little better for New York though. His ERA was a 2.90 for the Yankees although a respectable 3.44 for Boston. He pitched nearly twenty more innings for the Yankees and struck out thirteen more batters. Boston was able to get him for a little cheaper since they got him off waivers while the Yankees signed him for over a million as a free agent. Being a LOOGY, he was used by Boston primarily against left-handed Yankee batter Hideki Matsui, and then by New York to face Red Sox lefty David Ortiz. Ortiz was 5 for 17 with a .297 average and a single home run. Matsui faced Myers 9 times, getting 3 hits, one a home run for a .333 average. New York wins this one as well.

JOHN OLERUD

Spanning a 17 years career, Olerud was known for a couple of things. The first was his wearing a hard helmet as a first baseman. He had suffered a brain aneurysm in college so wore the hard hat in the field as a precaution. The second thing he is known for is being a Toronto Blue Jay. He spent eight years with that organization, jumping directly from college to the majors. He won the World Series with the 1992 and 1993 teams. He spent 3 years with the New York Mets and another 5 with the Seattle Mariners. His stops in Boston and for the Yankees were at the very end of his career when his value as a steady hitter and on-base guy had begun to diminish. Olerud was very talented at getting on base any way possible with a career .398 on-base percentage. He compiled 2,234 hits, 500 of which were doubles and 255 which were home runs. He also walked 1,275 times in his career. In his best year for Toronto, he had a .473 OBP to lead the league.

Yankees Year

Year	Age	G	AB	R	H	2B	3B	HR	RBI	SB	CS	BB	SO	BA	OBP	SLG	OPS	OPS+	TB	SH
2004	35	49	164	16	46	7	0	4	26	0	0	21	20	.280	.367	.396	.763	101	65	0

Red Sox Year

Year	Age	G	AB	R	H	2B	3B	HR	RBI	SB	CS	BB	SO	BA	OBP	SLG	OPS	OPS+	TB	SH
2005	36	87	173	18	50	7	0	7	37	0	0	16	20	.289	.344	.451	.795	106	78	0

Which Team Fared Better?

Although not in his prime when he played for the Yankees and Boston, he did have decent OBP of .367 and .344 respectively. His limited number of at-bats reflect his being the backup first baseman to the more productive hitters of Jason Giambi for the Yankees and Kevin Millar for Boston. His numbers are pretty close between the two teams with New York getting the better OBP and Boston getting more RBIs but not by much. Boston would have to get the nod because his slugging percentage is .451 as compared to .396 although both teams would have liked to have had Olerud in his prime.

Joe Oliver

A catcher, Oliver is perhaps most closely associated with the Cincinnati Reds, with whom he spent eight of his 13 seasons. He spent some time with the Milwaukee Brewers, Detroit Tigers, Seattle Mariners, and Pittsburgh Pirates before splitting a single season with the Yankees and the Red Sox in 2001. He had begun the year with the Yankees, signing as a free agent. In June the Yankees released him after only playing in twelve games. The Red Sox then signed him a couple of weeks later but he saw even less playing time with them.

Yankees Year

Year	Age	G	AB	R	H	2B	3B	HR	RBI	SB	CS	BB	SO	BA	OBP	SLG	OPS	OPS+	TB	SH
2001	35	12	36	3	9	1	0	1	2	0	0	1	12	.250	.263	.361	.624	62	13	2

Red Sox Year

Year	Age	G	AB	R	H	2B	3B	HR	RBI	SB	CS	BB	SO	BA	OBP	SLG	OPS	OPS+	TB	SH
2001	35	5	12	1	3	1	0	0	1	0	0	1	3	.250	.308	.333	.641	69	4	0

Which Team Fared Better?

There are no real winners here. Oliver's contributions to both teams were as a backup catcher to perennial All-Stars, Jorge Posada and Jason Varitek. He did get more plate appearances with the Yankees but they did not think enough of his services to keep him around the entire year. Yankees win, but the prize is like splitting a pot in poker, not very satisfying. In 2014 he was hired to be the manager of the single A Boston affiliate the Lowell Spinners.

Curtis Pride

Pride became the first deaf player to play in the major leagues since Dick Sipeck in 1945. Even though he had an 11-year career, Pride only amassed a total of 796 at-bats, playing with Montreal, Detroit, Atlanta, and the Angels. His most productive time was spent with Detroit where he had 267 at-bats with 10 home runs and 31 RBIs. He spent most of his career as a pinch hitter or a fourth outfielder, going back and forth between the minors and majors.

Red Sox Years

Year	Age	G	AB	R	H	2B	3B	HR	RBI	SB	CS	BB	SO	BA	OBP	SLG	OPS	OPS+	TB	SH
1997	28	2	2	1	1	0	0	1	1	0	0	0	1	.500	.500	2.000	2.500	508	4	0
2000	31	9	20	4	5	1	0	0	0	0	0	1	7	.250	.286	.300	.586	48	6	0
Totals		11	22	5	6	1	0	1	1	0	0	1	8	.273	.304	.455	.759	88	10	0

Yankee Year

Year	Age	G	AB	R	H	2B	3B	HR	RBI	SB	CS	BB	SO	BA	OBP	SLG	OPS	OPS+	TB	SH
2003	34	4	12	1	1	0	0	1	1	0	0	0	2	.083	.083	.333	.417	4	4	0

Which Team Fared Better?

He had two different stints with Boston that totaled only 22 at-bats, and he had only 12 at-bats with the Yankees in 2003. Because there were so few plate appearances this is a hard one to judge. Pride contributed only a single RBI to each team, each on solo home runs. That was actually the only hit he had for the Yankees. For Boston he at least contributed other hits so the scale tips in their favor.

Paul Quantrill

A very consistent spaghetti armed right-handed pitcher from the bullpen. Over the course of his 14-year career he pitched 75 innings or more ten times for the seven teams he played for. He was drafted by the Red Sox and played the first three years of his career in the majors with them until he was traded mid-way through the 1994 season to the Philadelphia Phillies. The team he pitched best for was the Toronto Blue Jays where he played for 6 years. He was an All-Star with them and went 11–2 with a 3.04 ERA, leading the league in games in 2001. He also led the league in games the next two years with the Los Angeles Dodgers. He came to the Yankees in 2004 as a free agent, signing a two-year deal. The Yankees released him halfway through his second year, going to the San Diego Padres and then the Florida Marlins, who released him as well.

Red Sox Years

Year	Age	W	L	%	ERA	G	GS	CG	SV	IP	H	R	HR	BB	SO	ERA+	WHIP	H/9	BB/9	SO/9	SO/BB
1992	23	2	3	.400	2.19	27	0	0	1	49.1	55	18	1	15	24	193	1.419	10.0	2.7	4.4	1.60
1993	24	6	12	.333	3.91	49	14	1	1	138.0	151	73	13	44	66	119	1.413	9.8	2.9	4.3	1.50
1994	25	1	1	.500	3.52	17	0	0	0	23.0	25	10	4	5	15	144	1.304	9.8	2.0	5.9	3.00
Totals		9	16	.360	3.47	93	14	1	2	210.1	231	101	18	64	105	133	1.403	9.9	2.7	4.5	1.64

Yankees Years

Year	Age	W	L	%	ERA	G	GS	CG	SV	IP	H	R	HR	BB	SO	ERA+	WHIP	H/9	BB/9	SO/9	SO/BB
2004	35	7	3	.700	4.72	86	0	0	1	95.1	124	54	5	20	37	96	1.510	11.7	1.9	3.5	1.85
2005	36	1	0	1.000	6.75	22	0	0	0	32.0	48	24	5	7	11	63	1.719	13.5	2.0	3.1	1.57
Totals		8	3	.727	5.23	108	0	0	1	127.1	172	78	10	27	48	85	1.563	12.2	1.9	3.4	1.78

Which Team Fared Better?

His ERA was better in Boston, 3.47 as compared to 5.23, and he pitched almost a hundred more innings for the Red Sox. But it is not these reasons the favor goes to Boston. It actually comes when Quantrill was a member of the Yankees, he served up a game winning home run ball to David Ortiz in inning number twelve of game four of the American League Championship Series. This allowed the Red Sox to avoid elimination, win the next three games, and then go on to win the World Series. For that the Red Sox thank him.

Carlos Rodriguez

Rodriguez played for only two teams in his professional career and they happen to be the Red Sox and Yankees. He was purchased by the Yankees and he stayed in their system for six years but only reached the majors in 1991. Boston signed him as a free agent in 1994 and he played two seasons with them.

Yankees Year

Year	Age	G	AB	R	H	2B	3B	HR	RBI	SB	CS	BB	SO	BA	OBP	SLG	OPS	OPS+	TB	SH
1991	23	15	37	1	7	0	0	0	2	0	0	1	2	.189	.211	.189	.400	12	7	1

Red Sox Years

Year	Age	G	AB	R	H	2B	3B	HR	RBI	SB	CS	BB	SO	BA	OBP	SLG	OPS	OPS+	TB	SH
1994	26	57	174	15	50	14	1	1	13	1	0	11	13	.287	.330	.397	.726	84	69	7
1995	27	13	30	5	10	2	0	0	5	0	0	2	2	.333	.394	.400	.794	106	12	3
Totals		70	204	20	60	16	1	1	18	1	0	13	15	.294	.339	.397	.737	87	81	10

Which Team Fared Better?

Even if you compare his limited 1995 season with the Red Sox to his limited 1991 season with the Yankees, Boston still comes out on top. He had more hits, RBIs, and doubles in this small sample. When you add the 1994 season where he had 174 at-bats, 50 hits, 13 RBIs, and 15 runs scored, it sends it over to the Red Sox without a doubt.

REY SANCHEZ

A journeyman utility man middle infielder, Sanchez was good for a pinch hit appearance, spelling defensively at second, third, or shortstop, or laying down a sacrifice bunt. He played for the Yankees twice, in 1997 and in 2005, and spent the 2002 season with Boston. His most time was spent with the Chicago Cubs where he played the first 7 years of his career. He also played 3 years for the Kansas City Royals, then bounced around from the Braves, Boston, Mets, Seattle, and Tampa Bay before finishing with the Yankees. His strength was definitely not the long ball as he had a total of 15 home runs in the 15 seasons he played professional baseball, but getting 1,317 hits and 389 RBIs over that span.

Yankees Years

Year	Age	G	AB	R	H	2B	3B	HR	RBI	SB	CS	BB	SO	BA	OBP	SLG	OPS	OPS+	TB	SH
1997	29	38	138	21	43	12	0	1	15	0	4	5	21	.312	.338	.420	.758	97	58	5
2005	37	23	43	7	12	1	0	0	2	0	1	2	3	.279	.326	.302	.628	71	13	2
Totals		61	181	28	55	13	0	1	17	0	5	7	24	.304	.335	.392	.727	91	71	7

Red Sox Year

Year	Age	G	AB	R	H	2B	3B	HR	RBI	SB	CS	BB	SO	BA	OBP	SLG	OPS	OPS+	TB	SH
2002	34	107	357	46	102	12	3	1	38	2	2	17	31	.286	.318	.345	.662	75	123	5

Which Team Fared Better?

Because he was more of a regular in Boston at second base, he got more at-bats in that single season than in the two he spent with the Yankees. As a result he got nearly double the hits, double the RBIs, and nearly triple the walks. Although it is difficult for a utility man to crack the lineup on a regular basis, doing so for the Red Sox allowed him to fare better with them.

MIKE STANLEY

Stanley started out as a catcher with the Texas Rangers, logging five years with that team. He spent the next ten years bouncing back and forth between Boston and the Yankees. He was with both organizations for five years and played for both teams at two different times. He finished up his career by going to the playoffs with the Oakland A's. He played in 1,467 games, finishing with a respectable .270 batting average and .320 OBP.

Yankees Years

Year	Age	G	AB	R	H	2B	3B	HR	RBI	SB	CS	BB	SO	BA	OBP	SLG	OPS	OPS+	TB	SH
1992	29	68	173	24	43	7	0	8	27	0	0	33	45	.249	.372	.428	.800	125	74	0
1993	30	130	423	70	129	17	1	26	84	1	1	57	85	.305	.389	.534	.923	150	226	0
1994	31	82	290	54	87	20	0	17	57	0	0	39	56	.300	.384	.545	.929	141	158	0
1995	32	118	399	63	107	29	1	18	83	1	1	57	106	.268	.360	.481	.841	118	192	0
1997	34	28	87	16	25	8	0	3	12	0	0	15	22	.287	.388	.483	.871	127	42	0
Totals		426	1,372	227	391	81	2	72	263	2	2	201	314	.285	.377	.504	.882	134	692	0

Red Sox Years

Year	Age	G	AB	R	H	2B	3B	HR	RBI	SB	CS	BB	SO	BA	OBP	SLG	OPS	OPS+	TB	SH
1996	33	121	397	73	107	20	1	24	69	2	0	69	62	.270	.383	.506	.889	122	201	0
1998	35	47	156	25	45	12	0	7	32	1	0	26	43	.288	.388	.500	.888	128	78	0
1999	36	136	427	59	120	22	0	19	72	0	0	70	94	.281	.393	.466	.859	115	199	0
2000	37	58	185	22	41	5	0	10	28	0	0	30	44	.222	.327	.411	.738	84	76	1
Totals		450	1,425	224	391	76	1	73	254	3	1	234	293	.274	.381	.483	.864	118	688	1

Which Team Fared Better?

His number of at-bats between the teams are fairly comparable. His hits match perfectly, 391 for each team. He hit only one more home run with Boston than with the Yankees. RBIs are fairly close as well, only 9 more with the Yankees than with Boston. It comes down to what did he mean for each of these teams. It seems he meant more to the Yankees. He was an All-Star in 1995 as well as a silver slugger in 1993. He also had his best single season with the Yankees in 1993 with 26 home runs, 84 RBIs, and a .305 batting average. The Yankees thought enough of him to get him back in August of 1997 to help them down the stretch, trading Jim Mecir to Boston in exchange for Stanley and Tony Armas.

Mike Stanton

Like most left-handed specialists out of the bullpen, Stanton had a fairly long career, playing 17 years with 9 different teams. He played for Boston and the Yankees twice in his career. His longest time was spent with the Yankees (7 years) and Atlanta Braves (7 years) while spending single seasons with the San Francisco Giants, Texas Rangers, and Cincinnati Reds. He also spent two years each with the New York Mets and Washington Nationals. Although not an official statistic, Stanton holds the major league record for the number of holds at 266. Stanton was mentioned in the Mitchell Report that named players who had tested positive for use of PEDs.

Red Sox Years

Year	Age	W	L	%	ERA	G	GS	CG	SV	IP	H	R	HR	BB	SO	ERA+	WHIP	H/9	BB/9	SO/9	SO/BB
1995	28	1	0	1.000	3.00	22	0	0	0	21.0	17	9	3	8	10	164	1.190	7.3	3.4	4.3	1.25
1996	29	4	3	.571	3.83	59	0	0	1	56.1	58	24	9	23	46	132	1.438	9.3	3.7	7.3	2.00
2005	38	0	0		0.00	1	0	0	0	1.0	1	0	0	0	1		1.000	9.0	0.0	9.0	
Totals		5	3	.625	3.56	82	0	0	1	78.1	76	33	12	31	57	142	1.366	8.7	3.6	6.5	1.84

Yankees Years

Year	Age	W	L	%	ERA	G	GS	CG	SV	IP	H	R	HR	BB	SO	ERA+	WHIP	H/9	BB/9	SO/9	SO/BB
1997	30	6	1	.857	2.57	64	0	0	3	66.2	50	19	3	34	70	176	1.260	6.8	4.6	9.5	2.06
1998	31	4	1	.800	5.47	67	0	0	6	79.0	71	51	13	26	69	81	1.228	8.1	3.0	7.9	2.65
1999	32	2	2	.500	4.33	73	1	0	0	62.1	71	30	5	18	59	109	1.428	10.3	2.6	8.5	3.28
2000	33	2	3	.400	4.10	69	0	0	0	68.0	68	32	5	24	75	118	1.353	9.0	3.2	9.9	3.13
2001	34	9	4	.692	2.58	76	0	0	0	80.1	80	25	4	29	78	175	1.357	9.0	3.2	8.7	2.69
2002	35	7	1	.875	3.00	79	0	0	6	78.0	73	29	4	28	44	148	1.295	8.4	3.2	5.1	1.57
2005	38	1	2	.333	7.07	28	0	0	0	14.0	17	11	1	6	12	61	1.643	10.9	3.9	7.7	2.00
Totals		31	14	.689	3.77	456	1	0	15	448.1	430	197	35	165	407	121	1.327	8.6	3.3	8.2	2.47

Which Team Fared Better?

When you look at his numbers for both teams, his WHIP (walks plus hits per innings pitched) is about the same as well as his ERA. He did the job of a lefty specialist for both teams admirably, but by number of years, he contributed that dependability for far longer in the Yankees organization. He was an important part of the bullpen in that incredible 1998–2000 Yankee team. Out of the six years he pitched in the postseason for New York, he had a mid-twos ERA. He pitched in four World Series for the Yankees, appearing in eleven games of the world championship. He also was an All-Star with the Yankees in 2001. Maybe if Boston had held onto him longer, he would have done the same for them. When he played for them the second time, they traded for him on September 29. The season ended three days later on October 2.

David Wells

Wells pitched for ten teams during his 21 year pitching career. That is over a third of the teams in both leagues, so the chances of him ending up on both the Yankees and Red Sox were pretty good. He also went to the playoffs with 6 of those teams (Toronto, Cincinnati, Baltimore, Yankees, Red Sox, and San Diego), showing he was a winner. He pitched in 27 postseason games with a 10–5 record. A left-handed starter, he amassed 239 wins in his career, most of them for the Toronto Blue Jays where he played for 8 years.

Yankees Years

Year	Age	W	L	%	ERA	G	GS	CG	SV	IP	H	R	HR	BB	SO	ERA+	WHIP	H/9	BB/9	SO/9	SO/BB
1997	34	16	10	.615	4.21	32	32	5	0	218.0	239	109	24	45	156	107	1.303	9.9	1.9	6.4	3.47
1998	35	18	4	.818	3.49	30	30	8	0	214.1	195	86	29	29	163	127	1.045	8.2	1.2	6.8	5.62
2002	39	19	7	.731	3.75	31	31	2	0	206.1	210	100	21	45	137	118	1.236	9.2	2.0	6.0	3.04
2003	40	15	7	.682	4.14	31	30	4	0	213.0	242	101	24	20	101	106	1.230	10.2	0.8	4.3	5.05
Totals		68	28	.708	3.90	124	123	19	0	851.2	886	396	98	139	557	114	1.204	9.4	1.5	5.9	4.01

Red Sox Years

Year	Age	W	L	%	ERA	G	GS	CG	SV	IP	H	R	HR	BB	SO	ERA+	WHIP	H/9	BB/9	SO/9	SO/BB
2005	42	15	7	.682	4.45	30	30	2	0	184.0	220	95	21	21	107	102	1.310	10.8	1.0	5.2	5.10
2006	43	2	3	.400	4.98	8	8	0	0	47.0	64	30	10	8	24	96	1.532	12.3	1.5	4.6	3.00
Totals		17	10	.630	4.56	38	38	2	0	231.0	284	125	31	29	131	101	1.355	11.1	1.1	5.1	4.52

Which Team Fared Better?

If you asked Wells (he had a habit of overstating his opinion) he would tell you the Yankees got the better of him. Wells loved playing for the Yankees, even complaining about not wanting to leave when New York traded him to Toronto for Roger Clemens. One wonders who made out

Often a controversial figure, Wells knew how to pitch, compiling a winning record in 15 of the 21 seasons he played. He finished with 2,201 strikeouts and 239 wins, and finished among the top 10 in WAR for pitchers four times (courtesy David Ferguson).

better in that deal. He had 37 wins in his two seasons with the Blue Jays. In those same two years Clemens won 27 for the Yankees. Wells eventually came back to the Yankees during the 2002 and 2003 season to be a teammate of Clemens. During this time Wells had 34 wins while Clemens had 30. Wells was always a huge Babe Ruth fan, sporting a tattoo of the Yankee great. When Wells signed as a free agent with the Yankees he asked for Ruth's retired number 3, which he was of course denied. Instead he bought an authentic hat that Ruth wore in 1935 for $35,000 and wore it to pitch in a game for the Yankees. More impressive was the fact that Wells pitched a perfect game as a member of the Yankees in 1998. By the time Wells got to the Red Sox he was in his forties and well beyond his prime. Boston did manage to flip Wells to the San Diego Padres for catcher George Kottaras, who became a backup. The Yankees got 68 wins while Boston only 17, giving the Yanks the victory.

Mark Whiten

A hard hitting outfielder, Whiten never stayed with a team more than a couple of years and played for eight different teams, logging two two-year stints with the Cleveland Indians. He probably had his best seasons when he played for the St. Louis Cardinals. In a doubleheader against the Reds he hit four home runs in the second game, tying a major league record. He also tied a major league record of 13 RBIs in that doubleheader. His time with Boston and New York was less memorable, garnering only six home runs in his time spent with both. Boston traded him mid-season to the Phillies. He bounced from the Atlanta Braves and Seattle Mariners before going to the Yankees. He ended his career with 423 RBIs and 465 runs scored in 3523 plate appearances.

Red Sox Year

Year	Age	G	AB	R	H	2B	3B	HR	RBI	SB	CS	BB	SO	BA	OBP	SLG	OPS	OPS+	TB	SH
1995	28	32	108	13	20	3	0	1	10	1	0	8	23	.185	.239	.241	.480	24	26	0

Yankees Year

Year	Age	G	AB	R	H	2B	3B	HR	RBI	SB	CS	BB	SO	BA	OBP	SLG	OPS	OPS+	TB	SH
1997	30	69	215	34	57	11	0	5	24	4	2	30	47	.265	.360	.386	.746	96	83	1

Which Team Fared Better?

With twice as many plate appearances Whiten was able to do more damage as a Yankee, hitting 5 home runs, 24 RBIs, and 11 doubles as compared to 1, 10, and 3 with Boston. Make no mistake that neither were stellar seasons and Whiten will hang his hat on his time spent with the Cardinals and the magical four home run game. The Red Sox also paid a lot for his limited services, his salary being $1.6 million. The Yankees on the other had got twice as many bats for a fraction of the cost, $1 million.

7. The Evil Empires
The Present and Future (2006–present)

Over the course of the last 15 years, the path of these teams has taken a turn. The lowly Boston Red Sox, who cobbled together teams that somehow found a way to get to but lose on the big stage, has given way to the development of one of the most lucrative teams in the league. In March of 2014, Forbes magazine reported the most profitable franchises in baseball. The Yankees were number one with $461 million in revenue, but the Red Sox were close behind in third, taking in $357 million. In 2013 they were ranked first and second, the Yankees with $471 million and the Red Sox with $336 million. Both teams have very profitable television deals, having their own sports networks to televise the games. In addition, because their rivalry is a known commodity, the two teams get more nationally televised games than any other teams in the baseball, especially if they are playing one another. Between ESPN, the MLB network, TBS, and Fox, they televised 17 games per team, including six games against one another in 2011. That same year small market teams such as Pittsburgh and Cleveland had none. This only intensified in 2014 when in the month of April alone, New York had 17 nationally televised games while the Red Sox had 15. In short; the rivalry has been good for business.

During the 2004 playoff run of the Yankees, the pinstripers were labeled the evil empire while the Red Sox were cast as the lovable losers, or the idiots as Johnny Damon coined them. They were the quintessential underdogs, the David versus the Goliath, and the viewing public ate it up. But what many failed to realize was that the Red Sox were just as much an evil empire as the Yankees, if only to a slightly less degree. While the Yankees have had the top payroll for the past 15 years in baseball (finally being outspent in 2014 by the Los Angeles Dodgers), the Red Sox are usually never far behind. Here is the amount of money each club has spent over the past 15 years and where they rank compared to other teams in baseball:

Year	Yankee's Payroll	Rank	Boston Payroll	Rank
2014	$203 million	2	$162 million	4
2013	$228 million	1	$150 million	4
2012	$197 million	1	$173 million	3
2011	$201 million	1	$161 million	3
2010	$206 million	1	$162 million	2
2009	$201 million	1	$122 million	4
2008	$209 million	1	$133 million	4
2007	$189 million	1	$143 million	2
2006	$228 million	1	$150 million	2
2005	$205 million	1	$121 million	2
2004	$182 million	1	$125 million	2
2003	$152 million	1	$99 million	6
2002	$125 million	1	$108 million	2

Year	Yankee's Payroll	Rank	Boston Payroll	Rank
2001	$109 million	1	$109 million	2
2000	$92 million	1	$81 million	5

Seven of those years the Red Sox were the second highest payroll. The lowest they ever were was in 2003 when they were the sixth highest payroll in the league. To put this into perspective, let us take the combined payroll of the rest of the three teams in that division, the Baltimore Orioles, Tampa Bay Rays, and Toronto Blue Jays, and compare them to the combined payroll of the Yankees and Red Sox.

Year	Yankees/Red Sox Payroll	Rest of Eastern Division Payroll
2014	$365 million	$316 million
2013	$386 million	$266 million
2012	$370 million	$220 million
2011	$363 million	$188 million
2010	$368 million	$214 million
2009	$322 million	$210 million
2008	$342 million	$207 million
2007	$332 million	$198 million
2006	$378 million	$178 million
2005	$326 million	$148 million
2004	$307 million	$130 million
2003	$251 million	$143 million
2002	$233 million	$170 million
2001	$221 million	$206 million
2000	$173 million	$193 million

As you can clearly see, since 2001 the empires are outspending the other three teams in their division, sometimes by more than double. Make no mistake that free agency has not dulled the rivalry between these two clubs. If anything it has heightened it and this is evident from the dollars they are spending to keep up with one another.

The question is, does that allow for any other teams in the Eastern Division to compete with the mighty empires? Over the course of the past 15 seasons, here are the division standings:

	1st	2nd	3rd	4th	5th
2000	Yankees	Red Sox	Toronto	Orioles	Tampa Bay
2001	Yankees	Red Sox	Toronto	Orioles	Tampa Bay
2002	Yankees	Red Sox	Toronto	Orioles	Tampa Bay
2003	Yankees	Red Sox	Toronto	Orioles	Tampa Bay
2004	Yankees	Red Sox	Orioles	Tampa Bay	Toronto
2005	Yankees	Red Sox	Toronto	Orioles	Tampa Bay
2006	Yankees	Toronto	Red Sox	Orioles	Tampa Bay
2007	Red Sox	Yankees	Toronto	Orioles	Tampa Bay
2008	Tampa Bay	Red Sox	Yankees	Toronto	Orioles
2009	Yankees	Red Sox	Tampa Bay	Toronto	Orioles
2010	Tampa Bay	Yankees	Red Sox	Toronto	Orioles
2011	Yankees	Tampa Bay	Red Sox	Toronto	Orioles
2012	Yankees	Orioles	Tampa Bay	Toronto	Red Sox
2013	Red Sox	Tampa Bay	Orioles	Yankees	Toronto
2014	Baltimore	Yankees	Toronto	Tampa Bay	Red Sox

The Yankees have finished in first 10 times and the Red Sox twice. The Red Sox did however finish second 8 times, the Yankees 3 times. Toronto has never finished in first and Baltimore just achieved it in 2014 (their first since 1997). It is not easy to be the other three teams in the division. Boston has given up their underdog status and passed it to the Tampa Bay Rays, who usually always field a pretty good team at a fraction of the cost. Anymore feeling sorry for the Red Sox is like feeling sorry for Donald Trump just because he is not as rich as Bill Gates. He is still filthy rich and there is no reason to feel sorry for him.

Players Who Spent Time with Both Teams, 2006–Present

DAVID AARDSMA

Aardsma spent his career as a reliever, pitching for seven teams in eight seasons. Used mostly in middle relief, he did spend two years as a closer with the Seattle Mariners. His college team, the Rice Owls, won the 2003 College World Series, and he was made a first-round draft pick by the San Francisco Giants. After throwing 10.2 innings with the Giants a year later, and then spending a season in the minors, he threw for the Chicago Cubs in 2006 and then went to the South Side to pitch for the White Sox the following season. He had his most successful years with the Mariners, saving 69 games over two seasons. After brief, forgettable stops with the Yankees and Mets, he found himself back in the minors in 2014. He briefly broke back into the majors with Atlanta in 2015, but he was gone again by 2016, released in May after a signing a minor-league contract with Toronto.

Red Sox Year

Year	Age	W	L	%	ERA	G	GS	CG	SV	IP	H	R	HR	BB	SO	ERA+	WHIP	H/9	BB/9	SO/9	SO/BB
2008	26	4	2	.667	5.55	47	0	0	0	48.2	49	32	4	35	49	84	1.726	9.1	6.5	9.1	1.40

Yankees Year

Year	Age	W	L	%	ERA	G	GS	CG	SV	IP	H	R	HR	BB	SO	ERA+	WHIP	H/9	BB/9	SO/9	SO/BB
2012	30	0	0		9.00	1	0	0	0	1.0	1	1	1	1	1	64	2.000	9.0	9.0	9.0	1.00

Which Team Fared Better?

Aardsma pitched poorly for both the Red Sox and Yankees. With Boston, he had a 5.55 ERA and a 1.726 WHIP, yielding 49 hits in 48.2 innings, meaning he gave up 9.1 hits per nine innings. The Yankees signed Aardsma to a half-million dollar contract after the success he had as closer with the Mariners, even though he was coming off Tommy John surgery. He was not activated until September of that year and went on to pitch in a single game in a single inning, giving up a single walk, securing a single strikeout, and surrendering a single home run. The Yankees wasted another half a million exercising a club option before releasing him right after spring training the following season. Neither team got much out of him, then, but the Yankees paid far more, spending $1 million for one inning of work. The Red Sox paid a little over $400,000 for 48.2 innings. They weren't always the best innings, granted, but at least Boston got *something* for their money.

ALFREDO ACEVES

Pitching on and off for seven years, Aceves pitched for only two teams in the majors, the Yankees and the Red Sox. He was known for his control and could throw any of his four pitches at any count, which made him a reliable reliever. He finished his career with a 31–16 record, a 3.64 ERA, 266 strikeouts, and 29 saves.

Yankees Years

Year	Age	W	L	%	ERA	G	GS	CG	SV	IP	H	R	HR	BB	SO	ERA+	WHIP	H/9	BB/9	SO/9	SO/BB
2008	25	1	0	1.000	2.40	6	4	0	0	30.0	25	8	4	10	16	185	1.167	7.5	3.0	4.8	1.60
2009	26	10	1	.909	3.54	43	1	0	1	84.0	69	36	10	16	69	131	1.012	7.4	1.7	7.4	4.31
2010	27	3	0	1.000	3.00	10	0	0	1	12.0	10	5	1	4	2	148	1.167	7.5	3.0	1.5	0.50
2014	31	1	2	.333	6.52	10	0	0	0	19.1	23	14	6	4	16	60	1.397	10.7	1.9	7.4	4.00
Totals		15	3	.833	3.65	69	5	0	2	145.1	127	63	21	34	103	122	1.108	7.9	2.1	6.4	3.03

Red Sox Years

Year	Age	W	L	%	ERA	G	GS	CG	SV	IP	H	R	HR	BB	SO	ERA+	WHIP	H/9	BB/9	SO/9	SO/BB
2011	28	10	2	.833	2.61	55	4	0	2	114.0	84	37	8	42	80	165	1.105	6.6	3.3	6.3	1.90
2012	29	2	10	.167	5.36	69	0	0	25	84.0	80	51	11	31	75	79	1.321	8.6	3.3	8.0	2.42
2013	30	4	1	.800	4.86	11	6	0	0	37.0	42	21	8	22	24	85	1.730	10.2	5.4	5.8	1.09
Totals		16	13	.552	3.94	135	10	0	27	235.0	206	109	27	95	179	108	1.281	7.9	3.6	6.9	1.88

Which Team Fared Better?

His tenure with the Red Sox started pretty well, as he went 10–2 in 2011 with 114.0 innings pitched (a career high for him) and a 2.61 ERA. Aceves became the closer for the Red Sox in 2012 when everyone else fell by the wayside. Jonathan Papelbon had left as a free agent to sign with the Phillies, Daniel Bard had been turned into a starter, and Papelbon's replacement, Andrew Bailey, was injured in spring training. Aceves wore out his welcome, however, by getting into an argument with manager Bobby Valentine. He was suspended for three games for the incident and banned from the team plane. Although he had 25 saves that season to lead the team, he also had a record of 2–10 with a 5.36 ERA. He bounced up and down from the minors to the Red Sox in 2013 before they finally released him in July. He was more successful with the Yankees, compiling a 15–3 overall record compared with 16–13 with the Sox, although in three of the four seasons he pitched for New York he got into fewer than 10 games. His best year was with the 2009 Yankees, for whom he went 10–1, pitched 84.0 innings, and contributed to a World Series win.

Mark Bellhorn

A scrappy, switch hitting utility infielder, Bellhorn made himself valuable enough to play for 10 years in the major leagues. He broke in with the Oakland Athletics, with whom he spent four seasons. It was in 2002, when he went to the Chicago Cubs, that he began to see regular playing time, getting over 500 plate appearances for the year. He played the second half of the 2003 season with the Colorado Rockies, mostly struggling, but cemented his place in the baseball history books by becoming the regular second baseman for the 2004 Red Sox. This team will forever be known as the one that broke the curse and battled back from a 0–3 deficit in the ALCS against the Yankees. Ironically, it was the Yankees that picked him up after Boston released him the following season, but he saw very little playing time in the Bronx. He bounced around with the San Diego Padres and Cincinnati Reds organizations before calling it a career in 2007.

Red Sox Years

Year	Age	G	AB	R	H	2B	3B	HR	RBI	SB	CS	BB	SO	BA	OBP	SLG	OPS	OPS+	TB	SH
2004	29	138	523	93	138	37	3	17	82	6	1	88	177	.264	.373	.444	.817	107	232	1
2005	30	85	283	41	61	20	0	7	28	3	0	49	109	.216	.328	.360	.689	81	102	0
Totals		223	806	134	199	57	3	24	110	9	1	137	286	.247	.357	.414	.772	98	334	1

Yankees Year

Year	Age	G	AB	R	H	2B	3B	HR	RBI	SB	CS	BB	SO	BA	OBP	SLG	OPS	OPS+	TB	SH
2005	30	9	17	2	2	0	0	1	2	0	0	3	3	.118	.250	.294	.544	46	5	0

Which Team Fared Better?

It merits repeating that Bellhorn was a part of the 2004 team that won it all for Boston and spared Red Sox Nation another year of heartbreak. That year was also his finest as a player, as he hit 17 home runs, drove in 82 RBIs, scored 93 runs, and posted a .373 on-base percentage. In a crucial Game Six versus the Yankees, Bellhorn hit the game-winning home run, and he hit another home run in the deciding Game Seven. In Game One of the World Series he hit a third home run, helping the Sox to beat the Cardinals. He also hit a two-run double in Game Two to allow Boston to go on for the sweep. After such a performance he would have had to put up Babe Ruth–like numbers for the Yankees to have gotten the better of him. Instead, he had only 17 at-bats for New York, with two hits and one home run.

CHRIS CAPUANO

Capuano's pitching career began with a lot of promise. In his first full year with the Milwaukee Brewers in 2005, he won 18 games. It was to be the only winning season over the course of his 10-year career. The next year he started strong again and was named to the All-Star squad but finished with an 11–12 record. He had Tommy John surgery and missed the entire 2008 and 2009 seasons. He made it back with the Brewers in 2010 in limited action but then was signed by the New York Mets the following year. He received a two-year contract from the Los Angeles Dodgers, the second year of which he was relegated to the bullpen because LA had too many starting pitchers. The Red Sox signed him for the 2014 season, but after a stretch in which he allowed 17 runs over 16.2 innings, they designated him for assignment. He joined the Yankees in July of that year. Heading into the 2016 season, Capuano had a career 76–91 record with a 4.39 ERA.

Red Sox Year

Year	Age	W	L	%	ERA	G	GS	CG	SV	IP	H	R	HR	BB	SO	ERA+	WHIP	H/9	BB/9	SO/9	SO/BB
2014	35	1	1	.500	4.55	28	0	0	0	31.2	34	17	3	15	29	86	1.547	9.7	4.3	8.2	1.93

Yankees Years

Year	Age	W	L	%	ERA	G	GS	CG	SV	IP	H	R	HR	BB	SO	ERA+	WHIP	H/9	BB/9	SO/9	SO/BB
2014	35	2	3	.400	4.25	12	12	0	0	65.2	67	34	7	19	55	91	1.310	9.2	2.6	7.5	2.89
2015	36	0	4	.000	7.97	22	4	0	0	40.2	52	38	6	22	38	51	1.820	11.5	4.9	8.4	1.73
Totals		2	7	.222	5.67	34	16	0	0	106.1	119	72	13	41	93	69	1.505	10.1	3.5	7.9	2.27

Which Team Fared Better?

Between the two teams in 2014 Capuano had a 3–4 record and a 4.35 ERA, hardly impressive numbers. He started strong with the Red Sox, going 15 consecutive scoreless innings, but then the wheels fell off and he could not get anyone out; his ERA ballooned to 4.55. He was not much better for the Yankees, posting a 4.25 ERA, but he at least gave them double the innings, 65.2. The Red Sox also paid him $2.25 million for 31.2 innings of work. The Yankees bought him from the Colorado Rockies at a much cheaper price. The Yankees win this one but do not get much of a reward for their victory.

Kevin Cash

A backup catcher who never had more than 200 at-bats in a season, Cash spent a lot of time going back and forth between the minor and major leagues. He started out in the Toronto organization, working his way up to 60 games in his third season. From there he was traded to the Tampa Bay Devil Rays, who eventually released him after he spent the entire 2006 season in the minors. He next caught on with the Red Sox, staying with them for a couple of years before pinballing between the Yankees, the Houston Astros, and back to Boston. His career line includes an unimpressive .183 batting average, 12 home runs, and 58 runners batted in, but his value as a player came in his ability to catch, and he finished his career with a .993 fielding percentage, committing only 10 errors in eight seasons played. After his playing days he became the bullpen coach of the Cleveland Indians under his old manager Terry Francona.

Red Sox Years

Year	Age	G	AB	R	H	2B	3B	HR	RBI	SB	CS	BB	SO	BA	OBP	SLG	OPS	OPS+	TB	SH
2007	29	12	27	2	3	1	0	0	4	0	0	4	13	.111	.242	.148	.391	4	4	0
2008	30	61	142	11	32	7	0	3	15	0	0	18	50	.225	.309	.338	.647	67	48	0
2010	32	29	60	1	8	1	0	0	1	0	0	6	16	.133	.224	.150	.374	3	9	1
Totals		102	229	14	43	9	0	3	20	0	0	28	79	.188	.279	.266	.545	43	61	1

Yankees Year

Year	Age	G	AB	R	H	2B	3B	HR	RBI	SB	CS	BB	SO	BA	OBP	SLG	OPS	OPS+	TB	SH
2009	31	10	26	1	6	2	0	0	3	0	0	0	5	.231	.250	.308	.558	43	8	0

Which Team Fared Better?

Cash has World Series rings with both the 2007 Red Sox and the 2009 Yankees. That being said, he did not have an at-bat in either World Series and saw very little playing time for either club. His value to the Red Sox is evident in the fact that after spending two years with them, they went back out and got him for their club in 2010. Cash acted as the personal catcher to Tim Wakefield, the knuckleball pitcher whom starting catcher Jason Varitek had great difficulty catching. Cash was a fourth-string catcher for New York, getting into only 10 games.

Bartolo Colon

The ups and downs of Bartolo Colon's career are enough to give anyone whiplash. He began his career on a high, pitching for the Cleveland Indians, with whom he won 75 games in 6 years. He then was traded first to the Montreal Expos and then the White Sox. He became a big-name free-agent signing in 2004 for the Anaheim Angels, pitching for them for four years at an average salary of $12 million. His best year was 2005 when he won the Cy Young Award, leading the league in wins at 21. Then the wheels fell off on his once promising career and he found himself winning one game the following year, and treading water with Boston, the White Sox again, and the Yankees before landing in Oakland and resurrecting his career, winning 18 games in 2013. He was able to parlay his success into a two-year contract with the New York Mets for $20 million. Colon was a three-time All-Star, getting the nod with Cleveland in 1998, the Angels in 2005, and with Oakland in 2013. He is still pitching, fairly effectively, and reached the milestone of 200 wins in August of 2014.

Red Sox Year

Year	Age	W	L	%	ERA	G	GS	CG	SV	IP	H	R	HR	BB	SO	ERA+	WHIP	H/9	BB/9	SO/9	SO/BB
2008	35	4	2	.667	3.92	7	7	0	0	39.0	44	23	5	10	27	119	1.385	10.2	2.3	6.2	2.70

Yankees Year

Year	Age	W	L	%	ERA	G	GS	CG	SV	IP	H	R	HR	BB	SO	ERA+	WHIP	H/9	BB/9	SO/9	SO/BB
2011	38	8	10	.444	4.00	29	26	1	0	164.1	172	85	21	40	135	107	1.290	9.4	2.2	7.4	3.38

Which Team Fared Better?

The Red Sox and Yankees both caught Colon when he was on the downside of his rollercoaster career. Although he had a winning record with Boston, he did not leave on good terms, going to the Dominican Republic to handle some personal matters and not returning, forcing them to place him on the suspension list. He was not even permitted to be on the playoff roster when the Red Sox beat his old team, the Angels. He pitched in far more innings with the Yankees (164.1) but finished below .500 (8–10) for them. He pitched as both a starter and reliever, though, and went to the postseason with the Yankees when they lost to the Detroit Tigers. The Yankees were the beginning of another resurgence of his career, as he went to the Athletics and had two pretty good seasons, making them the team that fared better.

Johnny Damon

Damon began his career with in Kansas City where he became a fantasy baseball player's dream. He scored a lot of runs, stole a lot of bases (leading the league in 2000), had nearly a .300 average, and even knocked in a decent number of runs. He was an all-around threat and because of this he was valuable to many teams. After a one-year stop with the Oakland Athletics, he went to Boston as a free agent and signed a four-year contract. It was a good contract for both parties as Damon when on to win a World Series with the Red Sox in 2004. The Yankees also signed him to a four-year contract, and Damon delivered a World Series with them in 2009. Toward the end of his career he had yearlong stints with the Detroit Tigers, Tampa Bay Rays, and the Cleveland Indians. Over the course of his 18-year career he was an All-Star twice, both times with Boston, and was in the top 20 for MVP voting on four different occasions. He finished with 2,769 hits, 235 home runs, 1,139 RBIs, 408 stolen bases, and a .352 on-base percentage.

Red Sox Years

Year	Age	G	AB	R	H	2B	3B	HR	RBI	SB	CS	BB	SO	BA	OBP	SLG	OPS	OPS+	TB	SH
2002	28	154	623	118	178	34	11	14	63	31	6	65	70	.286	.356	.443	.799	109	276	3
2003	29	145	608	103	166	32	6	12	67	30	6	68	74	.273	.345	.405	.750	94	246	6
2004	30	150	621	123	189	35	6	20	94	19	8	76	71	.304	.380	.477	.857	117	296	0
2005	31	148	624	117	197	35	6	10	75	18	1	53	69	.316	.366	.439	.805	110	274	0
Totals		597	2,476	461	730	136	29	56	299	98	21	262	284	.295	.362	.441	.803	108	1,092	9

Yankees Years

Year	Age	G	AB	R	H	2B	3B	HR	RBI	SB	CS	BB	SO	BA	OBP	SLG	OPS	OPS+	TB	SH
2006	32	149	593	115	169	35	5	24	80	25	10	67	85	.285	.359	.482	.841	115	286	2
2007	33	141	533	93	144	27	2	12	63	27	3	66	79	.270	.351	.396	.747	96	211	1
2008	34	143	555	95	168	27	5	17	71	29	8	64	82	.303	.375	.461	.836	118	256	2
2009	35	143	550	107	155	36	3	24	82	12	0	71	98	.282	.365	.489	.854	118	269	2
Totals		576	2,231	410	636	125	15	77	296	93	21	268	344	.285	.363	.458	.821	112	1,022	7

Which Team Fared Better?

This is a tough one to call. If Damon's career was placed on a balance scale, his time with the Yankees on one side, his time with Boston on the other, it would nearly be perfectly balanced. There is only ten points difference in his batting average (.295 Sox/.285 Yanks), one point in OBP (.362 Sox/.363 Yanks), three more RBIs for Boston 299 than New York (296). He had 21 more home runs for New York (77) but almost a 100 more hits for Boston (730). He won a World Series with each team and posted similar numbers in production. He was the face of the 2004 Boston Idiots with his mullet and beard, but left Boston with a bad taste in their mouth when he said he wouldn't sign with the Yankees and then did anyway. What would tip the scales ever so slightly in favor of the Red Sox is the amount of money each spent for their four years of service. The Red Sox paid $31 million and over the same amount of time with nearly the same production, the Yankees paid $52 million. Boston got more for their money.

Damon is the reason for a book like this, providing nearly identical offensive numbers for both the Yankees and Red Sox, spending the same amount of time with each, and winning a World Series with each. An all-around player, Damon had more than 2,700 hits, 235 homeruns, and 408 stolen bases in his career. He never won a Gold Glove, in part because of a below-average arm, but played an above average outfield, finishing his career with a .988 fielding percentage (courtesy KeithAllisonPhoto.com).

STEPHEN DREW

A shortstop who came out of Florida State University, Drew was drafted by Arizona in the first round of the 2004 amateur draft, and he spent the first seven years of his career with the Diamondbacks, which included four consecutive seasons of 12 or more home runs. He found himself traded to the Oakland Athletics to finish out the 2012 season, then went to the Red Sox as a free agent. He was on the 2013 World Series Championship team with Boston, hitting 13 home runs and 67 RBIs while playing in 124 games. He is the brother of former major leaguer J.D. Drew as well as pitcher Tim Drew.

Red Sox Years

Year	Age	G	AB	R	H	2B	3B	HR	RBI	SB	CS	BB	SO	BA	OBP	SLG	OPS	OPS+	TB	SH
2013	30	124	442	57	112	29	8	13	67	6	0	54	124	.253	.333	.443	.777	111	196	0
2014	31	39	131	11	23	6	1	4	11	1	1	14	39	.176	.255	.328	.583	62	43	0
Totals		163	573	68	135	35	9	17	78	7	1	68	163	.236	.316	.417	.733	100	239	0

Yankees Years

Year	Age	G	AB	R	H	2B	3B	HR	RBI	SB	CS	BB	SO	BA	OBP	SLG	OPS	OPS+	TB	SH
2014	31	46	140	7	21	8	0	3	15	0	0	13	36	.150	.219	.271	.491	39	38	0
2015	32	131	383	43	77	16	1	17	44	0	2	37	71	.201	.271	.381	.652	77	146	4
Totals		177	523	50	98	24	1	20	59	0	2	50	107	.187	.257	.352	.609	67	184	4

Which Team Fared Better?

In 2014 Drew became the first trade between the Red Sox and Yankees since 1997. At the start of the season he was holding out for a long-term contract and did not sign with Boston until mid–May. By the July trade deadline Boston had fallen out of contention and the Yankees were looking to add some middle infielders. Drew was acquired for Kelly Johnson and was penciled in as the second baseman, a position he had never before played in his major league career, which might account for his .150 batting average and lack of production (a 2.71 slugging percentage).

Jacoby Ellsbury

Ellsbury is in the middle of a solid career that has sometimes been marred by injuries. He was drafted by Boston, with whom he spent his first seven years. He was an All-Star for them in 2011, the same year he won a Gold Glove and Silver Slugger Award. He has led the league in stolen bases three times in his career (2008–2009, 2013), and he became the only Boston Red Sox member of the 30/30 club (30 stolen bases and 30 home runs) in 2011, the same year he was runner-up in the MVP balloting. He had two seasons in which injuries prevented him from playing in many games (2010, 18 games; 2012, 74 games) but has been a fairly steady producer in his other seasons. After winning his second World Series with the Red Sox in 2013, he signed a long-term contract with the rival Yankees.

Red Sox Years

Year	Age	G	AB	R	H	2B	3B	HR	RBI	SB	CS	BB	SO	BA	OBP	SLG	OPS	OPS+	TB	SH
2007	23	33	116	20	41	7	1	3	18	9	0	8	15	.353	.394	.509	.902	131	59	0
2008	24	145	554	98	155	22	7	9	47	50	11	41	80	.280	.336	.394	.729	88	218	4
2009	25	153	624	94	188	27	10	8	60	70	12	49	74	.301	.355	.415	.770	98	259	6
2010	26	18	78	10	15	4	0	0	5	7	1	4	9	.192	.241	.244	.485	30	19	0
2011	27	158	660	119	212	46	5	32	105	39	15	52	98	.321	.376	.552	.928	146	364	3
2012	28	74	303	43	82	18	0	4	26	14	3	19	43	.271	.313	.370	.682	84	112	0
2013	29	134	577	92	172	31	8	9	53	52	4	47	92	.298	.355	.426	.781	113	246	1
Totals		715	2,912	476	865	155	31	65	314	241	46	220	411	.297	.350	.439	.789	108	1,277	14

Yankees Years

Year	Age	G	AB	R	H	2B	3B	HR	RBI	SB	CS	BB	SO	BA	OBP	SLG	OPS	OPS+	TB	SH
2014	30	149	575	71	156	27	5	16	70	39	5	49	93	.271	.328	.419	.747	111	241	0
2015	31	111	452	66	116	15	2	7	33	21	9	35	86	.257	.318	.345	.663	83	156	1
2016	32	148	551	71	145	24	5	9	56	20	8	54	84	.263	.330	.374	.703	88	206	4
Totals		408	1578	208	417	66	12	32	159	80	22	138	263	.264	.326	.382	.708	94	603	5

Which Team Fared Better?

This is a call that cannot be made with great confidence because there is, most likely, much of Ellsbury's career with the Yankees yet to come. He has completed only three seasons in his seven-year, $152-million contract. If he plays out the length of the contract he will have spent equal amounts of time with both teams, but in light of the fact that he won two World Series (2007 and 2013) with the Sox and has appeared in only a wild card loss thus far with the Yankees, Boston has the advantage for now. Unless Ellsbury can find his old stroke in the seasons ahead, there would seem to be little chance of New York's catching up.

Left: Ellsbury is Johnny Damon revisited, having won a World Series with Boston before jumping ship to the Yankees. His Yankees career is still under way, but his performance has fallen off in his first three years in the Bronx. He has four more seasons to right the ship, though he'll have to do so in his middle thirties, when most players see their skills deteriorate (courtesy KeithAllisonPhoto.com).

Nick Green

In the majors on and off for eight seasons in 10 years' time, Green was a utility infielder mostly playing shortstop or second base. Like many utility infielders, he was deemed valuable enough to trade for but not to keep around long term, which accounts for his having moved around so much. He started with the Atlanta Braves before becoming a regular with the Tampa Bay Devil Rays, appearing in a career-high 111 games for them in 2005. He then went to the Yankees, Seattle Mariners, Red Sox, Los Angeles Dodgers, and Toronto Blue Jays before playing two seasons with the Miami Marlins, for whom he appeared in only 25 games.

Yankees Year

Year	Age	G	AB	R	H	2B	3B	HR	RBI	SB	CS	BB	SO	BA	OBP	SLG	OPS	OPS+	TB	SH
2006	27	48	75	8	18	5	0	2	4	1	1	5	29	.240	.296	.387	.683	75	29	1

Red Sox Year

Year	Age	G	AB	R	H	2B	3B	HR	RBI	SB	CS	BB	SO	BA	OBP	SLG	OPS	OPS+	TB	SH
2009	30	104	276	35	65	18	0	6	35	1	4	20	69	.236	.303	.366	.669	72	101	2

Which Team Fared Better?

One of the downsides of being a utility infielder is that even if your versatility makes you valuable, your overall value will never be greater than it is for an everyday player who produces on a consistent basis. Regardless, Green did provide some benefit to both teams, playing mostly second base and providing steady defense for the Yankees in his 48 games with them. (He did return to the Yankees in 2008 but played the entire year in the minor leagues.) Upon signing a minor league deal with the Red Sox in 2009, his value shot up when shortstops Jed Lowrie and Julio Lugo both went on the disabled list, leaving him the starting shortstop. He even expanded his utility role for them when he was asked to pitch a couple of innings for the Red Sox. (And he did well in that tiny sample size, giving up no runs.) Boston fared better with him.

Rich Hill

Pitching for seven teams in his first 12 years, Hill began with the Chicago Cubs, winning 18 games for them over 4 years. He then went to the Baltimore Orioles for a year before finding another home in the bullpen for Boston, although Tommy John surgery limited him to just 40 games during his tenure. He spent a little time with the Cleveland Indians and Anaheim Angels before being picked up in July of 2014 by the Yankees. He appeared in only 14 games but posted a 1.69 ERA. He then returned to the Red Sox for the 2015 season, posting a 1.55 ERA (278 ERA+) in 29 innings.

Red Sox Years

Year	Age	W	L	%	ERA	G	GS	CG	SV	IP	H	R	HR	BB	SO	ERA+	WHIP	H/9	BB/9	SO/9	SO/BB
2010	30	1	0	1.000	0.00	6	0	0	0	4.0	5	0	0	1	3		1.500	11.3	2.3	6.8	3.00
2011	31	0	0		0.00	9	0	0	0	8.0	3	0	0	3	12		0.750	3.4	3.4	13.5	4.00
2012	32	1	0	1.000	1.83	25	0	0	0	19.2	17	4	0	11	21	234	1.424	7.8	5.0	9.6	1.91
2015	35	2	1	.667	1.55	4	4	1	0	29.0	14	5	2	5	36	280	0.655	4.3	1.6	11.2	7.20
Totals		4	1	.800	1.34	44	4	1	0	60.2	39	9	2	29	72	327	0.973	5.8	3.0	10.7	3.60

Yankees Year

Year	Age	W	L	%	ERA	G	GS	CG	SV	IP	H	R	HR	BB	SO	ERA+	WHIP	H/9	BB/9	SO/9	SO/BB
2014	34	0	0		1.69	14	0	0	0	5.1	6	1	0	3	9	246	1.688	10.1	5.1	15.2	3.00

Which Team Fared Better?

If you look at Hill's ERA with both teams—1.14 for the Red Sox and 1.69 for the Yankees—it would seem that he was a very effective pitcher. But his 31.2 innings over three seasons were not enough for the Red Sox to want to keep him another year. He went to the Yankees mid-way through the season and was actually designated for assignment before being added back to the roster three days later. He saw limited time, appearing in only 5.1 innings over 14 games, meaning he was only brought in to face a single lefty batter before being replaced. The Red Sox did manage to get one decent year out of him, 2012, when he appeared in 25 games and pitched 19.2 innings. It was not much but still more than the Yankees got.

Eric Hinske

One of the most impressive things about Eric Hinske's career is that during the period 2007–2010, he played for four teams, all of which made the playoffs and three of which made it to the World Series. He started out with the Toronto Blue Jays, being named the Rookie of the Year in 2002 with 24 home runs and 84 RBIs. Unfortunately for Hinske, these would be career highs. Although he never reached that level of production again, he proved himself a valuable teammate. He was traded to the Red Sox where he won a World Series in the 2007 season before going to the Tampa Bay Rays, Pittsburgh Pirates, and New York Yankees in a two-season period, winning a World Series with New York in 2009. He stayed three years with the Atlanta Braves before finishing up with the Arizona Diamondbacks. His valuable clubhouse presence parlayed to his being hired as a first-base coach for the Chicago Cubs at the end of his playing career. His career numbers included a .249 batting average, 947 hits, 137 home runs, and 522 RBIs.

Red Sox Years

Year	Age	G	AB	R	H	2B	3B	HR	RBI	SB	CS	BB	SO	BA	OBP	SLG	OPS	OPS+	TB	SH
2006	28	31	80	8	23	8	0	1	5	1	1	8	30	.288	.352	.425	.777	97	34	0
2007	29	84	186	25	38	12	3	6	21	3	0	28	54	.204	.317	.398	.714	83	74	0
Totals		115	266	33	61	20	3	7	26	4	1	36	84	.229	.327	.406	.733	87	108	0

Yankees Year

Year	Age	G	AB	R	H	2B	3B	HR	RBI	SB	CS	BB	SO	BA	OBP	SLG	OPS	OPS+	TB	SH
2009	31	39	84	13	19	3	0	7	14	1	0	10	25	.226	.316	.512	.828	109	43	0

Which Team Fared Better?

Hinske provided value for both teams. He joined the Red Sox in August 2006, contributing 80 at-bats in their stretch run. He appeared in 84 games during the 2007 season, playing first base, left field, right field, and designated hitter. After he was traded to New York at the end of June, he filled in at several spots there too, playing third, right field, left field, and DH. His batting average was almost identical for each team: .229 for Boston and .226 for the Yankees. The difference-maker would be the value each team saw in him in its run to the World Series Championship. The Red Sox carried him on the roster throughout all three rounds of the postseason in 2007. Although he got into only three games over that time, they thought he was valuable enough to keep around, just in case. The Yankees, however, left him off the roster for the division and league series championships. They did add him to the World Series roster and he got into a single game, but it was obvious the Red Sox saw more value in him and thus fared better as a result.

BRENT LILLIBRIDGE

A utility player who in his career appeared at every position except pitcher and catcher, Lillibridge was a light-hitting defensive wizard. There was one year for the White Sox when he hit 13 home runs, 29 RBIs, and 38 runs, all career highs, but outside of that year he was a career .205 batter with six home runs over five other seasons. He started in the Atlanta Braves organization but eventually found a home in Chicago with the White Sox, for whom he played for four years. Over his last two years he bounced around between five teams, starting with the White Sox, who traded him to the Red Sox, who traded him to the Cleveland Indians. He then signed with the Chicago Cubs and then was bought by the Yankees.

Red Sox Year

Year	Age	G	AB	R	H	2B	3B	HR	RBI	SB	CS	BB	SO	BA	OBP	SLG	OPS	OPS+	TB	SH
2012	28	10	16	0	2	0	0	0	0	0	0	0	5	.125	.125	.125	.250	-32	2	0

Yankees Year

Year	Age	G	AB	R	H	2B	3B	HR	RBI	SB	CS	BB	SO	BA	OBP	SLG	OPS	OPS+	TB	SH
2013	29	11	35	2	6	1	0	0	3	1	0	1	8	.171	.194	.200	.394	9	7	1

Which Team Fared Better?

Lillibridge was equally ineffective for both teams, batting .125 with no home runs, no RBIs, no walks, and two hits for the Red Sox over the course of 10 games and hitting .171 with no home runs, three RBIs, one walk, and six hits with the Yankees in 11 games. His value came in the form of filling in when and where the team needed him. For the Red Sox he played mostly in right field and a little in center, giving the starters the occasional rest. With the Yankees both Derek Jeter and Alex Rodriguez were out of action, and Lillibridge filled the gap at third base until Rodriguez returned, stabilizing the left side of the infield, making him more valuable to New York.

Mike Lowell

Lowell was drafted and developed by the Yankees, and he had a cup of coffee with the big league club in 1998, getting 15 at-bats. He was traded to the Marlins before the next season, and it was in Florida that Lowell really came into his own. There he became one of the better third basemen in the league, winning a World Series with the team in 2003. In 2005, when Boston really wanted Marlins pitcher Josh Beckett and Florida wanted to unload Lowell's big contract, the two teams got together on a trade that landed both players in Fenway. The Red Sox did it to get Beckett but got a whole lot more from Lowell than they expected. He finished out his career in Boston, playing with them for five seasons.

Yankees Year

Year	Age	G	AB	R	H	2B	3B	HR	RBI	SB	CS	BB	SO	BA	OBP	SLG	OPS	OPS+	TB	SH
1998	24	8	15	1	4	0	0	0	0	0	0	0	1	.267	.267	.267	.533	42	4	0

Red Sox Years

Year	Age	G	AB	R	H	2B	3B	HR	RBI	SB	CS	BB	SO	BA	OBP	SLG	OPS	OPS+	TB	SH
2006	32	153	573	79	163	47	1	20	80	2	2	47	61	.284	.339	.475	.814	104	272	0
2007	33	154	589	79	191	37	2	21	120	3	2	53	71	.324	.378	.501	.879	124	295	0
2008	34	113	419	58	115	27	0	17	73	2	2	38	61	.274	.338	.461	.798	104	193	0
2009	35	119	445	54	129	29	1	17	75	2	1	33	61	.290	.337	.474	.811	103	211	0
2010	36	73	218	23	52	13	0	5	26	0	0	23	34	.239	.307	.367	.674	79	80	0
Totals		612	2,244	293	650	153	4	80	374	9	7	194	288	.290	.346	.468	.814	108	1,051	0

Which Team Fared Better?

Lowell has a World Series ring from his brief stop in New York, despite his not having been on the postseason roster in 1998. In the postseason with the Red Sox, though, he played an integral part, earning MVP honors for the 2007 World Series. During the regular season that year he knocked in 120 runs and batted .324. Although he will probably best be remembered as a Florida Marlins star, there's no question that meant more to Boston than New York.

Darnell McDonald

In the seven years McDonald played in the major leagues, he got into 100 or more games only once. Always good enough to fill in for an injured starter, McDonald was never quite good enough to become an everyday player himself. If his team avoided injuries, he was generally shipped off to the minor leagues. Over the course of his career he had 20 home runs and 83 RBIs, good statistics for a single season, but perhaps less impressive for a seven-year run for the Baltimore Orioles, Minnesota Twins, Reds, Red Sox, Yankees, and Chicago Cubs. He announced his retirement in April 2014.

Red Sox Years

Year	Age	G	AB	R	H	2B	3B	HR	RBI	SB	CS	BB	SO	BA	OBP	SLG	OPS	OPS+	TB	SH
2010	31	117	319	40	86	18	3	9	34	9	1	30	85	.270	.336	.429	.766	103	137	12
2011	32	79	157	26	37	6	1	6	24	2	3	14	33	.236	.303	.401	.704	88	63	0
2012	33	38	84	17	18	7	0	2	9	1	1	12	17	.214	.309	.369	.678	83	31	2
Totals		234	560	83	141	31	4	17	67	12	5	56	135	.252	.323	.413	.735	96	231	14

Yankees Year

Year	Age	G	AB	R	H	2B	3B	HR	RBI	SB	CS	BB	SO	BA	OBP	SLG	OPS	OPS+	TB	SH
2012	33	4	4	0	0	0	0	0	0	0	0	0	2	.000	.000	.000	.000	-100	0	0

Which Team Fared Better?

In the three years he played for the Red Sox, McDonald's value was apparent when he filled in for injured players. In 2010 when Jacoby Ellsbury went down with a rib injury, for instance, McDonald assumed his place in center field, and McDonald would end up playing in 117 games to Ellsbury's 18. When J.D. Drew appeared in only 81 games in 2011, McDonald likewise found himself filling in. In 2012 when the Red Sox outfield was relatively healthy, there was no room for McDonald, so they released him mid-season. The Yankees picked him up and he spent only 10 days with them before he was sent down to the minors, where he played the rest of the season. He fared much better with the Red Sox as a fill-in for their injured players.

Mark Melancon

A relief pitcher, Melancon has filled many roles in the bullpen, including long man, set-up man, and closer, but he has never started a game in the major leagues. He was drafted by the Yankees, enjoying a cup of coffee for 13 games in 2009 and only a sip in 2 games in 2010. From there he went to the Houston Astros, eventually pitching his way into the closer role in 2011 and saving 20 games, which led the team. He was traded to Boston where he gave up as many hits as innings pitched before being traded again, this time to the Pittsburgh Pirates. The Steel City is where Melancon really came into his own, first as the set-up man and then as the closer when regular closer Jason Grilli was injured. Melancon was named an All-Star for the Pirates in 2013, and when Grilli was traded in 2014, Melancon was named the team closer.

Yankees Years

Year	Age	W	L	%	ERA	G	GS	CG	SV	IP	H	R	HR	BB	SO	ERA+	WHIP	H/9	BB/9	SO/9	SO/BB
2009	24	0	1	.000	3.86	13	0	0	0	16.1	13	8	0	10	10	122	1.408	7.2	5.5	5.5	1.00
2010	25	0	0		9.00	2	0	0	0	4.0	7	5	1	0	3	52	1.750	15.8	0.0	6.8	
Totals		0	1	.000	4.87	15	0	0	0	20.1	20	13	1	10	13	96	1.475	8.9	4.4	5.8	1.30

Red Sox Year

Year	Age	W	L	%	ERA	G	GS	CG	SV	IP	H	R	HR	BB	SO	ERA+	WHIP	H/9	BB/9	SO/9	SO/BB
2012	27	0	2	.000	6.20	41	0	0	1	45.0	45	31	8	12	41	68	1.267	9.0	2.4	8.2	3.42

Which Team Fared Better?

Melancon pitched his best when in the role of the closer or set up man. Unfortunately, those roles were already filled in New York, by Mariano Rivera and David Robertson, and in Boston, by Andrew Bailey and Alfredo Aceves. He received a World Series ring with the Yankees in 2009, although he was not on the active roster. He appeared in only 20.1 innings over two seasons and posted a 4.87 ERA. His ERA with Boston was much higher, at 6.20, a number attributable in part to a disastrous April, but he pitched in twice as many innings as he had with the Yankees, logging 45.0. Because the numbers are close, his value is perhaps best determined not by his performance but by the players each team was able to get when they traded him. When the Yankees traded him to Houston, they got Lance Berkman in return. Berkman spent the rest of that year with the Yankees, hitting only one home run and knocking in nine. This from a guy whose career 162-game average was 32 home runs and 106 RBIs. Boston traded him to the Pirates in exchange for closer Joel Hanrahan. Unfortunately, after only nine games pitched, Hanrahan had Tommy John surgery and was out for the rest of the season. So neither team got much in trade for Melancon, despite landing high-profile players. But Berkman was at least able to finish the season and hit well in the playoffs for the Yankees, getting five hits, including a home run.

Andrew Miller

Miller had a promising start as a player being named the National Player of the Year by Baseball America while playing college ball at North Carolina. He was chosen in the first round of the 2006 draft, sixth overall, by the Detroit Tigers. He struggled to find his way as a starter, going from Detroit, to the Florida Marlins, and then to Boston. It was in Fenway that he was transitioned to relief pitching, and he found his groove in this role while playing for Baltimore. He finished the 2014 year with a 1.35 ERA for the Orioles and parlayed that performance into a four-year deal worth $36 million to play with the Yankees.

Red Sox Years

Year	Age	W	L	%	ERA	G	GS	CG	SV	IP	H	R	HR	BB	SO	ERA+	WHIP	H/9	BB/9	SO/9	SO/BB
2011	26	6	3	.667	5.54	17	12	0	0	65.0	77	43	8	41	50	78	1.815	10.7	5.7	6.9	1.22
2012	27	3	2	.600	3.35	53	0	0	0	40.1	28	15	3	20	51	127	1.190	6.2	4.5	11.4	2.55
2013	28	1	2	.333	2.64	37	0	0	0	30.2	25	12	3	17	48	158	1.370	7.3	5.0	14.1	2.82
2014	29	3	5	.375	2.34	50	0	0	0	42.1	25	13	2	13	69	171	0.898	5.3	2.8	14.7	5.31
Totals		13	12	.520	3.79	157	12	0	0	178.1	155	83	16	91	218	111	1.379	7.8	4.6	11.0	2.40

Yankees Years

Year	Age	W	L	%	ERA	G	GS	CG	SV	IP	H	R	HR	BB	SO	ERA+	WHIP	H/9	BB/9	SO/9	SO/BB
2015	30	3	2	.600	2.04	60	0	0	36	61.2	33	16	5	20	100	198	0.859	4.8	2.9	14.6	5.00
2016	31	6	1	.857	1.39	44	0	0	9	45.1	28	8	5	7	77	314	0.772	5.6	1.4	15.3	11.9
		9	3	.750	1.77	104	0	0	45	107.0	61	24	10	27	177	238	0.822	5.1	2.3	14.9	6.56

Which Team Fared Better?

The Red Sox had the brilliant idea of taking Miller and converting him from a so-so starting pitcher to an excellent relief pitcher. Unfortunately, they traded him away to Baltimore before discovering what they had created, and the Yankees reaped the benefits as Miller started his first season in pinstripes throwing 17 2/3 innings of scoreless baseball and finished the year with 36 saves. He won the 2015 American League Relief Pitcher of the Year Award, then was even better in his half-season with the team in 2016. The Yankees win this round.

Gustavo Molina

It seems that every player with a last name of Molina ends up being a catcher. There is Izzy Molina, who spent four years in the majors, mostly with Oakland. There are the famous Molina brothers—Bengie, Jose, and Yadier—all of whom became big league catchers, the best of that bunch being Yadier, who plays for the St. Louis Cardinals. Then there is Gustavo Molina, a catcher who played for five teams over a four-year career. He started with the Chicago White Sox before being claimed off of waivers by the Baltimore Orioles. He spent the next season with the New York Mets before spending a year in the minors. Molina finished out his last two years with the Yankees and Red Sox. In all of the time traveling between the minors and majors, he only accumulated 47 at-bats, getting six hits and 1 RBI.

Red Sox Year

Year	Age	G	AB	R	H	2B	3B	HR	RBI	SB	CS	BB	SO	BA	OBP	SLG	OPS	OPS+	TB	SH
2010	28	4	7	1	1	0	0	0	0	0	0	0	2	.143	.143	.143	.286	-23	1	0

Yankees Year

Year	Age	G	AB	R	H	2B	3B	HR	RBI	SB	CS	BB	SO	BA	OBP	SLG	OPS	OPS+	TB	SH
2011	29	3	6	0	1	1	0	0	0	0	0	0	0	.167	.167	.333	.500	30	2	0

Which Team Fared Better?

Molina had one hit for each club. He had a .143 average with Boston and a .167 with New York. At least for the Red Sox he scored a run, meaning he fared better with them but not by much.

JT Snow

During a six-year stretch of his career, Snow was one of the elite first baseman in baseball, winning six Gold Gloves in a row and averaging more than 20 home runs a season. The two teams he will best be remembered for playing with are the California Angels, with whom he spent four years, and the San Francisco Giants, with whom he played for 10. He had his best season in 1997 with the Giants when he hit 28 home runs and knocked in 104. He bookended his time with these teams playing one season with the Yankees at the beginning of his career and one season with the Red Sox at the end. Over the course of his 16 seasons in the big leagues, he had 189 home runs, 877 RBIs, 1,509 hits, and a .268 average.

Yankees Year

Year	Age	G	AB	R	H	2B	3B	HR	RBI	SB	CS	BB	SO	BA	OBP	SLG	OPS	OPS+	TB	SH
1992	24	7	14	1	2	1	0	0	2	0	0	5	5	.143	.368	.214	.583	69	3	0

Red Sox Year

Year	Age	G	AB	R	H	2B	3B	HR	RBI	SB	CS	BB	SO	BA	OBP	SLG	OPS	OPS+	TB	SH
2006	38	38	44	5	9	0	0	0	4	0	0	8	8	.205	.340	.205	.544	44	9	0

Which Team Fared Better?

Snow began his career on a cup of coffee with the Yankees in 1992, but there was no way he was going to see much playing time at first base with Yankees legend Don Mattingly still around. The Yankees traded Snow to the Angels, getting Jim Abbott, who would pitch a no-hitter for New York that same year. When Snow went to the Red Sox he was on the downward path of his career, having given his best to San Francisco. He found himself in a platoon situation with Kevin Youkilis and wanting more playing time, so he requested and was granted a release in June after only 44 at-bats. Because neither team got him in his prime, neither one benefitted all that much, but the Red Sox at least got a seasoned veteran while the Yankees had a wet-behind-the-ears rookie.

Justin Thomas

Thomas was a left-handed pitcher who began his career with the Seattle Mariners, who shuttled him back and forth between the minors and majors in a pattern repeated by his next team, the Pittsburgh Pirates. He split his 2012 season between Boston and New York, appearing in a combined 11 games.

Red Sox Year

Year	Age	W	L	%	ERA	G	GS	CG	SV	IP	H	R	HR	BB	SO	ERA+	WHIP	H/9	BB/9	SO/9	SO/BB
2012	28	0	0		7.71	7	0	0	0	4.2	10	4	0	2	4	59	2.571	19.3	3.9	7.7	2.00

Yankees Year

Year	Age	W	L	%	ERA	G	GS	CG	SV	IP	H	R	HR	BB	SO	ERA+	WHIP	H/9	BB/9	SO/9	SO/BB
2012	28	0	0		9.00	4	0	0	0	3.0	2	3	1	1	3	52	1.000	6.0	3.0	9.0	3.00

Which Team Fared Better?

This is another case of a sample size too small to really determine the benefit. He gave up fewer hits for the Yankees (two versus 10) but had more innings pitched with the Red Sox (4.2 versus 3.0). His ERA was higher with the Yankees (9.00 versus 7.71), but his WHIP was much lower (1.000 versus 2.571). He gave up four earned runs with the Sox and three with the Yanks, walked two with the Sox and one with New York, but all of this is really just splitting hairs. Thomas did not contribute mightily to either team, but the Red Sox thought enough of him to have him on the Opening Day roster while the Yankees waited until the rosters expanded in the fall to call him up. Give the Red Sox a slight edge.

Matt Thornton

A first-round pick by the Seattle Mariners in 1998, Thornton made his major league debut in 2004 as a left-handed middle-relief pitcher. He was traded to the White Sox in 2006, making a name for himself in Chicago as a solid bullpen guy. He was an All-Star with them in 2010, the same year he had a career-high eight saves. After his ERA rose over the next few years, the White Sox traded him to Boston in July 2013. Although he did not appear on the postseason roster, he did earn a World Series ring with them. The Yankees signed him the following year to a two-year contract but put him on waivers, allowing the Washington Nationals to pick him up for their run to the postseason.

Red Sox Year

Year	Age	W	L	%	ERA	G	GS	CG	SV	IP	H	R	HR	BB	SO	ERA+	WHIP	H/9	BB/9	SO/9	SO/BB
2013	36	0	1	.000	3.52	20	0	0	0	15.1	22	6	0	5	9	120	1.761	12.9	2.9	5.3	1.80

Yankees Year

Year	Age	W	L	%	ERA	G	GS	CG	SV	IP	H	R	HR	BB	SO	ERA+	WHIP	H/9	BB/9	SO/9	SO/BB
2014	37	0	3	.000	2.55	46	0	0	0	24.2	23	9	0	6	20	153	1.176	8.4	2.2	7.3	3.33

Which Team Fared Better?

Thornton saw limited time with both teams, but he gave the Yankees more innings (24.2 vs. 15.1), a lower ERA (2.55 vs. 3.52), a lower WHIP (1.176 vs. 1.761), and more strikeouts (20 vs. 9). New York wins in almost every category, including salary. Boston paid him $5.5 million for his 15 innings of work while the Yankees paid only $3.5 million for double the innings.

BILLY TRABER

Traber was a left-hander who threw his career high in innings during his first season in the majors (111.2 with the Cleveland Indians). He never pitched half as many in any of his four remaining seasons, as he sat out the next season with Tommy John surgery and then worked 83.2 innings with the Washington Nationals over the course of two seasons. He moved between the minors and majors while playing for the Yankees and only got into a single game with the Red Sox in his final year playing in the bigs. He had a career 12–14 record with 152 strikeouts and a 5.65 ERA.

Yankees Year

Year	Age	W	L	%	ERA	G	GS	CG	SV	IP	H	R	HR	BB	SO	ERA+	WHIP	H/9	BB/9	SO/9	SO/BB
2008	28	0	0		7.02	19	0	0	0	16.2	23	13	3	7	11	64	1.800	12.4	3.8	5.9	1.57

Red Sox Year

Year	Age	W	L	%	ERA	G	GS	CG	SV	IP	H	R	HR	BB	SO	ERA+	WHIP	H/9	BB/9	SO/9	SO/BB
2009	29	0	0		12.27	1	0	0	0	3.2	9	5	2	1	1	41	2.727	22.1	2.5	2.5	1.00

Which Team Fared Better?

The Yankees and Red Sox went through a lot of left-handed relievers during this time, and none seemed to work out all that well. Traber actually had two tours of duty with the Red Sox. In addition to the 2009 season, in which he appeared in a single game, the Red Sox had signed him during the 2004 offseason; but before he ever threw a pitch for them, he was placed on waivers and picked up by the Cleveland Indians. The Yankees made out better in their time with Traber, who pitched 16.2 innings and gave up 23 hits, 13 runs, and three home runs. How, one may wonder after seeing those numbers, could the Yankees have gotten more out of him? He was still worse with Boston, giving up two home runs, five runs, and nine hits in just over three innings.

KEVIN YOUKILIS

Youkilis was made famous by Michael Lewis's *Moneyball* before he ever played in the major leagues. Referred to in that book as the Greek God of Walks—he is in fact Jewish, not Greek—Youkilis mostly lived up to the hype, enjoying a 10-year career in the bigs with the Red Sox, White Sox and Yankees. His career stats include a .281 average, 1,053 hits, 150 home runs, 618 RBIs, and 539 walks, giving him a career on-base percentage of .382. Injuries and an ailing back took their toll early on Youkilis, who ended up playing the 2014 season in the Japanese League.

Red Sox Years

Year	Age	G	AB	R	H	2B	3B	HR	RBI	SB	CS	BB	SO	BA	OBP	SLG	OPS	OPS+	TB	SH
2004	25	72	208	38	54	11	0	7	35	0	1	33	45	.260	.367	.413	.780	99	86	0
2005	26	44	79	11	22	7	0	1	9	0	1	14	19	.278	.400	.405	.805	113	32	0
2006	27	147	569	100	159	42	2	13	72	5	2	91	120	.279	.381	.429	.810	106	244	0
2007	28	145	528	85	152	35	2	16	83	4	2	77	105	.288	.390	.453	.843	117	239	0
2008	29	145	538	91	168	43	4	29	115	3	5	62	108	.312	.390	.569	.958	144	306	0
2009	30	136	491	99	150	36	1	27	94	7	2	77	125	.305	.413	.548	.961	146	269	0
2010	31	102	362	77	111	26	5	19	62	4	1	58	67	.307	.411	.564	.975	157	204	0
2011	32	120	431	68	111	32	2	17	80	3	0	68	100	.258	.373	.459	.833	123	198	0
2012	33	42	146	25	34	7	1	4	14	0	0	14	39	.233	.315	.377	.692	87	55	0
Totals		953	3,352	594	961	239	17	133	564	26	14	494	728	.287	.388	.487	.875	126	1,633	0

Yankees Year

Year	Age	G	AB	R	H	2B	3B	HR	RBI	SB	CS	BB	SO	BA	OBP	SLG	OPS	OPS+	TB	SH
2013	34	28	105	12	23	7	0	2	8	0	0	8	31	.219	.305	.343	.648	79	36	0

Which Team Fared Better?

Youklis was the heart and soul of the Red Sox for many years. He was a core of players the Sox developed including Dustin Pedroia and Jacoby Ellsbury. Most of his career highlights came while wearing a Red Sox uniform. He was a three-time All-Star, won a Gold Glove in 2007, and was in the top six in MVP voting in both 2008 and 2009. He also holds the record for most errorless games played by a first baseman at 238, which included 2,002 fielding attempts. When the Yankees signed Youkilis they were hoping he would be able to man third base until they got Alex Rodriguez back from injury. Back injuries prevented him from producing his usual numbers, and he played in only 28 games—for which the Yankees paid him $12 million. In his years with the Red Sox he averaged a salary of $4.6 million. The Red Sox definitely fared better.

Appendix
Which Team Fared Better?

Player	Red Sox Years	Yankee Years	Red Sox	Yankees
David Aardsma	2008	2012	X	
Alfredo Aceves	2011–2013	2008–2010		X
Doc Adkins	1902	1903	X	
Ivy Andrews	1932–1933	1931–1932, 1937–1938	X	
Pete Appleton	1932	1933	X	
Andrew Bailey	2012–2013	2015	X	
Neal Ball	1912–1913	1907–1909		X
Scott Bankhead	1993–1994	1995	X	
Willie Banks	2001–2002	1997–1998	X	
Don Baylor	1986–1987	1983–1985		X
Mark Bellhorn	2004–2005	2005	X	
Juan Beniquez	1971–1975	1979	X	
Lou Berberet	1958	1954–1955	X	
Doug Bird	1983	1980–1981		X
Wade Boggs	1982–1992	1993–1997	X	
Darren Bragg	1996–1998	2001	X	
Ken Brett	1967–1971	1976	X	
Hal Brown	1953–1955	1962	X	
George Burns	1922–1923	1928–1929	X	
Bullet Joe Bush	1918–1921	1922–1924		X
Ray Caldwell	1919	1910–1918		X
Jose Canseco	1995–1996	2000	X	
Chris Capuano	2014	2014–2015		X
Roy Carlyle	1925–1926	1926	X	
Kevin Cash	2007–2010	2009	X	
Danny Cater	1972–1974	1970–1971		X
Rick Cerone	1988–1989	1980–1984, 1987–1990		X
Ben Chapman	1937–1938	1930–1936		X
Jack Chesbro	1909	1903–1909		X
Jack Clark	1991–1992	1988	X	
Tony Clark	2002	2004		X
Roger Clemens	1984–1996	1999–2007	X	
Tex Clevenger	1954	1961–1962	X	
Lou Clinton	1960–1964	1966–1967	X	
Michael Coleman	1997–1999	2001	X	
Rip Collins	1922	1920–1921		X
Bartolo Colon	2008	2011		X
David Cone	2001	1995–2000		X

Player	Red Sox Years	Yankee Years	Red Sox	Yankees
Dusty Cooke	1933–1936	1930–1932	X	
Guy Cooper	1914–1915	1914	X	
Lou Criger	1901–1908	1910	X	
Babe Dahlgren	1935–1936	1937–1940		X
Johnny Damon	2002–2005	2006–2009	X	
Al DeVormer	1923	1921–1922	X	
Patsy Dougherty	1902–1904	1904–1906	X	
Stephen Drew	2013–2014	2014–2015	X	
Joe Dugan	1922	1922–1928		X
Cedric Durst	1930	1927–1930		X
Mike Easler	1984–1985	1986–1987	X	
Jacoby Ellsbury	2007–2013	2014–	X	
Alan Embree	2002–2005	2005	X	
Clyde Engle	1910–1914	1909–1910	X	
Todd Erdos	2001	1998–2000		X
Steve Farr	1994	1991–1993		X
Doc Farrell	1935	1932–1933		X
Alex Ferguson	1922–1925	1918–1925	X	
Wes Ferrell	1934–1937	1938–1939	X	
Chick Fewster	1922–1923	1917–1922		X
John Flaherty	1992–1993	2003–2005		X
Tony Fossas	1991–1994	1999	X	
Eddie Foster	1920–1922	1910	X	
Ray Francis	1925	1925		X
Billy Gardner	1962–1963	1961–1962	X	
Milt Gaston	1929–1931	1924		X
Frank Gilhooley	1919	1913–1918		X
Joe Glenn	1940	1932–1938		X
Tom Gordon	1996–1999	2004–2005	X	
Nick Green	2009	2006	X	
Randy Gumpert	1952	1946–1948		X
Chris Hammond	1997	2003		X
Harry Harper	1920	1921	X	
Greg Harris	1989–1994	1994	X	
Joe Harris	1922–1925	1914	X	
Fred Heimach	1926	1928–1929		X
Charlie Hemphill	1901	1908–1911		X
Rickey Henderson	2002	1985–1989		X
Tim Hendryx	1920–1921	1915–1917	X	
Rich Hill	2010–2012	2014	X	
Eric Hinske	2006–2007	2009	X	
Butch Hobson	1975–1980	1982	X	
Fred Hofmann	1927–1928	1919–1925	X	
Ken Holcombe	1953	1945		X
Elston Howard	1967–1968	1955–1967		X
Waite Hoyt	1919–1920	1921–1930		X
Tom Hughes	1902–1903	1904	X	
Jackie Jensen	1954–1961	1950–1952	X	
Deron Johnson	1974–1976	1960–1961	X	
Hank Johnson	1933–1935	1925–1932		X
Roy Johnson	1932–1935	1936–1937	X	
Sad Sam Jones	1916–1921	1922–1926	X	
John Kennedy	1970–1974	1967	X	

Appendix: Which Team Fared Better?

Player	Red Sox Years	Yankee Years	Red Sox	Yankees
Red Kleinow	1910–1911	1904–1910		X
John Knight	1907	1909–1913		X
Andy Kosco	1972	1968		X
Jack Kramer	1948–1949	1951	X	
Frank LaPorte	1908	1905–1907, 1908–1910		X
Bill Lamar	1919	1917–1919	X	
Lyn Lary	1934	1929–1934	X	
Louis Le Roy	1910	1905–1906		X
Duffy Lewis	1910–1917	1919–1920	X	
Jim Leyritz	1998	1990–1996, 1999–2000		X
Brent Lillibridge	2012	2013		X
Tim Lollar	1985–1986	1980		X
Derek Lowe	1997–2004	2012	X	
Mike Lowell	2006–2010	1998	X	
Joe Lucey	1925	1920	X	
Sparky Lyle	1967–1971	1972–1978		X
Danny MacFayden	1926–1932	1932–1934		X
Jeff Manto	1996	1999	X	
Josias Manzanillo	1991	1995		X
Carl Mays	1915–1919	1919–1923	X	
Mickey McDermott	1948–1953	1956	X	
Darnell McDonald	2010–2012	2012	X	
Jim McDonald	1950	1952–1954		X
Lynn McGlothen	1972–1973	1982	X	
Bob McGraw	1919	1917–1919, 1920		X
Deacon McGuire	1907–1908	1904–1907		X
Marty McHale	1910–1911, 1916	1913–1915		X
Norm McMillan	1923	1922		X
Mike McNally	1915–1920	1921–1924		X
Mark Melancon	2012	2009–2010		X
Bob Melvin	1993	1994	X	
Ramiro Mendoza	2003–2004	1996–2002, 2005		X
Doug Mientkiewicz	2004	2007	X	
Elmer Miller	1922	1915–1922		X
Buster Mills	1937	1940		X
Fred Mitchell	1901–1902	1910	X	
Johnny Mitchell	1922–1923	1921–1922	X	
Gustavo Molina	2010	2011	X	
Bill Monbouquette	1958–1965	1967–1968	X	
Wilcy Moore	1931–1932	1927–1929, 1932–1933		X
Jerry Moses	1965–1970	1973		X
Johnny Murphy	1947	1932–1946		X
Rob Murphy	1989–1990	1994	X	
George Murray	1923–1924	1922		X
Mike Myers	2004–2005	2006–2007		X
Bobo Newsom	1937	1947		X
Gus Niarhos	1952–1953	1946–1950		X

Player	Red Sox Years	Yankee Years	Red Sox	Yankees
Harry Niles	1908–1910	1908		X
Otis Nixon	1994	1983	X	
Les Nunamaker	1911–1914	1914–1917		X
Mike O'Berry	1979	1984		X
Lefty O'Doul	1923	1919–1922		X
Steve O'Neill	1924	1925	X	
Bob Ojeda	1980–1985	1994	X	
John Olerud	2005	2004	X	
Joe Oliver	2001	2001		X
Spike Owen	1986–1988	1993	X	
Ben Paschal	1920	1924–1929		X
Herb Pennock	1915–1922, 1934	1923–1933		X
Bill Piercy	1922–1924	1917–1921		X
George Pipgras	1933–1935	1923–1933		X
Bob Porterfield	1956–1958	1948–1951	X	
Del Pratt	1921–1922	1918–1920	X	
Curtis Pride	1997–2000	2003	X	
Paul Quantrill	1992–1994	2004–2005	X	
Jack Quinn	1922–1925	1909–1921		X
Jeff Reardon	1990–1992	1994	X	
Bill Renna	1958–1959	1953	X	
Gordon Rhodes	1932–1935	1929–1932	X	
Aaron Robinson	1951	1943–1947		X
Carlos Rodriguez	1994–1995	1991	X	
Buddy Rosar	1950–1951	1939–1942		X
Braggo Roth	1919	1921	X	
Muddy Ruel	1921	1917–1920	X	
Red Ruffing	1924–1930	1930–1946		X
Allen Russell	1919–1922	1915–1919		X
Babe Ruth	1914–1919	1920–1934		X
Rey Sanchez	2002	1997, 2005	X	
Ray Scarborough	1951–1952	1952–1953		X
Wally Schang	1918–1920	1921–1925		X
Johnny Schmitz	1956	1952–1953		X
Dick Schofield	1969–1970	1966	X	
Everett Scott	1914–1921	1922–1925	X	
George Scott	1966–1979	1979	X	
Bob Seeds	1933–1934	1936		X
Howie Shanks	1923–1924	1925	X	
Rollie Sheldon	1966	1961–1965		X
Ben Shields	1930	1924–1925		X
Ernie Shore	1914–1917	1919–1920	X	
Bill Short	1966	1960		X
Norm Siebern	1967–1968	1956–1959		X
Camp Skinner	1923	1922		X
Elmer Smith	1922	1922–1923		X
Lee Smith	1988–1990	1993	X	
J.T. Snow	2006	1992	X	
Jake Stahl	1903, 1908–1913	1908	X	
Mike Stanley	1996–1997, 1998–2000	1992–1995, 1997		X

Player	Red Sox Years	Yankee Years	Red Sox	Yankees
Mike Stanton	1995–1996, 2005	1997–2002, 2005		X
Tom Sturdivant	1960	1955–1959		X
Frank Tanana	1981	1993	X	
Jesse Tannehill	1904–1908	1903	X	
Justin Thomas	2012	2012	X	
Lee Thomas	1964–1965	1961	X	
Jack Thoney	1908–1911	1904	X	
Hank Thormahlen	1921	1917–1920		X
Matt Thornton	2013	2014		X
Luis Tiant	1971–1978	1979–1980	X	
Bob Tillman	1962–1967	1967	X	
Mike Torrez	1978–1982	1977		X
Billy Traber	2009	2008		X
Frank Truesdale	1918	1914		X
Bob Turley	1963	1955–1962		X
Bob Unglaub	1904–1908	1904	X	
Bobby Veach	1924–1925	1925	X	
Sammy Vick	1921	1917–1920		X
Jake Wade	1939	1946		X
Jimmy Walsh	1916–1917	1914	X	
Roxy Walters	1919–1923	1915–1918		X
Pee Wee Wanniger	1927	1925		X
Gary Waslewski	1967–1968	1970–1971		X
Bob Watson	1979	1980–1982		X
David Wells	2005–2006	1997–1998, 2002–2003		X
Billy Werber	1933–1936	1930–1933	X	
George Whiteman	1907, 1918	1913	X	
Mark Whiten	1995	1997		X
Bill Wight	1951–1952	1946–1947		X
Stan Williams	1972	1963–1964	X	
Archie Wilson	1952	1951–1952		X
Harry Wolter	1909	1910–1913		X
John Wyatt	1966–1968	1968	X	
Kevin Youkilis	2004–2012	2013	X	
Bill Zuber	1946–1947	1943–1946	X	
			113	109

As you can see, it is really close. But when you consider some of the big names the Yankees got from the Red Sox—Babe Ruth, Herb Pennock, Sparky Lyle, and Roger Clemens—it seems as if the Yankees made out better, generally speaking, in the production received from a player who donned both uniforms. In addition, there are 11 members of the Red Sox Hall of Fame who began with Boston and went on to play for the Yankees, while only one who started with the Yankees and came to the Red Sox. There are few instances in which the Yankees sent or allowed the Red Sox to sign Hall of Famers. Only six players who played for both teams are in the National Baseball Hall of Fame: Wade Boggs, Jack Chesbro, Waite Hoyt, Herb Pennock, Red Ruffing, and Babe Ruth. All but Jack Chesbro started as a member of the Red Sox and then went to the Yankees. Like most big moments in this rivalry, the Yankees have the advantage.

Bibliography

Alderman, Joe. "Joe DiMaggio for Ted Williams, a Trade to Top All Trades, Almost Happened." Sportz Edge (website). Retrieved from http://sportzedge.com/2013/12/10/joe-dimaggio-for-ted-williams-a-trade-to-top-all-trades-almost-happened.

Bradley, Richard. *The Greatest Game: The Yankees, the Red Sox, and the Playoffs of '78*. New York: Free Press, 2008.

Fetter, Henry D. *Taking on the Yankees: Winning and Losing in the Business of Baseball, 1903–2003*. New York: W.W. Norton, 2003.

Frommer, Harvey, and Fredric J. Frommer. *Red Sox vs. Yankees: The Great Rivalry*. Boulder, CO: Taylor Trade, 2014.

Levy, Jane. *The Last Boy: Mickey Mantle and the End of America's Childhood*. New York: HarperCollins, 2010.

"Major League Baseball: Revenue by Team in 2013." Statista: The Statistics Portal (online). Retrieved from http://www.statista.com.

Newman, Mark. "'78 Boston Massacre Revisited." August 21, 2006. MLB.com. Retrieved from http://mlb.mlb.com/news/article.jsp?ymd=20060821&content_id=1621531&c_id=nyy

O'Nan, Stewart, and Stephen King. *Faithful: Two Diehard Boston Red Sox Fans Chronicle the Historic 2004 Season*. New York: Scribner, 2004.

Ozanian, Mike. "Baseball Team Values 2014 Led By New York Yankees At $2.5 Billion." *Forbes*. Retrieved from http://www.forbes.com/sites/mikeozanian/2014/03/26/baseball-team-values-2014-led-by-new-york-yankees-at-2-5-billion/#2135d43d5e79.

Vaccaro, Mike. *Emperors and Idiots: The Hundred Year Rivalry Between the Yankees and the Red Sox, from the Very Beginning to the End of the Curse*. New York: Random House, 2005.

The Rivals: The Boston Red Sox vs. the New York Yankees—An Inside History. Various authors. New York: St. Martin's Press, 2004.

Weintraub, Robert. *The House That Ruth Built: A New Stadium, the First Championship, and the Redemption of 1923*. New York: Little, Brown, 2011.

Zimmer, Don, with Bill Madden. *Zim: A Baseball Life*. New York: Total Sports Illustrated, 2001.

Index

Aardsma, David 174
Aceves, Alfredo 174
Adkins, Doc 16
Andrews, Ivy 47
Appleton, Pete 47

Ball, Neal 17
Bankhead, Scott 150
Banks, Willie 151
Baylor, Don 130
Bellhorn, Mark 175
Beniquez, Juan 113
Berberet, Lou 93
Bird, Doug 131
Boggs, Wade 132
Bragg, Darren 151
Brett, Ken 113
Brown, Hal 94
Burns, George 48
Bush, Bullet Joe 49

Caldwell, Ray 17
Canseco, Jose 152
Capuano, Chris 76
Carlyle, Roy 50
Cash, Kevin 177
Cater, Danny 114
Cerone, Rick 133
Chapman, Ben 50
Chesbro, Jack 18
Clark, Jack 133
Clark, Tony 153
Clemens, Roger 153
Clevenger, Tex 95
Clinton, Lou 115
Coleman, Michael 155
Collins, Rip 51
Colon, Bartolo 177
Cone, David 155
Cooke, Dusty 52
Cooper, Guy 19
Criger, Lou 19

Dahlgren, Babe 52
Damon, Johnny 178
DeVormer, Al 53
Dougherty, Patsy 20

Drew, Stephen 179
Dugan, Joe 54
Durst, Cedric 54

Easler, Mike 134
Ellsbury, Jacoby 180
Embree, Alan 156
Engle, Clyde 21
Erdos, Todd 157

Farr, Steve 135
Farrell, Doc 55
Ferguson, Alex 56
Ferrell, Wes 56
Fewster, Chick 57
Flaherty, John 157
Fossas, Tony 158
Foster, Eddie 58
Francis, Ray 58

Gardner, Billy 115
Gaston, Milt 59
Gilhooley, Frank 21
Glenn, Joe 60
Gordon, Tom 158
Green, Nick 181
Gumpert, Randy 95

Hammond, Chris 159
Harper, Harry 60
Harris, Greg 135
Harris, Joe 61
Heimach, Fred 61
Hemphill, Charlie 22
Henderson, Ricky 136
Hendryx, Tim 23
Hill, Rich 181
Hinske, Eric 182
Hobson, Butch 137
Hofmann, Fred 62
Holcombe, Ken 96
Howard, Elston 96
Hoyt, Waite 63
Hughes, Tom 23

Jensen, Jackie 98
Johnson, Deron 116

Johnson, Hank 64
Johnson, Roy 64
Jones, Sad Sam 65

Kennedy, John 117
Kleinow, Red 24
Knight, John 25
Kosco, Andy 117
Kramer, Jack 98

Lamar, Bill 25
LaPorte, Frank 26
Lary, Lyn 66
LeRoy, Louis 26
Lewis, Duffy 27
Leyritz, Jim 160
Lillibridge, Brent 183
Lollar, Tim 137
Lowe, Derek 161
Lowell, Mike 184
Lucey, Joe 67
Lyle, Sparky 118

MacFayden, Danny 68
Manto, Jeff 162
Manzanillo, Josias 162
Mays, Carl 28
McDermott, Mickey 99
McDonald, Darnell 184
McDonald, Jim 100
McGlothen, Lynn 119
McGraw, Bob 29
McGuire, Deacon 30
McHale, Marty 31
McMillan, Norm 68
McNally, Mike 31
Melancon, Mark 185
Melvin, Bob 138
Mendoza, Ramiro 163
Mientkiewicz, Doug 164
Miller, Andrew 186
Miller, Elmer 69
Mills, Buster 70
Mitchell, Fred 32
Mitchell, Johnny 70
Molina, Gustavo 186
Monbouquette, Bill 119

Moore, Wilcy 71
Moses, Jerry 120
Murphy, Johnny 101
Murphy, Rob 139
Murray, George 72
Myers, Mike 164

Newsom, Bobo 72
Niarhos, Gus 101
Niles, Harry 33
Nixon, Otis 139
Nunamaker, Les 34

O'Berry, Mike 140
O'Doul, Lefty 73
Ojeda, Bob 141
Olerud, John 165
Oliver, Joe 166
O'Neill, Steve 74
Owen, Spike 142

Paschal, Ben 74
Pennock, Herb 75
Piercy, Bill 76
Pipgras, George 77
Porterfield, Bob 102
Pratt, Del 78
Pride, Curtis 166

Quantrill, Paul 167
Quinn, Jack 79

Reardon, Jeff 142
Renna, Bill 103
Rhodes, Gordon 79

Robinson, Aaron 103
Rodriguez, Carlos 167
Rosar, Buddy 104
Roth, Braggo 80
Ruel, Muddy 81
Ruffing, Red 81
Russell, Allen 34
Ruth, Babe 82

Sanchez, Rey 168
Scarborough, Ray 105
Schang, Wally 35
Schmitz, Johnny 105
Schofield, Dick 121
Scott, Everett 36
Scott, George 143
Seeds, Bob 84
Shanks, Howie 85
Sheldon, Rollie 122
Shields, Ben 85
Shore, Ernie 37
Short, Bill 122
Siebern, Norm 123
Skinner, Camp 86
Smith, Elmer 86
Smith, Lee 144
Snow, J.T. 187
Stahl, Jake 38
Stanley, Mike 168
Stanton, Mike 169
Sturdivant, Tom 106

Tanana, Frank 144
Tannehill, Jesse 39
Thomas, Justin 188

Thomas, Lee 123
Thoney, Jack 39
Thormahlen, Hank 87
Thornton, Matt 188
Tiant, Luis 124
Tillman, Bob 125
Torrez, Mike 145
Traber, Billy 189
Truesdale, Frank 40
Turley, Bob 126

Unglaub, Bob 40

Veach, Bobby 87
Vick, Sammy 88

Wade, Jake 107
Walsh, Jimmy 41
Walters, Roxy 88
Wanninger, Pee-Wee 89
Waslewski, Gary 126
Watson, Bob 146
Wells, David 170
Werber, Billy 90
Whiteman, George 42
Whiten, Mark 171
Wight, Bill 107
Williams, Stan 127
Wilson, Archie 108
Wolter, Harry 42
Wyatt, John 128

Youkilis, Kevin 189

Zuber, Bill 109

www.ingramcontent.com/pod-product-compliance
Lightning Source LLC
Chambersburg PA
CBHW081159230426
43666CB00016B/2866